P9-CBB-545

Diary of an African Journey

Sir Henry Rider Haggard in Melbourne during the visit of the Dominions Royal Commission to Australia, 1913.

Diary of an African Journey

The Return of Rider Haggard

by

H. RIDER HAGGARD

edited, with an Introduction and Notes,
by Stephen Coan

NEW YORK UNIVERSITY PRESS
Washington Square, New York

This edition first published in the U.S.A. in 2001 by
NEW YORK UNIVERSITY PRESS
Washington Square
New York, NY 10003

Library of Congress Cataloging-in-Publication Data
Haggard, H. Rider (Henry Rider), 1856–1925
Diary of an African journey: the return of Rider Haggard/H. Rider Haggard
edited by Stephen Coan
p.cm.
Includes bibliographical references and index,
ISBN 0-8147-3631-9 (cloth: alk. paper)
1. Haggard, H. Rider (Henry Rider), 1856–1925—Journeys—Africa.
2. Haggard, H. Rider (Henry Rider), 1856–1925—Diaries, 3. Novelists,
English—19th century—Diaries. 4. Africa– Description and travel.
5. British—Africa– Diaries. I. Coan, Stephen. II. Title.
PR4732. A34 2000
828'.803—de21
[B]   00-045598

Printed in Malaysia

Cover design by Brett Armstrong
Beaded dancing stick courtesy Killie Campbell Collection
Background photograph courtesy *Natal Witness*
Portrait of H. Rider Haggard by William Strang (1916) courtesy
Cheyne Collection

Typeset and designed by the University of Natal Press

Contents

⁀⁀⁀⁀⁀

Illustrations & Maps

❧❧❧❧❧

Acknowledgements

෴෴෴෴෴

While many people have played a role in bringing *Diary of an African Journey* by H. Rider Haggard to its first publication, the greatest debt of gratitude must be to Commander Mark Cheyne DSC. RN. DL., Haggard's grandson. Firstly, I must thank him and his wife Nada for their kind hospitality during my stay at their home, Ditchingham Lodge, Norfolk, England, in October 1997 while researching items in the Cheyne Collection. Secondly, I must thank Commander Cheyne for presenting me with the typed manuscript of his grandfather's 1914 diary of his trip to southern Africa and charging me with the task of finding a publisher.

That the University of Natal Press, based in Pietermaritzburg, publish the book is entirely appropriate. Not only does *Diary of an African Journey* include Haggard's return to the city where he began his first African sojourn in 1875, but it also reflects much of the history of the province and features a number of prominent Natalians of the day, including John Dube and James Stuart, the latter with whom Haggard toured Zululand, the setting of many of his novels.

In steering the project to fruition I must thank the publisher Glenn Cowley, production editor Trish Comrie, and editors Philip Daniel and Sally Hines. Thanks are also due to Margery Moberly, former head of the University of Natal Press, for her encouragement and advice.

In researching the Introduction and Notes, and in editing the text of *Diary of an African Journey*, I have received generous assistance from many people to whom I now extend my thanks and make due acknowledgment:

Pamela Barlow, for access to the corrected typescript of the diary in the collection of her late husband, Peter Barlow.

Grant Christison, of The Book Man, who, while always keeping a weather eye out for Haggard references, gave me the pamphlet by H.M. Rex on the mooted restoration of Haggard's Pretoria house in 1967 which opened up a new perspective on Haggard's visit to the city in 1914.

Maria Bambus for her translation of the Afrikaans sections of the pamphlet.

Sharon Dell for research in Bulawayo, Zimbabwe.

Mary Gardner of the Diocesan Archives, Cathedral of the Holy Nativity, Pietermaritzburg, and the staff of the Collegiate Church of St Mary the Virgin, Port Elizabeth, for information on Anglican ecclesiastical buildings and personalities. Also Carol Archibald of the William Cullen Library, University of the Witwatersrand.

Johan Green of the Pretoria municipality who located the Ford family plot in the Heroes' Acre cemetery. Anne Lehmkuhl brought to light much information on Haggard's time in Pretoria in the 1870s and put me in touch with Peter Smits, historian of the Ford family, who has been unstinting in his assistance and also provided the photograph of Lewis Peter Ford and his wife Johanna Catherine, published here for the first time.

Bryan Hall for permission to reproduce photographs from Lilias Rider Haggard's photograph album.

Captain Brian Hockaday, master mariner, for information on the Port Captain of Durban in 1914, Captain John Rainnie.

Jean Kennedy, County Archivist, Norfolk Records Office, Norwich, England, and her successor John Alban for fielding queries by letter and e-mail.

Ian Knight for illuminating detail regarding several obscure references related to the Anglo-Zulu War of 1879.

Victoria Manthorpe for information concerning references to Norfolk personalities.

Lukas Anton Mettler CMM for information on the Mariannhill Monastery and its history, and for showing me the artefacts of which Haggard writes in Chapter Eight.

The *Natal Witness* for permission to use photographs and editorial material including the report included here as Appendix Three.

Sue Reece for permission to use the photograph of her grandfather, James Stuart.

Judy Stearn, Haggard's great-grandaughter, who compiled the initial index.

From the University of Natal, Pietermaritzburg campus:

The staff of the Cecil Renaud Library.

W.H. Bizley, English Studies, School of Language, Culture and Communication, gave freely of his encyclopedic knowledge of South African railways.

Toni Boddington of the university's cartographic unit for drawing the maps.

Adrian Koopman, Zulu Studies, School of Language, Culture and Communication, for assistance with Zulu translation and orthography, and information on various aspects of Zulu culture.

John Laband and John Wright, of the Faculty of Human Sciences, for reading the manuscript and for their comments and corrections. I must also thank John Wright for information on various historical figures of KwaZulu-Natal, especially James Stuart. Bill Guest also happily answered questions.

David Pike, Classical Studies, School of Language, Culture and Communication, for his translation of the Latin phrases in the text; and Michael Lambert of the same department.

Jo Walker of the heritage body Amafa aKwaZulu-Natali for details regarding the magistrates and storekeepers of Zululand.

Colonel Denys Whatmore for permission to reprint Haggard's letters to the Colonial Secretary, Lewis Harcourt, which appear here as Appendix One. They were first published in full in his *Rider Haggard's Good Deeds: Pamphlet Four.* The original letters are held by the Public Record Office, London, under references CO 879/115 and CO 881/14. British Crown Copyright material in the Public Record Office is reproduced by permission of the Controller of Her Britannic Majesty's Stationery Office.

The staff of the Killie Campbell Collection, Durban, especially Steven Kotze.

The staff of the Pietermaritzburg Archive Repository.

The staff of the Natal Society Library, especially David Buckley, Special Collections Librarian.

The following have also provided valuable assistance: Roger Allen, secretary, Rider Haggard Society; Tom Andrews; Lieutenant-Colonel Ian Bennett; Barry Bredenkamp (Malaria Research Institute, Durban); Ian Castle; Vincent Coan; John Conyngham; Jenny Davies; John Deare; Dave Fall; Janice Farquarson; Reverend Ivor Glass; Brian Kaighin; Maureen Klug (Lever Brothers); Steven Lunderstedt; Gordon Maclean; Mungo Park Ross; Olive Park Ross; Dorothy and Marion Robinson; Fred Schetler; Graham Warr; and Steve Watt.

A special debt is owed to Lindy Stiebel, Department of English, University of Durban-Westville, whom I first encountered when a letter from her arrived for Commander Cheyne during my stay at Ditchingham Lodge in 1997. I thank her for much useful and encouraging discussion and for happily sharing her extensive knowledge of Haggard and his work.

Finally I must repeat my gratitude to Commander Mark Cheyne who has been ever present with help and assistance during the preparation of his grandfather's diary for publication. I thank him again for the extraordinary gift of the manuscript and with it the trust placed in me. Now, in the hope of a bond honoured, I return it to him in published form.

Note on the text

৵৵৵৵৵

Throughout his life Henry Rider Haggard kept rough diaries-cum-note-books. In 1913 and 1914, during his tours of Australia, New Zealand and South Africa with the Dominions Royal Commission (DRC), Haggard used his rough diaries as *aides-mémoire* for writing up fuller accounts of his visits which retained the diary form.

On 5 August 1914, during the DRC's tour of Canada, Haggard heard of Britain's declaration of war on Germany following which the DRC was recalled. Thereafter Haggard continued to keep a detailed diary until his death in 1925.

The diaries dating from July 1914 to March 1925 have been published in edited form as *The Private Diaries of Sir Henry Rider Haggard*, edited by D.S. Higgins (London, 1980). Contrary to the title, the diaries were not private and Haggard had always envisaged publication. To this end, in 1921, he discussed with Rudyard Kipling the possibility of Kipling becoming his literary executor and the editor of the diaries. However, following Haggard's death in 1925, his wife, Louisa, was named his literary executor. Comments in the text of *Diary of an African Journey* also make it clear Haggard was writing with publication in mind.

Diary of an African Journey finds its origins in the rough diary Haggard kept during his trip to southern Africa in 1914. On the return trip to Britain aboard the *Gaika*, Haggard used his rough notes to work up a detailed diary. This handwritten manuscript was transcribed by his secretary, Ida Hector, to become a typed manuscript which Haggard subsequently corrected in pencil. This corrected typescript is in the collection of the late Peter Barlow, Rustenberg, Stellenbosch, Western Cape, South Africa, held by his widow, Pamela.

A later typed transcription was made from Haggard's handwritten original, probably during the 1950s. Identical copies of this typescript are held by the Norfolk Studies Library, Norwich, England, and Commander Mark Cheyne, DSC, RN, DL ,Ditchingham, Norfolk, England. This text contains a number of inaccuracies, in the main concerning South African terms and place names, attributable to the later transcriber not having access to the corrected typescript plus having to contend with Haggard's self-confessed poor handwriting.

Haggard's original handwritten manuscript appears to no longer be extant.

In editing *Diary of an African Journey* for publication I have worked with the Cheyne manuscript. This has been checked against the original typescript and Haggard's corrections and comments have been included.

The 1914 rendering of place names have been retained in the text and in the accompanying maps. Their present day equivalents are given in the Notes and in the Gazetteer. Similarly, Haggard's Zulu orthography has been retained. Current day usage is given in the Notes.

Editorial insertions in the text, other than Haggard's, are indicated thus: [   ].

Short sections of *Diary of an African Journey* have previously been quoted in *The Purple and the Gold: The Story of Johannesburg and Pretoria* by Joy Collier (Cape Town, 1960). Collier made use of the corrected typed manuscript in the Barlow collection.

Quotations from *Diary of an African Journey* can also be found in Lilias Rider Haggard's biography of her father, *The Cloak That I Left* (London, 1951). A comparison will show these quotations differ from the original due to Lilias adding her own gloss as well as combining passages from different sections of the diary.

Gazetteer

❧❧❧❧❧

In 1914, at the time of Haggard's visit, the Union of South Africa (established in 1910) consisted of four provinces: Cape Province, Orange Free State, Transvaal and Natal.

Names in 1914	Current Names
Amatikulu River	Matigulu River
Bechuanaland Protectorate	Botswana
Boven Vallei	Bovlei
British East Africa Protectorate	Kenya
Dugusa	Dukuza
Gwelo	Gweru
Gingindhlovu	Gingindlovu
Houw Hoek	Houhoek
Indondakasuka	Ndondakasuka
Ingome Forest	Ngome Forest
Inkandhla Forest	Nkandla Forest
Isandhlwana	Isandlwana
Lalapanzi	Lalapunsi
Lobatsi	Lobatse
Lourenço Marques	Maputo
Mafeking	Mafikeng
Mazoe	Mazowe
Northern Rhodesia	Zambia
Nyasaland	Malawi
Petrus	Petrusberg
Portuguese East Africa	Mozambique
Que Que	Kwekwe
Rhodesia	Zimbabwe
Salisbury	Harare
Seruli	Serule
Somkeli	Somekhele

Tugela River	Thukela River
Umbonambi	kwaMbonambi
Umfolozi River (Black and White)	Mfolozi River (Black and White)
Umhlatuze River	Mhlatuze River
Umkumbane Stream	Mkumbane Stream
Unzololo Stream	Nzololo Stream
Victoria	Masvingo
Zoutpansberg	Soutpansberg

Introduction

❧❧❧❧❧

Henry Rider Haggard's *King Solomon's Mines* was one of the inspirational texts of the British Empire during the late Victorian era. The book's appearance in 1885 effectively inaugurated the cult of the best-seller, while its brand of adventure-imperialism cleverly tapped into the British reading public's fascination with Africa, satifying a curiosity hitherto largely catered for by traveller's journals and tales of exploration. Following its success, Haggard was to remain best known as a writer of adventure stories, and as such comparatively uninterested in literary form or the interpretation of contemporary life.

But there was another, deeper side to Haggard, the romantic storyteller, that arose out of a yearning to be of service to his country and its empire. Haggard travelled widely in this weightier guise, writing extensively about the land, social issues, agriculture and developments in Africa. The pursuit of these interests finally earned him an appointment to the Dominions Royal Commission (DRC) set up in 1911 to examine the role that Canada, Australia, New Zealand and South Africa could play in the consolidation and furtherance of the British imperial endeavour.

The middle-aged Haggard who returned to South Africa in 1914 as a member of the DRC was far removed from the callow 19-year-old who had landed in Natal 39 years earlier – in 1875 – as a willing 'dogsbody' attached to the entourage of his father's friend, fellow Norfolk squire and the recently appointed Lieutenant-Governor of the British colony, Sir Henry Bulwer. For an Englishman of his class and background, Haggard proved remarkably adaptable in the pioneering environment of the colonies and his five years in South Africa were formative, if not particularly successful in financial terms.

The chief influence on the young Haggard was Sir Theophilus Shepstone, Natal's Secretary for Native Affairs, who exposed his young protégé to the conflicts between Boer and Briton and those between black and white that conditioned the struggle to bring order to a volatile colonial settler society. While Haggard was clearly on the side of the British in matters of governance, he was also unusually sympathetic to the plight of the 'native', most particularly the Zulu of Natal, for whom he developed a keen regard and empathy.

This concern shows through in the diary that he kept during his three-month visit in 1914, even though his language is shot through with somewhat patronising references to 'kaffirs' and 'natives' – terms that were the currency of the times but strike a discordant note today. Haggard was alert to the tensions that the white government of Louis Botha experienced in relation to an overwhelmingly black population and he was keen to canvass the opinions of prominent locals during his travels around South Africa. He did so with omnivorous enthusiasm, so it was not surprising, therefore, that the activities of John Dube, founder and first President of the African National Congress, should come to his notice and typical of Haggard that he should seek him out for an interview.

The Dube interview, Haggard's observations on racial tensions, migrant labour and the prevailing conditions in Zululand, together with those on South Africa's political future recorded during the course of the diary, serve often to cut against the grain of popular and academic perceptions of the author of *King Solomon's Mines*. The Haggard of 1914 was not the romancer of the 1880s and early 1890s – the period of his greatest creativity and the height of his fame as a writer of adventure stories. A measure of the change in Haggard is to be found in a newspaper report published during his 1914 visit: 'Sir Rider, who is 58 years of age, is a charming and delightful personality, with whom the stranger feels instantly at home. He looks more the "man of affairs" than the novelist, and more the farmer than the man of affairs. He is tall, spare of build, rugged yet homely, and with keen penetrating eyes and a mobile expressive mouth.' This was how an anonymous reporter of the *Natal Witness* described Haggard on 27 March, during his visit to Pietermaritzburg – his first to the city since his departure from South Africa in 1881 as a young man of 25 with a wife, a small baby and uncertain prospects.

In the years between his departure and return, Haggard had become a household name thanks to the phenomenal success of *King Solomon's Mines* (1885), *She* (1887) and *Allan Quatermain* (1887) – his three best-known books that have remained in print since first publication. By the time of his death in 1925, Haggard had written 48 adventure stories (or romances as they were then styled), as well as 12 novels dealing with contemporary subjects, and 10 works of non-fiction.

Since the mid-1890s Haggard had tried to shake off the mantle of the romantic novelist in favour of carving a career in public life. He did so with considerable success. Haggard's eventual knighthood was awarded not for services to literature but in recognition of his services to his country, an award that endorsed Haggard's perception of himself as a public servant, albeit, as shall be seen, an often frustrated one.

Haggard would have relished the *Witness* reporter's description of him as a 'farmer' and 'man of affairs'. He happily played both roles and it was his reputation as an agricultural expert and reformer to which Haggard owed his appointment to the Commission charged with visiting the dominions 'to report on the health of the British Empire and recommend any measures thought necessary to improve it'.[1]

Serving on the Commission brought Haggard back to South Africa, a long-anticipated return to the country and the sub-continent that inspired the romances to which he owed his initial fame.

While the *Diary of an African Journey* is a product of Haggard's public life and the older man, it nevertheless provides a mirror to the younger Haggard, and the historical events that formed the backdrop to his first stay in South Africa from 1875 to 1881. The diary also gives an indication of how his opinions and beliefs had changed since those early days. In conversation with Annie Botha, the Irish-born wife of Louis Botha, former Anglo-Boer War general and first Prime Minister of the Union of South Africa, Haggard finds that 'we both agreed that time and experience were wonderful softeners of strong views'. A few weeks later the expression of similar views at a public forum in Pretoria attracted vociferous disagreement from some quarters.[2]

If the diary holds up a mirror to Haggard the man, it also provides a mirror to South Africa – a South Africa radically different to that of Haggard's youth. In 1881 the southern African sub-continent consisted of several separate states settled by Europeans – mainly Dutch and English – with a long history of conflict, occasionally erupting into open warfare. War, however, was more commonly waged by the two groups of European settlers upon the indigenous peoples. Haggard had experience of both types of conflict: the Anglo-Zulu War (1879) saw him volunteering as a cavalryman and the First Anglo-Boer War (1880–81) precipitated his departure.

After his departure, the Second Anglo-Boer War (1899–1902) devastated the country. From the ashes rose the Union of South Africa in 1910, bringing together the former republican states and crown colonies. The war had its roots in the British policies of the 1870s concerning the Boer republics and the later discovery of gold on the Witwatersrand, which occasioned the explosive growth of the city of Johannesburg, a city not in existence when Haggard lived in South Africa as a young man.

The mines of Johannesburg were just one sign of the increasing industrialisation of the country; another was the railways that threaded the country. During his visit in 1914, Haggard found it hard to rediscover the Africa of his youth. When, in a bid to recreate old times, he requested a horse-drawn wagonette for his tour of Zululand after the work of the Commission was finished, none was to be found. The trip was made in an Overland car.

South Africa clearly played a pivotal role in Haggard's life and to better understand the significance of his return to the sub-continent, and to appreciate the man Haggard had become in late middle age, it is necessary to detail some of the biographical strands that find expression in the diary; and, in linking past to present, to uncover Haggard the 'farmer' and 'man of affairs' in contrast to Haggard the romantic story-teller.

If South Africa could claim the credit for igniting Haggard's literary imagination, it was also the place where Haggard embarked on a career in public service thanks to his father's friendship with Sir Henry Bulwer, whose estate at Heydon in Norfolk was close to that of the Haggards, who lived at Bradenham, Rider's birthplace. He was born in a cottage on the estate on 22 June 1856 and christened Henry Rider, the eighth of ten children. From the beginning, Rider, as he was always called, appears to have been the odd one out. 'Only fit to be a damned greengrocer', was the verdict of his father William, a mercurial Norfolk squire who, according to his grand-daughter, 'was a man of violent temper, impatient and autocratic . . . but (who) loved his children and worked hard in their interests'.[3]

At the age of 13, after being schooled by a series of governesses, Rider entered into more formal education. Unlike his brothers, Haggard's father decided against sending him to a public school. 'Not only was he apparently without any particular ability, but he completely lacked concentration, and had failed to absorb enough general knowledge to come up to even the modest requirements of the lesser public schools.'[4] Furthermore, William Haggard was feeling the financial strain of supporting a large family.

Accordingly Haggard was sent for coaching by the Reverend H.J. Graham of Garsington Rectory, near Oxford, and from there proceeded to Ipswich Grammar School in Suffolk, where his academic career was undistinguished. Alhough he won a school essay competition, he failed the Army entrance examination in 1872 – 'duly floored by my old enemy, Euclid'.[5]

His father was probably pondering what to do with this problem son when, in a move of 'characteristic suddenness',[6] he decided that Rider should be educated with a specific career in mind – the Foreign Office. He was packed off to London where he spent almost a year at the home of a private tutor. 'Then my father announced that I was to go to Scoones, the great crammer, and there make ready to face the Foreign Office examination.'[7]

Bulwer mission to Africa – August 1875

After a year-and-a-half at Scoones another sudden change of mind on the part of his father sent the young Haggard heading off in a different direction – Africa. Rider, along with the rest of his family was enjoying a summer holiday at Tours in France when his father William 'read in *The Times*, or heard otherwise',[8] that Sir Henry Bulwer had been appointed Lieutenant-Governor of Natal. The Bulwers were old Norfolk friends of the Haggard family, and Rider's mother, Ella, wrote from France asking Sir Henry if he would take her son to Africa as a member of his staff. Bulwer agreed, 'which was extremely kind of him, as I do not remember that he had ever set eyes on me'.[9]

Bulwer was to replace Sir Garnet Wolseley, who had been appointed Acting Governor by Lord Carnarvon, the Colonial Secretary, for an interim term after the recall of Sir Benjamin Pine over his handling of the Langalibalele 'rebellion' in 1873.[10] Wolseley had been given the task of reforming the colony's administration with a view to promoting Carnarvon's vision of a confederation of states in South Africa, a policy in which Haggard was destined to play a minor but dramatic role.

Haggard's holiday in France came to an abrupt end and he reported to his 'future chief in London, where he set me to work at once ordering wine and other stores to be consumed at Government House in Natal'.[11] Haggard was in charge of the catering arrangements – an unpaid post that helps to explain the young Haggard's financial dependence on his father for several years to come.

While Haggard's brother Bazett organised the purchase of guns, Rider kitted himself out in London and said his goodbyes.

Reflecting on his youthful self sailing towards Africa, Haggard described 'a tall young fellow, quite six feet, and slight; blue-eyed, brown-haired, fresh-complexioned, and not at all bad looking . . . Mentally I was impressionable, quick to observe and learn whatever interested me, and could already hold my own in conversation. Also, if necessary, could make a public speech.'[12] But the ingenuousness of youth masked a darker side: 'I was . . . subject to fits of depression and liable to take views of things too serious and gloomy for my age – failings I may add, that I have never been able to shake off.'[13]

After a brief stay in Cape Town, Bulwer and his staff landed in Durban on 26 August 1875. Sir Garnet Wolseley recorded the meeting with his successor in his diary and included this unflattering impression of Haggard: 'A leggy-looking youth not long I should say from school who seems the picture of weakness and dullness.'[14]

The Lieutenant-Governor and his staff departed from Durban for Pietermaritzburg, Natal's capital city, on the morning of 1 September 'and came up the fifty-four miles over most tremendous hills in five and a half hours, going at full gallop all the way in a four-horse wagonnette'.[15]

Travels with Shepstone — 1876

Established in Pietermaritzburg, Natal's capital, Haggard set about his catering duties and other general duties of a secretarial nature during the course of which he met many of the prominent Natalians of the day. Among them was John Colenso, Bishop of Natal. Colenso had been a rector at Forncett St Mary in Norfolk from 1846 to 1853 and 'he recognised my name the first time I saw him'.[16] But it was Colenso's former friend, Theophilus Shepstone, the Secretary for Native Affairs, who was to exert the greatest influence on the young Haggard, becoming in effect a surrogate father figure and mentor.[17] Shepstone had organised a tour of the province for Bulwer and his staff in May 1876 and it was during this tour that the young Haggard came under Shepstone's sway – 'the most interesting man of all whom I came into contact in Natal . . . who afterwards became my beloved chief and friend . . . not withstanding the wide difference in our years.'[18]

The up-country trip included a visit to the homestead of Phakade, chief of the Mchunu, where Haggard saw 'a great war dance which was organised in (Bulwer's) honour'. He described it in a letter home, later working it up for publication – 'it was the first thing I ever wrote for publication'[19] – in the *Gentleman's Magazine* of July 1877 under the title 'A Zulu War Dance'. Although the first to be written, it was, in fact, the second of Haggard's articles to be published. His first, 'The Transvaal', dealt with the annexation of the Transvaal Republic and appeared in the May 1877 issue of *MacMillan's Magazine*.

Haggard was not unaware of the tensions that led, in part, to the annexation. In a letter dated 6 July 1876, written from Durban where he was on holiday, he spoke of 'stirring news from the Transvaal'. There had been a skirmish between the 'Boers and Secocoeni, a native chief of very considerable power'.[20] While Haggard was holidaying in Durban, Shepstone was attending the confederation conference in London. He returned with a Commission from Lord Carnarvon empowering him to annex the Transvaal. Shepstone asked Bulwer to let Haggard go with him. '(Shepstone) wants me to come with him for two reasons. First, we are very good friends and he was kind enough to say he wished to have me as a companion. Second, I imagine there will be a good deal of what is called the champagne and sherry policy up at Pretoria and he wants somebody to look after the entertaining. It will be a most interesting business . . .'[21]

But Haggard found himself caught up in the antipathy between Bulwer and Shepstone. 'To my surprise the Governor has cut up very rough about it,' Haggard wrote to his father. 'I am very sorry as it would be a most interesting expedition, and probably an historical one. The fact is our chief is as jealous as he can be of Sir T. Shepstone who has come out here with higher powers than himself and cannot bear the idea of anybody connected with him having a finger in the fire.'[22] In the event he was permitted to accompany Shepstone as his guest, 'in a private capacity on the condition I hold no official position'.[23]

In mid-December Haggard departed for the Transvaal as a member of Shepstone's staff, which included Melmoth Osborn, Major Marshall

Clarke, Colonel Brooke, Captain James, Joseph Henderson, W.B. Morcom, Fred Fynney, Dr Vacy Lyle and Lieutenant Phillips, the latter in charge of the escort of mounted police. The party reached Pretoria on 27 January 1877. In later life, Haggard recalled with nostalgia the camaraderie experienced during those days of travel. 'Those camps were very pleasant, and in them, as we smoked and drank our "square-face" after the day's trek, I heard many a story from Sir Theophilus himself, from Osborn and from Fynney, who next to him, perhaps knew as much of the Zulus and their history as any living in Natal.'[24]

Osborn had witnessed the battle of Ndondakusuka fought between the rival heirs to the Zulu throne, the brothers Cetshwayo kaMpande and Mbuyazi kaMpande, in 1856. Haggard was to make use of Osborn's account of the battle in *Child of Storm* (1913), the second volume of his Zulu trilogy.

Haggard also heard stories from another individual attached to the Commission, 'a kind of head native attendant to Sir Theophilus'. His name was Mhlophekazi. A Swazi of high birth, he was 'a tall, thin, fierce-faced fellow with a great hole above the left temple over which the skin pulsated, that he had come by in some battle. He said that he had killed 10 men in single combat . . . always making use of a battle-axe. However this may be, he was an interesting old fellow from whom I heard many stories that Fynney used to interpret.'[25]

Under the name Umslopogaas, together with his axe the Woodpecker, Mhlophekazi featured in three books by Haggard: *Allan Quatermain* (1887), *Nada the Lily* (1892) and *She and Allan* (1921).[26]

Haggard's own servant was a Zulu named Mazooku with whom he was destined to have several adventures. One on occasion when Haggard got lost while hunting he credited Mazooku with saving his life.[27] Mazooku appears under his own name in Haggard's second novel, *The Witch's Head* (1885).[28]

In Pretoria, after pursuing a policy that was part diplomacy and part stone-walling, Shepstone annexed the Transvaal. The proclamation of annexation was read out in Pretoria on 12 April 1877. During his visit in 1914, Haggard was to be reminded by Johan Rissik, Administrator of the Transvaal, that he had stepped into the breach when Osborn froze halfway through the public reading of the proclamation. Rissik had been a young man in the crowd at the time. To avoid further inflaming local feeling, the raising of the British flag was postponed until 24 May, Queen Victoria's birthday, when Haggard helped to run it up the flagstaff.

Even before the proclamation was read, Haggard had indicated his intention of returning to England. Though it involved resigning, he would return with some status as he would be carrying despatches and unofficially provide information on the circumstances of the annexation to Lord Carnavon. Or so he told his father. In reality he was hoping to bring off an engagement with a young woman, Lilly Jackson,

whom he had met at a ball during his stay in London while studying at Scoones.

Lilly Jackson 'was to remain through his life his only true love'.[29]
This relationship was destined to take a tragic course that would leave
its imprint on the rest of Haggard's life. 'For it was to be his fate that the
deep emotional experiences, his loves and tragedies, were not as with
most men and women, if not forgotten, overlaid so deeply by the years
that they become mere remembrances,' wrote his daughter Lilias. 'They
remained active, insistent, his daily companions until the hour of his
death, no less present because jealously hidden, nor unspeaking, because of them he never spoke.'[30]

Master and Registrar — June 1877

Unaware of the intended engagement, Haggard's father wrote an angry letter to his son practically forbidding him to throw up a good career. Haggard destroyed this letter but it would seem that his father's
anger was provoked by Rider taking up with Shepstone and apparently
burning his bridges with Bulwer, a family friend. A distraught but
obedient son withdrew his resignation and recalled his baggage, which
had already been sent on to Cape Town. Thereafter, Haggard's career
prospects improved and on 1 June 1877 he was appointed Clerk to the
Executive Council. He had hardly settled into his new – and, incidentally, first paid post – when the Master and Registrar of the High Court
died and he was appointed to act in his place. This, when barely turned
21 and with no legal experience. But then his superior, John Kotze, the
High Court judge, was only 27.[31]

While in Pretoria, Haggard found a friend of similar age in Arthur
Cochrane, who had come to the Transvaal on the staff of William
Sergeaunt, a crown agent sent out by the home government to investigate the Transvaal's finances.[32] Together, Haggard and Cochrane
built a small cottage in Pretoria, ironically calling it 'The Palatial'.
It was during this time that Haggard learnt Lilly had become be-
trothed and on 4 June 1878 married Francis Bradley Archer, a banker
and stockbroker, a marriage 'that brought disaster and sorrow on
her and her relations'.[33]

In his autobiography, *The Days of My Life*, written in 1912 but not
published until after his death in 1925, Haggard confessed that Lilly's
marriage was 'a crushing blow, so crushing that at the time I should not
have been sorry if I could have departed from the world. Its effects upon
me also were very bad indeed, for it left me utterly reckless and unsettled. I cared not what I did or what became of me.' However, he
draws a veil over what happened exactly. 'I will leave this subject of
which even now I feel it painful to write.'[34] It is now known that he had
an affair with a married woman, Johanna Catherine Ford, wife of Lewis

Peter Smits

Lewis Peter Ford and his second wife Johanna Catherine. This photograph was probably taken in Kimberley shortly after their marriage.

Peter Ford, a lawyer and Acting Attorney-General of the Transvaal. She became pregnant with his child.[35]

Political affairs were not going much better. Two Boer deputations had gone to England to demand retrocession and Shepstone 'was summoned home to confer with the Colonial Office respecting the affairs of the Transvaal'.[36] While he was in England Sir Owen Lanyon was appointed to replace him, and Shepstone decided to retire.

In Pretoria, Haggard and Cochrane were living through troubled times. The Anglo-Zulu War began in January 1879 and the Boers were growing restive. With the constant alarums, Haggard took the Queen's shilling as a cavalry volunteer, eventually commanding a troop of the Pretoria Horse. But prospects were not promising for Haggard and Cochrane. With Shepstone's resignation, a new order had come to power in the Transvaal, and this, and the two young men's complicated personal lives, made them resolve to leave Pretoria.

With Cochrane to Hilldrop — April 1879

In April 1879 they resigned from government service to start a farming venture centred on ostriches. They bought a small estate in Natal, just outside Newcastle, from Melmoth Osborn, who had been resident magistrate there and had built the farmhouse known as Hilldrop on the 3 000-acre *Rooi Point* farm.

While Cochrane took over the farm and a herd of ostriches, Haggard returned to England in August 1879. It was there he learnt that on 16 September Mrs Ford had given birth to a baby girl named Ethel Rider. Mr Ford appears to have been blissfully unaware of the true paternity of the child and Cochrane was asked to be a godfather. 'I am afraid there will be a heavy reckoning for us two when we go to Pretoria,' wrote Cochrane.[37]

In the event Haggard was not to visit Pretoria again until 1914 and any heavy reckoning was effectively eliminated by the news contained in a letter sent to him by Cochrane in November. 'I enclose a telegram telling of the sudden death of my young God child and of your — ? Yes, the poor little thing is dead and perhaps it is a good thing for all concerned.'[38] It was perhaps especially good considering that Haggard had now become engaged to Louisa Margitson, an heiress to the small property of Ditchingham in south Norfolk. Nevertheless, events in Pretoria of 1879 were recalled in 1914 when Haggard visited the grave of his illegitimate child.[39]

Matters were not all going Haggard's way in the England of 1879. His fiancée's guardian, William Hartcup, possibly seeing Haggard as a fortune-hunter, placed obstacles in the couple's way and it was not until almost a year later, following a protracted courtship and legal action, that they were married – on 11 August 1880. By then Haggard was having second thoughts about farming in South Africa and considering either a legal career or a return to the colonial service. Lack of opportunity, plus his commitment to Cochrane, decided him to return to South Africa.

Haggard and his wife Louie, as she was known, arrived in Pietermaritzburg in time to spend Christmas with the Shepstones but 'the news that greeted them was anything but cheerful. The long-expected Boer rebellion had broken out in the Transvaal, the country was in an uproar, and Sir George Colley, now Governor and Commander-in-Chief in Natal, was about to move up-country with the few troops available.'[40]

The situation put Haggard in a quandary. 'Newcastle, whither we desired to proceed, lies very near the Transvaal border, and the question was, Did I dare take my wife thither? . . . Literally I was at my wits' end to know what to do. To advance seemed too risky; to remain where we were was both wearisome and, with our servants, ruinously expensive.'[41]

While Haggard dithered, Louie decided. Boers or no Boers she wanted to go to her new home. Moreover, Pietermaritzburg was 'fearfully hot'[42] and she was pregnant with their first child.

Shortly before their departure the couple dined at Government House. 'I think it was the night before Colley left Maritzburg to take personal command of the troops at Newcastle. I believe there were thirteen of us at table . . . of whom three were ladies – Lady Colley, another lady whose name I forget, and my wife. The other guests were officers and members of Colley's staff.'[43] Haggard recalled grimly that 'in a few months' time Lady Colley, the other lady, my wife and I were the sole survivors of that dinner party.'[44]

The Haggards set out for Newcastle on 14 January 1881, following the same route that Haggard had taken three years earlier with Shepstone to the Transvaal. For Louie the trip was a dramatic introduction to the delights of African travel, with its sudden thunderstorms and swollen rivers. At last they reached Newcastle and Hilldrop.[45] There Haggard was reunited with Cochrane and Mazooku. Also awaiting the Haggard's arrival was George Blomefield 'alias George Mayes, the illegitimate child of old Col. Blomefield of Necton Hall, Norfolk'.[46] He was a ward of Haggard's father and with £1 000 from his inheritance Haggard's father had purchased a partnership in the farm with Rider and Cochrane.

War comes to Hilldrop — January 1881

The arrival of the Haggards at Hilldrop coincided with the opening moves of the First Anglo-Boer War. On 24 January, the day of their arrival, Colley advanced on the Transvaal border. Two days later they heard gunfire – the sound of the British forces being defeated at the battle of Laing's Nek. On 8 February the sound of guns was heard again, signalling another defeat for the British at the battle of Ingogo, after which the victorious Boers invaded Natal. 'One night in the stillness, I heard the galloping of a vast number of horses,' wrote Haggard. 'Some five hundred of the enemy had taken possession of the farm next to our own, which they looted.'[47]

The climax of the war came on Sunday 27 February. 'Weather oppressively hot,' wrote Louie in her diary. 'In the afternoon Rider thought he heard guns but we all said it was thunder. Presently he and Mr Cochrane rode into town and came back with the startling news that an engagement had taken place near the "Nek"; our loss was great and Sir G. Colley missing.'

The next day Cochrane went into Newcastle and brought back the following news: 'Sir George, having gone with 500 men to take possession of a hill commanding the "Nek", was attacked by 7 000 Boers. Our men . . . ran short of ammunition . . . Sir George was shot through the head.'[48] The Boers had won a decisive victory on the mountain of

Majuba. On 6 March a truce was arranged with the Transvaal and 15 days later an armistice was signed agreeing to the appointment of a Royal Commission to negotiate the terms of the peace – the retrocession of the Transvaal was certain.

While retaining one room with a separate entrance for the heavily pregnant Louie, on 6 April 1881, Haggard let Hilldrop as 'a residence for H.E. Sir Hercules Robinson and staff and for the use and service of the Royal Commission about to assemble under H.E.'s presidency' in order to negotiate the peace terms. Haggard was not unaware of the irony of the Commission sitting in his home. 'It was a strange fate which decreed that the Retrocession of the Transvaal, over which I had myself hoisted the British flag, should be practically accomplished beneath my roof.'[49]

While the Commission was occupying Hilldrop, Louie gave birth to their first child on 22 May. The baby was named Arthur John Rider Haggard – after Cochrane and Haggard's brother Jack who had arrived for a visit in May – but he was always called Jock.

Events in the Transvaal and the subsequent war had undermined the Haggards' desire to stay in South Africa. 'Every day that passes has only strengthened my conviction that we can look for no peace and security in South Africa,' Haggard wrote to his mother.[50] In a letter to Shepstone, Haggard voiced similar sentiments:

> The fact of the matter is I do not like at all the aspect of affairs here. These seem to me the early prospect of a renewal of war. If the home Govt. insist on anything I am sure the Boers will fight again. At any rate I should hardly feel justified in risking it ... Therefore taking everything into consideration we have come to the conclusion that we had better go ... I don't see how respectable people can be expected to stop up here in this land of murder and sudden death.[51]

Cochrane was to return with them. Suffering from dysentery, it was thought a 'rest and change of air is the only thing that will pull him together again'.[52] The farm was left in the charge of George Blomefield. Two years later, on 29 April 1883, a settlement of farm ownership was signed at Ditchingham (now the Haggard home) by Haggard, Cochrane and Blomefield, dissolving the partnership. Assets after liabilities were £250.14s.6d., divided among the three signatories. This settlement would be the cause of an apparent blackmail attempt by the Blomefield family during Haggard's visit to South Africa in 1914.

Farewell to Hilldrop – August 1881

Before leaving Hilldrop the Haggards sold their imported furniture. 'It was a highly successful sale since such articles were then rare at Newcastle. A grand piano which I had bought second-hand for £40 in Eng-land, fetched £200, and the other things went at proportionately good prices.' In 1914 Haggard would meet the buyer of one of his wagons.[53]

The auction over, they were ready to leave. 'So at last we bade farewell to Hilldrop, which neither of us ever has, or I suppose ever will, see again except in dreams. I remember feeling quite sad as we drove down the dusty track to Newcastle, and the familiar house, sur-rounded by its orange trees, grew dim and vanished from our sight. There my son had been born; there I had undergone many emotions of a kind that help to make a man; there I had suffered the highest sort of shame, shame for my country; there, as I felt, one chapter in my event-ful life had opened and had closed.'

The saddest goodbye was to Haggard's servant, Mazooku. 'The poor fellow was moved at this parting, and gave me what probably he valued more than anything he possessed, the kerry [knobkerrie] that he carried ever since he was a man – that same heavy, redwood instrument with which more than once I have seen him battering the head of some foe. It hangs in the hall of this house, but where I wonder, is Mazooku, who saved my life when I was lost upon the veld? Living, perhaps, in some kraal, and thinking from time to time of his old master Indanda, of whose subsequent doings some vague rumours may have reached him. If so, were I to revisit Africa today, I have not the faintest doubt but that he would reappear. I should go out of my hotel and see a grey-headed man squatted on the roadside, who would arise, lift up his arm, salute me and say "Inkoos Indanda, you are here; I am here, come back to serve you". I do not know that I felt anything more in leaving Africa than the saying good-bye to this loving, half-wild man.'[54]

The Haggards left Hilldrop in the last week of August 1881, and 'on Wednesday, the 31st August, from the deck of the *Dunkeld*, we saw the shores of Natal recede from our sight forever.'[55]

Or so Haggard had believed in 1912 when writing his autobio-graphy. In 1914 Haggard and Louie, together with their youngest daughter Lilias, would return to Hilldrop; and Haggard was to meet Mazooku and travel with him through Zululand.

ৰ্ঝ ৰ্ঝ ৰ্ঝ ৰ্ঝ ৰ্ঝ

Once back in England, Haggard decided to embark on a legal career and applied to enter Lincoln's Inn, arguing, to no avail, that his experi-ence as Master and Registrar of the High Court in the Transvaal should exempt him from the entrance examination. After a course at a cram-mer he duly passed the exam. Another three years of study lay ahead and to offset what he found a boring and irksome prospect, he turned to writing. His first book *Cetewayo and His White Neighbours* (1882) was

Cheyne Collection

Haggard (seated) *and his friend Arthur Cochrane*
shortly after their return to England from South Africa in 1881.
Mazooku's knobkerrie is stuck in the flowerbed.

an historical work, largely an apologia for Shepstone and his policies in the Transvaal, combined with an attack on Wolseley's settlement of Zululand after the war in 1879. He then tried his hand at fiction but, after producing two potboilers, *Dawn* (1884) and *The Witch's Head* (1884), he decided to concentrate on his legal career until fate intervened, in the form of a chance conversation.

Lilias records how one day Haggard was travelling to London with one of his brothers when they began discussing the recently published and highly successful *Treasure Island* by Robert Louis Stevenson. 'Rider said he didn't think it was so very remarkable, whereupon his brother replied, rather indignantly: "Well, I'd like to see you write anything half as good, bet you a bob you can't." "Done," said Rider.' The result of the bet was *King Solomon's Mines* published in 1885.[56]

The book proved a sensation, owing much of its success to the novelty of its African setting. Haggard suddenly found himself a famous author, drawing praise from literary figures such as Andrew Lang and Stevenson. Now established as a best-selling author, a constant flow of books came from Haggard's pen, among them *She* (1887), *Jess* (1887), *Allan Quatermain* (1887), *Cleopatra* (1889), *Nada the Lily* (1892), *Montezuma's Daughter* (1893), and the later Zulu trilogy of *Marie* (1912), *Child of Storm* (1913) and *Finished* (1917).

The Haggard family also expanded, with the birth of Angela in 1883 and Dorothy in 1884. But Haggard's fame and success were marred by personal tragedy. His son Jock died in 1891 at the age of 10 while Rider and Louie were visiting Mexico. Haggard became depressed and began to suffer from influenza and digestive problems. Respiratory problems, particularly bronchitis, were to affect him for the rest of his life. The death of Jock also signals the end of Haggard's most creative period and, when he later began to emerge from his grief, the beginning of Haggard's life as a 'farmer' and 'a man of affairs'.

> Be it good or be it bad, the best that I can do in the lines of romance and novel-writing is to be found among the first dozen or so of the books that I wrote, say between *King Solomon's Mines* and *Montezuma's Daughter*. Also I would add this. A man's mind does not always remain the same. People are apt to say of any individual writer that he has gone off, whereas the truth may be merely that he has changed, and that his abilities are showing themselves in another form. Now, as it happens in my own case, in the year 1891 I received a great shock; also subsequently for a long period my health was bad. Although from necessity I went on with the writing of stories, and do so still, it has not been with the same zest. Active rather than imaginative life has appealed to me more, and resulted in the production of such works as *Rural England* and *A Farmer's Year*, and others.[57]

After the death of Jock, Haggard retreated to Ditchingham where he lived in 'a very quiet and retired fashion, rarely visiting London, wrote a few novels, and for recreation occupied myself with farming and gardening'.[58] With the birth of his daughter Lilias on 9 December 1892, Haggard noted his 'health and spirits began to mend and my energy to return'.[59] He also employed a secretary, Ida Hector, to whom he dic-

Cheyne Collection

H. Rider Haggard in the 1890s.

tated his later books. 'I was obliged to give up writing long books with my own hand, as the constant leaning over a desk affected my health.'[60]

His interest in the world beyond the borders of his Ditchingham estate was rekindled by the birth of Lilias, and in 1893 he began writing letters to *The Times* and making public speeches, many of them concerned with Rhodesia, then a subject of great public interest because of the Ndebele War. Consequently he was asked to contest the safe Conservative seat at King's Lynn. 'I declined because of the expense and the difficulty of getting backwards and forwards between my home and the borough, since this was before the day of motors.'[61]

Defeat at the polls — 1895

In 1895 when the call came again for Haggard to stand for parliament, he was ready. 'I was utterly weary of a retired life and of the writing of books, from which I sought eagerly for some avenue of escape.'[62] His letters and speeches on South Africa had attracted the attention of 'those interested in the affairs of that country' and he was elected chairman of the Anglo-African Writers' Club, 'a pleasant and useful dining society that is now defunct'.[63] He also accepted an offer from a friend, William Wills, to become co-director in a company publishing the weekly *African Review* – 'the most trustworthy Journal for Investors, and all those interested in the South African Industries'[64] – as well as actively speculating in those industries. Implicit in the agreement was the understanding that Haggard would stand for parliament 'with the general idea of giving my attention to African affairs in the House of Commons'.[65] Unlike King's Lynn, the East Norfolk division, the seat he was invited to stand for by the Conservatives as a Unionist and Agricultural candidate, was not a safe bet.

During his election campaign Haggard was accompanied by Arthur Cochrane who warmed up the audience with comic songs before Haggard delivered his speech. A campaign, Dickensian in character, ensued and Haggard often left the village halls and public houses where he spoke to be met with a deluge of stones. As a result of what became known as the Battle of Stalham Bridge, Haggard's opponent, Lord Wodehouse, and a drover were charged with assault and fined. Small comfort to Haggard who lost by 198 votes. He would not stand for parliament again.

> Now I understand I never was a real Tory – that, in short, as a party man I am the most miserable failure. As a politician I should have been useless from any whip's point of view. He would – well, have struck me off his list as neither hot nor cold, as a dangerous and undesirable individual who, refusing to swallow the shibboleths of his tribe with shut eyes, actually dared to think for himself and to possess that hateful thing, 'a cross-bench mind'.[66]

> In the same way, what place is there in politics for a man like myself who has the most earnest sympathies with the poor and who desires to advance their lot in every reasonable way, but who loathes and detests the Radical method of attempting to set class against class, and aiming all their artillery at the middle section of society – and the real prop of the race – for the reason that it is Conservative in its instincts and votes against them at the polls.[67]

Haggard found his own instincts at variance with the life of a businessman in the city – 'it was all much too speculative for me, while the burden of those companies weighed upon my mind heavily' – and when his partner Wills announced that he was heading out to South Africa leaving him to conduct the company's 'extremely intricate affairs', Haggard acted promptly to dissolve the partnership.[68] 'My town excitements over I returned to the country and the writing of books. Oddly enough, I found that the thorough change of thought seemed to have rested my mind, with the result that my imagination was fresher than it had been for some years before. Also the work itself was and has remained less irksome to me than during the years 1891 to 1895. Still the desire haunted me to do something in my day more practical than the mere invention of romance upon romance. By degree it came home to me that a great subject lay to my hand, that of the state of English agriculture and of our rural population.'[69]

Haggard first wrote of what he knew: a diary of life and work on the Ditchingham estate. A day-by-day account of the year 1898, it was published in book form as *A Farmer's Year* (1899). 'At first he saw himself in his father's image – certainly not as a reformer or crusader,' comments biographer Morton Cohen. 'It was the experience he gained on his land, and in writing a chatty journal, that translated the country squire into an aggressive reformer.'[70] Haggard came to the conclusion 'that the state of English agriculture was even more appalling than he had imagined'. His journal became, 'at least in part, a record of the plight of the man on the land and a plea for a vanishing way of life'.[71]

For Haggard, even when deep in the Norfolk countryside, Africa was never far away. With the declaration of the Second Anglo-Boer War in 1899, *Cetywayo and His White Neighbours* was reissued in an abridged version, *The Last Boer War* (1899), with a new Introduction, and in 1900 he was approached by *The Times* with a view to becoming a war correspondent in South Africa 'but this did not strike me as an attractive business at my age'.[72] Instead he entered into an agreement with the *Daily Express* to write a series of articles after the war dealing with 'The New South Africa'. 'This engagement was never fulfilled, for the reason that the war dragged on for another two years or so, before which time the British public was utterly weary of the subject of South Africa.'[73]

Rural rides — 1901–02

However when the *Express* suggested cancelling the contract, Haggard came up with an alternative proposal: that he emulate the eighteenth-century agricultural reformer Arthur Young, who toured the England of his day (between 1768 and 1771) reporting on the state of its agriculture. The *Express* agreed and commissioned a series of 50 articles. Haggard sent out the call for the faithful Cochrane and the two set off on a trip through the counties of England. As well as the commissioned articles, Haggard produced the two-volume *Rural England: Being an Account of the Agricultural and Social Researches Carried Out in the Years 1901 & 1902*. The work was published in November 1902 and chronicles visits to 26 counties. Haggard declared it 'the heaviest labour of all my laborious life'.[74]

His labours produced a 'picture of rural exodus, neglect, and decay'.[75] According to Haggard, the decline in English agriculture was the result of vast numbers of the rural population moving to the cities. To counter this phenomenon he suggested reviving smallholdings and making loans available to those wanting to buy land, thereby creating a class of new landowners. He also called for a reduction in agricultural taxes and the restriction of foreign imports. As Haggard well knew, such ideas flew in the face of the current orthodoxy of his class – both political and agricultural. 'What would be thought of one who, posing as a member of the Tory party, yet earnestly advocated the division of the land amongst about ten times as many as hold it at present, thereby spoiling a great many great estates, and often enough interfering with the interests and pleasures of those who shoot and hunt, or who seek this road to success? Assuredly for such a one there is no standing room upon any of our political platforms. "Away with him!", would be the cry. Therefore, he must be content to remain outside, doing whatever work may come to his hand which he conceives to be clean and, in however humble a measure, useful.'[76]

Though some might look askance at Haggard's views, his work brought him recognition as a major authority on agriculture and, at the same time, made him something of a thorn in the side of government. Indeed it was Haggard's potential nuisance value that led in part to an invitation from Alfred Lyttleton, Secretary of State for the Colonies, to become a commissioner appointed to visit the United States and report on the 'Labour Colonies' established there by the Salvation Army and 'used for the transmigration of persons from the big American cities. It is thought that if on inquiry this system is found to be financially sound and to be a real benefit to the poorer classes, it might prove a useful model for some analogous system of settlement from the United Kingdom to the Colonies.' Lyttleton baited his trap well, suggesting to Haggard that it was a post to which 'your experience as an observer both of men and agricultural affairs so eminently qualifies you'.[77]

Haggard had already met General William Booth, founder and Commander-in-Chief of the Salvation Army, during his researches for *Rural England*. Both men believed that smallholdings were the answer to keeping people on the land and the Salvation Army had established training camps in England and the United States to provide skills to the urban poor, thus enabling them to lead productive rural lives. Funded by the Rhodes Trustees, Haggard would not officially be a government representative. The trusting Haggard only discovered later the implications of his status. The Commission was a paper tiger, as the government had always intended it to be, serving to mollify General Booth 'whose constant revelations about the plight of the urban poor were even more damaging to the Cabinet than Haggard's writings'.[78] During an election year the Commission would safely divert the attentions of these two prominent critics from the home front.

Unaware of this official deviousness, Haggard, accompanied by his 22-year-old daughter Angela, sailed for New York on 22 February 1905 as a proud representative of his country. This was his first visit to New York since January 1891 when, en route to Mexico, Haggard had been fêted as the famous novelist. Once again the press descended but Haggard wasn't interested in talking about his writing. 'My mind is all on the commission,' he declared, leaving the reporter of the *New York Herald* to comment that 'Rider Haggard of the new crusade is another man from the jaunty romancer of a decade ago.'[79]

In Washington, Haggard met the newly re-elected President, Theodore Roosevelt. Of Dutch descent, Roosevelt was sympathetic to the Boers in South Africa, hoping that 'they would settle down, learn English, and become a dominant factor in that country under the British flag and rule'.[80] Haggard lunched at the White House with Roosevelt, who had read *Rural England*, and was pleased to find the President's views on agriculture coincided with his own. Roosevelt later sent a note to Haggard at his hotel asking to be kept informed on his findings with regard to the Salvation Army colonies.

The meeting with Roosevelt, together with an encouraging interview with James Wilson, the Secretary for Agriculture, saw Haggard begin his American journey with enthusiasm. In a coast-to-coast rail journey he managed to visit three Salvation Army colonies: Fort Romie near San Francisco, Fort Amity in Colorado and Fort Herrick in Ohio, as well as visiting Salt Lake City to investigate the smallholdings organised by the Mormons. In Canada his enthusiasm was matched by that of the Canadian government, which offered 240 000 acres of land as a gift for future settlement by British immigrants.

On his return to England, Haggard found the British government less responsive. Some weeks after the presentation of his report he had a brief interview with Lyttelton who, while expressing delight at the report, declaring it 'splendid', added: 'I wish the Prime Minister would take it up. But *Arthur* [Balfour] *won't read it – you know Arthur won't read it.*'[81]

In a bid to spur the authorities into action, Haggard persuaded Longmans to publish a copy of his report as a Blue Book for public consumption. Entitled *The Poor and the Land*, it placed the issue before a larger audience and received favourable mentions in the press. But to little avail. After some debate in the House of Commons, Haggard's report was referred to a departmental committee. 'The end of the matter may be briefly summarised. As was to be anticipated, "the bottom was knocked out" of my scheme in the most satisfactory official way.'[82]

Haggard was clearly hurt by the official cold shoulder. In the United States and Canada he had been treated as a statesman but at home he was relegated to the tradesman's entrance. 'I had worked hard and in all honestness, and, like many better men I had found myself thrown over. After all the Colonial Secretary's declarations as to the value of my work, etc., I never even received a letter of thanks from the government, or, for that matter, a copy of the Report and Evidence of the Committee, which I had to buy like any other member of the public. All I got was the privilege of paying the bill, for of course the small sum allowed by the Rhodes Trustees did not suffice to meet the expenses of my tour in a high official position through that very expensive country, the United States.'[83]

The strain of the experience appears to have affected Haggard's health and in 1906 he underwent a minor operation 'which the effects of my long journey made necessary'.[84] But his appetite for public service was still strong. Balfour's government fell at the end of 1905 and Haggard hoped that his talents might be utilised by the new Liberal government under Sir Henry Campbell-Bannerman. No invitations were forthcoming but when Haggard heard of plans to create a Royal Commission on Coast Erosion, he wrote to Lloyd George, then President of the Board of Trade, offering his services and stating his credentials.

Coastal erosion was (and is) a constant feature of the East Anglian coastline, as Haggard well knew. In the early 1900s he had bought Kessingland Grange on the coast near Lowestoft and to counter the force of the North Sea and the winds coming off it, he sloped the cliff on the edge of his property, planting it with marram grass, a dune plant that helped to bind the sand. The experiment proved successful, the slope increasing in height rather than diminishing.

Haggard was duly invited to join the Commission, on which he worked for five years. At the end of the first year, Haggard, deciding the 'Coast Erosion business . . . had been somewhat exaggerated',[85] suggested adding 'the question of Afforestation . . . to our reference'.[86] In due course the Commission presented a report suggesting that areas of wasteland be afforested. 'Needless to say it was not adopted; its fate was the fate of my Land Settlement Report, minus the appointment of a Committee to "knock the bottom out of it".'[87] The Commission then went back to examining coastlines. 'I wonder if there isn't a groin [groyne] or an eroded beach on the shores of the United Kingdom that I have not seen and thoughtfully considered.'[88]

In between his commission work, Haggard found time to write a book about the Salvation Army and its work in response to a request from Booth. Refusing payment, except for expenses, Haggard embarked on a three-month tour of the Salvation Army's institutions in cities throughout the country. On completion he signed over the copyright of *Regeneration* (1910) to the Salvation Army.

In 1911 Haggard published another work of non-fiction, *Rural Denmark*, the result of 'another task I undertook in the intervals of my Royal Commission'.[89] In other intervals Haggard continued the writing of romances and novels, which effectively subsidised his public service and agricultural interests. Between 1900 and 1911 he completed 14 books, including *The Brethren* (1904); *Ayesha* (1905), the sequel to *She*; and *The Ghost Kings* (1908), with a plot developed in collaboration with his friend Rudyard Kipling, to whom in 1906 he had dedicated *The Way of the Spirit*. In Kipling, Haggard had a friend who shared his belief that life should transcend writing – 'both of us believe that there are higher aims in life than the weaving of stories well or ill, and according to our separate occasions strive to fulfil this faith.'[90]

Depression and the death of Lilly – April 1909

Haggard's striving came to an end when the Royal Commission on Coast Erosion and Afforestation was finally wound up. Suddenly at a loose end, depression set in and he battled with bronchitis. 'I miss that commission very much,' he wrote in his autobiography, 'since its sitting took me to London from time to time, and gave me a change of mental occupation and interests. Indeed I do not remember ever being more consistently depressed than I was during the first part of the following winter. Here, as I no longer shoot, I had nothing to do, except the daily grind of romance-writing, relieved only by Bench business, my farm affairs, and an afternoon walk through the mud with the two spaniels, Bustle and Jeekie, and a chat after church on Sunday upon the affairs of the nation with my fellow churchwarden, friend and neighbour, Mr. Carr, the squire of this place.'[91]

Other factors probably contributed to his low spirits. In particular, the death of his first love Lilly Jackson in 1909. He had maintained if not direct contact, at least knowledge of her affairs, through his friendship with her brother Frederick Jackson. In 1895, following charges of embezzlement, her stockbroker husband had fled the country to Africa, leaving Lilly, their three young sons and her unmarried sisters in dire straits. Haggard took them under his wing and found a home for them at Snape, near Aldeburgh, on the Suffolk coast. In 1898, Lilly's husband asked her to join him in Africa and against all advice she did so. She returned in 1907 suffering from syphilis that she had contracted from her husband and from which he died. Once again she came under Haggard's protection and joined her sisters at Snape where she died on 22 April 1909 with Haggard at her deathbed.

Lilly's death had been preceded by that of Haggard's first grandchild, born to Angela and Tom Haggard, at less than seven months. The same year found him supervising the construction of the family vault at St Mary's, Ditchingham, with shelves for 20 urns. 'I could not help reflecting that the next time I went down into that vault it would probably be in a compacter form.'[92]

During this melancholy time Haggard began writing his autobiography 'for really it seemed as though everything had come to an end'.[93] This statement, from a man in his mid-fifties, along with the work's title *The Days of My Life*, give an indication of the sense of sadness that impregnates the book. Sadness and frustrated ambition, regret that he had been unable 'to gratify a very earnest ambition of my younger years, namely, to enter parliament and shine as a statesman'.[94]

The Days of My Life reads like the work of a far older man but in the final pages a new energy emerges – 'of a sudden things changed, as they have a way of doing in life'. A letter from the Prime Minister (Herbert Asquith) just before Christmas 1911 brought news of a knighthood, which Haggard accepted on the grounds that 'a title is useful in the public service, and especially so abroad. Moreover, it was Recognition, for which I felt grateful; for who is there that does not appreciate recognition particularly after long years of, I hope, disinterested toil?'[95]

Public recognition and honour – January 1912

There was more welcome news to follow. On 11 January 1912, shortly after Haggard was gazetted a Knight Bachelor in the New Year Honours List, a letter arrived from Lewis Harcourt, Secretary of the Colonial Office,[96] inviting him to be one of the commissioners appointed to the 'Royal Commission to visit the various Dominions and report upon them'.

The Colonial Office was responsible for the dependent crown colonies and the business of the self-governing colonies of white settlement: Australia, New Zealand, South Africa, Newfoundland and Canada, referred to as the dominions following an agreement at the Colonial conference in 1907. 'The inquiry will probably extend over three years,' wrote Harcourt, 'and it will entail three visits to the Dominions – one of three months to Canada and Newfoundland, another of three months to South Africa, and another of six months to Australia and New Zealand.'[97]

His publisher and friend Charles Longman enthused over Haggard's appointment: 'I would rather have heard this than they had given you a peerage. Anyone can be a peer, but to be one of the six men chosen to represent the United Kingdom on a great Empire inquiry of this sort is a real honour.'[98]

Though the British Empire covered around a quarter of the globe and accounted for the same number of its inhabitants, competition with other industrialised nations was growing fierce and there were signs of decline in both the economic and military spheres. 'The Weary Titan staggers under the too vast orb of its fate,' said Joseph Chamberlain, addressing the premiers of the white settler societies at the Colonial conference of 1902. 'We have borne the burden long enough. We think it is time our children should assist us to support it.'[99] How exactly, would be the task of the Dominions Royal Commission to find out.

The Commission was appointed on the recommendation of the Imperial conference held in London over 12 days in May and June 1911. Sir Wilfred Laurier, the first French-Canadian Prime Minister of Canada, proposed the appointment of 'a Royal Commission representing the United Kingdom, Canada, Australia, New Zealand, South Africa, and Newfoundland, with a view to investigating and reporting upon the natural resources of each part of the Empire represented at this Conference, the development attained and attainable, and the facilities for production, manufacture, and distribution, the trade of each part with the others and with the outside world, the food and raw material requirements of each, and the sources thereof available, to what extent, if any, the trade between each of the different parts has been affected by legislation in each, either beneficially or otherwise'.[100] This proposal, with an extra clause to safeguard the Liberal government's adherence to the principle of free trade, provided the foundation for the Commission.

There were to be six representatives from the United Kingdom and one from each of the five dominions. After a few reshuffles and resignations, the final appointments were: chairman, Sir Edgar Vincent, later Lord D'Abernon; Sir Alfred Bateman; Joseph Tatlow; William Lorimer; Tom Garnett; and Haggard. The dominions were represented by George Eulas Foster (Canada); Sir Jan Willem Langerman (South Africa); John Robert Sinclair (New Zealand); Donald Campbell (Australia); and Edgar Rennie Bowring (Newfoundland). The secretary was Edward Harding.[101]

The Dominions Royal Commission travelled to Australia and New Zealand in 1913 and to South Africa in February 1914. Their visit to Newfoundland and Canada, which began in July 1914, ended after the declaration of war in August 1914. The visit to Canada was resumed in August 1916 (minus Haggard). An interim report was issued after each visit and the Final Report was signed on 21 February 1917. 'The report constitutes the most complete record of any Imperial investigation that has yet been carried out,' declared *The Times*.[102]

ھ ھ ھ ھ ھ

Even before Haggard had embarked on his official duties, it was clear his appointment to the Commission brought with it a new lease on life. After a short visit to Egypt to shake off his ever-present bronchitis, he returned to England restored in mind and body. Perhaps in a bid to put the past behind him, he quickly finished his autobiography before consigning it to a safe at Longmans with the instruction that it should not be published until after his death. He then embarked on an Allan Quatermain adventure *Allan and the Holy Flower* (published in 1915). Another Quatermain novel, *Marie*, the first of his Zulu trilogy, had been published in 1912 and, by then, with Africa beckoning, it was only fitting that he should dedicate it to the man under whose wing he first went there, Sir Henry Bulwer.

Child of Storm, the second in the trilogy, had been written first. When it was published in 1913, it was dedicated to James Stuart (1868–1942), a Natal civil servant whose contact with the Zulus and other African peoples had led him to empathise with their situation while, at the same time, being responsible for implementing the policies of colonial control. Over several decades Stuart had collected and recorded the testimonies of nearly 200 informants on a range of topics concerning the history of the Zulus and their neighbours. The resulting archive has been described as 'one of the richest sources available to the student interested in the language, the literature and the history of the African peoples of Natal, Zululand and Swaziland'.[103]

Haggard met Stuart in London in 1912, ostensibly to discuss a mooted biography of Theophilus Shepstone, who had died in 1893 and as yet was without a biographer, a situation his son Arthur wished to remedy. In an attempt to induce Haggard to write the biography, he offered the services of Stuart to do the research, 'to help in collecting the necessary material, which is scattered about in all kinds of family records, documents, pamphlets, books and blue books, dating from as far back as 1833'. Stuart would be in England between May and August supervising publication of his *A History of the Zulu Rebellion* and Shepstone suggested that Haggard 'might wish to avail yourself of his services'.[104]

Haggard declined the invitation to write the biography as 'I have before me a very responsible and important piece of government work which will closely occupy me for some years to come and take me much from home.'[105] However, he offered to write an introduction and to meet Stuart to discuss the form and content of the book. When Stuart arrived in London, Haggard did indeed avail himself of his services, but with regard to *Child of Storm*. Stuart read the manuscript making various suggestions which Haggard incorporated, together with the Zulu national anthem, which, according to Stuart, had never been seen in print.[106] Haggard was to meet Stuart again in South Africa and during their tour of Zululand together obtained information that he used in the third volume of the Zulu trilogy, *Finished*, published in 1916 and dedicated to Theodore Roosevelt.

When *Child of Storm* was published in January 1913, Haggard was in Australia on his first trip as a royal commissioner. He had prefaced the visit with one to India where he visited his daughter Dorothy and her husband, Major Reginald Cheyne. He toured the country, visiting the Taj Mahal before continuing on to Ceylon where he joined his fellow commissioners when their ship, the *Medina*, called at Colombo.

'Sir Rider Haggard turned up safely at Colombo,' wrote Harding, the Commission's secretary, in a letter to his father, saying that as the Commission party was now complete he would attempt 'a few character sketches, but I may as well wait a few days, so as to get a better impression of Rider Haggard'.[107] Five days lapsed before he commented on Haggard. 'I suspend judgment on him. I think he is of the temperament which has very ordinary Imperial ideas, and thinks they are extraordinary. Perhaps that is the result of being a novelist with a really keen imagination.'[108] In Adelaide a few days later, when reporters came aboard, Harding sardonically noted that 'fortunately Rider Haggard is used to them, and, though he would disclaim it, obviously rather likes them.'[109]

Harding wasn't the only person aboard keeping a diary. Over the years Haggard had always kept a rough diary-cum-notebook and, while continuing this habit, he now worked them up into more detailed diaries. Before his departure for India, Haggard had also written to Harcourt, the Colonial Secretary, asking whether 'when I am in Australasia and elsewhere you would like me to send you some confidential letters, not, of course, on the affairs of the Dominions Royal Commission or, except indirectly perhaps, on anything which it has to do, but on general topics'. Harcourt agreed and the letters dealing with his visit to South Africa provide an appendix to *Diary of an African Journey*, as Haggard requested that they should in the event of publication.[110]

After visiting New Zealand with the Commission, Haggard returned to England by way of the Pacific and a crossing of the United States. By the .time he arrived home at Ditchingham, Haggard had been away from his family for six months. It had been a lonely experience and, anticipating his return to South Africa the following year, he resolved not to travel alone but accompanied by Louie and their 22-year-old daughter Lilias.

Africa beckons — February 1914

The trip to South Africa began with a private visit to Madeira. The Haggards had visited Madeira, the setting for Haggard's first novel *Dawn*, in 1881 during their return from Africa in the wake of the British defeat at Majuba Hill. Haggard joined his fellow commissioners on 11 February 1914 when the *Kinfauns Castle* docked at Funchal.

The Dominions Royal Commission arrived in Cape Town on 24 February. Its planned programme was to visit all four provinces – the Cape, Orange Free State, Natal and Transvaal – of the Union of South Africa

Natal Witness

Members of the Dominions Royal Commission.
Back row (from left to right): *Sandeman, Frank Robb (DRC's South Africa agent), H. Pearce (staff), Edward Harding (secretary), A.H. Bridgman (staff), J.H. Law (shorthand reporter).*
Centre row (from left to right): *William Lorimer (United Kingdom), Edgar Bowring (Newfoundland), Joseph Tatlow, Tom Garnett (United Kingdom), John Sinclair (New Zealand).*
Front row (from left to right): *Sir Jan Langerman (South Africa), Donald Campbell (Australia), Sir Edgar Vincent (chairman), Alfred Bateman, Sir Henry Rider Haggard (United Kingdom).*

during its stay. Once the Commission had completed its work, Haggard planned to travel on to Rhodesia and then tour Zululand. Throughout the trip he kept a rough diary and during the return journey up the East African coast on the *Gaika* worked it up into its final publishable form, adding his extended thoughts and reflections. Among them he noted that 'racial animosities are beginning to die down'. He was referring to those between Boer and Briton, the burning race issue of the day 12 years after the end of the Second Anglo-Boer War. But Haggard was not blind to the aspirations of the black majority in South Africa, observing that 'the black man is driving a wedge into the fabric of European civilisation, is permeating it through and through . . . He is beginning to think for himself and to demand a fair share for the rewards of his labour.'

Haggard records how Sir Meiring Becke saw a solution to South Africa's racial problems in the fusion of the black and white races. While not in agreement, Haggard did think that 'in a time to come . . . that these will in effect rule in their own land is not at all incredible'. He dismissed as absurd a plan proposed by Henry Nourse, a prominent Rand mine owner, 'for segregating all the natives'.

In the discussion with Mrs Louis Botha touched on earlier, he agreed with her that 'the Native could no longer be suppressed, or even oppressed: he must follow his destiny and often was an able and a capable person.'

Observing the conditions of migrant labourers on the diamond mines at Kimberley he noted it a 'strange and unnatural life that these slaves of Vanity endure . . . To isolate thousands of men without their womenkind, cannot be good.' But Haggard the romancer is not kept completely at bay. There are plenty of imaginative flourishes to be found in the diary, for example during his visit to the Cango Caves or while scaling the Zimbabwe Ruins and reflecting on the destruction of the Ndebele. 'Conquest, conquest, conquest! that is history in the blood-stained land of Africa. Perhaps one day their turn will come again, either with steel or bullet, or more probably by mere weight of numbers and the ballot box.'

Surprisingly perhaps, considering his depiction of Africa's indigenous peoples in his earlier books and even in the later Zulu trilogy, his sympathies clearly lay with the Zulus, who had endured 'an unnecessary war in which 10 000 were killed, then all the subsequent troubles'. He was highly critical of land-hungry whites occupying the crown lands in Zululand. 'The white population, I was told is about 100 and the native population about 16 000, yet the whites are supposed to require twice as much land as the Natives! This is typical of what is going on all over S. Africa.'

Land was one of the issues dealt with in Haggard's interview with John Dube. 'I am bound to say that he impressed me most favourably while the case which he advanced seems to me a hard one to answer.' Hard or not, Haggard was not optimistic concerning the outcome of Dube's petition to the Union government or the British King with regard to reform of the Native Land Act (1913). But the black majority 'cannot be permanently neglected – or is oppressed the word? – by one million and a quarter whites. Compressed steam will escape somehow and somewhere.'[111]

In conversation with Maurice Evans, Haggard agreed that the 'white man has a very heavy bill to pay to the Native and certainly he will be called upon to discharge it in this coin or that. Those who persistently sow the wind must expect to reap the whirlwind.' He also noted the opinion of John X. Merriman, former Prime Minister of the Cape Colony, that the African 'has wrongs to be righted which gives him a moral advantage, a great support in any national struggle'.

Within weeks of returning from South Africa, Haggard had resumed his travels, sailing from Liverpool for Canada with members of the

Dominions Royal Commission on 17 July. They arrived at St John's, the capital of Newfoundland, on the 25th to hear reports of the crisis in Europe arising out of the June assassination of Archduke Ferdinand and his wife in Sarajevo. 'Today we heard that there is a grave peril of a European war, news which racks us with anxiety,' Haggard wrote in his diary on 29 July.[112]

In Halifax, Nova Scotia, on 5 August he recorded that 'this morning we learned that England had declared war against Germany on the ground of the violation of the neutrality of Belgium by that power.' The commissioners wired home for instructions on what to do. In response they received 'a peremptory telegram from H.M.'s Government recalling us home after we have completed our work in the maritime provinces'.[113]

Two days later at a dinner held for the commissioners, Haggard made an impromptu speech extemporising on themes 'that had been simmering in my mind for days'.[114] It was a clarion call to the Empire to come to Britain's aid. 'For today we stand at desperate straits with Fate. The Angel of Death appears in a dawn of blood; the Armageddon which has long been foretold has at length fallen upon us.'[115]

Harding, the Commission's secretary, was not impressed. 'Haggard distinguished himself by making a speech which some people think the extreme of pessimism, and others a "trumpet-call" . . . I think the speech in the very worst of taste. But Haggard prides himself on his diplomacy!'[116]

On 21 August the commissioners sailed for England where, in November, the Commission was 'adjourned till the conclusion of the war'.[117]

His work on the Dominions Royal Commission proved to be the high-water mark of Haggard's career as a 'man of affairs'; he would never enjoy such a high public profile again.

کی کی کی کی کی

Safely restored to England, Haggard was soon busy putting his shoulder to the war effort. In September a recruitment speech by Haggard was produced in pamphlet form as *A Call to Arms*, with a print run of 10 000, although his suggestion that a Royal Commission be created to investigate alleged German atrocities in Belgium was turned down.

Meanwhile, the staging of 'Mameena', a stage version of *Child of Storm* mounted by Oscar Asche, provided some distraction although Haggard thought the production should be postponed as inappropriate to the times. Haggard was not particularly impressed with the production, which attracted favourable notices. 'London had never before seen what appeared to be real Zulus in all their war rig-out.'[118] That such authenticity was achieved was thanks to James Stuart, who had been hired to purchase costumes and supervise the Zulu dances in the play. But Haggard was right, the times were inappropriate. Wartime lighting restrictions discouraged theatre-goers and 'Mameena' had its last performance on 14 January 1915, when Asche's lease on the Globe Theatre expired. He lost at least £8 000, although this he recouped a couple of years later with his hit 'Chu Chin Chow'.[119]

As the lights went out in London, and, more famously, 'all over Europe', Haggard was beginning to feel like one of yesterday's men. Though he served on two committees under the banner of the Royal Agricultural Society, offers of service to his country in more concrete ways were declined. 'It would appear that men like myself who have life-long experience and much accumulated knowledge are practically of no value to the country . . . I feel sore, and not altogether for my own sake, since I know well enough that I could still do good work for the nation, if only I were given the chance.'[120]

There was a glimmer of hope in July 1915 when it was suggested that Haggard be despatched around the dominions to investigate the possible settlement of servicemen overseas at the end of the war. Then a silence until, to Haggard's surprise, he heard that he was to head a small commission created by the government for this purpose. In the event the investigation into post-war land settlement was funded by the Royal Colonial Institute. Haggard was to visit South Africa, Australia, New Zealand and Canada – 'a long and arduous business. I can only hope the mission will be fortunate and fruitful. At any rate it is my duty to take the risks, go ahead and do the work to the best of my ability. Here is my war offering!'[121]

On 27 February 1916, Haggard found himself back in Cape Town where he spent two weeks being unusually circumspect in the light of advice that the political situation was 'very strained and that I must be most careful in my public utterances re land settlement which would instantly be seized on by the Nationalist party'.[122]

In Cape Town he met again with several of the personalities he had seen during his visit with the Royal Commission in 1914, including John X. Merriman and the Prime Minister, General Louis Botha. He dined with his old friend John Kotze and met his wife 'whom I have not seen for thirty-seven years (and) is now a handsome old lady, but deaf. The unmarried daughters are curiously early Victorian in appearance.'[123] He also reminisced with Sir William Beaumont, another old friend, about people and friends they had known in the 1870s. 'They are nearly all dead, but a few remain, retired like Beaumont himself.'[124]

He found his meeting with General J.B.M. Herzog, founder of the National Party, less congenial. 'A thin dark-eyed man,' with 'a dangerous face, that of a fanatic, brooding, intense and rather cruel.'[125]

African farewell – March 1916

On 13 March he sailed for Australia. 'So for the fourth time I bid farewell to the shores of South Africa, leaving them as usual peopled by

problems and political trouble. I think that I have done everything possible in the time and am fairly satisfied with the results.'

After touring Australia and New Zealand, he sailed for Vancouver
celebrating 'a very lonesome' 60th birthday aboard the *S.S. Niagara*.
'Today I have definitely entered upon old age, for at sixty a man is old,
especially when he begins young as I did. My work, for the most part,
lies behind me, rather poor stuff too – yet I will say this: I have worked.
My talent may be of copper not of gold – how can I judge of my own
abilities? – but I have put it to the best use I could. My opportunities
have not been many, and for the most part I have made them for myself; the book writing, the agricultural research business, the public
work for instance.'[126]

In Canada his spirits were raised by the favourable response to his
mission and the proposal that a peak and a glacier in the Rocky Mountains be named after him. 'It is a curious world. Here they give my
name to a towering Alp; in Norfolk they would not bestow it on a
"pightle".[127] Truly no man is a prophet in his own country.'[128] By August
Haggard was back at Ditchingham, when the local doctor prescribed
'rest and strychnine tonic and says I am not to travel again at present.
That mission has taken it out of me.'[129]

Despite the interest in post-war settlement he encountered on his
travels, and the promises of land for serviceman he brought back, the
British government was unmoved. In the third year of war, provision
for servicemen after the fighting was not a priority. Haggard's report to
the Royal Colonial Institute – *The After-War Settlement and the Employment of Ex-servicemen* (1916) – was published and largely ignored.

Another casualty of the war was Haggard's farm. 'Now when I grow
old and the responsibilities and worries are so many, the time has come
for me to stop.' No longer economically viable, he had been advised to
sell the farm and eventually did so. Following the sale of his animal
stock, he reflected that 'I have made nothing, if return on capital is
taken into account, but I have gained a vast amount of experience,
without which I could not have written my books on agriculture, which
will, I trust humbly, prove of permanent value and interest in time to
come.'[130]

Around the same time he donated the bound manuscripts of his
novels (those written by hand prior to his employment of a secretary)
and some letters to the Castle Museum in Norwich, together with Cochrane's notebooks, which had formed the foundation for *Rural England*.[131]

February 1917 saw the final dissolution of the Dominions Royal
Commission and the publication of its 24-volume report. The following
month Haggard was elected vice-president of the Royal Colonial Institute and in April he was appointed a member ('though of course I would
have liked the Chairmanship')[132] of the Empire Settlement Committee,
which had largely come about as a response to his endeavours.

During 1917, somewhat to Haggard's chagrin, it was announced that D'Abernon and Harding were to be decorated for their services on the Dominions Royal Commission – a GCMG (Grand Commander of St Michael and St George) and a CMG (Companion) respectively – 'the five-year-long labours and journeyings of the rest of us are not acknowledged.'[133]

Some comfort was to be had when he was appointed a Knight Commander of the British Empire [KBE] in the New Year Honours List of 1919. 'Though what I have always wished to become is a Privy Councillor . . . However, one mustn't look a gift horse in the mouth, and it is a recognition of my work for Empire.' He hoped it would lead to more 'honorary work before I grow too old for it'.[134]

The end of the war found Haggard at a low ebb. His chronic bronchitis had led to emphysema and in January 1919 his health forced him to abandon an appointment as an inspector for the Agricultural Wages Board. He was to have visited the West Country with the faithful Cochrane once more in tow. But that undertaking was called off when in Truro, Cornwall, a doctor declared that 'Sir Rider is running grave risk in going about the country in a motor-car and stopping at casual inns.'[135] Haggard sent in his resignation.

He continued to campaign on behalf of post-war settlement but by now the impetus had passed from his hands. When, in April 1922, the Empire Settlement Bill, aimed at subsidising settlement schemes in the Empire, was given its Second Reading in the House of Commons, Haggard was at least able to feel that although his share 'in the business is now forgotten, I look upon this advance with some pride since surely I have had some part in bringing it about'.[136]

In July 1919, a Royal Commission on Agriculture was appointed but Haggard was not among its members despite his offer of service – 'on the whole I daresay I am well out of it.'[137] In 1920 he became a prime mover in the Liberty League, an anti-Bolshevik movement which ended in disarray when one of the officials absconded with the funds. After this, his last prominent involvement in public affairs, Haggard returned to Ditchingham where he was to spend the rest of his life in between wintering on the south coast to avoid the bleak Norfolk winters.

Final thoughts

Unpaid and unsung, Haggard continued to serve on committees such as those considering the National Birth Rate, the Relief of the Allies, and the Commission on Imperial Communication. In 1924, he asked to be considered for a place on a committee that the Colonial Office was considering appointing to investigate political, social and economic issues in East Africa. He was indeed appointed but health problems saw him unable to take an active role.

After several years of failing health, Arthur Cochrane, his 'oldest remaining and nearest friend, with whom in my youth in Africa I lived as a brother', died in January 1925.[138] Haggard was not well enough to attend his funeral. He had taken ill after attending the lunch to celebrate Longmans bi-centenary and after a brief rally he had returned to Ditchingham where he took to his bed and 'fought a losing battle with pain, weakness and depression'.[139]

Less than two months before his death, Haggard dictated a 14-page letter to Rudyard Kipling in which he attempted an assessment of his life's work. It is worth quoting at some length as it focuses almost entirely on his public life:

> ... under many disabilities and in the teeth of much official opposition (Lord! how officials hate the outsider with ideas) I have done my best to serve my country to the full extent of my small opportunities which, generally, I have had to make. Some fifteen years solid of it I have put in as one of the great unpaid on these accursed Commissions, etc., which really are trying because of the small minds that often you have to fight upon them. You argue and wear yourself out and they vote you down, and then in after years come and say they are so sorry, as now they see you were absolutely right and they were absolutely wrong.
>
> However, so far as the R. Commissions are concerned, the effort seems to have been utterly wasted, that is, if anything earnest is ever wasted in the end. When they had served the Government purpose they were chucked aside on the national rubbish heap at Whitehall.
>
> The only things that appear to have succeeded at all are what I have done off my own bat – such as the 'Rural England' work and my mission on behalf of the R. Colonial Institute during the war.
>
> To take the latter first. It was bitterly opposed by the Colonial Office at the time, I never quite found out why. Partly I think, however, from a kind of jealousy of such important matters being put into the hands of one whose findings carried some weight with the Public because they were known, at any rate, to be earnest and honest; and partly from fear lest I should make trouble with the Governments of the Dominions at a critical time, or stir up the passions of Labour thereby advocating the settling in them of migrants.
>
> Do you know I even found out that they even went the length of writing round to the various Governors to caution them heavily against me? Well, the results of it all were far different from what was anticipated. Instead of angering the Dominions, I conciliated them, and I may say honestly that I converted a hostile

Australia to my views, and brought home offers that were worth millions – which were thrown away by our Government.

These developments were received with official amazement, because you see duly appointed missions do not often produce much effect, and the end of it was they were driven to appoint a Committee upon which I served. Out of the findings of that Committee sprang the present Migration Act (Empire Settlement Act) which is imperfect and insufficient enough, but still a beginning – an egg out of which great things will, I hope, grow in time – and, honestly, I believe I had something to do with that egg.

It's all forgotten now (and indeed would be denied probably with indignation) except perhaps by my kindly old friend who thinks I ought to be sworn of the Privy Council, and, apparently at intervals so informs those who dispense the carrots. Quite without avail of course, for who wishes (especially if of the Conservative faith I have observed) to decorate the manes and tails of worn-out old horses with ribbons? But that don't matter one way or the other. Still honestly I believe the truth to be as I have stated.

The same thing with *Rural England*. After that Lloyd George consulted me on sundry occasions about the setting up of his Development Board,[140] its possible Chairman, etc. Indeed he went further, announcing that I was to be a member of that Board, sending Ashby St. Ledgers, now Lord Wimborne, to me to say so, with the result that, Lord Richard Cavendish in the chair, I attended the preliminary meeting. Ultimately, however, he threw me over to suit a political convenience. So the Board was established without me, to whom no explanations were offered. Only I think I had something to do with its origin.

But what is the use of dragging up all this past history, of which there is plenty more, I only wanted to show you that I have done the best I can single-handed, fighting against principalities and darksome, unknown powers in Government offices, and on the whole, since in such matters one should put oneself out of the question, I am not dissatisfied with the results.[141]

In April 1925, his health rapidly failing, Haggard went to a hospital in London for an operation. 'The operation, the doctors said, was "entirely successful",' recorded his daughter Lilias, 'and Rider lay there, pain more or less kept at bay, quiet and speaking little for three days. Then a new abscess gathered. He lapsed into semi-consciousness and on May 14th about midday, without speech or any struggle except to protest voicelessly against some effort to feed him, he died.'[141]

Haggard's grave is in the chancel of St Mary's, Ditchingham, his ashes interred in the vault he had caused to be made in 1909. Not only

The Haggard memorial window at St Mary's, Ditchingham. The centrepiece of the Risen Christ is flanked by the angels Michael and Raphael. Below on the left is a view of the pyramids and on the right is his farm Hilldrop in South Africa.

Inset: Haggard's farm Hilldrop outside Newcastle, South Africa, as depicted in the same window.

did Haggard choose his final resting place, he also composed the epitaph engraved on the black marble marble slab above the vault. The epitaph makes clear that it was for his public service and not his writing he wished to be remembered:

> *Here lie the ashes of Henry Rider Haggard*
> *Knight Bachelor*
> *Knight of the British Empire*
> *Who with a Humble Heart Strove to Serve his Country.*

Stephen Coan
Pietermaritzburg
2000

Notes

1. Tom Pocock, *Rider Haggard and the Lost Empire*, London, 1993, p. 163.
2. See Chapter One, p. 73 and Chapter Five, p. 130 and Note 13.
3. Lilias Rider Haggard, *The Cloak That I Left*, London, 1951, p. 70.
4. Ibid., p. 29.
5. Henry Rider Haggard, *The Days of My Life*, Vol. 1, London, 1926, p. 28. Haggard's autobiography, completed in 1912, was published posthumously according to his instructions.
6. Ibid., Vol.1, p. 35.
7. Ibid., Vol.1, p. 36.
8. Ibid., Vol.1, p. 44.
9. Ibid.
10. The refusal of Langalibalele of the Hlubi to surrender arms to a local magistrate provided a *casus belli* for the colonial authorities, who dispatched a force to arrest him at his homestead in the foothills of the Drakensberg. In an action at the summit of a pass over the Drakensberg, this force was repulsed in a confused skirmish that led to the death of three colonial volunteers and two African auxiliaries. Thereafter the Natal authorities embarked on a brutal policy of suppression. The handling of Langalibalele's subsequent trial by Theophilus Shepstone, Secretary for Native Affairs, ended the long friendship between himself and Bishop John Colenso. See W.R. Guest, *Langalibalele: The crisis in Natal, 1873–1875*, Durban, 1976; Norman Herd, *The Bent Pine: The Trial of Langalibalele*, Johannesburg, 1976; and John Wright and Andrew Manson, *The Hlubi Chiefdom in Zululand-Natal: A History*, Ladysmith Historical Society, 1983.
11. H.R. Haggard, *The Days*, Vol.1, p. 44.
12. Ibid., Vol.1, p. 49.
13. Ibid.
14. Adrian Preston (ed), *The South African Diaries of Sir Garnet Wolseley*, Cape Town, 1971, p. 249.
15. Letter to his mother quoted in H.R. Haggard, *The Days*, Vol. 1, p. 52.

16. Letter written on Easter Sunday, 16 April 1876 quoted in H.R. Haggard, *The Days*, Vol. 1, p. 56.
17. The friendship between Shepstone and Colenso had ended on a matter of principle involving Shepstone's role in the handling of the Langalibalele affair and the chief's subsequent trial. See Note 10 above.
18. H.R. Haggard, *The Days*, Vol. 1, p. 68. *Nada the Lily*, London, 1892, contains a three-page dedication to Shepstone.
19. H.R. Haggard, *The Days*, Vol. 1, p. 57.
20. Ibid., Vol. 1, p. 61. Sekhukhune (*c.*1810–82) was paramount chief of the Pedi from 1861 and fought with the Boers for the independence of his people. Following the British annexation of the Transvaal in 1877, the Pedi were defeated, after a period of successful resistance, by British forces and their Swazi allies in 1879.
21. Letter dated 2 December 1876 quoted in H.R. Haggard, *The Days*, Vol. 1, p. 62.
22. Cheyne Collection, Norfolk: H.R. Haggard to his father, 24 November 1876.
23. Cheyne Collection, Norfolk: H.R. Haggard to his mother, 13 December 1876.
24. H.R. Haggard, *The Days*, Vol. 1, p. 76.
25. Ibid.
26. When Haggard met Mhlophekazi he was about 60. He died in 1897 and was buried in Pietermaritzburg in the Native cemetery on Town Hill. Clarendon Primary School now occupies the site. In *She and Allan* (London, 1960, p. 45), Umslopogaas refers to himself as Umhlopekazi. See Chapter Four, p. 114 and Note 36.
27. See H.R. Haggard, *The Days*, Vol. 1, pp. 137–40, and 'Lost on the Veld', *Windsor Magazine*, 1903.
28. Though Haggard calls him Mazooku, James Stuart and the *Natal Witness* refer to him as Masuku. The name should be correctly rendered Mazuku. Haggard's form of the name has been retained to conform with its usage in the diary as well as Haggard's autobiography and fiction. According to the *Witness*, his name meant 'day' and he was 'a member of the Buthelezi tribe, a very famous tribe, to which many notables in Zulu history belonged'. He was born in 1854, two years before the battle of Ndondakusuka. 'His father fought on the side of Cetshwayo on that occasion, but owing to the induna under whom he served being suspected of disloyalty, the said induna, with Masuku's father and others, was obliged to take refuge in Natal.' *Natal Witness*, 30 March 1914.
29. Because of incidents in her later life and the circumstances of her death, Haggard does not mention her name in his autobiography. In her biography of her father, Lilias refers to her as Lilith. Her identity as Lilly Archer née Jackson was revealed for the first time in D.S. Higgins, *Rider Haggard: The Great Storyteller*, London, 1981, p. 13.
30. L.R. Haggard, *The Cloak*, pp. 31–2.
31. See Chapter Two, p. 62 and Note 38.
32. 'He [Cochrane] was not a brilliant man, but extraordinarily hardworking and conscientious, also of an affectionate nature – at any rate towards myself. (It was his native name, by the way – Macumazahn – that

I took for that of Allan Quatermain.)' D.S. Higgins (ed), *The Private Diaries of Sir Henry Rider Haggard,* London, 1980, p. 283. According to Haggard, the name means Watcher by Night. It is of obscure Nguni origin.

33. L.R. Haggard, *The Cloak,* p. 72.

34. H.R. Haggard, *The Days,* Vol. 1, p. 116.

35. The relationship between Haggard and Johanna Catherine Ford was first brought to light by Victoria Manthorpe in *Children of the Empire: The Victorian Haggards* (London, 1996, see p. 89 *et seq.*).

Lewis Peter Ford (1846–1925), lawyer, businessman and Johannesburg pioneer. Ford came to South Africa with his parents in 1851. After reading law at South Africa College (now the University of Cape Town), he was enrolled as an attorney in 1866 and thereafter appointed deputy sheriff of Richmond and Murraysburg from 1866–71. He moved to Kimberley following the discovery of diamonds where he built up a successful practice as well as becoming actively involved in the diggings.

In Kimberly he was deserted by his first wife and subsequently married Johanna Catherine Lehmkuhl (1854–85) in 1876, the daughter of a German immigrant.

Following the annexation of the Transvaal in 1877, Ford went to Pretoria where he was appointed Acting Attorney-General, also acting as a judge on two occasions. He was chancellor of the Anglican diocese of Pretoria, 1879–89.

In Pretoria, Ford became friendly with Haggard and Arthur Cochrane. As well as Haggard's liaison with Mrs Ford, Cochrane had a relationship with her unmarried sister Josephine. Haggard, Cochrane and Josephine Lehmkuhl were godparents to another of Ford's children, Rollo Theodore.

After the retrocession of the Transvaal, Ford remained in Pretoria acting on behalf of the British government. Johanna died in 1885. Ford married twice more before his death and had a total of 19 children.

When gold was discovered on the Witwatersrand in 1886, Ford became a partner of the Randjeslaagte Syndicate and one of the founders of Johannesburg. In partnership with the Jeppe family, he was responsible for developing the townships of Jeppestown and Fordsburg.

Ford returned to England in 1888 due to illness. After returning to South Africa in 1889, his health gave way again and he left the country for good. During the 1890s he was involved in a number of commercial African enterprises, notably developing areas of East Africa. He appears to have maintained contact with Haggard during this time.

36. H.R. Haggard, *The Days,* Vol. 1, p. 121.

37. Manthorpe, *Children of the Empire,* p. 92.

38. Ibid.

39. See Chapter Five, p. 131 and Note 15.

40. L.R. Haggard, *The Cloak,* p. 103.

41. H.R. Haggard, *The Days,* Vol. 1, p. 175.

42. Letter from Louisa Haggard quoted in H.R. Haggard, *The Days,* Vol. 1, p. 177.

43. H.R. Haggard, *The Days,* Vol. 1, p. 176.

44. Ibid., p. 177.
45. The farmhouse, Hilldrop, appears renamed as Mooifontein in *Jess* (London, 1887): 'It was a delightful spot. At the back of the stead was the steep boulder-strewn face of the flat-topped hill that curved round on each side, embosoming a great slope of green, in the lap of which the house was placed. It was very solidly built of brown stone, and . . . was covered with rich brown thatch. All along its front ran a wide verandah, up the trellis-work of which green vines and blooming creepers trailed pleasantly, and beyond was the broad carriage-drive of red soil, bordered with bushy orange trees laden with odorous flowers and green and golden fruit.' H.R. Haggard, *Jess*, 1900 edition, p. 22.
46. See Chapter Five, p. 134 and Note 29.
47. H.R. Haggard, *The Days*, Vol. 1, p. 183.
48. Cheyne Collection, Norfolk: Lady Haggard's Diary, 'South Africa 1880–81', 27 February 1881.
49. H.R. Haggard, *The Days*, Vol. 1, p. 190.
50. Quoted in L.R. Haggard, *The Cloak*, p. 109.
51. Shepstone Papers, Vol. 47, pp. 74–80, Pietermaritzburg Archives Repository: Haggard to Shepstone, 2 August 1881.
52. Letter to William Haggard, 30 July 1881, quoted in H.R. Haggard, *The Days*, Vol. 1, p. 195.
53. See Chapter Two, p. 53 and Note 2.
54. H.R. Haggard, *The Days*, Vol. 1, pp. 201–2.
55. Ibid.
56. L.R. Haggard, *The Cloak*, p. 121.
57. H.R. Haggard, *The Days*, Vol. 2, p. 12.
58. Ibid., p. 84.
59. Ibid.
60. Higgins, *Private Diaries*, p. 114.
61. H.R. Haggard, *The Days*, Vol. 2, p. 110.
62. Ibid.
63. Ibid.
64. The wording of an advertisement on the unnumbered end pages of W.A. Wills and L.T. Collingridge, *The Downfall of Lobengula*, London, 1894, and reprint Bulawayo, 1971.
65. H.R. Haggard, *The Days*, Vol. 2, p. 111.
66. Ibid., p. 106.
67. Ibid., p. 108.
68. Ibid., p. 119.
69. Ibid., p. 131.
70. Morten Cohen (ed), *Rudyard Kipling to Rider Haggard*, New Jersey, 1956, p. 40. See also Chapter 7, 'Agricultural Reformer' in Cohen's *Rider Haggard: His Life and Works*, London, 1960.
71. Cohen, *Rudyard Kipling*, p. 41.
72. H.R. Haggard, *The Days*, Vol. 2, p. 134.
73. Ibid., p. 134.
74. Ibid., p. 140.
75. Cohen, *Rudyard Kipling*, p. 48.

76. H.R. Haggard, *The Days*, Vol. 2, p. 108.
77. Letter to Haggard from Alfred Lyttelton, 14 January 1905, quoted in H.R. Haggard, *The Days*, p. 173.
78. Higgins, *Rider Haggard*, p. 189.
79. Quoted in Peter Berresford Ellis, *H. Rider Haggard: A Voice from the Infinite*, London, 1978, p. 170.
80. H.R. Haggard, *The Days*, Vol. 2, p. 178.
81. Ibid., pp. 191–2.
82. Ibid., p. 196.
83. Ibid., p. 198.
84. Ibid., p. 204.
85. Ibid., p. 211.
86. Ibid.
87. Ibid., p. 212.
88. Ibid., p. 213.
89. Ibid., p. 220.
90. From dedication H.R. Haggard, *The Way of the Spirit*, London, 1906.
91. H.R. Haggard, *The Days*, Vol. 2, pp. 225–6.
92. Quoted in Pocock, *Rider Haggard*, p. 151.
93. H.R. Haggard, *The Days*, Vol. 2, p. 226.
94. H.R. Haggard, *The Days*, Vol. 1, Introduction, p. xx.
95. H.R. Haggard, *The Days*, Vol. 2, p. 226.
96. Lewis Harcourt (1863–1922). Secretary of State for the Colonies 1910–15.
97. H.R. Haggard, *The Days*, Vol. 2, p. 227.
98. Ibid., p. 228.
99. Julian Amery, *The Life of Joseph Chamberlain*, Vol. 4, London, 1951, p. 421. Quoted in Stephen Constantine (ed), *Dominions Diary: The Letters of E.J. Harding 1913–1916*, Halifax, 1992, p. 18.
100. Constantine, *Dominions Diary*, pp. 21–2.
101. Sir Edgar Vincent (1857–1941). 'He had once been in the Coldstream Guards but resigned to develop a distinguished career in the Balkans and Middle East in a variety of financial and administrative posts, at one time as Governor of the Imperial Ottoman Bank in Constantinople, and from 1899 to 1906 as a Conservative MP. He was appointed Chairman of the Central Control Board to restrict the drink trade during the First World War and was later a notable Ambassador to Berlin 1920–26, Chairman of the Medical Research Council 1929–33 and even for a while Chairman of the Lawn Tennis Association. He became Baron D'Abernon on 2 July 1914, in part at least for his services on the Dominions Royal Commission, and he was promoted G.C.M.G. when it was all over in 1917.' Constantine, *Dominions Diary*, p. 23.
    Haggard's fellow United Kingdom representatives were:
    Sir Alfred Bateman (1844–1929): originally a civil servant with the Board of Trade later Controller-General for Commerce, Labour and Statistics; Chairman of an Advisory Committee on Commercial Intelligence; and President of the Royal Statistical Society.
    Joseph Tatlow (1851–1929): railwayman from 1890 until 1912 as

general manager and thereafter director of the Midland Great Western Railway of Ireland. His memoirs were entitled *Fifty Years of Railway Life in England, Scotland and Ireland* (1920).

William Lorimer (1844–1922): Chairman of the North British Locomotive Company and Chairman of the Steel Company of Scotland.

Tom Garnett (no dates available): 'He was evidently a cotton manufacturer from the north of England and the director of an engineering company'. Constantine, *Dominions Diary*, p. 25.

Representing the Dominions were:

Canada – George Eulas Foster (1847–1931): He missed the tour of South Africa owing to pressure of domestic politics.

South Africa – Sir Jan Willem Stuckeris Langerman (1853–1931): member of the Union House of Assembly, President of the Rand Chamber of Mines and Managing Director of the Robinson Group of Mines.

New Zealand – John Robert Sinclair (1850–1940): lawyer and member of the Legislative Council (parliament's upper house).

Australia – Donald Campbell (1866–1945): journalist, engineer and Labour member of the South Australian legislature since 1906. His defeat in the election of 1912 released him for service on the Commission.

Newfoundland – Edgar Rennie Bowring (1858–1943): businessman and member of the Legislative Council.

The Secretary to the Commission was:

Edward Harding (1880–1954): a civil servant, Harding kept a diary of the Commission's various journeys. Published in 1992 it provides an informed and, on occasion, ironic window into the work of the commissioners.

The commissioners received no remuneration but their governments paid their representatives' personal expenses. The United Kingdom commissioners received 4 guineas a day (£4. 4s.) for subsistence plus travel. See Constantine, *Dominions Diary*, Introduction for a comprehensive overview and assessment of the work of the commissioners.

102. *The Times*, 27 March 1917, p. 33.
103. See Introduction to C. de B. Webb and J.B. Wright (eds), *The James Stuart Archive of Recorded Oral Evidence Relating to the History of the Zulu and Neighbouring Peoples*, Vol. 4, Pietermaritzburg and Durban, 1986.
104. Killie Campbell Collection, Durban: Stuart Papers, File 19, p. 172. Copy of letter from A.J. Shepstone to H.R. Haggard, 30 December 1911.
105. Ibid., p. 178. Copy of letter from H.R. Haggard to A.J. Shepstone, 23 January 1911.
106. See H.R. Haggard, *Child of Storm*, London, 1952, p. 184.
107. Constantine, *Dominions Diary*, p. 62.
108. Ibid., p. 65.
109. Ibid., p. 107.
110. The complete letters have been compiled by D.E. Whatmore (comp) in *Rider Haggard's Good Deeds: Pamphlet Four – Letters to The Right Hon. Lewis Harcourt*, Cheltenham, 1998. The fourth in a series published 'to acknowledge Rider Haggard's public spirit and devoted work in support of his country and the lost Empire'. The preceding three pamphlets collate

material related to 'Deeds for the Church', 'Deeds for Children and Young People', and 'Deeds for the Salvation Army'. The original letters are held by the Public Record Office, London, references CO 879/115 and CO 881/ 14.

111. According to the census of 1911, the population of South Africa was 5 973 965, of which 23 per cent were white.

112. Higgins, *Private Diaries*, p. 3.

113. Ibid.

114. Ibid., p. 4.

115. L.R. Haggard, *The Cloak*, p. 246.

116. Quoted in Pocock, *Rider Haggard*, p. 184.

117. Higgins, *Private Diaries*, p. 14.

118. Oscar Asche, *Oscar Asche, His Life*. Quoted in Higgins, *Rider Haggard*, p. 220.

119. In February 1913, Haggard was in Melbourne, Australia, on the first tour of the Dominions Royal Commission when he received copies of *Child of Storm* and where he also attended a production of 'A Midsummer Night's Dream' mounted by Oscar Asche. Afterward Asche told Haggard that 'he would much like to stage a Zulu play. So I promised to send him *Child of Storm* to read, which I did upon the morrow' (Quoted in Higgins, *Rider Haggard*, p. 214). There followed another meeting and correspondence in which the two men discussed a playscript. During the rest of his visit to Australia Haggard worked on a script called 'Mameena', the heroine of the story. He continued to work on the script during the Commission's tour to New Zealand and on his return to England. By the time he arrived at Ditchingham he had completed the work.

120. Higgins, *Private Diaries*, p. 33.

121. Ibid., p. 49.

122. Ibid., p. 53.

123. Ibid., p. 55.

124. Ibid., p. 55. See Chapter Eight, p. 230 and Note 4.

125. Ibid., p. 55.

126. Ibid., p. 67.

127. In Norfolk, a small field.

128. Higgins, *Private Diaries*, p. 71.

129. Ibid., p. 75.

130. Ibid., p. 116.

131. These included all the manuscripts written up to 1892 with the exception of *Mr Meeson's Will*, given to Haggard's literary agent A.P. Watt, and *Allan Quatermain*, given to his publisher Charles Longman. The latter remained in the hands of the publishing firm until 1940 when it was presented by W. Longman to the Lord Mayor's Appeal for the Red Cross. It appeared on auction at Sotheby's in 1951 and again on 24 February 2000 when it was sold for £45 500.

132. Higgins, *Private Diaries*, p. 96.

133. Ibid., p. 107.

134. Ibid., p. 155.

135. Ibid., p. 129.

136. Ibid., p. 241.

137. Ibid., p. 172.
138. Ibid., p. 283.
139. L.R. Haggard, *The Cloak*, p. 278.
140. 'The Development Commission administered the Development Grant, created in 1909 under the Development and Road Improvement Fund Act and the Development Act Amendment Bill. The Grant was used to promote "schemes which have for their purpose the development of the resources of the country".' (Lloyd George, quoted in *The Times*, 30 April 1910, p. 9), Cohen, *Rudyard Kipling*, Note on p. 143.
141. Ibid., pp. 141–3.
142. L.R. Haggard, *The Cloak*, pp. 278–9.

Chapter One

From youth to age

✒✒✒✒✒

Sir Henry Rider Haggard, accompanied by his wife Louie and daughter Lilias, left England ahead of the Dominions Royal Commission to spend a fortnight on Madeira. The island had been a Portuguese colony since 1419, although it was briefly occupied by Britain during the Napoleonic wars. It was a regular stopping point for Union-Castle liners en route to and from Cape Town. Haggard had spent a fortnight there on his way home from South Africa in 1881.

Saturday, 7 February 1914

Whilst we wait for the *Kinfauns Castle*[1] (which is late) to take us to the Cape with the rest of the Dominions Royal Commission I will set down my impressions of Madeira revisited.

In October, two and thirty years ago, my wife and I stayed here for a fortnight with our infant son (Jock, aged five months) and old Gibbs his nurse.[2] We hunted out the hotel where we put up on our way back to England after disastrous experiences in the shadow of Majuba. In those days it was called Miles, now it is named Carmo and belongs (as it did then) to Reids, the proprietors of the gigantic establishment known as The Palace Hotel which, or rather an annexe of which, we now inhabit. The Carmo is just as it was a generation gone – a large old Portuguese house in a narrow street not far from the cathedral, with a beautiful garden. The trees therein are a little larger that is all. Some of them have fallen also, notably the great fig whereof I speak in *Dawn*, which local superstition declares died because a negro hung himself on its boughs.[3]

We lunched there and revisiting it was somewhat sad to me who has passed from youth to age since my feet crossed its threshold. They told me that our names were in the book of 1881 but search revealed that the page had been torn out by some autograph hunter. So we re-entered them at the right place – as near as might be – and I added a note explaining the circumstances under which we did so.

Another place we revisited was the Quinta Vigia, described in *Dawn* under the name of the Quinta Carr, where the hero of that odd and very Victorian tale and one of the heroines (Mildred Carr) made love. The garden is still beautiful and more or less kept up, but the house which has come into the hands of the government is falling into ruin. It is odd to walk its rooms and, in fancy, to see them peopled with the creatures of one's own imagination. Well they are quite as real as those generations of owners and tenants – the late Empress of Austria among them – whose its walls have sheltered.

Madeira is much the same as it was so many years ago. There are a few more houses on the hill slopes above Funchal, a railway line climbs the mountain, a huge, empty 'sanitorium' built by Germans to serve, it is unkindly suggested in the island, as a barracks, but now in the hands of the Portuguese government, which was forced to repurchase it at no small price with other property acquired for a 'coaling station', stares down upon the ocean. Motors have come however. Shrieking and stinking they rush up and down the narrow streets and make them dreadful. Surely Madeira might have been content with the peace and dignity of its gliding ox-cart.[4] Last but not least there is the new Palace Hotel that I have already mentioned where many English dwell during the winter months. Some of these are here for this or that ailment, though Madeira is no longer the health resort that once it was. The climate has been proved too damp for consumptive patients. Also it can be bitterly cold, though the thermometer denies it, especially when rains fall constantly, gales blow and the snow lies low upon the mountains as it did during the fortnight of our visit. 'Unexpected weather', said the inhabitants but then in every land they make the same remark. A big umbrella and a leather-lined ulster will not come amiss in the outfit of the winter visitor to the isle.

When I asked the [British] consul, Capt. Boyle, what the majority of the guests at the hotel might be, he answered with energy 'loafers'. Perhaps this is too severe a word but it is certainly extraordinary what numbers of English there are with money who seem to take pleasure in wandering about the Earth with no definite object. This leisured class too is composed of very various elements. Thus among those at the Palace were ladies of a certain age sitting alone at little tables, young men who appeared to lack occupation and a tribe of the sportsmen known as 'bookies' reposing themselves before the spring race meetings.

One afternoon, Canon de Gouvea, a most broad-minded priest, born of peasant parents on the island, who speaks English well, was so kind as to shew us over the cathedral.[5] The building itself, erected about 350 years ago, is neither imposing nor beautiful, but the panelled roof of, I think, cedar wood, is a really wondrous work, rather Moorish in taste and design. Among the treasures which were brought out for us to see was a collection of splendid and ancient Portuguese church plate given by certain of the kings in the great days of that fallen country; also of antique, broidered vestments. The canon lives in terror lest these splendid possessions should be seized by the republican government, which has already taken an inventory of them, a disaster which, he says, has overtaken many churches in Portugal. He declares that he will go to prison before he delivers them. I suggested that he should open one of the ancient vaults and hide them in coffins among the bones of the dead, an idea he appeared to think worthy of consideration. He seemed to entertain wild hopes that in some way England might intervene in the matter, which of course she will never do. I believe that all the real property of the churches has already been annexed with the result that the priests must live on the offerings of the faithful.

The nunneries, too, have been taken and most of their inhabitants driven away – as Henry VIII drove them out in England, to begin life afresh in the outer world. Some of these poor 'religious' cast forth in their age would starve were it not for charity. The conventual buildings themselves are falling into ruin.We visited one of them, Santa Clara, which is gradually tumbling down.[6] Only a few ancient lay sisters remain here, who eke out a livelihood by making feather flowers. The damp, stained walls and dilapidated shrines, their hangings tawdry and decayed, look sad to the eye – like relics of a faith bygone. Which is the cruellest, I wonder, in the day of its triumph, Religion as she has often shewn herself, or her foe, raw and savage Infidelity?

Some of the Quintas in Madeira are ancient and interesting. Thus we visited one owned by Dr. Grabham, a most intelligent man possessed of a wide and varied learning ranging from botany to the heights of geological science and medicine; one, too, who carries the vigour of youth into the depth of age. A collector of old clocks and a musician also who, in summer, when in England, plays the organ at St. Paul's cathedral. His beautifully situated house was one of the first built in the island by some Portuguese nobleman. It passed to an English merchant named Murdoch, who entertained Capt. Cook and his party here on their way to the discovery of New Zealand.[7] The grounds contain many splendid trees, some of them primeval and of the laurel tribe. Also there is a gigantic tulip tree, about 20 feet in circumference, which records that came to Dr. Grabham with the title deeds of the house shew was planted by Capt. Cook during his visit, to say nothing of a magnolia whereof the bole has a girth of 10 feet or more.

The loveliest spot we visited however is the Quinta Palheus-Ferreiro, the property of Mr. Herbert Blandy, which stands at a height of about 1 700 feet on the promontory known as Brozen Head.[8] Here there is a very fine house built (twice, for once it was burnt) by Mr. Blandy's father, to reach which we motored up a precipitous and winding road. The beauty of the surrounding grounds is a revelation to the dweller in colder climes. It is said that these contain 10 000 camellia trees alone. Then there are huge and ancient magnolias, araucarias of various sorts, including some magnificent Norfolk Island pines, while all about the surrounding slopes grow forests of conifers. In the great garden blooms every flower, violets in profusion and arums springing wild among others. There are ranges of greenhouses also filled with exotics and in a deep glen tall New Zealand ferns, which flourish almost as they do in their native home. In short the place is a floral and arboreal paradise – not cramped moreover as are so many of the Madeira gardens.

Another beautiful demesne is that of Mr. Hilton. This gentleman is a kind of sugar king in the island. When I was here over 30 years ago no sugar cane was grown; now it is everywhere. Mr. Hilton has a 14-year contract with the government under which he is bound to buy all the cane at a certain price. In return he has the privilege of importing the sugar into Portugal, as I understand, duty-free, and, of course, the benefit of a highly protected local sale. I believe he has experienced some difficulties with the Portuguese government but if one may judge by the price of sugar in Madeira the business should be profitable. Under a free-trade system it could not exist. It is very curious to note how all the great businesses in the place fall into the hands of the English, perhaps because here they have no Jews with whom to compete.[9]

Of these businesses, I suppose, the greatest is that of Messrs. Blandy, who have been established here for over a century. Herbert Blandy was so kind as to take me over the wine stores which were established by, I think, his great-grandfather. These are enormous places containing I know not how many huge pipes and barrels of Madeira wine, of which from a million to a million-and-a-half gallons are produced annually in the island. Some of these identical barrels were in use 100 years ago and still appear quite sound. The quality of the wine depends chiefly on the vineyard in which it is grown; thus that which comes from the north side of the island, where there is less sun, is very inferior. Also, here as elsewhere, the vintages vary. The palmy days of the trade in Madeira have departed because so much less of it is now drunk, largely Mr. Blandy thinks owing to the introduction of cigarette smoking immediately after dinner, which ruins the taste of wines; also whisky has proved itself the great enemy of all wine drinking.

In the old days it was thought necessary or desirable to send Madeira in cask once or twice round the world in a sailing vessel. The same ripening and softening results are now attained by placing them for from three to four months in a store where the temperature is raised to 130 degrees by means of hot-water pipes. I suggested that it might be further improved by a machine which imitated the rocking motion of a ship and he seemed to think this was possibly true though scarcely feasible. Madeira as sold is generally a blended wine. At Messrs. Blandy's this blending is effected by pumping from barrel to barrel (often set on different floors) through enamelled iron pipes. I tasted three sorts of Madeira, one a good matured wine worth about 40s. [£2] a dozen, the second a 'Reserve' wine 30 or 40 years old, and the third 'Oldest Reserve', of which a portion of the blend was stored 100 or 120 years ago. Between the first and second the difference was very marked, but between the second and third I could detect little, save in the aroma.

On 14 February, with the arrival of the *Kinfauns Castle* bringing the other members of the royal commission, our stay at Madeira came to an end. I enjoyed it much.[10]

Notes

1. *Kinfauns Castle*: 9 664 tons, Clyde-built for the Castle Line, launched 1899; 250 passengers first class, 200 second and 136 third; sold to Dutch shipbreaker in 1927. The 6 760-ton *Gaika* on which Haggard returned to England via the East Coast route entered company service in 1897; sold to a shipbreaker in 1928. The *Gaika* was named after Gaika (Ngqika) (1775–1828), a Xhosa chief recognised as the paramount chief of the Gaikas (Ngqikas) by the authorities of the Cape Colony after the Fifth Frontier War (1818–19). The Castle and Union lines amalgamated in 1900 to form the Union-Castle Line, which was operating 41 vessels by 1910 and became part of the Royal Mail Group in 1912. Royal Mail steamers left Southampton every Saturday for South Africa, taking 17 days to Cape Town and 22 days from Durban, where return journeys began. The commissioners sailed on 7 February. For further details see Constantine, *Dominions Diary*, p. 178, and Marischal Murray, *Union-Castle Chronicle 1853–1953*, London, 1953.
2. Lucy Gibbs was Louisa (Louie) Margitson's maid and accompanied her to South Africa after her marriage to Haggard. The Haggard's son, Arthur John (Jock), was born 23 May 1881 and died 9 February 1891.
3. *Dawn* (London, 1884). Haggard's first novel – a three-volume Victorian melodrama. The hero, young Arthur Heigham, falls in love with Angela Caresfoot. Her dominating father is against the union and Arthur agrees to a year's separation. He goes to Madeira where an older woman, Mildred Carr, falls in love with him. He returns to England to find Angela has married her wicked cousin George. After his return to Madeira he learns that Angela was forced into the marriage. George conveniently dies and Arthur returns to marry Angela, leaving Mildred with a broken heart. In an earlier and possibly more autobiographical draft, entitled *There Remaineth a Rest*, Arthur, has a child by the older woman and later he also goes to South Africa where he is killed in a native rebellion.
4. *Carros du bois*, open carriages on runners drawn by oxen.
5. Funchal cathedral. 'Built between 1485–1514, during the reign of King Manuel I of Portugal, the cathedral reflects the "Manueline" style current in the Portuguese architecture of the period. Its plainness is a little daunting, but the details are interesting . . . It has a fine ceiling of cedar wood inlaid with ivory, in the Moorish style.' Extract from *See Madeira and the Canaries* by Annette Pink and Paul Watkins, London, 1976, p. 135.

6. A Franciscan convent founded in the late fifteenth century by the grand-daughters of Joao Goncalves Zarco, the first European to discover the island in 1419. His tomb is in the convent church.

7. Captain James Cook visited Madeira in 1768 during his circumnavigation of the globe in the *Endeavour*.

8. The Blandy dynasty of Madeira was founded by John Blandy, a quarter-master posted to the island as a member of the British garrison sent to assist the Portuguese in resisting any attempted invasion by the French. He returned to Madeira in 1811 and founded the company that still bears his name. He died in 1855.

9. Haggard was partly Jewish. His grandfather had married a German Jewess, Elizabeth Meybohm, whose father was a banker in St Petersburg. Despite this he shared the prejudices of his time. 'There was an anti-Semitic miasma in English society, mostly of wariness against the foreign, the parvenu and those who lived by trade. (Haggard) seems to have seen the Jews as an heroic race that had been dispossessed by being too clever and ambitious for their own good; his admiration for their early tribal leaders was reduced by his dislike of any modern man who made money by its manipulation; and he had paid little attention to their more recent history of persecution that had left them landless. Thus he liked to refer to his paternal grandmother's family as Russian – since they had been living in Russia – rather than Jewish. Yet he was so stirred [by a letter calling for his support for the Zionist movement in 1910] that he telegraphed his reply: "YOUR MOVEMENT HAS MY HEARTY SYMPATHY. THE JEWS BELONG TO PALESTINE AND PALESTINE SHOULD BELONG TO THE JEWS. WHY DO NOT YOUR RICH MEN LEAD THEM FROM THEIR LANDS OF BONDAGE BACK TO THEIR APPOINTED HOME?" ' Pocock, *Rider Haggard*, pp. 153–4.

10. The commissioners on the *Kinfauns Castle* included Vincent, Bateman, Garnett, Lorimer and Tatlow, plus Campbell (Australia), Sinclair (New Zealand) and Bowring (Newfoundland), together with A.H. Bridgman (staff) and various commissioners' wives. Langerman (South Africa) would join them on arrival at Cape Town while Foster of Canada was absent due to pressure of business. In a letter to his mother, Edward Harding, secretary of the DRC, noted that Haggard, his wife and daughter had 'apparently enjoyed their fortnight, and were full of the Blandys and their works. I had hardly realised that they (I mean the Blandys) had been in the island for a century or so and are the English people of the place. They specialise, I gather, in Madeira wine.' Constantine, *Dominions Diary*, p. 181.

    During the voyage to Cape Town Harding spent his evenings playing bridge with 'Sinclair (the New Zealander), Lady Haggard and Mrs. Garnett . . . As to Lady Haggard, she improves greatly on acquaintance. She is stout and placid and what might be called an "outdoor person" – very practical and full of commonsense – just the reverse of Haggard.' Constantine, *Dominions Diary*, p. 183.

    Harding found Lilias a 'curious mixture of her Father and Mother – she has some of the placidity of the one, and some of the nervousness of the other: the result is rather nondescript, and I don't feel able to give at all an accurate description. Anyhow, she is quite good fun, whatever one's final opinion.' Constantine, *Dominions Diary*, pp. 183–4.

Another passenger on the *Kinfauns Castle*, Sir Hartman Just (1854–1929) composed a poem featuring his fellow travellers.
Alphabet of the D.R.C. (written with a J pen).

> *A for Sir Alfred whom figures do cheer,*
> *B is for Bridgman, the old marinere.*
> *C is for Campbell, Australia's boast,*
> *D is for the dungeon, of duty the post.*
> *E for Sir Edgar, Apollo so spruce,*
> *F for the food which he brought for his use.*
> *G is for Garnett, most courtly of men,*
> *H is for Harding's right diligent pen.*
> *I for Lord Inchcape, whose loss we regret,*
> *J for Sir Jan, who has not joined us yet.*
> *K is for the Kinfauns, which this trip is making,*
> *L for the ladies, all five very taking.*
> *M is for the minerals – Lorimer's quest,*
> *N for Newfoundland, and Bowring, its best.*
> *O for the ocean we're traversing now,*
> *P for the porpoise that plays at our prow.*
> *Q for the Quinta, a farm in Madeira,*
> *R is for Sir Rider's yarns, queerer and queerer.*
> *S is for Sinclair, whose law never fails,*
> *T is for Tatlow, our expert on rails.*
> *U for the Union-Castle, our line,*
> *V for the voyage for which we combine.*
> *W for whales, which spout and pass by,*
> *X for the cross on our quoits and the sky.*
> *Y for Young Rosemarie, witchingly curled,*
> *Z for New Zealand, the pick of the world.*
>
> – Constantine, *Dominions Diary*, p. 185.

Just was a high-ranking official of the Colonial Office travelling with the Commission as far as Cape Town en route for Australia and New Zealand on a six-month tour which was to include Fiji and Vancouver.

Lord Inchcape (1852–1932), mentioned in line 9 of the poem, was appointed the first chairman of the Dominions Royal Commission on 15 April 1912. A former member of the Legislative Council of the Viceroy of India and an important figure in commerce and shipping, he resigned shortly afterwards for business reasons. He was replaced by Arnold Morley (1849–1916), a former Liberal Chief Whip and Postmaster-General who resigned on 12 October due to the death of his wife and his own ill-health. On 26 November 1912, the chairmanship devolved upon Sir Edgar Vincent. For details of Vincent and the other commissioners named in the poem see Introduction p. 24 and Note 101.

'Young Rosemarie' mentioned in the penultimate line of the poem was the three-year-old daughter of Lady Helen Mitford, a passenger on the *Kinfauns Castle*.

Chapter Two

This land of troubles

క్వక్వక్వక్వ

The Royal Commission landed in Cape Town, 'mother' city of South Africa on 24 February and was quartered at the Queen's Hotel in Sea Point, a beachfront suburb. Over eight days – between 25 February and 6 March, with a break for the weekend – the Commission gathered evidence from 35 witnesses before moving to other parts of the Cape Province.

From 1652 until the Union of South Africa came into being in 1910, the region was known as the Cape Colony and was founded by Jan van Riebeeck, an employee of the Dutch East India Company, when he landed in Table Bay to set up a revictualling station to serve company vessels on the sea route to the East Indies. The British occupied the Cape in 1795. It reverted briefly to Batavian rule from 1803 to 1806 but thereafter remained in British hands. The colony's northern border was extended to the Orange River in 1847. Separate crown colonies were incorporated later – British Kaffraria in 1866, Griqualand West in 1895, while the Transkeian territories were incorporated between 1879 and 1894. When the Cape Colony entered the Union, Cape Town became the seat of parliament.

Wednesday, 25 February

Yesterday we landed from the *Kinfauns Castle* after an uneventful but pleasant voyage. The Bishop of Nyasaland [J.L. Fuller, Bishop of Lebombo 1913–21] was the most interesting and informing of our companions.

It was with pleasure, mingled with a certain melancholy, that once more I saw the cloud cap hanging like poured water down the kloofs and steep sides of Table Mountain. Cape Town of course has changed a good deal during the last 33 years. Motors fly everywhere; there are electric trams crawling along the sides of Lion's Head and so forth. But the sunshine is the same – the eternal glorious African sunshine – there is the same spirit everywhere which is best represented by the South American word *manana*, the spirit of 'tomorrow' which makes this

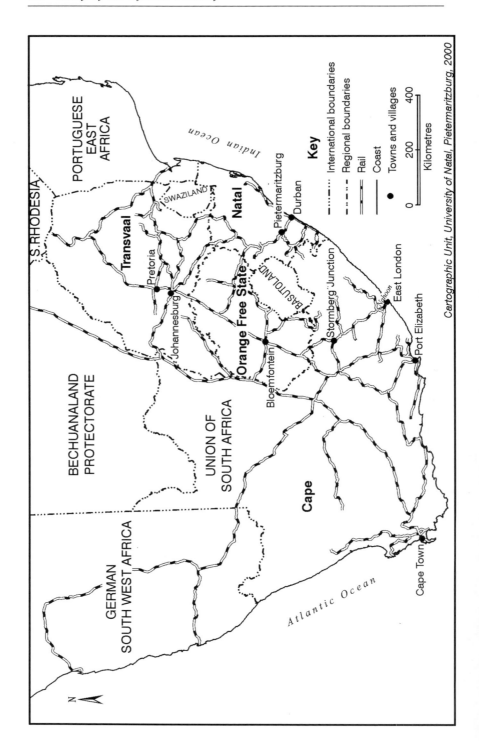

Cartographic Unit, University of Natal, Pietermaritzburg, 2000

land of troubles so restful through them all. To me it feels as though the 33 intervening years had vanished, and once more I were back in the years 1875 to 1881.

Our first function was to attend a luncheon at a government agricultural show at Rosebank [a Cape Town suburb]. There was a large company, many of them Dutch, who paid but small attention to the speeches which were smothered by the hum of conversation. Sir Edgar[1] was listened to when he responded for the DRC but a reference he made to King George V produced not a single cheer. Here I met Mr. Struben who recognised me after the passage of 33 years, now an old man of 74. He reminded me that he bought a wagon and a span of oxen from us when we left Newcastle, Natal, in 1881. I used to know him well in Pretoria in the annexation days.[2] I also met Sir Abe Bailey,[3] who asked Vincent and myself to stay the nights of 25th and 26th with him to meet General Botha[4] and Sir Thomas Smartt, Leader of the Opposition.[5] The gathering at the lunch was a typical farmer audience of whom I have addressed so many, interested only in the show and their exhibits. All the world over farmers are the same.

In the evening we went to a banquet at the Nelson Hotel,[6] given to us by the Union government. I sat next to Mr. Van Heerden,[7] the Minister of Agriculture, and Mr. Malan,[8] the Minister of Mines, and opposite to the Minister of Justice [Jan Smuts], who gave me a lively account of how he came to deport the (foreign) labour leaders who reached England yesterday amid much excitement.[9]

Observing Botha I saw at once that he was of French Huguenot origin, no Dutchman. The motions of his hands and face shewed it and today when some of us lunched with him at the Parliament house, he told me that this was so. Of his forefathers, the *emigré*, he knows little, and French-speaking died out of his family generations ago, since that the dominant Dutch element would not allow. Returning I slept at this charming hotel [Queen's Hotel] some miles from Cape Town. In the afternoon Louie and I went for a delightful but hot walk along the seafront to Hout Bay whence we took a steam train back.[10]

Thursday, 26 February — first sitting

Today we held our first sitting at Huguenot Buildings and lunched with General Botha at Point House. I sat next to and had a long talk with him. He narrated incidents in his early life and of the war. He declared that had it not been for Lord Milner the war would have come to an end 18 months earlier, thereby saving some thousands of lives and millions of money. Kitchener would have agreed (Kitchener, he said, was easy to negotiate with, a man who once he had come to an agreement stuck to it), but with Milner it was otherwise; he was a hard and obstinate antagonist.[11] The point on which they split was that of granting an

amnesty to all the rebel Boers who had fought against us. Botha pointed out that it was impossible for him to accept safety for himself and
leave these out, but Milner would not yield, so the war went on. In the
end these men were amnestied so nothing was gained and, as a matter
of fact, in practice, England would never have taken vengeance upon
them after the conclusion of a war. It was an interesting luncheon.

At dinner again I sat next to Gen. Botha at a party at Rust en Vrede,[12]
Muizenberg, whither I came with Vincent to stay for a couple of nights
with Sir Abe Bailey. On this occasion he [Botha] talked of the labour
situation at Johannesburg, which he said has a population containing
many of the most evil people on the earth, red anarchists and repub-
licans. He described his great anxiety during the rioting [by mine-
workers] some months ago when, he told me, he thought Johannesburg would have been destroyed. That is why he took strong measures
on the second occasion. It is evident that Gen. Botha favours the employment of more natives and fewer troublesome and highly-paid whites
at nine times the wages of the latter, viz. about £360 p.a. He told me
that he thought these skilled natives, and some of them are very skilled,
were the worst treated men in South Africa. I could see that the drift of
his mind is towards protecting them and bettering their state. There is
no 'down with the kaffir'[13] about Gen. Botha. In every way Botha im-
presses me enormously. He is indeed a fine man. Though some say he
is weak. Mrs. Botha is very nice also.[14] I had a long talk with her about
old times in Pretoria and the politics of England. I liked her very much.
Sir F. de Waal, the Administrator,[15] was also at the dinner and Sir
Thomas Smartt. He is a very pleasant man but I do not think he has the
same enterprise as Botha. Their relations seem to be most amicable;
indeed I fancy that this labour trouble has drawn all parties together.

This is a beauteous place about eight miles from Cape Town. It stands
right on the sea and is very cool. The house, built by our host Sir Abe
Bailey, one of the South African millionaires, is lovely – rooms marble-
lined etc. Next door is one of more interest, for in it died Cecil Rhodes.
I looked through the window at the little chamber where this remarkable man gave up his breath. A pathetic place. The house however has
been somewhat altered, the tin roof changed for thatch, etc. It is not
inhabited except by a caretaker.[16]

Friday, 27 February

Yesterday was very hot in Cape Town. After our morning sitting I attended the wedding breakfast of a Mr. and Mrs. Healy. The young lady
came out on our ship and as her wedding dress got spoiled Lilias has
lent her one. The husband, a nice fellow, is a game ranger somewhere
upon the Swazi border. He is 50 miles from his nearest white neighbour
and two days journey from any kind of a town. Matrimony under these

Lilias Rider Haggard (left) *and Mrs Healy on her wedding day at the Queen's Hotel, Cape Town. From Lilias Rider Haggard's photograph album.*

From left to right: *Mrs Garnett, Rider Haggard and his wife, Louie, at Sea Point.*

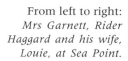

circumstances seems something of an adventure. Tatlow, my colleague,[17] in proposing the bride's health, said that she rode boldly to hounds; I in following added that I hoped she would also ride boldly to lions! I should not like the responsibility of a woman on my hands in so lonely a situation.

In the afternoon we went round the harbour and heard evidence to the effect that it will be easy to construct docks for which a plan is already prepared with a depth of 42 feet. This means the feasibility of a scheme of great ocean liners running round the Cape to Australia which is, I have always maintained, the true Imperial route, and one which avoids many possible dangers inherent to the passing of mails through foreign territory and the possible blocking of the Suez Canal.

Returning to Muizenberg we had a very interesting dinner. Among the guests were Sir T. Cullinan of diamond fame, the chairman of the Premier Mine, and Mr. Nourse of Nourse's Mines, whom I used to know nearly 40 years ago in Pretoria.[18] Late in the evening the conversation worked round to the subject of the Jameson Raid in which Sir Abe Bailey seems to have been deeply concerned.[19] He said that Rhodes planned the whole thing and that Jameson was only a tool. E. Vincent led the conversation on, and I, perhaps incautiously, remembering the company I was in, expressed disapproval of the business. Sir Abe Bailey remarked 'you are old-fashioned' and I pleaded guilty. He then went on to justify the raid and in answer to another remark of mine to the effect that it was a wretched failure, to allege that on the contrary it was a splendid success since it had 'led to the war which was its whole object' and all that has followed. I said it had cost England £350 millions and 20 000 lives. 'What does that matter,' asked A.B., 'lives are cheap'; also he intimated that South Africa did not have to pay the money.

If the only argument for this raid is that it led to a great war, it seems to me to be both weak and worthy of a buccaneer. A.B. alleges that Joseph Chamberlain knew every detail of the affair in advance, if he did not help to plan it.[20] For external proof he pointed to the concentration of Indian troopships at Table Bay at that moment and the grant to the Chartered Company of the strip of land [at Pitsani in Bechuanaland] whence Jameson 'jumped off'. He added that when Harcourt was told of Joseph Chamberlain's complicity he at once ceased his attacks, as striking instance of loyalty to a political adversary.[21] Bailey added that Rutherfoord Harris was Rhodes's agent in all their raid transactions and that subsequently he blackmailed Rhodes out of 96 000 *Cape Times* shares, worth £150 000. Rhodes said to him (here he imitated Rhodes's high and rather squeaky voice), 'He (R.H.) had the knife at my throat!' Harris it appears, who Bailey declares was worth £750,000, has now lost all, or nearly all, his money. He was concerned deeply in all this melancholy business I know well. But that story I have, I think, written down in my memoirs.[22]

Altogether the conversation was most instructive, but I cannot say that it raised my opinion of the group who were responsible for the raid. The truth is that they looked at matters from a different, and I think, a lower point of view than that which is prevalent at home, at any rate among some people. Well, they have won the game, and the evil that they did is now practically forgotten. Also out of this evil good has come since there seems to be little doubt that racial animosities are beginning to die down. So at least Botha and everyone else of weight with whom I have spoken, declare with emphasis and I hope with truth. Bailey and others say it is true that the Boers only remain British subjects 'for what they can get' and this may be so. Exuberant loyalty is not common in South Africa and perhaps can scarcely be expected. One of the company told a story last night illustrative of this statement. An intelligent visitor not long ago after travelling through South Africa on a journey of investigation ascended Table Mountain. One of the party shouted 'God save the King'. Back, sharp and clear from an opposing precipice, came the echo 'God save the King'. 'That', remarked the intelligent traveller, 'is the only really loyal sentiment I have heard in South Africa!'

I do not know which is the more remarkable, the strange diversity of opinion on every point of local importance that one hears in this country or the really abysmal ignorance of facts and odd lack of appreciation of obvious deductions whereby one is constantly confronted among those who should be in a position to weigh the truth. Thus Mr. Nourse, a successful man of my own age who has spent his life here, gravely propounded to me a plan, which he appeared to think quite feasible, for segregating all the natives, even to the extent of allowing none of them to enter domestic service, although in Cape Town alone there are very many thousands of such servants who are the prop of every household, and indeed of every farm and industry throughout the land. Their places, he advanced, should be filled by white people, mostly young women, who were to be emigrated from home. He had never realised that these exportable myriads did not exist in the United Kingdom; that if they did exist they would never come to South Africa to do servants' work or that it would be easier to cast Table Mountain into the sea than to persuade a people animated with the traditions of the Boers to give up their black labour.[23]

Indeed the tendency is all the other way. The black man is driving a wedge into the fabric of European civilisation, is permeating it through and through. He is becoming skilled in many ways, and is acquiring education. (I find the dusky housemaids outside my door wrapped in the study of works by the author of *Three Weeks!*).[24] He is beginning to think for himself and to demand a fair share of the rewards of labour. The white worker on the other hand is falling back, hence his fury and his violence. Thousands of them, to take an example, who were imported to the Rand, mainly perhaps that they might be turned into white voters, find their occupation gone, or in danger of going, since the native can do what they do at half or a quarter of their cost, and is moreover more tractable and often harder working. One very able gentleman with whom I lunched today at Parliament House, Sir Meiring Becke, went so far as to suggest that an ultimate solution of many of the problems of this country might be reached by a fusion of the white and the black races, not only of South Africa, but of the Western world generally.[25] His idea was that if and when the European peoples fail through race suicide and exhaustion, the Aryan and yellow East might flow in and absorb instead of slaughtering the remnants.

I can express no opinion, but all things are possible. Certainly fusion has gone and is going far in Cape [Province]. The streets are full of half and quarter breeds, mostly of Hottentot blood on the side of the female ancestor, which mingles better with the white than that of the Bantu kaffir, and some of the young women born of such unions are by no means unpleasing to behold. I am told that a considerable number of lower-class white men live with or marry more or less coloured women because they make better and more economical companions than do females of their own blood and status who often want much and work little. Certainly it is true also that the various sections of black folk who inhabit Southern Africa are by no means incapable of advance and adaptation to the civilized needs and ideas. In a time to come once more that these will in effect rule in their own land is not at all incredible.

Saturday, 28 February

Today we have made a long expedition in great heat to visit the Rhodes Trust Farms in what I think is known as the French Valley, as an inscription we saw upon a rock proclaims.[26] It was cut about 1740, the exact date I was not close enough to read. Here the Huguenots settled and it is said were shut in by the Hollanders till they had learnt Dutch. This valley in the mountains situated about 25 miles from Cape Town is very fertile and is now chiefly devoted to fruit farming. After leaving the suburbs we crossed the Cape Flats,[27] a wide stretch of somewhat arid land and finally entered the valley. The first place we stopped at was the farm of Mr. Pickstone,[28] who gave evidence on the fruit industry before the Royal Commission the other day. It is a beautiful old Dutch house filled with antique furniture and shewing every mark of refinement down to a visitors' book. Here our numerous party – there were many motor cars full of us – were regaled with wonderful fruit, tea, etc., after which I meandered through the garden and looked at the orchards.

I also met and had a most interesting conversation with Sir Benjamin Robertson, the officer detailed by the government of India to assist at the deliberations of the committee appointed by the Union government to consider the grievances of the Indian coolies in Natal, who have recently attracted so much attention by their determined strike.[29] He informed me privately that he had little doubt that their obvious wrongs would now be righted and the obnoxious poll tax mitigated or removed. Their case is clear. They were invited into the country and have a right to just treatment as fellow citizens of the Empire. He agreed with me that it would be most desirable that, before it finally concludes its labours, the DRC should visit India.

It is high time that the great self-governing dominions came to understand that India is a part of their inheritance, as well as that of the United Kingdom, and that its inhabitants cannot be flouted and treated as outcasts merely because its peoples are dark-skinned, saving and industrious. Sir Benjamin added that he would bring this matter to the notice of the Indian authorities and to that of those at home also should he visit England before his return to India.

Leaving Mr. Pickstone's house we motored some miles to Groot Drakenstein, one of the Rhodes farms.[30] Here we inspected the plum and

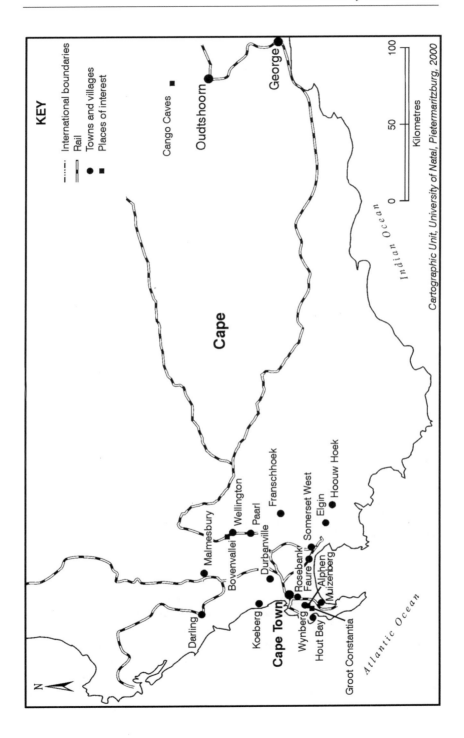

Cartographic Unit, University of Natal, Pietermaritzburg, 2000

other trees still loaded with fruit, which I noted is quite unmolested by wasps or birds; after lunching on the stoep the toast of the Royal Commission was proposed by Mr. [John] Parker, the mayor of Cape Town. I responded, I think, with some success, making a note or two on the top of a cigar box while he was speaking. He gave me one opening by talking of the Huguenots, of whom I know something having the blood in me through the Amyands.[31] I also pointed out that it had given Gen. Botha to South Africa.

After lunch and more fruit farming we motored across the mountains to a beautiful old house owned by Mr. John X. Merriman,[32] the well-known statesman. Here we lost our way in the orchards which gave us an opportunity of seeing how grand they are, especially the pears. When we had drunk tea and eaten more fruit whereof the manager of the farm, a relative of Mr. Merriman, told me he had learned to loathe the very sight, we departed for Cape Town, reaching this hotel after an 80-mile round, about seven o'clock.

The very able gentleman who drove us, Mr. Strong, who I believe is manager of the Mount Nelson Hotel, told me what I have heard in other directions, that Lord and Lady Gladstone are not too popular here as they insist upon every formality of vice-regal state, such as bowing on entering the presence and so forth. This the South Africans, and especially those of Dutch blood, do not like at all. When all the recent circumstances of this country are considered, I think, were I governor here, that I should adopt a very different attitude. It is not the place or the occasion for excessive and somewhat antiquated court ceremony. I do not suppose that Lord Gladstone can be a very strong character or one who has produced much impression as I have so far, save once, not heard his name even mentioned by any statesman. That was when General Botha told me that he took down the Deportation Bill to Government House late at night and 'persuaded Lord Gladstone to sign it' in a hurry. His name is not one of good omen in South Africa and perhaps it is as well that he is giving up the post. Still, as a man, he seems to be much liked.[33]

Sunday, 1 March

Mr. Merriman, with whom I had a long talk today when he kindly came to call on me, also spoke of Lord Gladstone. He said that he was a mere figurehead and had no power whatsoever. Merriman, notwithstanding his age of over 70 years, still is undoubtedly one of the most remarkable men living in South Africa. Tall, gaunt, handsome, personally most popular, extremely well read, quite honest and of an original mind distinguished by its many unexpected turns of thought, a strange mixture of philosopher and politician, he is yet in some ways a disappointment.

It is said of him that he has drawn more false conclusions from sound premises than any other individual in the land. His mind is essentially of the cross-bench order which, however high its type, and it is high, is not of much service in practical politics. He is supposed to be a great radical, yet he told me that his remedy for the present difficulties in the Union was to 'raise the franchise', a most conservative sentiment. He is entirely opposed to the policy which has culminated in the deportations and the introduction of the new and most drastic bill aimed against trade unionism with its picketings and violence, yet he considers that Botha and Smuts shewed 'moral cowardice' in the way they handled the July strike and in the measures they took a little while ago. They should, he said, have declined to parley with the mob and have shot more of them, while the deportees should have been put on trial under the ordinary law. Now, he urges, they have been furnished with that most valuable asset, a legitimate grievance, and transformed into heroes who will find many imitators and followers, an argument for which there is a good deal to be said.

The present scheme of government, in his opinion must end in the setting up of a system of rule in Africa scarcely to be distinguished from that of a South American republic. Of Gen. Botha he holds no high opinion, *nominis umbra* [34] he called him, intimating that he was without ideas and, in fact, stupid. Smuts, he declared was the power behind the throne and the man with the brains, but in truth he did not seem to think much of any of the present Union politicians.

On South African history he was particularly interesting. He knew Shepstone and spoke of him as a 'great' man.[35] Had he remained in the Transvaal, he said, all would have gone well and the course of South African history would have been changed. The madness was in moving him and replacing him by a military martinet like Lanyon.[36] All of these mistakes he attributed to Frere with his Indian training and ideas.[37] Shepstone, he declared, understood the Boers so well that practically he was a highly educated Boer. He would sit while they smoked and spat about him remarking that this and that was a 'lie' and take no offence. (This is true for I have often seen him do it.) He would have given them the Volksraad he promised and all would have ended in talk and smoke instead of in war. He considered that Shepstone's subsequent treatment was disgraceful, as indeed it was. I pointed out that the result of all this was the re-establishment of Shepstone's policy by means of the expenditure of 20 000 lives and £350 millions. He replied, yes, but it had left the Dutch on top. They were the real rulers of the country.

Of the mining 'magnates' he spoke with bitterness and indignation, stigmatising them as unprincipled, selfish and cruel in their dealings with all, even the natives in their employ. They were worshippers of Mammon of the worst sort with the usual attributes.

For the natives he seemed to have great liking. He anticipated that much of South Africa in the end would become practically native. Mr. Merriman seems generally to think well of the natives and to have considerable appreciation of their powers. He pointed out how fortunate it was that they are not animated by a single religion. If for instance, he said, the Zulus chanced to turn Mahommedan what would happen to white South Africa when the standards of Islam were raised against it?

Of Rhodesia he spoke as 'a land under a curse' because of the manner of its acquisition, adding that the true history of the business could not possibly be printed.

In the afternoon I, or rather we, went to lunch with my old friend and chief Judge Kotze.[38] I enjoyed our talk of old times, when we used to trek and work together in the Transvaal, very much indeed. My own memory is pretty good, at any rate for those things which happened in my youth, but that of Kotze is certainly better. Several times he corrected my recollection of particular events, even to the words used in connection with them. Thus he reminded me that the bar and solicitors of Pretoria gave me a public dinner in recognition of my work before I left the Transvaal, a circumstance that I had altogether forgotten.[39] Kotze said that he was the youngest judge as I was the youngest master of a court who had ever held office under the Crown, our respective ages in 1877 being 27 and 21. He has aged a good deal but his mind and manner remain identical. It gave me great pleasure to meet him again – even if it be for the last time. *Eheu feugaces!*[40]

After dinner we were motored to the famous Cape Town Observatory and were shewn the starry heavens through the great telescope, by the Astronomer Royal and his assistants.[41] There was something very impressive and even mysterious about that darkened iron dome with an opening in it, as though a gore had been torn out of the roof of a tent, through which was visible a section of the spangled sky. At a touch the whole round room rose up or down or turned, as did a huge object like a hundred-ton gun, which was the famous telescope. In the semi-silence, for here instinctively everyone spoke low, as was befitting in the presence of these mysteries, the *click-click* of a clockwork machine which, I understood, turned the dome so that it might keep its relative position in relation to the heavenly objects under observation, sounded almost startling. Here we set our eyes to a little peephole and upon our sight burst the glory of Saturn with its double ring and attendant moons. Something was touched, the dome rose, the telescope lifted itself and we looked again at the fiery planet Mars. Again we looked, this time at the blazing splendour of the sun named Sirius (what is it named up there? I wonder). Then at nebulae of flaming gas, then at what to the naked eye seemed to be pits of blackness that proved to be peopled with a score of orbs, pinpoints of fiery light and every point another sun. And so on and on till we grew weary.

The majesty of the sight, as it chanced one of the few I had never seen before, crushed and saddened me. The old truisms which we speak about the stars came home to me with the new force of an individual experience. My God! what are they all? My God! didst thou make them all? My God! are these Thee? My God! is Thy name Design or Chance? Answer and tell us. Tell us too what is man? Are those eternal splendours his inheritance? Or do they and will they for ever and ever know as little or less of him and his petty works and hopes and sorrows as now he knows of them?

Monday, 2 March

Today, which was as hot as ever till evening when a grateful breeze sprang up bringing with it a mist that veiled the fury of the sun, I lunched with Mr. Merriman at the Parliament House. Here I met Sir William Solomon, the brother of our late colleague, Sir Richard.[42] He told me that Sir Richard was the strongest man he had ever known and yet, a sudden operation and in three days, death! Well perhaps now he has learned the answer to the questions I have written above, as before these words are printed, if ever this should chance, I also shall have done. It is a grateful thought that *if* for us there is nothing to be learned we shall never learn that we have *not* learned. Some few sighs and struggles, then sleep and an infinite gulf of blackness, till every star has crumbled and reformed ten million million times. Or mayhap, let us hope so, an infinite lake of light. This at least we do know, that *matter* is eternal. So, too, I think is spirit. But what is spirit? Perchance they are the same thing and we lose ourselves in names.

Merriman told me an amusing story of Rhodes. One day he (Rhodes) was sitting at the exact spot where we lunched – then it was the debating chamber of the House. Next to him was a very stiff and sanctimonious old gentleman whom Rhodes disliked. The bill under discussion was one to raise the age of consent in women – "I say, B," squeaked Rhodes to his pious foe, "if this bill goes through *you and I will have to leave the country!*" Merriman said that B. (I do not give his name, because I have forgotten it) nearly burst with rage, answer he could not.

Tuesday, 3 March

We made a tremendous expedition by motor over the Cape Flats to a place called Koeberg[43] where we visited the farms of two gentlemen named Starck,[44] a father and son, in the company of Mr. Rose, an officer and chemist attached to the agricultural department. Unfortunately they were both from home, but we saw their large and well-cultivated holdings, worth, I was told, about £4 the acre. Corn is grown in this district in wide stretches on the hillsides, as the stubbles shewed. The system seems to be to crop for three years, then fallow for three years. An average return of oat and wheat was stated to be 25 bushels the acre, which if it *is* an average compares very well with the Australian 11 bushels. Basic slag is given occasionally, a light dressing of about 200 lbs. per acre; also superphosphates of which Mr. Rose does not approve, as he says they merely stimulate the land and are washed away by the rains. One of the difficulties here is the ploughing of these hillsides (mules are used for the most part) owing to the dongas caused by the heavy rains now that the low natural scrub which held the soil together has been cut away. If neglected these dongas become impossible to deal with. I saw them in process of formation – a network of meandering dykes on fallow land. The remedy is open drains but these few farmers attempt.

Passing through a village called Durbanville[45] in the neighbourhood of which I noted a good many Friesland cattle, we travelled over 20 miles or more of desolate-looking plain with few houses and little stock to a town of about 4 000 inhabitants called Malmesbury.[46] Here we lunched and guided by the assistant magistrate, Mr. Bowen, went on for another 25 miles or more to a settlement of the name of Darling[47] where we saw a rather dilapidated co-operative creamery which has a capital of £5 000, one of the few that has succeeded in this neighbourhood. It turned out over 20 000 lbs. of butter last year, paid a dividend of 5 percent and is to be rebuilt on a larger scale. Here at 4.30 I discovered that we were about 70 miles from our Seapoint hotel which we must reach by seven o'clock in order to dress for the public dinner to be given to us by the Chamber of Commerce. Off we went stopping only for a few minutes to drink a cup of tea at the house of a very progressive farmer of the name of Duckitt.[48] I regretted much we had no time to inspect his farm. He keeps about 70 cows in milk and grows much grain. We journeyed back to Cape Town at a fearful rate but without accident and ended our 150 miles of motoring at the Queen's Hotel punctually at 7pm. It was a very arduous day's work.

The city hall where the banquet was held, of which there is nothing to record, contains some interesting relics, including a carved stinkwood chair made for the first governor, Van Riebeeck, whose Rembrandt-like portrait hung above.[49] Also there are some rare prints of old Cape Town, very curious to see when it has changed so much. Today I attended the sitting of the R.C. and called on the Imperial Secretary, Mr. Rodwell, to make arrangements about my proposed tour in Rhodesia and Zululand.[50] Drew £100 at Standard Bank for our expenses up country.

Wednesday, 4 March

Sat on R.C.

Thursday, 5 March

With Mr. Robb[51] in charge, Garnett, Bowring[52] and I motored over somewhat barren veld, diversified by patches of vines, to the State Agricultural College of Elsenburg,[53] about 25 miles from Cape Town. The house, in the old Dutch style, is thatched, of remarkable beauty, and dated 1761. A ship's lantern is set in the fanlight over the door. The hall and rooms, including the students' dining chamber, are large and cool with beamed ceilings, the walls very thick and the doors are made of Batavian teak. In front runs a watercourse, probably an imitation of a Dutch canal, bordered by curious castellated walls built for ornament without regard to cost. Close by on masonry pillars hangs the bell which was used to call the slaves to labour and meals. It is dated 1729, and inscribed, perhaps in satire seeing its purpose, with the motto *Omnia vincit amor.*[54]

The adjoining college buildings are modern but in keeping with the house. In front are the recreation grounds, vineyards, and further off a plot of tobacco where some of the heads were being iron-fertilised, the entire site of the farm being ringed in by a distant wall of mountains. At this charming spot we were met by Dr. Perod,[55] the government viticulturist, a brisk and capable-looking gentleman – like so many of the ablest citizens of the Cape he is Huguenot by descent. It is extraordinary how that blood tells wherever it is found. There are at present 27 students resident at the college. They pay a sum of £50 per annum, which includes the price of their board and lodging, medical attendance and lecture fees, a moderate charge indeed. This number it is hoped will be raised to 50. Their ages vary from 16 to 22 and some of them come from London to be instructed in South African farming.

The course, in addition to practical work which occupies half their time, includes scientific agriculture and stock-keeping, veterinary science, fruit-growing, viticulture, agriculture, dairying, blacksmith's and carpenter's work, etc. It occupies two years, after which a diploma is obtainable. Dr. Perod hopes to arrange for a separate course for women to be held in the vacation at which they would be taught the care of poultry, dairying and so forth. The total cost of the upkeep of this college appears to be £13 000 per annum and its total present income from £5 000 to £6 000, the balance being defrayed by the state.

Two bulls are kept, a splendid Friesland animal of which the mother yielded 14 000 pounds of milk in a lactation period of 290 days with a butter-fat percentage of 3.8, and a Jersey, imported I think, but like all Jerseys and Alderneys in warm climates, larger than those to be seen in the Channel Islands. The young bulls bred here sell at from £60 to £150 according to age, some being held till they are two years old. The stallion in use is a fine grey Percheron, which took a championship in France and cost £4 000. There are blacksmith's and carpenter's shops for the use of students, the former with four forges and the latter for the making of farm woodwork such as gates and doors.

Also we saw a tin Dutch barn about 150 feet in length that was full of forage, and two brick silos of a capacity of 40 tons each. Here green maize ensilage is stored, which is blown into the silos after chaffing by means of an engine. The pigs (very well housed) are imported Large Blacks and Berkshires. The young boars bred from these sell at from two to three guineas but there is always a tendency for the snouts of the Berkshires to elongate in this climate where, as I saw later at a bacon factory, the progeny of imported swine quickly approximate to the original native type. Beyond the pig quarters is the wine-pressing house or cellar where grapes were being crushed by a machine to remove the stalks, the liquor running to the fermenting tanks inside the building. Also there are fowl houses and a place where Turkish tobacco, of which about 1 000 pounds is grown here, was being dried. The wheats grown are mainly the Keith rust-resisting and Gluyas Early, and an average yield is about 24 bushels per acre. No irrigation is practised as with a rainfall of 28 inches, which is precipitated in the winter months i.e. from the beginning of April to September, this is not necessary. There is a proper wired-in wheat hybridisation enclosure where experimental hybridisation is carried on. Another big crop which is being tried here is that of the herb known as buchu,[56] which is valuable in medicine. It grows wild in the Cape Province and its leaves sell for 10s. a pound. The vineyards are extensive but these we could only inspect from a distance. I understood that the total area of the farm is about 1 700 acres, of which, including fallows, about 1 200 are under the plough. In addition to the students 20 hands are employed, coloured men who receive a good wage.

Taken as a whole this up-to-date and progressive establishment impressed me very much. It cannot fail to exercise a most benificent influence on the agriculture of the Union, turning out as it will do year by year, a number of instructed farmers whose education has been supervised by so skilled and enterprising a teacher as Dr. Perod. The only criticism I have to make is that the legs and feet of the stallion showed great lack of attention, perhaps because – as he explained – horses are not Dr. Perod's speciality. If the cost seems to be somewhat high per head of students, it must be remembered that experimental as well as educational work is carried on.

Leaving Elsenburg we motored a distance of 14 miles to Paarl,[57] a very beautiful town of 15 000 inhabitants, situated in a hot but most fertile valley. Paarl is so called after certain weather-worn granite rocks on the top of the mountains by which it is dominated. These gigantic boulders, one of them so huge that I was informed it takes half an hour to walk round, shine white after rain like pearls. Hence the name of the town and district. Looked at from above Paarl presents to the eye a great stretch of vineyards, dotted over with houses, which lie between Paarl Mountain and the Berg River. The streets are shaded and made charming by lines of ancient oaks planted by the early settlers and, in all, the scattered town is six to seven miles in length. Wagon-making is the chief industry of the place.

Dr. Perod valued the virgin land in the neighbourhood of Paarl, all or nearly all of which will grow grapes, at about £4 the acre. But to trench the shaly soil or loosen it by exploding charges of dynamite and plant it with vines costs about £50 the acre, of which £20 is the price of the 2 000 vines that are planted on each acre. This dynamiting, I should explain, is said to be excellent when the soil is strong, but useless if clay prevails, since in the latter case it merely makes a pothole that holds water. On the whole, trenching to the depth of about 30 inches, seems the more profitable, if rather more costly method. The average yield for an acre of grapes is about four tons in this district. On rich *irrigated* alluvial lands in other parts the yield sometimes reaches the enormous total of 150 tons the acre, or so we were assured by Dr. Perod, and not infrequently to 100 tons. The wine from these great crops however is stronger and of an inferior quality.

The manure given to the vines is 300 pounds per acre of guano annually (containing 12 percent of nitrogen) and 2 600 pounds of what is known as Karoo ash, i.e. burnt sheep droppings from the Karoo (containing 10 percent potash). The government guano is seabird excrement collected from islands on the west coast. The price charged by government to farmers is £5 per ton, but Dr. Perod valued it at £10. The cost of collection from the bird islands is £3 per ton and the annual crop of droppings is about 6 000 tons. The Karoo ash also costs about £5 the ton.

From Paarl we went about eight or nine miles to Wellington,[58] a town with 7 000 inhabitants, which contains two boot factories and one for tanning; also two co-operative fruit companies and two co-operative vineries. On our road from Paarl to Wellington we passed some grain farms. The common rotation on such farms is one dry fallow (known as *brakland* [Afrikaans: dryland]) or rape, two wheat grown with superphosphate or basic slag, three oats, often unmanured, four oats again or sometimes fallow, five whole fallow, for either one or two years. After luncheon we visited the farm of Mr. P.J. Cillie of Frucht Baar, Boven Vallei, a most intelligent and progressive agriculturist who farms 600 acres of very fertile soil.[59] The house is charmingly situated, with the Drakenstein range to the east and in front the wide and lovely valley. Here are grown apricots, oranges of the mandarin variety locally known as naartjies[60] (which require irrigation every month or so, a process we saw in operation), peaches, figs and, of course, grapes.

First we visited the great wine cellar and saw the grapes arriving in wagons whence they were carried in baskets to the press, which is driven by electric power. The juice flows into a cement vat where it ferments for from 36 to 48 hours. Next it goes into huge wooden vats where it ferments again and stands for 14 days. From these it is pumped into other receptacles where it remains for the winter. Each of the big vats holds about 1 500 gallons. The wine is sold at an age of from three to four months. Last year the quantity was 240 leaguers [a cask of wine or oil of a certain size], which fetched £7 a leaguer. On this farm there are 70 acres under vines, 50 acres under fruit, the rest of the arable being devoted to cereals. The husks of the grapes that emit a most unpleasant sour smell, are given to pigs.

Leaving the wine cellar we were shewn the wooden trays on which various fruits were drying in the sun. The Adriatic or Verdone figs sell, when dried, for £75 the 2 000 pounds, which is the Dutch ton, the prunes that return £100 the acre for from £25 to £30 the ton, and the raisins for the same price. I forget what the apricots are worth but nearly 100 tons of these were grown here this season. We saw the great apricot orchard where the soil is coarse and sandy, with a subsoil of decomposed granite, which is the best combination for apricots. Also we were shewn the sulphuring house where apricots, peaches and pears are fumed for some hours before sun-drying and also partially evaporated by means of hot water pipes. This treatment disinfects them and causes them to keep their colour.

Near to the house was a patch of Hermitage vines bearing a splendid crop though many of the bunches were somewhat burned by the recent fierce sunshine. This vineyard is owned by the coloured labourers. Mr. Cillie pays such men from 2s. 3d. to 2s. 6d. per diem. Also they are given a house and garden and a number of vines and fruit trees out of which some of them do much better than others, as is common all over the world. Thus last year one boy sold his produce for £18 while another for an equal number of trees only realised from £2 to £3.

Bidding goodbye to Mr. Cillie, who is a splendid specimen of a successful and enterprising Cape fruit farmer, we went on to the South African Dried Fruit Co. at Wellington. This company is co-operative and fruit farmers alone can hold shares. Its capital is £10 000, of which half is paid up. It pays a dividend of 6 percent and a bonus of from 7° to 10 percent on the price of the fruit supplied, which price is fixed by the board. The building, which is a fine one, cost £4 000. A 10 h.p. oil engine drives a prune-grading machine. After grading the prunes are improved by what is known as 'processing' with boiling water. We saw girls packing dried apples and evaporating apple rings from the Orange Free State, also prunes of which 25 pounds are placed in a box, each prune being carefully shaped with the fingers before boxing. Other fruit is taken from the 50-ton storage bins and packed in large tins that by a special method are closed without soldering with the help of machinery worked by a native. Also there were boxes of prime apricots and prunes which sell respectively from 11d. and 7d. per pound at the factory. Another speciality which is made in South Africa only is the 'Melbos' apricot, consisting of two fruits pressed together. These fetch 2s. a lb at the factory, and 3s. 6d. a lb in the shops.

An expert Californian packer with whom I spoke told me that the best of the dried fruits equalled those prepared in California but that as much could not be said for the average. Twelve years ago this factory turned out 70 tons of dried fruit; today the output is 600 tons. All is consumed in South Africa leaving no balance for export, but owing to the number of trees being planted it is estimated that in five years the supply of apricots will be doubled.

Our next visit was to the Wellington Co-operative Vinery over which we were shewn by two of the directors, Messrs. Emerson and Joubert. The capital of this society is £10 000. The shareholders are paid for the grapes they supply and the profits are divided. The grapes, of the Hermitage variety, are forked from the wagon into an iron bin which runs on a tramline, their weight being recorded by a scale over which they pass and registered by a clerk in a glass box. This bin was handled by a white man and a kaffir working *together*, a sight I never saw in the old days in Africa and one which suggests a great change in sentiment, brought about, I suppose, by the pressure of necessity. In those times whites and blacks would not have worked on an equal footing. The subsequent processes were similar to those we saw on Mr. Cillie's farm, though on a larger scale.

This factory deals with 133 000 gallons of Drakenstein and Hermitage wines per annum. The grape husks are fed to pigs or used for manure. In the old days they were made into the potent and poisonous 'dop brandy', the manufacture of which is now forbidden by law.[61] In no country that I have visited do such excellent regulations exist concerning the manufacture of spirituous liquor as are in force in South Africa. The result is that the consumer of Cape wine and brandy may be sure that the article he drinks is of a perfect purity. Here we saw the best wine being distilled into brandy, of which about 300 gallons a day are produced during the month of vintage.

Close by was the South African Bacon and Provision Co., a private venture which deals with 160 pigs a month only owing to the lack of swine in the locality, although the plant can treat 200 a week. The supply however is increasing slowly and the company is importing a number of Large Blacks, very fine animals, from England at a purchase price of eight guineas [£8 8s.], from which they hope to rear about 150 pigs a month for their own use. The factory is fitted with all the usual machinery, store and cold rooms. It pays 5d. the pound live weight of pigs delivered at the station, the animals, which are fed on barley meal, mixed with one-third of mealie meal, averaging 160 pounds in weight at the age of from seven to eight months. Some of the local pigs which we saw were very inferior. Their appearance was that of wild pigs crossed with Tamworth.

Returning to Paarl by the lower road we drove to the Government Viticulture Station, a beautifully situated old farmhouse with eight acres of vines. It was bought in 1910 by the government at a price of £2 500. The view from this spot is one of particular loveliness, embracing as it does the wide Paarl valley, down which the river runs to the scarped heights of the sheer Drakenstein Mountains to the east, stained with a hundred hues by the reflected lights of sunset. In the excellent cellar we tasted various kinds of wine made from grapes grown upon the property. Dr. Perod has travelled through most of the wine-producing countries of Europe and in each of them has collected those kinds of vines that produce the famous vintages. Thus he has brought many sorts from the port-producing parts of Portugal, sherry grapes from Ceres and so forth. Now on this experimental farm he is engaged in imitating all these wines, and, if our taste may be trusted, with no small success. The port though young, struck us as particularly excellent, and likely to make a fine sample.

Indeed, there is no doubt but that the Cape, where the sun always shines and the rain falls in winter thus making sure of a good set of grapes and a fine season for the vintage, ought with skilled direction and viticulture, to produce wines which will equal or almost equal those of Europe. At present however there seems to be little market for them outside of the Union. The balmy day has gone by since the time that Mr. Gladstone lowered the duty on the light French wines.[62] In the vineyards of this government station, of which the work is purely experimental, we saw the remarkable sight of about 206 different sorts of fruiting grapes whereof we ate till we were tired. This institution should be of the utmost value to the Union and its existence is proof of the enlightened agricultural policy of the government. Leaving Paarl and bidding farewell to Dr. Perod at Elsenburg college, we had a long drive to the hotel, which we did not reach till 9.30. It was not made easier or safer by the lights of one car failing on a wild and lonely road.

Friday, 6 March

On this day under the guidance of Sir Thomas Hyslop[63] and Mr. McEwen, commissioners of the railway board, and of Mr. Van der Byl, a forest officer, we motored to inspect the forests which have been planted by the Union railway department in the neighbourhood of Elgin, about 40 or 50 miles from Cape Town.[64] In all, the department has afforested 16 200 acres in various parts of the Union at a total cost (inclusive of that of the land) of £158 612. The trees planted include pines of various varieties, eucalypts and Lebanon cedars. These last have been growing wild in the Clanwilliam district, about 150 miles to the north-east of Cape Town for generations but whether they are indigenous or were planted there by the early settlers is not known.[65] The main object of this afforestation is to provide sleepers for the railways but its indirect benefits are and will be almost incalculable in a land where the remaining natural forests are so few.

The cost of the undertaking is not charged to capital account but paid for out of revenue. It began in an expenditure of £10 000 per acre in 1902, sinking during the bad times to £5 000 per acre. Now in 1914 it has risen to £25 000 per acre, which is distributed over the plantations in Cape Province, Orange Free State and Natal. On the hill-tops and stony slopes where the soil is Table Mountain sandstone, pine seedlings are set out in holes dug for them. On lower lands of poor quality the soil is ploughed at an average cost of £1 the acre and pine seed broadcast before the rains. On lower, clayey lands, eucalypts of different kinds are planted in rows. In no country have I seen plantations more flourishing or freer from mioses and disease. I can only describe them as splendid and of a phenomenal growth. Already after a few years, 10 at the outside, one drives through miles of dense and shady forests of pines & gums.

We lunched at a place called Hoouw Hoek[66] where at this elevation, on the top of Sir Lowry's Pass, the rainfall amounts to 45 inches, the climate seemed almost perfect even at this hot season and Ribston pippins thrive, though they are somewhat soft in the flesh. Indeed I never saw more lovely moorland made gay with flowers than that which prevails in this Elgin district. After lunch we visited the farm of Dr. Viljoen, which is situated 1 135 feet above sea level at a place called Oak Valley.[67] The industries here are wine, fruit and afforestation, and the stock Merino sheep and pigs. Twelve hundred acres of black wattle have been planted of which the value of the bark, used in tanning, is at present £5 10s a ton. The stems are used for pit props and the crooked boughs are converted into a hard and most excellent charcoal in a scientifically built kiln, which sells for £5 the ton. There are also 300 acres of oaks of which, although the trunks of Cape oak is of no great worth, the acorns form a valuable food for pigs and, in moderate quantity, for sheep. There are also 10 000 apple and pear trees whereof about 100 are planted to the acre. Cleopatra is the most prolific apple on this farm. Warners King is also a valuable cooking sort and Cox's Orange does well.

After leaving Dr. Viljoen's we motored through a magnificent forest of eucalypts, down Sir Lowry's Pass, and so back to Cape Town through Somerset West and Faure.[68] This was the last of our agricultural expeditions in the neighbourhood of Cape Town, and I close this brief record of them by expressing my admiration of the progressive intelligence with which every problem connected with the land and its fruits is being faced and overcome. Of the fertility of the district there can be no doubt, reinforced as it is by a wonderful climate and a sufficient rainfall which comes at the right time of the year. Great as is the development also it can be very largely increased, as there are still thousands of acres capable of bearing grapes and fruit to perfection. As regards the former, however, the output must be limited by the demand for wine produced at a profitable price, which of course is circumscribed by the consumption in the Union since but little finds a market abroad. For fresh fruit, however, there seems a great outlook among the European populations which it reaches in the winter months and the same may be said of it in its dried form though of this but little is exported at present since the local demand absorbs the supply.

Saturday, 7 March

On this day, together with a number of other people, we were invited by the government to what might be termed a 'joyride' round Table Mountain. For one of our party, Mrs. Tatlow, it proved nothing of the sort. The motor she was in collided with another. She was thrown or fell out and has been left behind in bed at the Queen's Hotel (I write this at Oudtshoorn) suffering from something like slight concussion.[69] We lunched in a tent at the famous house of Groot Constantia. This place was granted in 1684 to Van der Stel, who was the next governor to Van Riebeeck. He built the house and began to cultivate the vines from which the well-known wine Constantia was made. Its last owners were the Cloetes who sold it in 1885 with 280 acres of land to the government for the small sum of £5 500. Since that time the state could have done well on their bargain if, as I was informed by the manager, they refused an offer for it of £28 000. Here there are 103 acres under vines and 56 under fruit trees. The house with its large cool rooms all adorned with ancient and appropriate furniture is really beautiful.[70]

At luncheon which was given in a tent I sat next to, and had an interesting conversation with, Mrs. Botha, who expressed herself as very pleased that I agreed with her husband, the Prime Minister, as to the uselessness of attempting to emigrate poor white folk to South Africa when already there were enough of them. Such people, unskilled and resourceless, she said, would come right up against the competition of the native, and their exclusion, which in some quarters was set down to race feeling, was really in their own interests. The only openings were for farmers with some capital, a scarce class. We discussed the outlook of the white inhabitants of South Africa in the future and both agreed that it seemed very doubtful – chiefly because of this native question. The native could no longer be suppressed, or even oppressed: he must follow his destiny and often he was an able and a competent person. In practice South Africa must face the fact that all it has to rely on, so far as the whites are concerned, is its present population and their progeny. But here came the trouble – the restriction of population (i.e. race suicide) is creeping in, even among the Boers, except quite in the backveld districts where it would reach ere long. One no longer saw the large families of 30 years ago: they grew smaller and smaller. Moreover those who were growing up, for some subtle reason, in enterprise, in virility and femininity in their widest sense, were not the men and women of the stamp of our generation. She had often said as much to her own children. What was to be the end of it? She could not tell but the future was dark and dubious. Perhaps at last South Africa would be the heritage of the black races with an admixture of white blood. The danger of war between whites and Bantu had gone by, but there were other dangers. Thus what I saw on the previous day, white man and black, working side by side was one of them: it meant the approach of equality. Once that was established how could the dwindling white people hold their own against an increasing race, already four or five times as numerous?

She said it was hard work for a man like her husband to be Prime Minister of the Union in these days and hard for his wife also. It was both exhausting and difficult to deal with politics continually and keep his hands quite clean. We both agreed that time and experience were wonderful softeners of strong views. Thus today I should not write another *Jess* and she would not think about the English as she had thought even a dozen years ago.[71] She told me that although it seemed a strange thing for her to say, the deportation of the captured Boers had been a very good thing for the people. The sight of other lands had opened their minds and made them more progressive; also they had learnt what the British Empire meant. Such is a summary of this enlightening talk made from notes taken that evening, and I think one that is accurate, although compressed. Mrs. Botha struck me as an able woman in a quiet way and I liked her very much.

After luncheon the manager took me to see the sights of Constantia. First there was the wine cellar where the wine is ripened with ozone generated by electricity, but this scientific achievement I pass over without attempting a description. Suffice it to say that what it took three years to bring about is now completed in half an hour. I was shewn the slave vaults, unventilated holes beneath the house where two or three hundred of these unfortunates who worked the great estate of about 8 000 morgen [about 16 000 acres] were herded in at night.[72] Above the masters feasted; below the poor stolen wretches sweated and stifled in misery. The married slaves' quarters were a little better. These had heavily iron-barred windows places with a kind of cupboard in the wall where the babies were laid upon shelves. Imagine the noise that must have issued from that cupboard! From these vaults runs an underground passage which I saw, ending about 100 yards away in what now is a stable, but was once the house of the Jongheer, or heir.[73] Its use no man knows: it may have been designed as a means of escape in case of an *émeute*,[74] or to facilitate the arrival of guards, or to enable the women's quarters to be approached in secret for other purposes.

Near by also is the cement kennel where the fierce watchdog was chained – part of its rusted chain still remains – and the old hen house with masonry nests, a much more comfortable place than the slaves' quarters. One wonders what the death rate among those slaves may have been! Also there is an annexe where meat was hung in the smoke drawn from the kitchen fire. Still more interesting is the bridge over what was once a canal that ran between the house and the old wine cellar. The seats on this bridge remain. They are slabs of stone much worn by the portly persons of the old Dutchmen who sat upon them for generations. One can see how they were accustomed to dispose their legs. It reminded me of similar sights at Pompeii.

I forgot to state that on the evening of the 6th we dined with the Governor-General, not at the old Government House where I stayed in 1875, but at a residence in the suburbs that is, or was, the property of Sir [Leander] Starr Jameson (the famous Dr. Jim of Raid fame).[75] I took in Mrs. Garnett and sat next but one to His Excellency with whom I had a good deal of talk. He seemed glad to learn that my views as to the Zulus and Lord Wolseley's wretched settlement of that country accorded with his own.[76] He told me that these people seem bewildered by the lack of any tangible head to look up to, which I can well believe, remembering their monarchial traditions. Lord Gladstone struck me as a kindly and sympathetic man, but not as one of any great force of character, such as one might have expected from his parentage (if there is really anything in personal and immediate heredity as distinguished from race heredity). The same description, perhaps applies more or less to Lady Gladstone, who suffers from poor health or nerves or both, which is alleged as the excuse of their approaching retirement. On my other side was Lady Muriel Paget, a daughter of Lord Winchilsea, who did, or tried to do, so much for British agriculture. She thanked me very heartily for what I had written about her father in *A Farmer's Year*. It was an agreeable dinner party. [77]

Sunday, 8 March

Went with Louie to call on the Tennants[78] out beyond Wynberg.[79] It was a long drive in a steam car.[80] One of the difficulties at Cape Town is the great distance at which everybody seems to live away and the expense of locomotion, especially motors. Mrs. Tennant was a Miss Plewman, an old school friend of Louie.

Here I met Henry Cloete who had become a member of the bar at Pretoria before I left in 1879.[81] Judge Kotze, Cloete and I are almost the only ones left alive who had to do with the administration of justice at

Pretoria at that time. He stopped on after the retrocession and knowing Dutch, made a great deal of money at the Bar. Also for a while he acted as British Agent though it would appear that subsequently his wife, whom we also met, did services to the Boers during the war, as is indicated in that very frank work called *The Petticoat Commando*.[82] She is a pleasant lady of Hollander extraction. Her father was a Predicant [preacher] at Heidelberg; she says I knew him. Subsequently Cloete succeeded to his father's estate, Alphen,[83] where the wine is made, became a Member of Parliament and gave up law. I asked him if he was Sir Henry now. He replied: 'No – only a CMG' [Commander of the Order of St Michael and St George]. This astonished me after his services in a land where almost everybody seems to have a title. How they all came by them I do not know, but I suppose through the war and the establishment of the Union – except in the case of the 'magnates', who have a road of their own to such distinctions. It is, in effect, rather absurd to find oneself in considerable gatherings where everybody is called Sir 'So-and-So'.

Cloete was of the opinion that race hatred is fading in South Africa and will ere long die, also that the idea of repudiating the British connection is a madness which will never again have power in the land. The Dutch, he declared, know too well what such folly would mean. The fear of Germany looms large before their eyes. Mr. Tennant was of the same mind. He held that if it were not for the professional politicians, whom he considered a curse in South Africa, and the newspapers on both sides, already there would be no bitterness left. These, however, kept it flickering by their blasts of recrimination. Mr. Haarhof, one of the directors of De Beers, expressed himself to me in a similar sense, as have sundry informants who are in a position to judge.[84] He said, as did others, that Hertzog has greatly injured, if he has not actually destroyed, his influence amongst all except the more backward of the Free State Boers by his virtual alliance with the socialistic Labour Party whom the Dutch detest.[85] I rejoiced to hear these views. But on the other hand a very well-informed and experienced gentleman, who gave evidence before us at Oudtshoorn told me that in this neighbourhood there is still a great deal of bad feeling towards the English which doubtless is true of this and some other districts.

Monday, 9 March

This morning I was occupied on commission business in struggling, with ultimate success, to secure a cabin to myself on the *Gaika* sailing from Durban on 4 May via the East Coast, and in interviewing Mr. Rodwell, the Imperial Secretary, and Mr. Apthorpe of the native department, as to my proposed trips to Rhodesia and Zululand.[86] At 6.30 most of us started by a special train for Oudtshoorn–Port Elizabeth, Louie and

Lilias going by sea with Sir Edgar Vincent and Sir A. Bateman.[87] The train was as comfortable as could be expected though hot.

Tuesday, 10 March

Woke up to find that we were running over bush-clad sourveld with a few ostriches wandering round lonely Boer steadings. While I was dressing the iron lid of the washbasin fell on and crushed the top plate of the false teeth which were recently fitted with so much discomfort. A most annoying incident. Luckily I have the old temporary set with me which the dentist wanted to destroy.

At lunch time we came to a range of mountains called Outniqiua, or some such name, that tower above a little township of about 2 000 inhabitants, called George, which is largely inhabited by retired persons in search of quiet.[88] The situation is fine on a flat plain dominated by tall grassy peaks down which run waterfalls that look like lines of wandering silver. At the beginning of the pass we went through government plantations of gums [eucalypts] of about 10 years of age which are doing splendidly. There are several of these here. Next we passed through some native bush in the kloofs, then came broom, heather and bracken, clothing the broad hill shoulders. From the crest of the pass the view was grand. The flat plain below diversified with plantations surrounding the scattered town of George and in the distance the great sea. All this district might be afforested, the hills with pines and the plains with gums. As the land seems to be worth no more than 10s. an acre it would be an excellent purpose to which to put it. About 4 o'clock we entered the Oudtshoorn valley,[89] a hot and fertile place surrounded by hills, and everywhere saw ostriches feeding on lucerne in their wired camps.

On arrival we were met by the mayor and notables and taken off to see the farm of Mr. John le Roux where, after 34 years or so, I renewed my acquaintance with that ungainly but profitable fowl, the ostrich.[90] By the way, at the station a gentleman whose name I think was Rex came up and asked me if I remembered him – as I did not he produced from his pocket an official order of the Pretoria High Court, written and signed by myself in 1878, appointing him a sworn interpreter. I wonder if he always carries it about with him. I was glad to see that the order was properly drawn and written in a better hand than I can boast nowadays. The signature, however, is identical with that I use at present.

At Mr. Le Roux's we, or some of us, armed ourselves with thorn boughs tied on long poles to ward off the possible attack of the infuriated cock (*vide Jess*) and advanced into an ostrich camp to inspect an ostrich's nest.[91] The cock had just gone onto the nest as like a good family bird he always does for the night about four in the afternoon, giving the hen an 'easy' till the following morning and had to be driven out of the kind of wigwam set up over the nest, at the back of which he stood glowering at us. Then followed much information about ostriches and the district, where the irrigated land is so valuable that it has fetched up to £150 the acre or more.

Even at the prevailing high prices there is none in the market for notwithstanding the present slump in feathers owing to change of fashion, ostrich farming is a most profitable business. It is said that some of the Oudtshoorn farmers get returns of £10 000 and even £20 000 a year. The reasons of the suitability of this neighbourhood to ostrich stock are its hot, dry climate which prevents the feathers from becoming bedraggled (the rainfall is not more than 10 inches per annum), the deep soil, in which lucerne does splendidly and will stand for 20 years, though it is advisable to plough it up and re-sow after six or seven years, after which it begins to be choked by twitch, and the abundance of water for irrigation purposes that flows down from the mountains.

Next and also on the following day, in the store of Mr. Martin who deals in them, we were shewn thousands of feathers sorted into lots, according to character, quality and sex, and very beautiful they were. No one knows how long the ostrich will live as the industry is not 50 years old but I saw some perfect feathers, taken from a cock, known to be over 30 years of age. The chicks however are subject to many diseases, which often kill two-thirds of them. One cock is generally put with two hens only but by nature the ostrich is polygamous. Its flesh is good to eat if made into curry and the eggs are excellent for omelettes. Up to the present slump the average return per bird has been about £6 per annum (three pluckings are taken in two years) but now it is down to £3 or £4. There is an enormous variation in the quality and quantity of feathers given by different birds, some of which are scarcely worth keeping, but an attempt is being made to raise the standard of the stock by close interbreeding between those which have proved the best producers, as I understood with a great deal of success. Ostriches, however, lose stamina under these artificial conditions so much that although when wild one may gallop them for half a day, the camp-born birds can be run to death in a quarter of an hour. Their hearts give out. But for all particulars see the evidence tendered to us.

Wednesday, 11 March

After our sitting some of us went to see the Chambers De Jager Tobacco Factory Co., which has a capital of £12 000. Tobacco is largely grown in this district and pays as well, some say, as do the ostriches. First the leaves are dried in thatched sheds about 50 feet in length where they hang for a long while from scaffoldings of sticks. At the factory they are plunged for 24 hours in lye made by mixing burnt ash bush with boiling water, which acts as a preservative. Then they are sweated in a box and twisted into the familiar Boer tobacco rolls. This is done by girls with Hottentot blood in them, who looked pretty in their turban-like headdresses, and some men. As they worked these girls sang, a very sweet and plaintive native song, the men joining in from time to time. It sounded like a dirge inspired by a sense of the sadness and vanity of all things human and I confess that it delighted and moved me. Never are such songs heard in Europe. Only the dark races with their age-long record of bloodshed, slavery and sorrow can conceive and utter them.

In the afternoon, through heat like to the breath of Nebuchadnezzar's furnace, we motored about 18 miles to the famous Cango Caves from which (I was told locally) I had taken those written of in *King Solomon's Mines*.[92] This, however, is apocryphal as I never saw them before. My model in the story were certain stalactite caves in the neighbourhood of Potchefstroom, which I had visited when a lad.[93] Our road, a very good one, wound in and out and up and down by a river and above the slopes of rugged mountains. In the old days this Groblaar river had to be crossed 20 or 30 times to reach the caves and it took a long day to travel there and back from Oudtshoorn. As we went standing on a rock quite close to us we saw an old dog baboon, a splendid fellow.

Arrived at the caves we entered. They are enormous, some of the finest in the world indeed. Through them the visitor may wander for three miles or more, but he had better not try to do so without a guide, as the slopes are slippery and in darkness it is easy to fall over some subterranean cliff. Here is every kind of fantastic shape fashioned during thousands or hundreds of thousands of years by the slow drip of the lime-charged water. Here are what might be titanic curtains and draperies, pulpits, fonts and baths. Here stands Lot's wife upon a towering pillar. Here are vast and echoing roofs, steep steps and paths, and mysterious pits and valleys. What struck me most, however, in that chill yet stifling place was the sight when I stood alone on one side of an enormous rock-roofed dome and from a distance of some 50 paces watched our companions, men and women, climbing down a precipitous path in single file, each with a lighted taper in the hand. Either they were silent or too far away for their voices to reach me and they looked – what did they look like, those quiet men, and veiled, light-bearing women? Ghosts, I think, or a procession of priests and priestesses bearing one of their number to burial in some measureless Egyptian tomb.

Outside of these caves are bushmen paintings still discernable on the rocks, but doomed soon to fade away. They are full of spirit. Here a bat hangs from an arching roof, here men hunt a speeding ostrich, here others fight their petty, forgotten wars. Wonderful savages, the lowest of the low, yet with art innate in their blood, otherwise how came it that in the idle hours when they were filled with their wild meat, and the sun was too hot for them to be abroad, they sat here under the shadow of the overhanging rock, hundreds of years ago perhaps, and with ochre mixed in water, recorded in pictures those things wherewith they were familiar? Now all, or nearly all their race is dead – shot out by the white man as cattle thieves. Yet they were artists as well as thieves, yet their poor bellies were empty and craved meat, yet once, before the Bantus came, all this wide land was their possession.

We left Oudtshoorn after dinner. I was not sorry to go for though the place is pretty and prosperous, the heat was terrible – 100 degrees in the draught at moonrise. One also wearies of the sight of ostriches countless as the sand, and the smell of their feathers in the salerooms.

Thursday, 12 March

We reached Port Elizabeth in the morning.[94] It has grown much since last I was here a generation ago and is now a wealthy, well-built city of, I think, about 50 000 inhabitants, which battens [thrives] on ostriches and the Johannesburg trade.

Friday, 13 March

I lunched with Mr. W.C. Scully,[95] the Resident Magistrate at Port Elizabeth, whom I had met in England. He is a very clever man and has no mean repute as a writer both of fiction and other books. But, as Irishmen are so prone to be, he is an extreme radical and a pro-Boer whom, I have heard, it was thought well to watch during the war – temporarily to remove from his magistracy to another. However, he is, I believe, quite honest in his views with some of which, such as his hatred of the magnates and the state of affairs that they have brought, it is easy to have a certain sympathy. These are expressed with vigour and perhaps not quite fairly, in a book of his that I have read since we met called *The Ridge of the White Waters* in which he draws a dreadful picture of Johannesburg. He told me that no African paper would even mention this book for fear of offending their moneyed supporters and shareholders and at a shop in Port Elizabeth I was informed loftily that 'we do not keep Scully's books'. He is a great pessimist about all things African and says that he hates the cities, and means to retire to Rhodesia. He added that phthisis[96] is making awful ravages among the natives, both at Johannesburg and in the kraals whither probably it has been brought from the city. Also, he declared that the Union is being run on far too extravagant lines as the gold of the Rand, on which it draws, is rapidly coming to an end. More interesting to me were some of the stories of kaffir tribes that he narrated at lunch.

Saturday, 14 March

Today Archdeacon Wirgman, who came to South Africa in 1874, took me for a motor drive. First we visited his church, St. Mary the Virgin, of which he is justly proud. It was burnt down by a mad woman some years ago and rebuilt at a cost of £14 000, Rhodes paying for the cloisters.[97] In this church is a fine 15th-century window that came from a nunnery in Cologne whence it was taken at the time of the French Revolution. It was bought by an Englishman in 1802 and for 80 years was in a church at Highgate whence it drifted here. Also, there is a piece of Purbeck marble from the porch of Westminster Abbey let into the wall, several colours that were used during the war and certain memorials to those who fell.

During our drive round Port Elizabeth (where I saw mixed surf bathing in progress – an amazing sight), the archdeacon told me that the calling out of the burghers during the Johannesburg troubles had done much to bring Englishmen and Boer together. He seemed to think that racial feeling between the two races would die out in time. Of Scully he had no high opinion; indeed he called him a fanatic. I was much interested in the account he gave me of the success of the native parliament in the Transkei, where the resident magistrates, sitting together, act as a 'House of Lords'. Why cannot something of this sort be done in Zululand? In a long letter I have received from Lord Gladstone he tells me that the state of things there is not at all satisfactory. But all this I hope to investigate for myself.

Sunday, 15 March

We left Port Elizabeth last night after dinner and I awake to find that we are passing through thornveld. A few hours later we ran through beautiful country covered with rich green grass. It is a great and fertile plain bordered on one side by a range of hills clothed to their crests with native bush. This was a welcome sight, especially as many people think that South Africa is drying up gradually as Tripoli and other places did in the time of the Roman Empire, owing to the destruction of the trees during the last few centuries by the Bantu invaders and others. Once the trees are gone the land will no longer hold the rainwater which rushes to waste or evaporates in the hot sun. In this district there are many kraals, the huts being built of mud and thatched. Round these played scores of children, but alas here civilisation is doing its work. Instead of being naked as in my day, they were nearly all clothed in dirty shirts. The women wear the most horrible garments, broken stays and ill-fitting dresses out of which they burst and bulge. I prefer the fig leaf, or rather *mucha,* costume.[98]

East London is a nice town though like all minor South African cities not very interesting.[99] Also, it gives me the idea that it is spending much more than it can afford in electric trams (which are very empty and I hear do not pay) and other ways. The harbour, such as it is, has already cost £200 000 and they are asking for another £500 000. The sea is beautiful and opposite to the Beach Hotel, where we are staying, the great rollers break continually upon the rocks. On the Sunday afternoon of our arrival all the population seemed to be gathered on the beach, except those who were fishing – with the usual negative results. Scores were fishing but I only saw one fish.

Monday, 16 March

After we had taken evidence, we went in a launch round the harbour and saw the 35-ton concrete blocks being cast by a huge crane into the sea in order to lengthen the breakwater. After this we were taken in a launch up the Buffalo River. The banks are formed of steep hills clothed with virgin bush, among which are thousands of euphorbias[100] – pretty and reminded me of some of the Australian rivers. After this the owner of our hotel, Mr. Hoppé, motored me to a farm he owns where the soil is extraordinarily rich and water plentiful. The land is full of sea shells. I wonder how they got there several miles from the sea. He does not know. Thence we drove to another beautiful river called the Nahoon. All good land but not much use being made of it so far as I could see. This is a favoured part of the country, with a splendid rain fall of about 35 inches, when anything will grow. Now that dipping has conquered the tick and both cattle and sheep thrive it should flourish exceedingly. Only it wants more population. Land about here is worth £3 the acre. Cotton is being grown experimentally, with every prospect of success.

Tuesday, 17 March

We slept in the train and started at 6 a.m. for Kimberley. At breakfast time we were passing through lonely rolling veld. Such cattle as we saw were fat on the rich green grass but they were not very numerous. Pity more use is not made of this fair land. The big farms should be broken up. Throughout the day the scenery grew even grander till at a pass in the neighbourhood of Stormberg, where poor Gatacre[101] was trapped, the prospect of water-carved mountains and kloofs and endless plains was in truth stupendous and awe-inspiring. Here we were over 5 000 feet above sea level.

Notes

1. Sir Edgar Vincent (1857–1941). See Introduction, p. 24 and Note 101.
2. Hendrik Willem Struben (1840–1915), gold-mining pioneer, trader and farmer. He was a member of the Volksraad at the time of the Transvaal annexation in 1877. Though he disapproved of the annexation, he accepted an appointment as Justice of the Peace. He organised the defence of Utrecht during the Anglo-Zulu War of 1879. His model farm, *The Willows* near Pretoria, was looted in April 1881 during the First Anglo-Boer War. He played an important role in the discovery of gold on the Witwatersrand and was the first president of the Chamber of Mines. The purchase of Haggard's wagon is referred to in his *Recollections and Adventures*, Cape Town, 1920, p. 166.
3. Abe Bailey (1864–1940), Rand magnate and politician, friend and ally of Cecil Rhodes. As a member of the British South Africa Company, he acquired extensive land and mining properties in Rhodesia. Knighted for his work in promoting the unification of South Africa in 1910.
4. Louis Botha (1862–1919), Anglo-Boer War general and statesman, first Prime Minister of the Union of South Africa. After the Second Anglo-Boer War (1899–1902), and in alliance with Jan Smuts, he pursued a policy of conciliation and unification among the whites of South Africa.
5. Thomas Smartt (1858–1929), doctor, farmer, politician and leader of the Unionist Party. He was knighted for his contribution to the formation of the Union at the National Convention (1908–09) where he advocated a colour-blind franchise. He gave evidence to the DRC on Wednesday, 4 March.
6. The Mount Nelson Hotel opened on 1 March 1898. It was built by the Castle Line to surpass its rival, the Grand, built by the Union Line. Both hotels were intended to extend the luxurious accommodation found on their respective company's ships and to replicate the standards of luxury hotels in Europe. Haggard stayed at the Mount Nelson during his brief visit to South Africa in 1916. He recorded that 'this hotel seems fairly comfortable, but food indifferent as is usual in S.A.', Cheyne Collection, Norfolk: H.R. Haggard, 'War Diary of Sir Rider Haggard', Vol. 5, 29 January 1916 to 23 November 1916, p. 303.
7. Hercules (Harry) van Heerden (1862–1933), progressive farmer and politician.
8. François Stephanus Malan (1871–1941), newspaper editor, politician and cabinet minister. In 1900, following the publication – in his absence – of a letter in *Ons Land* describing conditions in a concentration camp at Howick, Natal, he was sentenced to one year's hard labour for defamation of Major-General John French. At the time of Haggard's visit, Malan was Minister for Mines and Industry.
9. Jan Christiaan Smuts (1870–1950), statesman, soldier, philosopher and driving force behind the constitution of the Union. In July 1913, a dispute over recognition of trade unions and conditions of service at Kleinfontein mine ended in violence in the centre of Johannesburg. Many died before Botha and Smuts intervened. In the negotiations that followed, the government acceded to almost all the demands of the Labour Party. However, less than six months later, workers at coal and gold mines and on the

railways were involved in renewed strike action. Smuts quickly sent in troops and two people were killed. The strike leaders surrendered and Smuts deported nine non-South Africans without trial. This was a serious blow to the Botha administration and both he and Smuts were labelled merciless dictators by their opponents. In the Transvaal provincial council elections of March 1914 the Labour Party achieved a major victory over the South African Party.

10. Hout Bay, a famous scenic attraction on the Cape peninsula. However, it is almost 20 km (12 miles) from the hotel in Sea Point so it is likely Haggard is referring to Camps Bay, which is closer.

11. First Viscount Alfred Milner (1854–1925), British statesman, Governor and High Commissioner of South Africa.

    Kitchener, Horatio Herbert, Earl of Khartoum (1850–1916), initially chief of staff to Field Marshal Lord Roberts during the Second Anglo-Boer War (1899–1902); he succeeded him as C-in-C in 1900. Botha wanted to accept Kitchener's peace terms. See Thomas Pakenham, *The Boer War*, London, 1979, p. 568. In 1901 Kitchener opened negotiations with Botha but was opposed by Milner. 'This will always remain one of the great might-have-beens of the war', Pakenham, *Boer War*, pp. 487–99.

12. Rust en Vrede meaning Rest and Peace, Bailey's home in Muizenberg, a popular Cape resort on the shores of False Bay. The name is derived from Wynand Muys, an early official of the Dutch East India Company.

13. Kafir or kaffir, derived from the Arabic word *kafir*, meaning infidel. It was the term commonly used to describe black Africans in South Africa at the time.

14. Annie Frances Botha (1864–1937), English-speaking of Irish descent.

15. Sir Nicolaas Frederic de Waal (1853–1932), Cape politician and Administrator of the Cape Province.

16. Cecil Rhodes (1853–1902), British imperialist, politician, financier and founder of Rhodesia. Prime Minister of Cape Colony 1890–95. Rhodes bought Barkly Cottage, now known as Rhodes Cottage, in 1899, and died there in 1902. He was buried in the Matopos Hills in Rhodesia. Barkly Cottage is now a museum.

17. Joseph Tatlow. See Introduction p. 24 and Note 101.

18. Sir Thomas Cullinan (1862–1936), diamond mine owner. In 1902 he established the largest single diamond property in the world, the Premier (Transvaal) Diamond Mining Company near Pretoria. In 1905, the largest diamond found – the 'Cullinan', weighing 3 023 carats – was discovered there.

    Henry Nourse (1857–1942), soldier, mining magnate and sportsman, he went to the diamond fields at Kimberley in 1870. In 1874 he helped to raise the Kimberley Light Horse. In February 1877 he went to the Transvaal during the British Annexation and became a captain in Ferreira's Horse operating against Sekhukhune in the north-eastern Transvaal and later in the Anglo-Zulu War (1879). During the Second Anglo-Boer War (1899–1902), he commanded Nourse's Horse in the defence of Pretoria. He founded Nourse Mines in 1886.

19. Sir Leander Starr Jameson (1853–1917), doctor and politician, and a leader in the Jameson Raid, a failed attempt by Cecil Rhodes to topple Paul Kruger's republican government in the Transvaal. After the failure of the raid he

was handed over to the British government for trial. He was sentenced to 15 months' imprisonment but was released after four months on grounds of ill-health. Later Prime Minister of the Cape Province and member of the National Convention that drafted the constitution of the Union of South Africa. In 1912 he retired to London.

20. Joseph Chamberlain (1836–1914), British Secretary of State for Colonies at the time of the Jameson Raid. Abe Bailey was correct.

21. Sir William Harcourt (1827–1904), Liberal Party Chancellor of the Exchequer, England.

22. Dr Frederick Rutherfoord Harris (1856–1920), Rhodes's confidant and assistant. He was a physician in Kimberley where he met Rhodes in either 1882 or 1883. In 1889 he assisted Rhodes in the creation of Rhodesia and was appointed secretary of the British South Africa Company in South Africa. He was elected as one of four Kimberley representatives to the Cape Legislative Assembly in 1894. One of the Jameson Raid conspirators, he was Rhodes's agent in all raid transactions, especially the provision of arms. Harris was much disliked; John X. Merriman nicknamed him 'Cactus'.

    Haggard writes of his meetings with Rhodes in his autobiography. However, he does not record the topics mentioned here. See H.R. Haggard, *The Days*, Vol. 2, pp. 115–19.

23. 'Met Nourse? – his absurd ideas about segregation'. NRO, MC 32/51: H.R. Haggard, 'Rough Diary', 25 February 1914.

24. Elinor Glyn (1864–1943), British romantic novelist. 'The scandalous *Three Weeks* (London, 1907) dealt with an affair between a young Englishman and a much older woman, a Balkan queen, and included the famous "tiger-skin episode".' See *The Macmillan Dictionary of Women's Biography*, London, 1998, p. 228.

25. Sir Johannes Hendricus Meiring Beck (1855–1919), Cape politician, delegate to the National Convention (1906–09). He was Minister of Posts and Telegraph's in Botha's cabinet in 1914. A similar policy of miscegenation was posited as a solution to South Africa's racial problems in William Plomer's satirical novel *Turbot Wolfe*, London, 1926.

26. French Valley or Franschhoek in Dutch, meaning French Corner or French Glen, derived from French Huguenots who settled there in 1688 after fleeing persecution in France.

27. Cape Flats, area extending from Cape Peninsula and occupying the greater part of the isthmus between Table Bay and False Bay.

28. Harry Ernest Victor Pickstone (1865–1939), nurseryman and fruit farmer. After experience as a cultivator in California he decided to use his skills to develop the British Empire and, realising conditions in the Western Cape were similar to those of California, set about developing a fruit industry in South Africa. In 1896, on instructions from Rhodes, he bought 29 farms in the Franschhoek Valley, which became a trust company known as Rhodes Fruit Farms.

29. Indians were brought to Natal as indentured labourers to work on the sugarcane plantations from 1860. Immigration for such purposes was suspended from 1866–84 but thereafter continued until stopped by the Government of India in 1911. Many Indians remained after the completion of their contracts, while other Indian immigrants had established them-

selves as traders. They were placed under various restrictions, being denied the vote in Natal in 1896, and being subjected to finger printing in the Transvaal in 1907. Such discriminatory practices led to the creation of the passive resistance movement led by Mohandas Gandhi (1869–1948) who had been in South Africa since 1893. This movement eventually forced the government to appoint a Commission of Enquiry into the Grievances of Indians. Sir Benjamin Robertson (1864–1953), Chief Commissioner of the United Provinces 1912–20, gave evidence on behalf of the government of India. Some restrictions were lifted by the Indian Relief Act of 1914. Gandhi left South Africa for the last time on 14 July 1914, sailing to London on the *Kinfauns Castle.*

30. Groot Drakenstein, a farm in the Drakenstein Valley. In 1867 it was named in honour of High Commissioner Hendrik Adriaan van Rheede tot Drakenstein, who had visited the Cape two years earlier. Surplus grapes exported from here for the first time in 1886 marked the birth of the South African fruit export industry. By 1910 fresh fruit exports were worth £34 714 and £93 049 in 1914.

31. Haggard's great-great-grandfather William Henry Haggard (1757–1837) had married Frances Amyand in 1781. The Amyands were of French extraction. 'It was said in the family that the Haggard stock had been undermined by intermarriage with the excitable Amyands, causing an unstable temperament and an inclination to sexual passion,' Manthorpe, *Children of the Empire*, p. 29.

32. John X. Merriman (1841–1926), Cape politician and last prime minister of the Cape Colony. 'The father of the Union parliament' and a favourite candidate for first prime minister of the Union. He refused a cabinet post in Botha's administration but supported the South African Party during the rest of his parliamentary career. Regarded as an upholder of the liberal tradition of the Cape.

33. Herbert John Viscount Gladstone (1854–1930), wife Dorothy (née Paget) (n.d.–1953), British politician and younger son of the the Liberal Prime Minister, W.E. Gladstone, was Liberal Home Secretary 1906–10 before his appointment as the first Governor-General of the Union of South Africa. He chose Botha in preference to Merriman as the Union's first Prime Minister on his own authority after consultations with leading South African statesmen. He left his post as Governor-General in 1914. His name not being 'one of good omen' is due to his father having been in office at the time of the Retrocession of the Transvaal. Haggard and other colonials regarded this as a betrayal by the home government.

    In a letter to his father Harding writes that 'neither he (Gladstone) nor the "Governess" is exactly popular in South Africa. In fact – I trust you won't be shocked! – he is known as "Lord God" and she as "Lady God". Need I say more?' Constantine, *Dominions Diary,* p. 199.

34. *Nominis umbra,* Latin for the 'shadow of a name'.

35. Sir Theophilus Shepstone (1817–93). He was appointed Diplomatic Agent to the 'Native Tribes' of Natal in 1846. Subsequently he was appointed Secretary for Native Affairs in Natal from 1856 to 1876. In 1877, under instructions from Lord Carnarvon, he annexed the Transvaal, thereafter administering the territory for two years.

Shepstone's system of administering the indigenous populations of Natal via re-settlement in reserves where they were subject to 'Native Law' was one of the origins of later segregationist policies. See Norman Etherington, The 'Shepstone system' in the colony of Natal and beyond its borders, in A. Duminy and B. Guest (eds), *Natal and Zululand from Earliest Times to 1910: A New History*, Pietermaritzburg, 1989. See Introduction p. 6 *et seq.*

36. Sir (William) Owen Lanyon (1842–87), British soldier and colonial administrator, was appointed acting administrator of the Transvaal under the direction of Sir Garnet Wolseley, High Commissioner for Natal and the Transvaal. He became permanent administrator in April 1880.

37. Sir Bartle Frere (1815–84), Governor of the Cape Colony and High Commissioner for South Africa. 'On the North West Frontier Frere learned the merits of undivided command, of keeping the civilian population unarmed, and of dealing with problematic neighbouring states by a combination of continuous communication, straight dealing, and firm assertion of diplomatic rights, which he was later to apply with less happy results in South Africa' – W.J. de Kock and others (eds), *Dictionary of South African Biography*, Vol. 2, Pretoria, 1972, p. 243. Appointed High Commissioner in 1876 by Lord Carnarvon who considered Frere as the best man to carry out his plans for the confederation of South Africa.

38. Sir Johannes Gysbert (John Gilbert) Kotze (1849–1940), lawyer and judge, was appointed chief of justice to the Transvaal Republic by President T.F. Burgers in 1876. While en route from the Cape he learnt of the annexation but decided to proceed. His appointment was confirmed by Shepstone. He was referred to as the 'boy judge' by Anthony Trollope in *South Africa*, London, 1878. A judge for 50 years barring a four-year interruption, he made a significant contribution to Roman-Dutch law in South Africa.

39. Kotze again had cause to correct Haggard. In his *Biographical Memoirs and Reminiscences*, Cape Town, n.d., he refers, on p. 487, to the 'dramatic description' of a judicial execution recorded by Haggard in H.R. Haggard, *The Days*, Vol.1, pp. 112–3, as 'pure romance, and not in keeping with fact. It was not Mr Juta, the High Sheriff, as stated by (Haggard) that was overcome that morning and retired sick into the corner of the gaol yard, but Sir Rider himself; nor was the hangman intoxicated; and the statement that Haggard was consequently left alone to force the unfortunate hangman to do his duty is wholly imaginary'. Kotze adds in a footnote: 'I do not for a moment desire to suggest that my old friend wrote with any intent to misrepresent the truth. His passion for fiction and romance carried him away when writing about an occasion which should have been described by him with judgement and discretion. Those who knew Haggard recognised in him a man of honour and truth. But his was an extraordinary mind. He was emotional and much given to romancing. His imagination impelled him into a world of fancy which for the time had complete hold of his sense, and hence he described as fact what was mere fiction.' Haggard met Kotze again during his visit to South Africa in 1916. See Introduction, p. 8.

40. *Eheu feugaces,* Latin for 'alas for the fugitives'.

41. The Royal Observatory, established 1821 and designed by John Rennie. Sydney Samuel Hough was the Astronomer Royal at the time of Haggard's visit.

42. Sir William Henry Solomon (1852–1930), judge and one of the first judges of appeal in the Union of South Africa, and later Chief Justice. His brother Sir Richard Solomon (1850–1913), barrister and politician, was the Union of South Africa's first High Commissioner to the United Kingdom and died in London. He was initially appointed to represent South Africa on the DRC. After his death he was replaced by Sir J.W.S. Langerman. See Introduction, Note 101. A pencilled note by Haggard in the original typescript reads: 'Sir William Solomon, I hear, died a week or two ago. H.R.H. 23.1.15'.

43. Koeberg, now site of South Africa's only nuclear power station.

44. Probably Walter Thomas Starck and his son George Henry Starck (1882–1958). The son was a leader in the furniture-making industry and also a director of Rhodes Fruit Farms.

45. Durbanville was originally called Pampoenkraal (pumpkin corral). It was renamed in 1836 after the Governor, Sir Benjamin D'Urban (after whom the city of Durban is named).

46. Malmesbury, established 1745, was first named Zwartland (Black Country), being in the centre of the area of that name. It was renamed in 1829 by Sir Lowry Cole, Governor of the Cape, in honour of his father-in-law, the Earl of Malmesbury.

47. Darling, founded 1853 and named after the then Lieutenant-Governor of the Cape, Charles Henry Darling.

48. He was probably one of the descendants of William Duckitt (1768–1825), an agricultural pioneer who was selected to introduce modern farming techniques to the Cape Colony four years after British occupation in 1806.

49. The city hall, built from sandstone imported from England, is in an Italian Renaissance style with classical facade and central campanile. It was completed in 1905. Johan van Riebeeck (1619–77), first Dutch Governor of the Cape.

50. Cecil Hunter Rodwell (1874–1953). After service in the Second Anglo-Boer War (1899–1902), he joined the staff of British High Commissioner Alfred, Lord Milner (1901–03) and became Imperial Secretary. Later Governor of Fiji (1918–24), Governor of British Guiana (1925–28) and Governor of Southern Rhodesia (1928–34).

51. Frank Robb (b.1864), the DRC's South African agent. He worked for the Cape government railway department but moved to the harbour board in 1890, becoming dock manager in Table Bay in 1908 and superintendent of South African Railways in 1911.

52. Tom Garnett and Edgar Bowring, see Introduction, p. 24 and Note 101.

53. Elsenburg, a Cape Dutch mansion originally built in 1698. It is now home to the agricultural faculty of the University of Stellenbosch. The older house was rebuilt with additional decoration in and after 1754.

54. *Omnia vincit amor*, in Latin 'love conquers all'.

55. Abraham Izaak Perod (1880–1941), viticulturalist and key figure in the development of the Cape wine industry. He was head of Elsenburg Agricultural College 1912–17, thereafter Dean of Agriculture at the University of Stellenbosch.

56. Buchu (*Agathosma betuliana*), shrub native to South Africa and used to give a peppermint flavour to wine and brandy. It is much used by

indigenous peoples as a folk remedy, and popular worldwide today as a diuretic and antiseptic.

57. Paarl, established 1690, takes its name from huge domed granite boulders in the vicinity. When Abraham Gabbema saw them in 1657 glistening with dew at dawn he declared them 'paarl' (Dutch for pearl).

58. Wellington, established 1840, and named by Governor Sir George Napier after the Duke of Wellington.

59. Petrus Johannes Cillie (1856–1942), pioneering fruit farmer. In 1892 the Cape provincial government sent him to study fruit cultivation in California. An apricot developed by the Research Institute for Fruit was named the Piet Cillie in 1974. Boven Vallei, now named Bovlei, is on the outskirts of Wellington.

60. Naartjie (pronounced 'narchy'), South African name for a type of tangerine probably derived from Indian *Tamie Nartel*, a citrus fruit.

61. Dop brandy, colloquial phrase for brandy. It refers to Cape Smoke, the earliest, rough Cape brandy.

62. Duties on French wines were lowered in 1859 when William Gladstone was Chancellor of the Exchequer.

63. Sir Thomas Hyslop (1859–1919), Natal farmer and politician, was commissioner on the Railways and Harbours Board in 1914.

64. Elgin, site of refrigerated packhouses for storing the apples for which the surrounding area is famous.

65. The Clanwilliam Cedar (*Widdringtonia cedarbergensis*) is indigenous and restricted to the Clanwilliam district.

66. Houw Hoek (now Houhoek) and Sir Lowry's Pass. Haggard lunched at the Houw Hoek Inn, established 1834, the oldest surviving coaching inn in South Africa. The pass over the Hottentots-Hollands Mountains was built on the initiative of Cape Governor Sir Lowry Cole and carries the main road to Port Elizabeth via the Garden Route. The summit is 402 m (1 319 ft).

67. Sir Antonie Gysbert Viljoen (1858–1918), doctor, politician and farmer, pioneered growing of apples in Elgin area.

68. Somerset West, established 1822, and named after Lord Charles Somerset (1767–1831), Governor of the Cape Colony 1814–26. Faure, small hamlet, site of *kramat* or tomb of Sheik Yusuf (1626–99), Islamic mystic who led the revolt against the Dutch East India Company in Java and was banished to the Cape. His shrine is a place of pilgrimage for Muslims.

69. Mrs Tatlow, wife of Commissioner Joseph Tatlow. In a letter to his father Harding records 'the day was rather marred on the way home by a collision which ended in Mrs Tatlow falling out of her car and getting concussion of the brain – she is better now, fortunately, but has to stay in Cape Town, and won't join the party again until Kimberley,' Constantine, *Dominions Diary*, p. 200.

70. Groot Constantia, one of the grandest of the Cape Dutch homesteads, possibly named after Constantia, daughter of Commissioner Rijekloff van Goens who made the original grant of land. After the Van der Stel family – Simon van der Stel (1639–1712) was the second Governor of the Cape – it was owned by the Cloetes from 1773–1885 when it was acquired by the Cape government for use as an experimental wine farm. After a devastating fire in 1925 it was restored to its condition *circa* 1793.

71. *Jess*. Set against the backdrop of the First Anglo-Boer War and the retro-cession of the Transvaal (1880–81), the novel is highly prejudicial in its depiction of the Boers.

72. Morgen, a South African unit of area equal to about two acres or 0.8 hectare.

73. *Jongheer*, Afrikaans for young man.

74. *Émeute*, French for revolt or riot.

75. When Sir Henry Bulwer arrived in Cape Town on 17 August 1875 en route to Natal to take up his post as Lieutenant-Governor, his party, which included Haggard, stayed at the residence of the governor of the Cape, Sir Henry Barkly (1815–98). In a letter to his father, Haggard wrote that the Cape Town newspapers referred to him as 'Waggart'. See H.R. Haggard, *The Days*, Vol. 1, pp. 47–8.

76. Sir Garnet Wolseley (1833–1913) and the settlement of Zululand. See Chapter Seven, Note 1.

77. Lady Muriel Paget, sister of Lady Gladstone. Lord Winchilsea (1851–98). 'The Times announces the death of Lord Winchilsea. Opinions may differ as to his schemes and ideas, which have been attacked by some, but there is no doubt that in him the agricultural interests, and especially the agricul-tural labourers, have lost a true and earnest friend. The last sentence of his will, "God save Agriculture", echoes the spirit that animated his life' – H.R. Haggard, *A Farmer's Year: Being His Commonplace Book for 1898*, Lon-don, 1899, p. 335.

    'The G.G.'s dinner was also amusing in its way – more formal, of course (than a dinner with the Chamber of Commerce attended earlier in the week), but happily less so than in Australia. There were no curtseys by the ladies, and when Vincent and Haggard sat down on a sofa while the G.G. was still standing, nobody seemed to mind!' Constantine, *Dominions Diary*, p. 199.

78. Hercules Tennant (1850–1925), jurist, politician and civil servant, was aide-de-camp to Sir Bartle Frere 1877–80. His wife was Mary Cathcart Gra-ham.

79. Wynberg is a suburb of Cape Town.

80. Probably a Stanley Steamer made in Bridgeport, Connecticut, US. The twins, Francis (1849–1918) and Freelan (1849–1940) Stanley invented the first American steam car in 1897. They continued to manufacture Stanley Steamers until they retired during the First World War but produc-tion continued until 1927.

81. Henry (Hendrik) Cloete (1851–1920), a barrister at Inner Temple 1877; advocate to the Supreme Court, Bar of the Cape Colony 1878 and ap-pointed to the High Court Transvaal Bar in 1879. During the First Anglo-Boer War (1880–81), he served as lieutenant and adjutant of a volunteer unit and took part in various engagements around Pretoria. He was ap-pointed British Agent in the Transvaal after the Jameson Raid in 1896. He was a member of the Cape Province Assembly in 1902, 1904 and 1908. He married Johanna, daughter of the Rev. Van Warmelo in 1893 (see note that follows).

82. Johanna Brandt, *The Petticoat Commando or Boer Women in Secret Ser-vice*, London, 1913. The book details the exploits of the Van Warmelo family during the Second Anglo-Boer War (1899–1902), especially those of Hansie van Warmelo, Mrs Cloete's sister.

83. Alphen, historic wine farm in Constantia Valley, established 1714.
84. Daniel Johannes Haarhof, member of the Afrikaner Bond sympathetic to Cecil Rhodes. In the elections of 1894 in the Cape Colony he became member of parliament for Kimberley after Rhodes had persuaded another candidate to step down in his favour. He was apppointed a board member of De Beers in 1907, holding this position until he died in 1917.
85. James Barry Munnik Herzog (1866–1942), lawyer, Boer general and statesman, founded the National Party in 1913. He was elected Prime Minister of the Union in 1924. Haggard met Herzog during his brief visit to South Africa in 1916. 'I saw Herzog today; a dangerous face, that of a fanatic, brooding, intense and rather cruel. A thin dark-eyed man. Why are all or nearly all who think much thin?' Higgins, *Private Diaries*, p. 55.
86. For details of the *Gaika*, see Chapter One, Note 1. Marmaduke Gwyn Apthorpe, appointed Principal Clerk, Native Affairs Department, October 1910. Director, Native Affairs in 1914.
87. Alfred Bateman, commissioner. See Introduction p. 24 and Note 101.
88. Outeniqua Mountains, derived from the name of a people who lived in the area, the Outeniqua Khoekhoen, 'the people who carry bags of honey'. George was the first town established after the British occupation of the Cape in 1806. It was named after George III who donated a bible to the church, and was originally called Georgetown.
89. Oudtshoorn, 'capital' of the Little Karoo, established 1847 and named after Baron Pieter van Rheede van Oudtshoorn, who was a Cape official in 1741 and 1766. Thereafter he returned to Holland. In 1773 he was appointed Governor of the Cape but died at sea on his way to take up office. The commissioners tooks evidence in Oudtshoorn from five witnesses on Tuesday and Wednesday, 11 and 12 March.
90. Haggard had farmed ostriches outside Newcastle, Natal, in 1881. The ostrich feather export industry boomed when they became a Victorian fashion vogue. 'In 1913 there were over 750 000 birds, nearly all in the Cape Province, and over one million feathers were exported, worth nearly £3 million . . . at the time of the Commission's visit the peak was past, fashions had changed, and the business collapsed during the First World War.' See Constantine, *Dominions Diary*, p. 197.
91. In the opening chapter of *Jess*, entitled 'John Has an Adventure', the hero, Captain John Niel, on his way to the farm of Silas Croft, saves Bessie Croft, Silas's daughter and sister of the heroine, Jess, 'from an infuriated cock ostrich'.
92. Cango Caves, one of South Africa's great natural wonders in the foothills of the Swartberg mountains, 27 km (17 miles) from Oudtshoorn. They extend at least 5 km (3 miles) into the mountains, though the exact extent is not known. The name is a corruption of the Bushman/Hottentot words *!a!-! kanub*, meaning 'the valley between the hills'.
93. Potchefstroom, town in North West Province (formerly western Transvaal). Haggard visited it with Kotze during one of their court rounds. Outside the town is a range of hills called the Gatsrand so-named because they are filled with caves and holes – the Dutch word for hole is *gat*. Kotze records a visit he made with Haggard to the caves at Wonderfontein near Rustenberg. 'We had each provided ourselves with a packet of candles, and

by the light of these the moist and glistening stalactite formations presented an unusual and pretty sight. The dripping water from above, charged with lime, had formed numerous pillars of varying thickness, which, when struck by a stick, emitted different notes, sounding rather pleasantly, and doubtless with a little practice a tune might be played on these calciferous strings. In the centre, about eight feet from the floor, there was an opening in a very thick pillar resembling a pulpit. This evidently made an impression on Haggard, who took good note of what he saw, for a decade later he well described and immortalized this cave, including the pulpit, in his *King Solomon's Mines.'* Kotze, *Biographical Memoirs*, p. 482.

94. Port Elizabeth, city on Algoa Bay, landing site of the 1820 Settlers. First established as a military outpost in 1799 and named Fort Frederick, its foundation really dates to the arrival of the 1820 Settlers. It was named Port Elizabeth in 1820 by Sir Rufane Donkin (1773–1841), Acting Governor of the Cape, after his wife Elizabeth Frances who died of fever in India in 1818. The Commission took evidence from five witnesses in the Port Elizabeth town hall on Friday, 13 March.

95. William Charles Scully (1855–1943), magistrate, author, poet and botanist, emigrated to South Africa with his parents from Co. Wicklow, Ireland, in 1867. He prospected for diamonds at Kimberley in 1871, sharing a tent with three brothers – Frank, Herbert and Cecil Rhodes. After prospecting for gold in the Transvaal he embarked on a career as a civil servant in 1882. He was known as an impartial champion of the oppressed. His books include *The White Hecatomb and other stories*, London, 1897, *By Veld and Kopje*, London, 1907, *Ridge of the White Waters*, London, 1912, *Reminiscences of a South African Pioneer*, London, 1913, and *Daniel Vananda*, Cape Town, 1921.

96. Phthisis, any disease causing wasting of the body but here referring to pulmonary tuberculosis.

97. Augustus Theodore Wirgman (1846–1917), Anglican priest and scholar, author of *The History of the English Church and People in South Africa*, 1895, and *A Short History of the Church and Parish of St Mary*, 1892, extended edition 1925. It was largely due to Wirgman's perseverance that the Collegiate Church of St Mary the Virgin was rebuilt after the fire in 1895. Cecil Rhodes and Paul Kruger were among those who contributed to the rebuilding.

98. Mucha, properly *umutsha*, Zulu for loin-covering.

99. East London, at mouth of Buffalo River, developed from landing place of British soldiers during the War of the Axe (the seventh Frontier War) in 1845. First called Port Rex, after its surveyor John Rex, second son of George Rex, founder of nearby Knysna, it was renamed East London in 1848 following formal annexation of the area to the Cape Colony. The Commission took evidence from seven witnesses at the town hall on Monday, 16 March.

100. Euphorbias. See Chapter Seven, Note 80.

101. The battle of Stormberg Junction (10 December 1899). Following a badly executed night march, a force commanded by Lieutenant-General Sir William Gatacre was ambushed by the Boers. More than 600 British troops surrendered.

Chapter Three

A sad story in truth

९९९९९

From Port Elizabeth, the Commission travelled overnight by train to
Kimberley, journeying through the former Afrikaner republic of the
Orange Free State. The Voortrekkers passed through the area in the
1830s on their way north, across the Vaal River, and east, across the
Drakensberg Mountains into what became, briefly, the Republic of
Natalia. After the latter's annexation by the British in 1843, many re-
turned to farm in the land of the Griqua. The resulting tension led to
British intervention and the proclamation of the Orange River Sovereignty (1848–54). In 1854 the area was named the Orange Free State
under the Bloemfontein Convention in which the British formally recognised the independence of white farmers in the area. The Orange
Free State allied with the Transvaal Republic during the Second Anglo-
Boer War (1899–1902). When the British occupied Bloemfontein in
1900, the republic was renamed the Orange River Colony but reverted
to the Orange Free State on entry to the Union in 1910. The Commission began its visit to the region by taking evidence from five witnesses
in Kimberley, which geographically lies within the Cape Province but
is adjacent to its north-eastern border with the Orange Free State.

Wednesday, 18 March

I woke (we had passed Bloemfontein in the night) to find that we were
running through the deadest and barest veld I ever saw. At Petrus [Petrus-
berg, a village midway between the provincial capital, Bloemfontein,
and Kimberley], which we reached after breakfast, I found the reason
why. A railway man and an agent with whom I spoke described the
drought as *terrible*. Little rain for four years and none to speak of this
summer. 'The cattle stagger out to eat stones,' said one of my informants. Many of them have perished, more have been sent away. Others
have eaten 'tulip'[1] and other green but poisonous herbs and died. One
poor farmer who could get no trucks to remove his cattle lost all his
herd thus the other day while trying to drive them 40 miles to where
there is grass. Only the donkeys seem to survive but 'they eat paper or

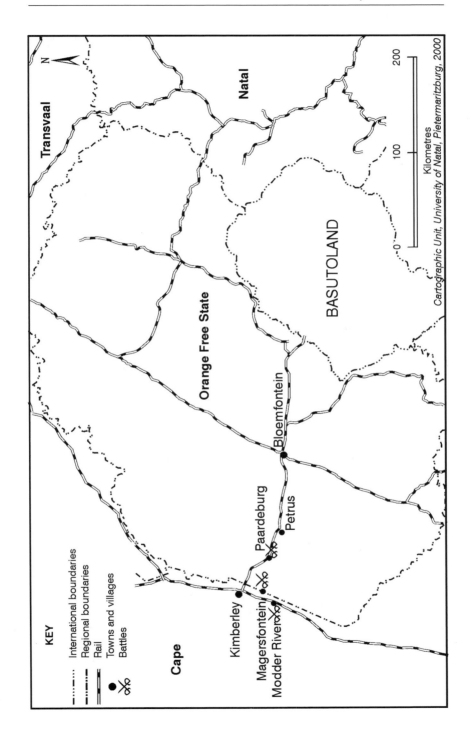

Cartographic Unit, University of Natal, Pietermaritzburg, 2000

anything'. On one farm of 10 000 morgen [about 20 000 acres], which
was pointed out to me, that used to carry 13 000 head there is now
nothing. Most of the farmers, the majority of whom are Dutch, have
'gone down' i.e. become bankrupt. A sad story in truth.

From Petrus we ran at a great rate to Paardeburg where Cronjé
surrendered.[2] We passed the graveyard where so many English and
Dutch are buried but could not see it from the train. Truly this veld is a
sad sight with its scattered mealies[3] not 18 inches high and its few
wandering half-starved sheep and cattle trying to fill themselves on
withered bushes. Of grain there is practically none and winter comes
on! Now, even if it fell, rain could not save the situation. But the time of
rain has passed. The land here is now only worth about £1 the acre –
with no buyers.

Arriving at Kimberley we were driven to the Belgrave Hotel, which
like everything else in this place is owned by the De Beers Co., who
were our hosts here.[4] It was built by Rhodes as a sanatorium for con-
sumptives but as the population of Kimberley objected to such an institution in their midst, was turned into an hotel which the company runs
at a loss of several thousands a year. Needless to say it is perhaps the
most luxurious and best-appointed hostelry in South Africa. Soon after
our arrival, Mr. Oates,[5] chairman of the De Beers Co., took two or three
of us for a motor drive. There are some good streets and buildings in
Kimberley but on the whole it is a mean-looking town, full of houses
built largely of tin that were, I suppose, occupied by the first diamond
seekers. As the place is approached by rail, the chief features are towering headgears marking the mouths of the shafts, huge and hideous
blue-grey dumps of the refuse ground dug from the mines, great areas
or 'floors', acres big, covered with the same stuff 'weathering' after its
arrival at the surface, and miles of tall barbed-wire fences with a kind
of birdcage arrangement on the posts, all designed to make them un-
climbable and to ensure that electric warning bells shall ring if they are
touched. Mr. Oates motored us to Kenilworth, a suburb where we saw
a vine avenue that seemed nearly a mile long. Notwithstanding irrigation, many of the vines were suffering severely from drought and the
same was the case with the fruit trees. We returned to a public luncheon where I sat next to the bishop,[6] an agreeable cleric with whom I
had an interesting talk. He said that the Church of England is doing
well in South Africa.

After lunch we took evidence in the council chamber of the town
hall, which was hung with truly awful pictures of many mayors. In the
evening we were entertained to dinner at the hotel by the De Beers Co.
I observed that no diamonds were worn even by the Jewish ladies.[7] I
suppose that being so common, they are looked on as vulgar here. I
forgot to say that Mr. Oates took us to see the De Beers machinery

works, a huge place. Machines are repaired here but not made as it is cheaper to import them. He told me that the mines employ about 2 000 white men, the average wage being 25s. a day. No smoking was allowed in the works but everybody seemed to have a pipe or a cigarette in his mouth. He added that, do what they would, there was still a good deal of IDB (Illegal Diamond Buying).[8] He put the loss from these thefts at about 5 percent.

The most interesting building I saw at Kimberley was the memorial to those who fell in the siege, before which stood the cannon that was made in the De Beers works and called 'Long Cecil'. This pillared monument is in excellent taste and, to me, appears to have been copied from Pharoah's Bed at Philae.[9]

Thursday, March 19

I went with Garnett and Mr. Greene [a member of the DRC staff] to inspect the irrigated and irrigable lands on the Modder and Reit rivers about 25 miles from Kimberley. Here the soil is splendid, 50 feet deep of alluvial I should say, and when it is put under water will produce enormous crops of lucerne, fruit, mealies, pumpkins, etc. Messrs. Wolhuter and Nightingale drove us from place to place shewing us everything. There is great wealth here but first bridges must be built as the weirs necessary to irrigation will make the rivers unfordable. The tree-clad Modder reminded me somewhat of the Jordan.

Both on our way out and back we visited the site of the battle of Magersfontein.[10] The koppies are a long bent line of stony hills with hollows in the centre of their crest where the Boers encamped. To me they seemed impregnable by direct assault. At their foot lies a vast level plain. We struggled up over the brown stones to the Scottish memorial at the top. Here the emplacements for the Boer guns are still visible, also *schanzes* [breastworks of stones or earth] built to hold [and protect] riflemen. Some of the stones are broken by our shell-fire and we picked up fragments of the burst shells, also a Boer knife and other relics. Below on the plain, perhaps 600 yards from the base of the main koppie, is the long Boer trench which would, I imagine, hold 1 000 men. It was onto this trench, or rather the wire entanglements in front hung with tins, that the unfortunate Black Watch, marching in close formation, stumbled on that fatal night. General Wauchope who, it is said, had protested against this mad attack, came on the silent trench almost alone and had only time to blow his whistle before he was shot down. Then the Boer firing began. What it must have been is shewn by the numbers of cartridge cases which still lie about – Mausers, Martinis and Sniders, also some of our Lee Metford bullets. Mr. Wolhuter told me that his uncle, who was fighting with the Boers here, shot till his rifle was too hot to hold. About 1 000 yards from the road is a great grave covered with stones, 30 feet long perhaps, in which lie many of our dead. They were not placed here at first, however, as I understand they were interred where they fell; certain white patches about the veld mark the spots. Some years later the 'Ladies Guild'[11] moved the remains to this grave and erected an obelisk on which is engraved the names of the fallen. It was indeed a desolate place to visit on that bleak and rainy morning with not a living thing in sight.

To a layman Lord Methuen's enterprise seems one of the maddest military undertakings on record, especially as he could have encircled the koppies by marching round them on the plain where the Boers would never have ventured to attack so strong a force, and, I should think, might have cut them off from their water supply and forced their retreat. To attack a fearful position of this kind with the knowledge of what happened at Laing's Nek[12] and elsewhere in past years was to court what ensued, disaster. However it was done and there's an end. Poor victims! Well, Sir Abe Bailey declared that the war was 'a magnificent success', and, as I think he intimated, lives are cheap. Just in the trenches where the firing must have been most fierce, I picked some blooming iris, the only flowers to be seen on that drought-scorched veld.

On reaching Kimberley we drove straight to what is called the Pulsator where the diamonds from all the mines are recovered by means of wondrous machinery too intricate to describe. Suffice it to say that finally they are shaken onto sloping, grease-covered boards, where, for some mysterious reason which no one seems able to explain, the grease holds the diamonds and lets the rubbish go. Then they are put into peculiar draining vessels, which are heated to remove the grease and taken to the sorting tables, £20 000 worth of them per diem. Here on the tables we saw them of all sizes and colours, and noted that the gems from each mine had characteristics of their own. I picked up a large 'off-coloured' one and was told that its value was about £600. It is strange to think of anybody paying so much for a bit of coloured crystal of which, after all, the value is purely artificial. There are enough diamonds in the various African mines to flood the market, the output could be indefinitely increased, but the price is kept up by means of a 'combine' or trust. The smallest stones are sorted from the remaining rubbish by *convicts,* who sit at a table and separate them with a knife-like piece of metal. It is a curious use to make of prisoners.

To me the native compound that we visited afterwards was of much more interest than the mines. Here numberless kaffirs live for four or six months at a time in a state of strict imprisonment. From the day they enter till the day they take their discharge they cannot set foot outside of these walls, or rather outside of the wire fences that ring the mines. They work eight hours a day in the mines reaching the shaft by an underground passage. At the gate we saw a number of new arrivals being searched before they were admitted, but the only thing discovered was a fragment of some charm or medicine (*mouti*)[13] hidden beneath a hatband. This the searcher took and threw away, I do not know why. Also they are medically examined. Here are members of many tribes, among them but few Zulus though I saw one, gigantic Matabele[14] who would have looked better in his warpaint than he did in dirty European clothing. These boys receive an average wage of about 3s. a day, out of which they have to pay about 1s. for the cost of their living. There are butchers' shops & grocery stores, etc. where they can buy everything they require, down to aerated waters and hop beer and all kinds of clothing. Also there is a place in the centre of the compound which, I should say, covers about four acres, where they wash their garments. Further we saw the night quarters where the men sleep in bunks, perhaps 20 or 30 in a compartment, the large room where religious services are held and the hospital where, most of them lying on beds in the verandah which they prefer, we found a good number of cases under treatment. Some were suffering from scurvy, which is prevalent notwithstanding the onions that are served out free with the purchased beef, others from stomach complaints or accidents. The great scourge however is pneumonia, which is often fatal. Thus in a recent outbreak of a virulent nature about 20 died out of 30 who sickened. The disease is contracted in the tunnels of the deep mines, but of its real cause little seems to be understood. I forgot to ask where they buried their dead, but the cemetery must be crowded. Firewood is supplied gratis and the boys cook their own food. They seemed happy and contented. In one of the meeting rooms two men were playing on harmoniums very well indeed. Outside, another strummed on a banjo and another read the Bible and so on. Occasionally savage tribal fights occur but these are not very frequent, though it has been necessary to call in troops. When all is said, however, it is a strange and unnatural life that these slaves of Vanity endure in order to net their 2s. a day. To isolate thousands of men without their womenkind cannot be good. Before they take their discharge they are shut up for four or five days for fear lest they should have swallowed any diamonds, a horrid and humiliating business for all concerned, but perhaps necessary.

While I was at the Pulsator, a Norfolk man who is employed here, Mr. Valpy, son of the late rector of Elsingham, came up to speak to me. He had last seen me making an election speech in 1905.[15] Oddly enough another Norfolk man, who keeps an hotel at Bloemfontein, has just called on me in that town where I write this note, who also last saw me at that election. Both of them seemed delighted to see one from their own country.

Friday, March 20

Leaving our hotel where we had been so hospitably entertained, we travelled through the night to Bloemfontein,[16] which we reached early this morning. It is a pretty country town of about 15 000 white inhabitants, lying at the foot of a flat-topped mount known as Naval Hill, because the Naval Brigade occupied it during the war. The place is one of sad memory for Englishmen and Boers alike. While here I have visited the old graveyard now so full that it has been closed. In this drought it is a plain of brown earth. As one enters by the old gate, a bar of wood from which hang chains to prevent cattle from getting through, hundreds of numbered iron crosses are seen, on the reverse of each of which is the name of some English soldier who perished in the war, nearly all of them from typhoid. Those crosses stand in rows so endless that the eye grows bewildered in looking at them. Here and there is a monument erected among them by some loving relative or by friends in the regiment to which the deceased belonged, and here and there a headstone telling that beneath lie the bones of a 'nursing sister'. I believe that these crosses were set up by the Ladies Guild.[17]

To the left of the central path the sight is, if possible, even sadder. There are countless mounds of brown earth, some of them only two or three feet in length. These cover the bones of unrecorded Boer women and children who died in the concentration camp not far away, but none can tell whose are the mortal remnants that each of them hides from sight, for of these no record was kept. The fine monument that has recently been erected to these unfortunates about half a mile from the burying ground states that over 26 000 women and children perished in the camps. On it are two figures in bronze of mourning women, very noble and pathetic figures, bronze plaques of children dying in tents, and patriotic sentiments in the Dutch language such as 'For Freedom, Nation and Fatherland'.[18] Sad indeed must have been the processions which passed that gate day by day for many months as the carts with their loads of blanket-wrapped dead arrived continually from the crowded hospital tents and from the wire-surrounded concentration camp beyond. Now friend and foe they lie here, separated only by a few feet of ill-kept pathway, shaded by some scattered shrubs dying in the drought.

I visited these sites afterwards. Almost where the hospital stood a university has been built, but that of the concentration camp, which was placed beneath a koppie, is still bare veld, save for one little desolate hut. Hardly a sod of all this space of land can there be that has not borne the weight of a dying human creature. But if all were known the same might be said of much of this earth's surface. I spoke above with admiration of the monument to the Boer women and children. Now I must add how deeply I regret that it should ever have been erected to perpetuate sentiments which I admit to be most natural, set as it is, doubtless by design, in such a situation that it can be seen not only by wayfarers but by every passenger in the passing trains. The deaths of all these poor people were most unfortunate but it is difficult to avoid the suspicion that more might have been done to avoid some of them. Thus Mr. Fichardt, the president of the chamber of commerce, told me that the water was brought to them tepid and in dirty, typhoid-infected iron carts, which were never – or rarely – washed.[19] Also it does seem sad that as many or more women and children should have perished than were lost by wounds and sickness in the whole war. All these facts this memorial with its noble and pathetic sculptures will commemorate for centuries. Well *stet et stabit* [20] for good or ill.

Sir Edgar, Mr. Fichardt and I lunched together at the club. Mr. F., who in the war days was a supporter of the Boer cause and one of those who refused to take the oath of allegiance after the occupation of Bloemfontein (although he did take the oath of neutrality), told us the most painful and extraordinary stories of his treatment by British officers, especially by two named Hitchcock and Salmon, young captains, I think, who successively filled the office of provost marshal, a kind of headship of police. The language used towards him on many occasions, according to his account, by these officers was so unutterably foul that I cannot even write it in this private diary and (again according to his account) it was well matched by the petty persecutions to which he was subjected for, I think, nearly two years. The thing seems incredible and yet the worst of it was that neither Vincent nor I could disbelieve his story. Either it is true, or the lying was of such a masterly character that it quite disarmed the doubts of two not inexperienced men.

I will only give the *mildest* example that I remember. Mr. F.'s father died early in the war and was buried by his own wish at a farm he owned about six miles out from the town of Bloemfontein. Again and again, he said, did his aged mother, for a period of, I think, two years, pray for permission to visit his grave, where as I saw afterwards she also lies today. The invariable answer was a savage refusal, accompanied by such words as these, 'you b . . . s won't do anything for us and we b . . . y well won't do anything for you.' Again, he informed us that the treatment of his pregnant wife was abominable in its brutality. On the other hand it must be recorded that he spoke with warmth and even with affection of some of the senior officers with whom he came into contact later, and those in authority, rightly or wrongly, perhaps rightly, regarded Mr. F. with the gravest suspicion. At the best, however, his story leaves a most unpleasant taste in the mouth. There is no doubt also that young men suddenly placed in a position of almost absolute power often do not know how to behave. It is possible also that those of whom he complains were of the quartermaster class promoted.

In the afternoon, after attending a tea party given by the Victoria League,[21] we were motored by Mr. Fichardt to see his farm. It was indeed a desolate sight. All the larger gum trees planted by his father about 30 years ago were dead or dying from the attacks of a horrible beetle which lays its eggs in the bark. The grubs, when hatched, work their way up and down cutting grooves beneath the bark and stopping the flow of sap which results in the death of the tree. Finally they bore into the heart of the tree and there become perfect beetles. On chopping with an axe at an affected tree we found the grubs to have mouths like nippers and saw the whole process of destruction. The younger plantations of firs and gums, also the fruit orchard, were dead or dying of drought, which has endured in this district for about four years. So melancholy was the aspect of the place that I think the well-kept graves of Mr. F.'s father and mother and infant son were almost the most cheerful objects we were shewn. Also there were some good stall-fed Friesland cattle. Truly South Africa is a land in which the 10 plagues of Egypt have become endemic.

At Bloemfontein I saw Colonel Du Toit, the head of the police of whom Mr. Merriman spoke to me as having witnessed an extraordinary performance by a kaffir witch-doctor, which he, Merriman, supposed quite erroneously to have been the origin of sundry mystic scenes in *She*.[22] He is, I should say, a most able and energetic officer, indeed that is his reputation. Here is Col. Du Toit's story as I wrote it down within a few hours. He has promised to let me have it in writing, stipulating only that no use should be made of his name, as he says that in past days this tale has brought ridicule on him and even suggestions that he, a teetotaller, had been drinking. A good many years ago he, a government officer, was on the Zoutpansberg[23] border with two other scientific gentlemen. I think they were surveying.

At the kraal of some chief whose name I forget, they lost two of their salted horses, which because of the prevalent sickness were very valuable. After long search, they consulted the local witch-doctor. He was an old, weak-looking man who wore some of the ordinary trappings, including a number of human finger bones strung about him. He threw the bones, which are called 'dumb-oxen' because Boer children are in the habit of setting these particular knuckle bones before wagons made of mud and pretending to drive them. After inspecting them the 'doctor' declared that the two horses would be found on the following morning, one by a certain spring and the other in a neighbouring kloof. One of the horses he described as white. Du Toit denied that the horse was white (in fact it was blue-grey). The doctor threw his bones a second time and asserted it was white. Ultimately it transpired that in his language there was no word for 'blue-grey'– that used for 'white' included this particular colour. The doctor had desired that one of the white men's own servants should be sent to look for the horses, not one of the local natives. The man told to go protested as he had already searched the place that day, it being the only one in the neighbourhood where there was water. However, at dawn he went and found the horses exactly as the doctor had promised that he would.

After the horse episode, the chief was asked to allow the doctor to shew further examples of his skill and consented. The doctor produced about a dozen rods of round blackwood – Col. Du Toit described them as like office rulers only crooked. These he laid one over the other on the ground, criss-cross in a pile. He then sent for some dry, sweet-smelling grass, which he packed between the interstices of the black sticks. Next he asked for fire. Matches were proffered to him but of these he refused to make use, sending to the kraal for embers that were brought upon a sherd. He placed the embers against the grass and blew. It took, fire burning with a steady blue flame like to that of a spirit lamp. From the flame arose a cloud of dense white smoke such as is caused by *black* powder. This flame and its smoke the doctor several times drew upwards by the lifting of his hands and pressed downwards by the lowering of his hands till they almost vanished. In fact they seemed to obey the motions of his hands. (It was this circumstance that caused Merriman to conclude that the similar scene in *She* was taken from the performance of this doctor, of whose feats I had never even heard. The particular scene alluded to was as much – or as little – of an invention as the rest of the book.)[24]

In the end the dense white smoke spread out like a fan, hiding the doctor altogether, except the tips of the fingers of both his hands, which projected on either side of the smoke. Then he asked what the white chiefs wished to see. The first thing Du Toit could think of was the new government buildings at Pretoria, just finished about that time. He asked that these might be shewn. Presently on the smoke appeared their image, so absolutely clear that the white men *could read the time shewn by the clock in the tower*. They all consulted their watches and found that it agreed with none of them by some minutes. On their return to camp, however, they compared their watches with the chronometer they had with them for their work and found that the time shewn on the smoke was correct to a second. The inaccuracy was due to their watches. The picture faded by degrees, but not before Du Toit had been able to point out thereon the window of his own office to his companions.

One of these wished to see another picture and thinking that he would discomfort the magician asked for a smoke shadow of the 'black water', having first ascertained that the man had never seen the ocean or, for the matter of that, Pretoria. The business was gone through once more and on the smoke (more clearly on one side of it than on the other) appeared first a rock, then breakers dashing against it, then (between the rock and the shore) a three-masted ship at anchor, and lastly, far out, a steamer battling against a heavy head sea, the smoke from her funnel tracking behind here. This picture faded also, the fire went out, and the performance came to an end leaving the old doctor quite exhausted and the white men equally bewildered. Du Toit took the black sticks into his hand and found that although they were *warm* there was no mark of fire on them.

On his return to Pretoria he told the story to General Joubert, who accepted it with a shrug and the remark 'Yes, yes the devil teaches the black wizards how to do those things.'[25] He also told it to another friend, I think he said it was the surveyor-general (Ressek?), an educated, scientific and sceptical Hollander, who laughed at him and said that as he was going to visit that part of the country he would look into the matter and find out how the trick was done.[26] Over a year afterwards Du Toit asked him the result of his inquiries. He replied humbly that he was nonplussed. The old doctor, at his request, had actually shewn him friends of his own walking about the streets of a town *in Holland* so clearly that he recognised them at once.

Here the story ends for this *inyanga*, a very ancient man, died a few years ago.[27] Personally I have no explanations to offer, nor has Du Toit. If it can be accepted, as for one I accept it, having heard it in full detail from his own lips – then – what? Then such a thing as magic *does* exist, and if this be so what becomes of the proud foundation of 'facts' on which we stand? Well, we must enlarge it, that is all. I should repeat that Du Toit begged that his name might not be published in connection with this tale, as in past years it had already brought much ridicule upon him and his companions, to say nothing of the suggestion that he, a lifelong teetotaller, was drunk at the time.

At Bloemfontein I was entertained at lunch by the 'African Club' and made a speech on agriculture, which was well received by a considerable company. It seems to be a thriving town and the market where ox wagons still appear laden with produce is crowded.

Sunday, March 22

We left Bloemfontein [last] night and woke to find ourselves running through fine green veld with many table-topped mountains, very different to the eye from the parched expanses in the neighbourhood of Bloemfontein. Later on Harrismith[28] appeared, a pretty little tree-clothed town lying beneath a range of hills, most of them with the familiar table tops. Afterwards we passed two of the blockhouses, tall stone, loop-holed buildings with iron roofs that were erected in numbers by the British during the war and surrounded by barbed wire. Now they stand deserted.

Notes

1. 'Tulip', familiar name for various wild bulbous plants of the Homeria group fatal to cattle and sheep.
2. Pieter Cronje (1836–1911), Boer general. After a battle lasting several days, Cronje's surrender at Paardeberg on 27 February 1900, the anni-

versary of Majuba, was the first significant British victory of the war and a
major blow to Boer morale, with more than 4 000 Boers captured.

3. Mealies, maize, Indian corn. 'Though it is not indigenous to South Africa,
    the mealie could almost qualify as our national vegetable,' *Evening Post*,
    27 October 1973, quoted in J. Branford with W. Branford, *A Dictionary of
    South African English*, Cape Town, 1991.

4. Kimberley grew from the diamond mining camp established after the ini-
    tial finds in 1867, then boomed in 1871 after the discovery of a diamondi-
    ferous volcanic pipe. It was named after the British Colonial Secretary, the
    Earl of Kimberley, who annexed the diamond fields in 1871. The De Beers
    Consolidated Mines Ltd. Company was founded by Cecil Rhodes in 1888.

5. Francis Oates (1848–1918), mining engineer, prospector and leader of the
    diamond industry, became director of De Beers after amalgamating the
    diamond mines at the behest of Cecil Rhodes, Alfred Beit and Barney
    Barnato.

6. Wilfred Gore Browne, Bishop of Kimberley, 1912–28.

7. See Chapter One, Note 9.

8. Illegal Diamond Buying provided a plot element for the novel *Finished*,
    London, 1917, written after Haggard's visit to South Africa.

9. The memorial was designed by Herbert Baker (see Chapter Five, Note 18)
    and is based on the fourth-century BC Nereid monument at Xanthos in
    Asia Minor. A two-storey structure – the upper part a pillared canopy or
    temple – it is constructed of Rhodesian marble quarried near the Matopos
    Hills. The gun 'Long Cecil' is an artillery piece built in the De Beers work-
    shops by George Abrams at the request of Cecil Rhodes during the siege of
    Kimberley.

10. Battle of Magersfontein (11 December 1899). Lieutenant-General Lord
    Methuen (1845–1932) was officer commanding the British force. The
    Highland Brigade suffered heavy casualties, among them their command-
    ing officer, Major-General Andrew Gilbert Wauchope (1846–99).

11. Ladies Guild. See Note 21.

12. Battle of Laing's Nek, 28 January 1881. The Haggards heard the sound of
    the battle from their farm outside Newcastle. As at Magersfontein, a Brit-
    ish force attacked an entrenched position over open country.

13. Mouti, *umuthi*, Zulu medicine, both herbal and animal products believed to
    have the power to heal and protect.

14. Zulu (see Chapter Seven, Note 1). Matabele (see preamble to Chapter Six).

15. Presumably on behalf of the Conservatives, whose leader, Arthur Balfour,
    resigned as Prime Minister on 4 December 1905. In the general election
    held on 12 January 1906 there was a landslide victory for the Liberals and
    Henry Campbell-Bannerman (1836–1908) became Prime Minister. Ten
    years earlier, in 1895, Haggard had stood as a Unionist and Agricultural
    candidate in parliamentary elections.

16. Bloemfontein, provincial capital of the Orange Free State, established 1846.
    The name literally means 'flower fountain' but this also could be the name
    of a man, horse or an ox. The Commission took evidence from eight
    witnesses at the Bloemfontein town hall.

17. Ladies Guild. See Note 21.

18. The National Women's Monument erected to the memory of 26 370 women

and children who died in the concentration camps and the other women and children who died elsewhere during the Second Anglo-Boer War. These internment camps were part of Lord Kitchener's plan to deny Boer combatants civilian assistance. 'The camps have left a gigantic scar across the minds of the Afrikaners: a symbol of deliberate genocide,' Pakenham, *Boer War*, p. 495. The ashes of Emily Hobhouse (1860–1926) are interred at the foot of the monument, which was unveiled on 16 December 1913. Hobhouse, an Englishwoman, publicised conditions in the camps and campaigned for their reform.

19. Charles Gustav Fichardt (1870–1923), businessman and politician. During the Second Anglo-Boer War, he escaped from Paardeberg prior to the surrender. He was subsequently captured at Poplar Grove on 7 March 1900, after his horse was shot dead under him and he sustained serious hip injuries. A founder member of the National Party.

20. S*tet et stabit,* Latin for 'let it stand and it will remain'.

21. Victoria League, founded in London on 2 April 1901 in memory of Queen Victoria, with the object of fostering friendship throughout the British Empire and alleviating distress in the concentrations camps in South Africa and aiding any British war refugees. It was created as a direct result of an appeal from the Guild of Loyal Women in Cape Town to give immediate attention to those in distress on both sides during the Second Anglo-Boer War.

22. Michiel (Mike) Siebert Wiid du Toit (1868–1938), policeman and politician, was Divisional Commissioner of the South African Police in the Orange Free State in 1914. During the First World War, he was responsible for camps for German internees in Pietermaritzburg and Durban. Joined the National Party in 1929, winning Pretoria West from the Labour Party.
    'Witch-doctor': prejudicial and incorrect term. See Note 27.

23. Soutpansberg, mountainous range in the northern Transvaal (now Northern Province), named after the saltpan used by the Voortrekkers.

24. Ayesha uses a 'font-like vessel' containing water to similar effect. 'That water is my glass; in it I see what passes if I care to summon up the pictures.' H.R. Haggard, *She*, 1991, p. 152.

25. Petrus Jacobus Joubert (1831–1900), politician and Boer Commandant-General.

26. Ressek was probably Johann Rissik (see Chapter Five, p. 128 and Note 7). In 1891 he was responsible for the Transvaal Survey Law (No. 9) and in 1895 was appointed Surveyor-General of the Transvaal.

27. *Inyanga*, Zulu doctor or herbalist as opposed to an *isangoma*, a diviner.

28. Harrismith, established 1850, and named after Sir Harry Smith (1787–1860), Governor of the Cape 1847–52.

Chapter Four

Chief from of old! Father!

After leaving Bloemfontein, the Commission travelled to the former British colony of Natal, which acquired its name from the Portuguese explorer Vasco da Gama when sailing past the Pondoland coast on Christmas Day 1497. At that time the region was occupied by Bushman hunter-gatherers and Nguni-speaking farmers. Towards the end of the 18th century a power struggle among chiefs north of the Thukela River led to the emergence of the Zulu kingdom under Shaka. The first white settlement was established at Port Natal – later Durban – in 1824, sowing the seeds for the conflicts that lay ahead, culminating in the Anglo-Zulu War of 1879. Natal was a district of the Cape Colony until 1856 when it was given its own Legislative Council, based in Pietermaritzburg, and became a separate British colony. It became self-governing in 1893. Zululand was absorbed as a province of Natal in 1897. It was to the Natal capital that Haggard had come, aged 19, in 1875, and there, in 1914, that the Commission interviewed 12 witnesses in the provincial council building.

The descent of the Drakensberg by Van Reenen's Pass[1] by which the Free State burghers advanced into Natal at the commencement of the war (no provision having been made by our generals to fortify and hold these passes and the railway line) is one of great beauty and so steep that in places the line is built in zigzags. Here we began to see graves by the rail side, of whom I do not know.[2] Ladysmith looks charming in its hill-surrounded hollow, but a more hopeless place to choose as a military arsenal and camp it would be difficult to imagine, commanded as is the hollow in which the little town is built from many huge and almost impregnable hills.[3]

The afternoon we spent in inspecting battlegrounds, a melancholy business, under the guidance of Mr. Duncan, who was in charge of the railway transport in these parts during the war. We visited the [Royal] hotel with a kind of grave in the back yard into which I descended. Here the visitors took refuge whenever an Indian up a tree rang a bell to warn them that one of the guns had been fired on a hill miles away.[4]

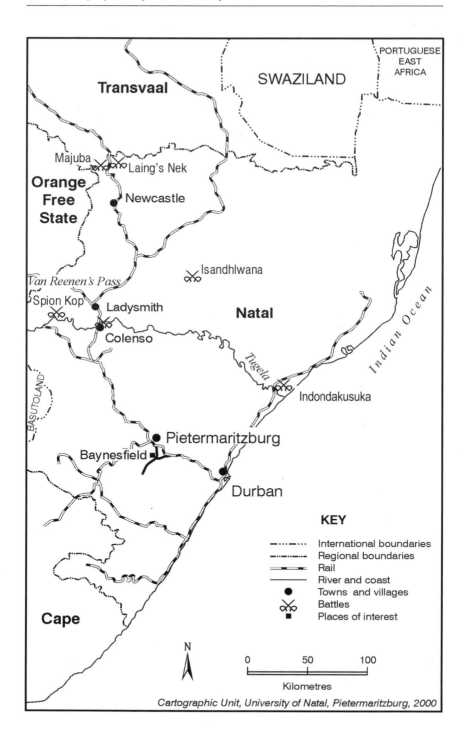

PORTUGUESE
EAST
AFRICA

SWAZILAND

Transvaal

Majuba ⚔ Laing's Nek

**Orange
Free
State**

Newcastle

Van Reenen's Pass

Spion Kop ⚔ Ladysmith

⚔ Colenso

⚔ Isandhlwana

Natal

Tugela

Indian Ocean

BASUTOLAND

Indondakusuka

● Pietermaritzburg

Baynesfield ■

Durban

KEY

—··—··— International boundaries
—··—··— Regional boundaries
━━━━━ Rail
─────── River and coast
● Towns and villages
⚔ Battles
■ Places of interest

Cape

N

0   50   100

Kilometres

Cartographic Unit, University of Natal, Pietermaritzburg, 2000

They had time to do this as the shell took five minutes to arrive. On the verandah however, a scientist, Dr. Stark,[5] was killed. Also we saw the clock tower [on the Town Hall] remaining partly shot away, the clock being supported by iron bars.[6] Thence we went to the church, which is full of memorials, tablets and windows to the fallen.[7] Then on to the graveyard where hundreds lie buried, among them poor G.W. Steevens, the *Daily Mail* Correspondent, and many officers.[8] Some of the crosses are merely inscribed 'Here lies a British Soldier', the dead man's identification card having been lost and his body too disfigured to be recognised. Others indicating 'Here lies a brave Burgher' are the resting places of the Boers who penetrated to and were shot down in the town during the Caesar's Camp engagement.[9] This cemetery is beautifully kept and offers a pleasing contrast to that at Bloemfontein. We went also to the convent[10] and from that eminence were shewn the whole plan of attack and defence. Afterwards Vincent and I motored out of the town to the other end of Caesar's Camp hill. Here I recognised the Maritzburg road and remembered the very spot where I had halted my horse in 1876 and admired the stars with Sir Henry Bulwer as we rode into Ladysmith.[11]

Taking the train again we proceeded 20 miles or so to the Colenso battlefield, which lies on the town lands over much of which we walked.[12] To me today Buller's 'bull at a gate' plan of attack seemed even madder than that of Methuen at Modderfontein. A vast, flat plain guarded by impossible mountains, a river, the Tugela, in front of it, and on the hither side of the river Boer trenches lined with sharp-shooters. Such was the position. Naturally the troops never even reached the river; they were shot down on the plain in heaps. Monuments mark where they fell, among them that of the gallant young Roberts died of wounds sustained while trying to rescue abandoned artillery,[13] and the graves in which they were buried are everywhere. Mr. Duncan told me that a shallow trench was dug, the dead laid in and covered over, often with only a few inches of soil over them. In some cases, often engagements in which any of the latter had fallen, English and Boers were placed in the same trench.

The terrible part of this Colenso battle is that there is a formidable hill that might presumably have been occupied by Buller, thereby commanding the Boer positions, which is situated on this side of the Tugela. Duncan and others pointed this out to Buller's staff, but they were working from a school map which shewed this hill on the further side of the Tugela, and would not believe them. Imagine an army in its own territory being supplied only with a child's atlas! According to Mr. Duncan it was always the same story, the imperial officers invariably treated the information offered by loyal English having local knowledge with supercilious contempt. 'They always thought we wanted to make something out of them,' he said. Of this I have no personal knowledge so far as the second Boer war was concerned but that it was the case in both the Zulu and the first Boer war I know. To take but a single instance, well do I remember Sir Melmoth Osborn[14] writing, I think to Lord Chelmsford,[15] warning him from his intimate knowledge of the Zulus and their tactics of what would happen if precautions of 'laagering' etc. were not taken. His letter was not even acknowledged and Isandhlwana followed. I myself knew all this so well that I wrote to friends in another part of the world telling them to be prepared for a great disaster. The letter reached them simultaneously with the telegraphed news of that disaster – to their great surprise.

Mr. Duncan saw our troops march out on the morning of this Colenso fight. They were singing, as he thought at first a hymn after the fashion of the old Puritans. When they came nearer however the supposed hymn resolved itself into a music hall song popular at the time, of which the refrain is 'What ho! she bumps'! Well, it is a cheerful ditty. Poor fellows, in a few hours many of them were dead. I should add that he spoke with the utmost enthusiasm of the conduct of the rank and file throughout all this Natal fighting, saying that it was simply *splendid*. They never knew when they were beaten and even at Colenso cursed because they were recalled from their hopeless attack. If the officers had been equal to the men there would have been a different tale to tell. After this and other battles Mr. Duncan insisted on collecting the wounded, placing them in railway carriages and removing them to the hospital. 'I remember,' he said, pointing to the little platform of Colenso station 'that while we were filling up, five men died. We took them out and laid them there. We had no room for corpses.' Bullets still lie about on the battlefield, for a member of our party picked one up – a martini ball from a Boer rifle. Also there is a hole in a small mimosa tree[16] over one of the graves shewing that a bullet had entered there. Perhaps the most suggestive place on this plain is the little water-cut depression, it cannot be called a donga for it is scarcely two feet deep, where the survivors of the artillery men took refuge from the hellish hail of bullets that screamed over them, not daring to lift their heads. The guns it will be remembered were left and as we did not send to fetch them during the night, the Boers did. We also saw the sites of other battles, notably one at a bridge where I think we lost 600 in killed and wounded. Spion Kop, where we met such terrible loss owing to the quarrel between Buller and Warren, we only looked on from a distance.[17]

Colenso does not seem to have changed much during the last 40 years. It is a collection of tin-roofed houses and hovels with no population to speak of. The foundations of the military bridge (now destroyed) seem to occupy the site of the drift over the Tugela where I remember being so badly stuck in bygone years that it took 32 oxen to pull the wagon through.[18] At Colenso our coach was detached from the special train and in it Bowring, Garnett and I travelled through the night to Newcastle attached to the mail train in which were Louie and Lilias who had come to meet me.

Monday, 23 March

At seven in the morning, once again we (Louie and I) trod the streets of the little town of Newcastle, which we left in 1881.[19] It has grown a good deal, the hotels have changed and there are more trees but, speaking generally, is much the same. After breakfast the committee of the royal commission was formally received in the town hall.[20] There were perhaps 30 gentlemen present, none of them young but not one of these was here when I departed from Newcastle. There was the usual speech of welcome to which I responded, after which we visited a coal mine. In the afternoon we took evidence concerning coal and agriculture, which is flourishing here since dipping for cattle was invented, and later visited another coal mine. This mine is just over the river opposite to the Rooi Point farm Cochrane and I used to own. Here I was shewn the very spot in the banks of the Ingagane River to which I used to send a cart to be filled with the coal that outcrops at this place, imagining it was on my property (which it was not). Every little memory of this sort connected with me seems to have been treasured up by the inhabitants of Newcastle.

Garnett and Bowring having departed by the night mail for Durban, we were entertained that evening at a reception which ended in a dance. Here I was marched onto a platform where the mayor [Albert Dunton, JP] made another speech of welcome to me, personally, to which of course I had to reply. I escaped early.

Tuesday, 24 March

In the morning I revisited Hilldrop, the last place on earth I ever expected to see again.[21] Hilldrop that for me has so many memories. After sundry vicissitudes it is now owned by a couple of the name of Mackenzie, who have improved the house and gardens. Until I told them I do not think they knew that the fatal Convention giving back the Transvaal to the Boers had been signed here in this historic house.[22] I looked at all the rooms, including that in which my dear son [Jock] was born. They are practically the same. I could even remember where my pipe rack hung upon the wall. Then I went outside, ate a fruit off the old naartjie trees, inspected the wagon house where in my book *Jess* was incarcerated, the stone kraal that we built to hold the ostriches, the new road up the hillside on which I am told the *dassies*, or rock rabbits, still sit as they used to do, and the water bore just completed by Mr. Mackenzie and this day working for the first time.

Natal Witness

*The farmhouse Hilldrop just outside Newcastle where Haggard
and his family lived in 1881. Haggard visited the farm in 1914.
Hilldrop was declared a national monument in 1981.*

After this I walked down through the sloping garden grounds where
the trees have grown greatly, especially one oak, though the lightning
has killed some of them, past the spring whence we drew water, now
nearly hidden in willows, to the spot where we made bricks. Lo! there
still lay some of the bricks, likely enough fashioned by my own hands
and even a little heap of the coal that we used to burn them. I picked
them up with a strange emotion. Well, they are not bad bricks. By the
spring I took from my pocket the knife that Andrew gave me when I
was 15 which has rested there from then till now, 43 years, and told Mr.
Mackenzie how once I lent it to Cochrane with the result that he lost it
for a month near this spring after which a kaffir found it again. So back
to the house presently to step off that well-remembered stoep, I presume for the last time.[23]

In the afternoon we went in a kind of bus with four horses to visit a
farm nine miles away that stands in a beautiful situation in a bay of the
[Drakens]Berg. We never reached that farm because of the awfulness
of the road but, except for the bumps, the drive was charming. Also I
visited what used to be Fort Amiel where now there is nothing but a
little stead and a graveyard full of the bones of the victims of the Boer
war.[24] Last time I was here the mount was covered with cantonments
and hospital tents in which, I remember, were many dying of wounds

and gangrene. Hither it was that once I galloped to learn if it were true that Colley had met with a great disaster on Majuba.[25] They knew nothing at the camp but at the post office I learned all the dreadful truth. It had not occurred to anyone to inform those left in command of the soldiers!

Wednesday, 25 March

We left Newcastle early, reaching Maritzburg after a journey through the lovely scenery of Natal, about four in the afternoon.[26] As soon as I reached the Imperial Hotel,[27] after the usual attentions from the photographer (which resulted in a picture in *The Natal Witness* [28] that looks exactly like that of the mummy of Rameses the Second), to my delight my friend, Mr. James Stuart, arrived.[29] I feared that he had left for

A picture of Haggard in the Witness *'that looks exactly like that of the mummy of Rameses the Second'.*
On Friday 27 March 1914, the front page of the Natal Witness *featured photographs of Haggard taken at the Imperial Hotel during his visit to Pietermaritzburg.*

England in connection with the production on the stage of 'Mameena'.[30] He told me that he had succeeded in finding my old Zulu servant Mazooku, who was coming to see me on the following morning.[31] We went for a walk up Loop Street to where Stuart lives and then on to the old Government House.[32] It is now a seminary for lady teachers and as it was already getting dark I had some hesitation in asking to be admitted. However, Mrs. Millard, the lady in command, was delighted to see me and I was shewn all over the old house so full of memories for me. I saw where I used to sit at the end of the table – there were 60 young ladies supping there who stood up when I 'said a few words' to them, (Stuart following in Zulu). This chamber is unaltered except that the folding doors have been built into the wall. The drawing room too is quite the same. I can remember where the card table stood.

Then I went upstairs and penetrated into my bedroom, now occupied by three young ladies. I remarked that there used to be a yellow-wood cupboard at the end of the room. 'There it is, Sir,' said the old caretaker triumphantly, pointing to the identical thing standing in the passage. I knew it again at once, it is one of the few pieces of the original furniture that has remained in the place. The drawing room mantelpiece with twisted columns seemed unfamiliar to me, I think it must have been put in since my time. My office in the executive council chamber has been pulled down, more's the pity – and with it the little bedroom where I tossed a coin with Sir George Colley [who was] in his bath as to the price of a gun, where also my watchfulness saved Cox's life, when the artery broke out again.[33] So out through the old porch where the big yellow spider used to make its web, back to the hotel. Stuart coming to dine.

Thursday, 26 March

Mazooku came in the morning and oh! he was pleased to see me. He has worn very well, his hair shewing no grey, but I fear has not prospered, as he lost his cattle by the East Coast Fever.[34] We had a conversation in the true Zulu style, Stuart interpreting. I told him that the *inkosikazi* (Louie) and the maiden (Lilias) were going to stay awhile at Eshowe in Zululand, that he was to go with them and that I put them 'into your hand'. He answered in the old way – "*Inkoosi y pagate! Baba!*" (chief from of old! Father!) thereby signifying obedience to the order.[35] Also that if possible I wished him to accompany me through Zululand afterwards. Subsequently I relieved his difficulties as to his rent to another native for which he was being sued. The talk between him and Stuart on this matter was amusing. Here is the substance:

> *Stuart*: 'In truth, O Mazooku, you should return thanks to the spirit of your ancestors. See now, in a most unexpected fashion

Mazooku, Haggard's servant from his days in South Africa as a young man. Mazooku was reunited with Hagggard during the latter's visit to Pietermaritzburg in March 1914 (when this photograph was taken), subsequently accompanying him on the tour through Zululand.

Natal Witness

your own, your very father, has descended from the heavens, has taken you by the hand and dragged you out of a deep pit!'

Mazooku, with fervour: 'Indeed I do thank the spirits and my father also, etc. etc.'

I asked him where he meant to live in future. He replied that he did not know, adding naïvely: 'If you were staying in this land, with you of course, my father.' There we have the old Zulu feudal idea of chief and retainer. I reminded him of how he had given me his kerrie when we parted, remarking that I still had and valued it.[36] He replied that he remembered but had never thought it possible that such a thing should be preserved for so long. Mazooku is the man who continued to search for me when others had abandoned the quest, and found me at last at one in the morning lying half frozen, starved and hurt by a fall of my horse on the winter high veld, thereby, as I think, probably saying my life. Such is the fidelity of the Zulu.

On this same morning I saw Mr. Addison, the chief magistrate of Zululand, as to my tour in that country.[37] On leaving Mr. Stuart took me outside to where a number of chief, headmen and Zulu messengers and policemen were waiting to see officials, etc. He explained to them that I was 'Sompseu's child' whom he had loved.[38] The effect was strange

Cheyne Collection

Mhlophekazi (the fictional Umslopogaas) with his axe.

Cheyne Collection

Mhlophekazi (the fictional Umslopogaas) as an old man.

– a volley of enthusiastic salutes. Such is still the magic of that name. Also I saw and had a long talk with John Shepstone, Sir T.S's brother. He is now 87 but wonderfully hale and well.[39] He was *very* pleased to meet me again. So were his daughter and his son. To the latter old Umslopogaas had given the hunting knife I sent him years ago by the hand of Osborn, that he might keep it safe lest it should be stolen away. If at any time he came to claim it, good, if not it was to be his. Mr. Shepstone now proposes to give this knife to the museum.

I heard a great deal about old Umslopogaas from a gentleman whose name I forget at the moment, and others. This gentleman, who sent me the photograph of him [Umslopogaas] taken as he was dying, told me

that he shewed him the pictures of himself in the illustrated edition of
Allan Quatermain. He said that the old fellow's interest in them was
extraordinary, especially in that of 'Umslopogaas holding the Stair'. He
jumped up, got hold of a chopper and enacted the whole scene. He said
also that 'my heart is white towards Lundanda' (i.e. myself) meaning
that he regarded me with affection.[40] This brings me to the matter of
my true native name. I always thought it was Indanda meaning 'a
pleasant man' or 'a quiet man'. According to Mazooku, however, it is
Lundanda in' Ndand' okalweni, which means 'The tall man who walks
along the ridges or on the mountains.' As I was never addicted to this
form of exercise I presume that the interpretation is metaphorical and
spiritual, i.e. one who keeps on high ground or it may mean one who
appears to be thinking of far away things.[41] This day I went over the
Voortrekker Museum where are to be seen many interesting mementoes of the old Dutch.[42]

In the evening I dined with Stuart at the old Victoria Club, now
housed in a fine building.[43] Here with Mr. Koch (Osborn's legal adviser
in Zululand) and others, I met Henrique Shepstone, Sir Theophilus's
son, now a man of well over 70.[44] We were indeed pleased to see each
other again. I forgot to say also that I inspected Sir T.'s statue. It is good
on the whole, especially the back which I recognised from 20 yards
away, but there is something wrong about the eyes and the hair is
represented as growing too far back on the forehead. At dinner we had

James Stuart in 1905. Stuart
accompanied Haggard on his trip
through Zululand. See Chaper Seven.

an interesting discussion on various disputed points in Zulu history on which Stuart is so great an authority. Some of these, notably the exact manner of the killing of Nandie, Chaka's mother by Chaka himself, and of the death of Umbelazi, Panda's son at the battle of the Tugela. I tried to elucidate on the following day, in a conversation with an old Zulu named Socwatsha, who is noted for his marvellous memory and historical knowledge.[45] There were also present Stuart, who interpreted, and Mazooku, whose father fought for Cetywayo in the battle in 1856, and afterwards fled into Natal as his chief was suspected of disloyalty. It was wonderful to watch old Socwatsha as he told his story of these events, enacting them as he spoke, as only a Zulu can. Thus he gave Chaka's words when mourning for his mother – see *Nada the Lily* – in the same weeping voice, repeating his epithets of endearment.[46] Some of these were of the strangest, referring as they did to her amorous propensities. Both he and Mazooku asserted that it is universally believed among the Zulus that Chaka did kill his mother, whether as Socwatsha alleged outright with a kerrie, after he had destroyed his child whom she was hiding and 'hung its body on a post of the hut fence', or by wounding her in the abdomen with a little assegai so that she subsequently died while he was away hunting, as Fynn thought from dysentery.[47] Of Umbelazi's death he had nothing *certain* to tell, one version, with a curious authentic touch, which he gave us is that he was last seen after the rout by a younger brother of his own, whom he hid in a bush *'lifting the grass with his spear* when he had finished hiding him, so that it might not be seen that men had walked there'. The mystery will never now be solved. I thought that I had invented the story of the hidden child of Chaka in *Nada the Lily*, but perhaps heard it somewhere.

Friday, 27 March

After the morning sitting of the committee I was entertained by the African Club at what was said to be the largest luncheon ever given in Maritzburg. My reception was *most* enthusiastic, affectionate and touching. I made a long speech, beginning by saying that I really wondered if my name was H.R.H. or Rip van Winkle, and paying the best tribute I could to the honoured memory of Sompseu (which I heard pleased the Shepstone family very much). I ended by invoking all good things in Natal 'this dear and lovely land'. The applause was great.[48] In the evening the R.C. (Vincent being absent at Johannesburg) was entertained at dinner by the Administrator.[49] After Bateman had responded, I made a few remarks on a passage in the Administrator's speech in which, among compliments, he suggested that I have 'idealised the native' in my books. The effect of these was that it is difficult to paint the Lily of Loyalty or to gild the Rose of Honour, as these have often been worn by the Zulu savage, whereof I gave examples. Still in details the charge is true. The artist must idealize, that is unless he desires to be a mere photographer. It rained heavily at Maritzburg this day which was unlucky for us but fortunate for the country in this year of drought.

Saturday, 28 March

I accompanied some of the R.C. on a visit we made by train to the beautiful 24 000-acre farm of Mr. Baynes, which is called Nel's Rust, about 17 miles from Maritzburg.[50] Here we took evidence and saw something of the creamery. To Mr. Baynes belongs the credit of having introduced the practice of dipping cattle into South Africa from Queensland. At 10 that night we started with Louie and Lilias for Pretoria and on the morning of the 29th once more passed Rooi Point and Hilldrop. Then appeared all the scenes of the war of 1881, notably the sad Majuba where poor Colley rests with others. It is a high conical hill with a cone at the south end and a long ridge down which the rout took place, very easy to attack as its flanks are somewhat hollow. I noted a little bush-clothed kloof up which the 90 Boers crept on that fatal morning. At its foot is a nice farmhouse. I should not care to live in the shadow of Majuba.

Notes

1. Named after Frans van Reenen (1816–1914), owner of a farm at the foot of the pass and the planner of the route.
2. Burial places of those killed in skirmishes during the early stages of the Second Anglo-Boer War (1899–1902). During the 1970s the bodies were exhumed and reburied in Ladysmith.
3. Ladysmith, established 1847, was named after the Spanish wife of Sir Harry Smith, Juana, Lady Smith, who he had rescued during the storming of Badajoz in 1812 during the Peninsular War. It was besieged by Boer forces during the Second Anglo-Boer War (1899–1902) from 2 November 1899 to 28 February 1900.
4. The Indian's name was Parbudhan Singh. Singh was an indentured labourer employed by the Dundee Coal Mine. During the siege of Ladysmith he was given the task of signalling whenever he saw a flash from one of the Boer Long Toms. The firing of these Creusot guns was characterised by a puff of white smoke followed by an interval of 20–22 seconds before the arrival of the shell.

    Among those who were in Ladysmith when it was invested by the Boers, there were besides Englishmen, a few stray Indian settlers. Some of these were traders, while the rest were indentured labourers, working on the railways or as servants to English gentlemen, one of whom was Parbusingh (sic). The officer in command at Ladysmith assigned various duties to every resident of the place. The most dangerous and most responsible work was assigned to Parbusingh who was a 'coolie'. On a hill near Ladysmith the Boers had stationed a pom-pom, whose operations destroyed many buildings and even occasioned some loss of life. An interval of a minute or two must pass before a shell which had been fired from the gun reached a distant objective. If the besieged got even such a short notice, they could take cover before the shell dropped in the town and thus save themselves. Parbusingh was to sit perched up in a tree, all the time that the gun was working, with his eyes fixed on the hill and to ring a bell the moment he observed a flash. On hearing the bell, the residents of Ladysmith instantly took cover and saved themselves from the deadly cannon ball whose approach was thus announced.

The officer in charge of Ladysmith, in eulogizing the invaluable services rendered by Parbusingh, stated that he worked so zealously that not once had he failed to ring the bell. It need hardly be said that his own life was constantly in peril. The story of his bravery came to be known in Natal and at last reached the ears of Lord Curzon, then Viceroy of India, who sent a Kashmir robe to the Natal Government for presentation to Parbusingh, asking them to carry out the presentation ceremony with all possible publicity. This duty was assigned to the mayor of Durban who held a public meeting in the Town Hall for the purpose.

The Selected Works of Mahatma Gandhi, Volume 3, Satyagraha in South Africa, Bombay, 1968, pp. 107–8.

5.   Arthur Cowell Stark (1846–99), doctor and ornithologist, volunteered as medical officer during the Second Anglo-Boer War (1899–1902). 'He lived at the Royal Hotel in the centre of town, and as he was fearful of gunfire he left the hotel every morning at daybreak, seeking security in a dugout on a bank of the Klip River; he took with a him a long overcoat, and an angler's basket in which he carried a kitten, and returned each evening at dusk. On Saturday 18.11.1899 at about 6.30 p.m. he was standing in front of the hotel when he was hit by a shell. He was critically wounded and died a few hours later. A bronze plaque on the pavement marks the spot where the shell landed.' De Kock and others (eds), *South African Biography,* Vol. V, 1987, p. 730.

6.   The clocktower on the Ladysmith city hall was not repaired until 1924.

7.   All Saints, an Anglican church.

8.   George Warrington Steevens (1869–1900). 'The most brilliant man in journalism I have ever met,' Winston Churchill, *My Early Life,* London, 1930, p. 219. 'Jauntiest of the war correspondents,' Pakenham, *Boer War,* p. 265. As correspondent for the *Daily Mail,* Steevens was caught up in the siege of Ladysmith during which he founded and edited the satirical siege newspaper *The Ladysmith Lyre.* He died of typhoid on 15 January 1900, sipping a last glass of champagne and sighing: 'This is a sideways ending to it all', *The Encyclopaedia of the British Press 1422–1992,* London, 1992, p. 535. His books include *With Kitchener to Khartum,* London, 1898; *In India,* London, 1899; and the posthumously published *From Cape Town to Ladysmith,* London, 1900.

9. The Boers attacked Platrand (Caesar's Camp and Wagon Hill) on 6 January 1900. They were repulsed after bitter fighting and a charge by the Devonshire Regiment.
10. Convent run by Augustinian nuns and now a hospital.
11. Sir Henry Ernest Bulwer (1836–1914), Lieutenant-Governor of Natal September 1875 – April 1880 when he was succeeded by Sir George Pomeroy Colley. He returned as Governor of Natal and Special Commissioner for Zululand in March 1882. Haggard and Bulwer admired the stars on their trip around Natal in May 1876 with Shepstone, during which Haggard witnessed the Zulu ceremonies he wrote of in his first article written for publication, 'A Zulu War Dance', *Gentleman's Magazine* (July 1877).
12. Colenso, established 1880s, was named after Bishop J.W. Colenso. The battle of Colenso (15 December 1899) was the first of several attempts by General Sir Redvers Buller (1839–1908) to break through the Boer lines and relieve Ladysmith.
13. Lieutenant Frederick Roberts, only son of Field Marshal Lord Roberts. Lord Roberts later succeeded Buller as C-in-C British forces in South Africa.
14. Sir Melmoth Osborn (1834–99), Natal civil servant, was Resident Magistrate at Newcastle before joining Shepstone's staff in the Transvaal in 1877 as Colonial Secretary. From there he moved to the post of British Resident in Zululand in 1879. After the British annexation of Zululand in 1887 he became Resident Commissioner and Chief Magistrate of Zululand with headquarters at Eshowe. 'He remained the most important colonial official in Zululand through the decade,' Jeff Guy, *The Destruction of the Zulu Kingdom: The Civil War in Zululand, 1879–1884*, London, 1979, p. 82.
15. Lieutenant-General Frederic Augustus Thesiger, second Baron Chelmsford (1827–1905), Commander-in-Chief of British forces during the Anglo-Zulu War (1879), who famously didn't 'laager' at Isandlwana, which was seen as a contributory factor to the overwhelming Zulu victory of 22 January 1879. 'The disaster I for one expected. Indeed I remember writing home to friends prophesying that it would occur, and their great astonishment when on the same day that they received the letter the telegraph brought the news of the great destruction. This farsightedness, however, was not due to my own perspicacity, but to the training that I had received under those who knew the Zulus better than any other men in the world.' H.R. Haggard, *The Days*, Vol.1. pp. 117–8.
16. Mimosa, popular name for *Acacia karoo*, one of the commonest African trees. It has sweetly scented yellow blossoms.
17. No such casualties were incurred in any of the battles of Buller's campaign to relieve Ladysmith, and the battle of Colenso was the only battle involving an existing bridge. Total casualties at Colenso were 138 men killed, 43 officers and 719 men wounded, and 21 officers and 199 men missing or captured. At the battle of Spioenkop (25 January 1900) the British lost 350 dead, 1 000 wounded and 350 captured. The Boers lost 75 dead and 100 wounded. There was no quarrel between Buller and Lt-Gen Sir Charles Warren, although Buller subsequently blamed Warren's indecision for the defeat. Buller: 'Old Warren is a duffer and lost me a good chance.' Pakenham, *Boer War*, p. 307.

18. Probably in December 1876 while on his way to the Transvaal with Shepstone.
19. Newcastle, established 1864, was named after the Duke of Newcastle, the Colonial Secretary. The rest of the Commission went on to Durban, staying there from Monday 23 March until Thursday 26 March when they left for Pietermaritzburg where they rejoined Haggard. In Durban they collected evidence from 20 witnesses.

Lilias recalled that the Haggard family spent the night at Newcastle 'in a somewhat primitive inn' where she was disturbed by a 'procession of small, round, dark objects on her bedroom wall. Hitherto unknown in her experience, they aroused her deepest suspicions. After a closer inspection by the light of a flickering candle, she paddled off down the passage to where Rider was sleeping, and found him beautifully ensconced behind his carefully tucked-in mosquito net.

'Daddy,' she remarked in awed tones, 'there are *bugs* in my room, I can see them walking down the wall.'

'Of course there are, my dear,' replied her father placidly, 'dozens of them, but bugs won't give you malaria, and you have a mosquito net which is all that matters – good night.' L.R. Haggard, *The Cloak*, pp. 222–3.
20. 'Drove out on way to gathering at Town Hall to have a look at Hilldrop fr. a distance. Never thought to find myself on t road again. Well remember my feelings as I passed over it in 1881 as I thought f last time.' NRO, MC 32/51: 'Rough Diary', 23 March 1914.
21. Hilldrop was declared a national monument in 1981.
22. See Introduction, p. 12.
23. 'Saw the room where J(ock) was born & my dressing room beyond. Holy ground to me – also old drawing & dining room. Stoep just same. The blackjacks grow where they used, some in my trousers now & the buck still comes to eat the rose fence & vegetables. Trees, especially gums, willows and oaks much grown but a good many struck by lightning. Wonder if I shall ever see the place more?' NRO, MC 32/51: 'Rough Diary', 24 March 1914.

Andrew Haggard (1854–1934), soldier and author. After service in the Sudan he left the army in 1886 and, possibly inspired by his brother's success, embarked on a writing career that produced 28 novels and histories. 'Andrew never wrote anything outstanding, with the result that he was often reduced to penury. It was a terrible shock to the man who had been Governor of Massowah and had stood shoulder to shoulder with the heroes of the Sudan, and from time to time he bitterly resented Rider's success.' Manthorpe, *Children of the Empire*, p. 164.
24. Fort Amiel, Newcastle, established 1876, a strategic base for military operations until 1902. It is now a national monument with the guard house restored. A room is devoted to Haggard mementoes, including his son Jock's birth certificate.
25. Sir George Pomeroy Colley (1835–81), British soldier and Governor-General of Natal 1880–81, died at the battle of Majuba, 27 February 1881.
26. Pietermaritzburg (frequently rendered Maritzburg), provincial capital of Natal, was established 1839 by Voortrekkers from the Cape. It came under British control when Natal was annexed in 1843. Here the Commission interviewed 12 witnesses on 27 March in the Provincial Council buildings.

27. Imperial Hotel, Loop Street, opened 1878. It has since been substantially altered but the inner tiled courtyard remains. This is where Haggard posed for the photograph published on the front page of the *Natal Witness*, 27 March 1914.

28. The *Natal Witness*, South Africa's oldest newspaper, was founded in 1846 by David Dale Buchanan. See Simon Haw, *Bearing Witness: The Natal Witness 1846–1996*, Pietermaritzburg, 1996.

29. See Introduction, p. 25.

30. See Introduction, p. 29 and Note 119.

31. Mazuku. See Introduction p. 7.

32. With the incorporation of Natal into the Union of South Africa in 1910, the Governor of Natal departed and the archives were removed to the Governor-General's office in Pretoria and the building, after alterations, became a teachers' training college.

33. Both incidents are recorded in Haggard's autobiography. In the 1870s Colley 'was staying with us at Government House, and I remember a curious incident concerning him. He was leaving Natal and wished to sell a shotgun which I wished to purchase . . . We had a difference of opinion as to the price of the article. Finally I interviewed him one morning while he was taking his bath, and he suggested that we should settle the matter by tossing. This I did with a half-sovereign, he giving the call, but who won, I forget.' H.R. Haggard, *The Days*, Vol. 1, p. 51.

     Captain W. Cox, 1st battalion, 13th Light Infantry, was private secretary to Bulwer, Lieutenant-Governor of Natal in the 1870s, and thus a colleague of Haggard. He received a blow playing polo which severed his carotid artery. After an operation to tie off the artery 'he seemed to get better, and at last was allowed to eat a snipe which I went out and shot for him. That evening some circumstance or other made me uneasy about him, and of my own motion I passed the night sitting up in the office, going into look for him from time to time. He slept well and when the dawn came I thought that I would retire to bed. By an afterthought I returned to give him another look, and found him still lying asleep, but with blood spurting from his head in a little fountain. I pressed my thumb on the artery and held it there until assistance came. Another operation was performed, and ultimately, he fully recovered though one of his eyes was affected.' H.R. Haggard, *The Days*, Vol. 1, p. 72.

34. East Coast Fever or tick fever swept away a large proportion of the cattle in Natal during the 1900s. Initially kept under control by the veterinary department, the Bhambatha Rebellion of 1906 contributed to its spread. 'Refugees trekked into the Vryheid town lands from the more distant and infected portions of the district, moving through the cleared areas and spreading infection as they travelled, while the military exigencies of the situation necessitated the use of ox transport in and around areas known to have been previously affected with the disease.

     'A further catastrophe occurred when looted cattle, captured in Zululand, were sold by public auction against the express warning of the veterinary authority. This introduced the disease into the coastal areas. By 1908 it had reached the western boundary of the colony and by 1910 the southern boundary. Cases were known where cattle farmers were left without a single beast . . . it was long after Natal's entry into the Union before the disease was brought substantially under control.' E.H. Brookes and C. de B. Webb, *A History of Natal*, Pietermaritzburg, 1965, p. 215.

35.   *Inkosikazi*, in Zulu 'chief or first wife'. *Inkoos! Inkoos y umcool! Inkoos y pagate* should be rendered as *Nkosi! Nkos' enkulu! Nkos' ephakade!* Meaning 'Chief! Great chief! Chief from olden times!' See also Chapter Seven, Note 92. Lady Haggard and Lilias stayed at Eshowe while Haggard visited Rhodesia. For Eshowe see Chapter Seven, Note 16.

36.   Kerrie or knobkerrie: a stick cut from a single piece of wood with a heavy knob on the end. In Zulu *iwisa*. Haggard was given the knobkerrie when he and his family left their farm Hilldrop in 1881. 'It was sad to part with the place, and also to bid goodbye to my Zulu servant Mazooku. The poor fellow was moved at this parting, and gave me what probably he valued more than anything he possessed, the kerry (sic) that he had carried ever since he was a man – that same heavy, redwood instrument with which more than once I have seen him battering the head of some foe. It hangs in the hall of this house (Ditchingham House), but where I wonder, is Mazoo-ku, who saved my life when I was lost upon the veld.' H.R. Haggard, *The Days*, Vol.1, p. 201.

37.   Michael Hallowes Addison, appointed Chief Native Commissioner, Natal, February 1913. He was a political adviser with Natal Police Force during Bhambatha Rebellion, 1906. When arranging the Zululand trip, Haggard had requested the tour be undertaken in a mule-drawn wagonnette, a common form of transport when he lived in South Africa 1875–81. Addison was unable to meet the request. 'I have tried every Government department as well as local contractors for such a conveyance. They either have no mules or won't risk them in certain parts of Zululand.' It was decided to hire a car instead. 'It is extraordinary how motor has super-seded other traffic in Zululand during the last year or so.' Chief Native Commissioner (2nd series), Minute Paper, File No: CNC 330/1914, Item 10: R.H. Addison to J.Y. Gibson, 13 April 1914.

38.   'Sompseu's child' correctly Somsewu – Father of Whiteness, the Zulu name of Sir Theophilus Shepstone.

39.   John Wesley Shepstone (1827–1916), Natal public servant and judge, an adviser to Sir Garnet Wolseley on post-war settlement of Zululand while Acting Secretary for Native Affairs. Zulu name Misjan. The son referred to was Percy (1864–1944) and the daughter, Averil (n.d.).

40.   The name Umslopogaas is a corruption of Mhlophekazi, a servant of Theophilus Shepstone, whom Haggard first met in 1875. His fictionalised persona first appeared in *Allan Quatermain* (London, 1887) where he dies a heroic death. He also appears in *Nada the Lily* (1892) and *She and Allan* (1921). Mhlophekazi 'is stated to have come to Natal in 1859 as an emissary from the Swazi king Mswazi, and thereafter entered the service of Sir Theophilus Shepstone in whose employ he remained until the death of the latter in 1893. One of his chief duties was to lead his master's saddled horse Nqakamatshe down to the office daily. After the death of Sir Theo-philus, Mhlopekazi became a sort of pensioner of the Shepstone family until in turn he died in 1897. At the time he was occupying a room in the old Native Barracks at Ortman's Drift. Since converted into a hostel by the

municipality. The room is No.1.' H.C. Lugg, *Historic Natal and Zululand*, Pietermaritzburg, 1949, p. 44.

The story regarding Umslopogaas's hunting knife is to be found in H.R. Haggard, *The Days*. 'One day long after I had left Africa, he (Umslopogaas/Mhlophekazi) had a long talk with Osborn, whom the natives called Mali-mat. "Is it true, Mali-mat," asked Umslopogaas, "that Indanda (i.e. myself) has been using my name largely in books that he has written?" "Yes, it is true, Umslopogaas." "So! Now what does Indanda do with the books when he has written them?" "He sells them, Umslopogaas." "Then, Mali-mat, say to the Inkoos Indanda when you meet him across the Black Water that, as he makes money about writing about me, it is right and just that he should send me half the money!" I took the hint and sent him, not money, but a very fine hunting-knife with his name engraved upon it.' H.R. Haggard, *The Days*, Vol. 1, p. 74.

The gentleman whose name Haggard forgets is William Lucas (1860–1939). An architect by profession, he restored the Ladysmith town hall after the siege during the Second Anglo-Boer War (1899–1902). He also designed the General Post Office and Diamond Jubilee Pavilion in Pietermaritzburg. He was elected President of the Natal Institute of Architects in 1906. *The Natal Who's Who* of 1906 lists his hobbies as 'travel, study of geography, biography and theology; and delivery of occasional sermons and addresses'. In one of these, dated 1 January 1898, Lucas recalls visiting Mhlophekazi the day before his death. He gave a talk on Mhlophekazi in Pretoria on Sunday, 29 March 1914 (reported in *Pretoria News*, 1 April 1914). The Commission arrived at Pretoria by train the same day at 9 p.m. In his unpublished Rough Diary Haggard refers to their meeting but cannot recall his name.

The photograph of Mhlophekazi on his death-bed appears in H.R. Haggard, *The Days*, Vol.1. Mhlophekazi died on 24 October 1897, and received obituaries in the *Natal Witness*, *Times of Natal* and the *Natal Mercury*.

41. Haggard's Zulu name was *Lundanda u Ndandokalweni* meaning 'the tall one who travels on the heights'. *Lundanda* means 'tall person', and the verb *ndanda* (to glide along, move lazily) has been chosen as a play on words. *Okhalweni* means 'on the ridge'. With modern spelling and word division, the sentence behind the name would be *undanda okhalweni* ('the tall one who walks on the ridge'). The phrase *Ondande ngokhal' olude* ('He who glided along the long ridge') occurs in the praises of King Shaka.

42. Voortrekker Museum. The original Church of the Vow built by the Voortrekkers to commemorate their victory over the Zulu at the Battle of Blood River on 16 December 1838. It was a place of worship until 1861. After being used for commercial purposes it opened in 1912 as the Voortrekker Museum.

43. Victoria Club, founded in 1859. The club adopted the Union Jack as its flag on 25 March 1960. As a club flag and not a national one, it is allowed to be flown from morning to evening. The club's premises from 1897 to 1997 were in Longmarket Street, one of the city's main thoroughfares. In 1997 the club amalgamated with the Pietermaritzburg Country Club, now the Victoria Country Club, and moved out of the centre of town.

44. Henry Christian Koch (1858–1930), appointed legal adviser to the

Imperial Government in Zululand, 18 April 1889. He acted several times as magistrate of Eshowe. He was Legal Adviser and Registrar-General to the Government of Zululand in 1889. He was appointed Crown Prosecutor and Legal Adviser, Zululand, in December 1897. He was appointed Master of the Supreme Court in August 1900. 'Judge Koch . . . wanted to sell me the house at Eshowe in the grounds of which is the waterfall that I have used in the last scene of *Finished* as the death place of Zikali.' Cheyne Collection, Norfolk: 'War Diary of Sir Rider Haggard', quote from 5 March 1916.

Henrique Charles Shepstone (1840–1917), Natal civil servant, was Theophilus Shepstone's eldest son. He accompanied his father to the Transvaal in 1877. In 1906 he was one of the judges appointed to try Dinuzulu charged with treason following the Bhambatha Rebellion. His first name was chosen by Juana, Lady Smith the Spanish wife of Sir Harry Smith (1787–1860).

45. Shaka (*c.*1787–1828), King of the Zulus, eldest son of Senzangakhona by Nandi (*c.*1764–1827). The sons of King Mpande (*c.*1798–1872), Cetshwayo (*c.*1826–84) and Mbuyazi (*c.*1826–56) fought over the succession to the Zulu throne at the battle of Ndondakusaka in 1856 when Cetshwayo defeated and killed Mbuyazi.

Socwatsha: 'son of Papu of Ngcobo tribe', NRO, MC 32/51: 'Rough Diary', n.d.

46. H.R. Haggard, *Nada the Lily*. See Chapter 18, 'The Curse of Baleka'.

47. Henry Francis Fynn (1803–61), one of the first Europeans to settle in Natal. In 1824 he helped establish a trading station at Port Natal (later Durban). See *The Diary of Henry Francis Fynn*, Pietermaritzburg, 1951, p. 132, for the version of Nandi's death referred to by Haggard.

48. 'The objects of the [African] club are to promote social intercourse during the luncheon hour, which are paid for by the members individually at 2s. per head. They are held at irregular intervals, but generally once a month and are usually addressed by some distinguished visitor to town.' *The Natal Directory 1915*, Pietermaritzburg, 1914, p. 809.

Haggard was the invited guest and speaker at the African Club's monthly luncheon. A record attendance was expected, especially as 'the committee desires it be known that on this occasion ladies may be brought as guests of members', *Natal Witness*, 24 March 1914. When booking for the lunch closed 150 seats had been reserved. 'The luncheon is the largest ever held in Maritzburg.' *Natal Witness*, 27 March 1914. Haggard concluded his speech: 'What remains? To wish well to South Africa? Well, I do that with all my heart, but perhaps as an old Natalian, I may be allowed to wish the best of all things to this dear and lovely land of yours – to this fair Natal. She has beauty, great beauty, if ever country had it; she has fertility to a marvellous degree; she has history, much history for so short a career. May she also have peace, prosperity and progress from generation to generation and from age to age. Advance, Natal! God bless Natal, white and black together, and bless her gates of mountain and sea!'

'Sir Rider resumed his seat amidst enthusiastic cheering,' *Natal Witness*, 28 March 1914. For full speech see Appendix Two.

On the day of the luncheon the *Natal Witness* led with front-page pictures of Haggard together with a long article on his career. An editorial sang his praises: 'The benefactors of the human race are many and their benefactions various. High up on the list must stand the name of who for 30 years has been giving to the English-speaking world volume on volume of healthy, wholesome and thoroughly entertaining literature, in no page of which is there anything of a degrading or unmanly tendency. Today when our libraries and bookstalls are flooded with productions of a more or less questionable nature, this is a record of which a man might well be proud. That record is held, and held worthily, by Sir Rider Haggard . . .

'The heart of Africa was . . . enshrined for the reading public only between the covers of costly books of travel; Haggard bared it in the pages of his stories and placed it within the reach of all . . .

'Who shall say how many strong and sturdy pioneers have been attracted from the pleasant Homeland to help in winning the African wilds to civilisation as the result of romantic interest aroused in them when as boys they read and revelled in these romances? It has been said that Rider Haggard did more to advertise South Africa to the world when it was less known than it is now than any man of his time.' *Natal Witness*, 27 March 1914.

49. Charles John Smythe (1852–1918), Administrator of Natal in 1914 and the first to hold the post after union in 1910. He was Colonial Secretary of Natal (1899–1903) and Prime Minister and Colonial Secretary from May 1905 to November 1906.

50. Sir Joseph Baynes (1842–1925), Natal farmer, politician, dairy industry pioneer and businessman.

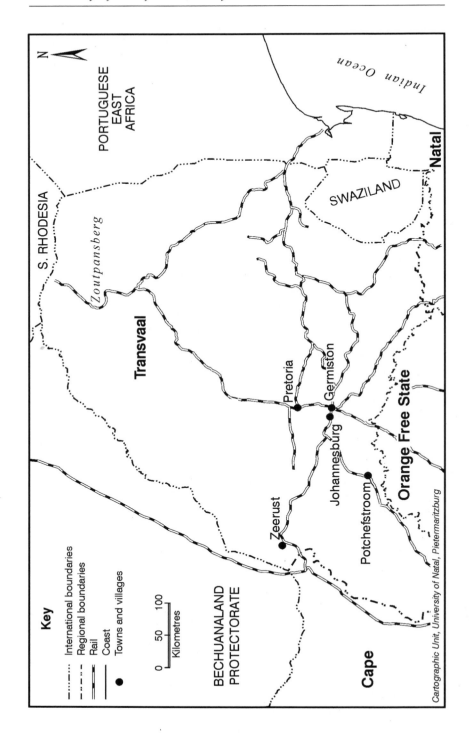

Cartographic Unit, University of Natal, Pietermaritzburg

Chapter Five

I felt like one returned from the dead

৶৶৶৶৶৶

The Commission travelled next to the Transvaal, the 'land across the Vaal river', which was annexed by the British in 1877 and in which Haggard played an impromptu role, described in this chapter. During the 1820s much of the territory – home to the Sotho and Tswana-speaking peoples – was disrupted by the Mfecane, *a Zulu term meaning 'the crushing'. Later, Mzilikazi, who had fled the Zulu kingdom to set up a Ndebele state north of the Vaal, came into conflict with the Voortrekkers and retreated across the Limpopo in 1837. The British recognised the independence of whites in the area at the Sand River Convention of 1852 and, in 1858, four republics founded by the Voortrekkers around Potchefstroom, Utrecht, Lydenburg and the Soutpansberg were united as the South African Republic, with Pretoria as its capital. Following the British annexation of 1877 and after the British defeat of the Pedi, Afrikaner unrest provoked the First Anglo-Boer War of 1880–81, which culminated in a British defeat at Majuba. The Transvaal regained its independence as the South African Republic but the discovery of gold on the Witwatersrand in 1886 excited British interest and led, in part, to the Second Anglo-Boer War (1899–1902), after which the republic became a Crown colony. In 1910 it joined the Union and Pretoria became its administrative capital.*

Sunday, 29 March

At length we emerged on the Transvaal high veld which I had not seen since 1879 when I rode across it on the way to Natal. It is suffering from the bad drought which has smitten most of South Africa for the last two or three years. Many new villages have sprung up on the Pretoria road. After dark at Germiston[1] we passed a blaze of lights, then a column of lights on a mine head, then some single lights, then a long range of distant, twinkling lights – Johannesburg of which it may well be said 'thou art a marvel and a hell'. Then darkness and once more the silence of the veld whence it arose and into which perchance it will sink again in a day to be.

We reached the fine railway station at Pretoria about 10 at night, a different arrival indeed to that of my first here by ox wagon in 1877.[2] The Grand Hotel where we stayed is in Church Square where we outspanned on that occasion. Trams (with not too many passengers) clank and clang beneath the windows, electric lights are flaring and on every side appear huge and costly buildings: government offices, law courts and so forth. This hotel, rightly named 'Grand' is, I think, on the site of the old European, which was kept by poor Carter, the brother of the present Archbishop of Cape Town, who afterwards was killed by lightning.[3]

The whole aspect of the place has utterly changed. Who would know it for the same that I described in *The Witch's Head* whereon the Boers used to assemble in their wagons at *nachtmaal*.[4] The old Dutch church, the 'house with horns' as the kaffirs used to call it, has been pulled down – in these colonial towns they always seem to pull down such historical monuments as they possess.[5] Oh! I hate this grandeur – give me the Pretoria of the 1870s. Alas, as well might I ask for my lost youth! The Union of South Africa has taken away its pride of place for Maritzburg, reducing it from the capital of a province to a country town,[6] but it has made Pretoria the official capital of this great land and here the gold of the Rand has been lavished in buildings of unnecessary splendour.

Opposite to the hotel where stand the government offices, which are being supplanted by others of unparalleled magnificence at a cost, it is said, of nearly £1 500 000, was the low, thatched building in which I had my office. All the time that I was sitting there on the royal commission I kept thinking of it. From the verandah of that building was read the proclamation annexing the Transvaal to the empire. The Hon. J. Rissik, the present Administrator, has reminded me of an incident connected with this historical event that I had forgotten.[7] It seems, and indeed I now remember, that when Sir Melmoth Osborn was reading the document, he grew so nervous in face of the crowd that he found it difficult to proceed. Thereon I took the paper from his hand and completed its public utterance. 'At that moment,' said Rissik, who of course was an ardent Dutchman, or rather Hollander, 'I would gladly have shot you.' It would seem that I did not lack for assurance in those days.

Monday, 30 March

As soon as we had breakfasted, sundry old inhabitants of Pretoria arrived to welcome me most kindly. Also there came a gentleman connected with the *Transvaal Leader*, Mr. David Pollock, a cousin of my old friend Walter Pollock, who kindly took me to The Palatial, the house

Bryan Hall

Jess's Cottage, The Palatial. Taken during Haggard's visit to Pretoria in March 1914. The left side of the house with the bay window is an addition to the original building built by Haggard and his friend Arthur Cochrane in 1878. From Lilias Rider Haggard's photograph album.

built by Cochrane and myself, which is now known as Jess's Cottage, which I should never have found alone.[8] Indeed I have scarcely been able to identify one of the houses in Pretoria with which I was familiar. Wandering there I felt like one returned from the dead. Near to the railway station we reached a gateway still fronted by a running sluit[9] and I saw nailed to a willow a notice 'rooms to let'. We went down a path bordered on one side by a line of great blue gums, the largest I saw in Pretoria (those corresponding on the other side have, most of them, been cut down). These gums, 100 feet or more in height, I should say, Cochrane and I planted with our own hands. Then appeared the house, much altered, for the original building, together with the stable behind it, is now embedded and surrounded by alien masonry, the thatch has been replaced by tin and the stoep has been made or added.[10] In what used to be our sitting room was a lady lodger packing apples, the place one confusion. Looking at it I could not but recall it as it used to be, with its pretty English furniture and the engravings on the walls. Beyond was the sleeping room, unoccupied I am glad to say. There also were the kitchen, the bathroom and the stable where stood my two fine horses, Black Billy and Moresco. By the way an old gentleman who I think said he was writing seated in what was my chair and at my desk, wrote the other day informing me that Black Billy had gone to the chief Khama as a stud horse, so I hope that he ended his days in honour and felicity.[11] The garden is a terrible sight, a mere tangle, the whole two acres of it. Of the vines we planted only one or two survive climbing up trees. The roses are all gone. *Hesternae Rosae!*[12] Part of our old bridge over the sluit lies in front of the new stables, about it strange legends have arisen and portions appear to have been carried away by relic hunters. Standing among those noxious growths I seemed to forget all the intervening years and grow young again. I saw the walls rising. I saw the sapling gums, the infant vines and the new planted roses and gardenias. The place is a lodging house, not of the highest class, kept by an honest but struggling couple who were delighted to show me everything. I went away with a sad heart. Oh! where are they who used to pass in and out through that humble gate?

At the public luncheon I was called upon to speak later in the day, at which I met with a reception that was more enthusiastic even than usual, I made a plea for the preservation of this place, which is for sale under a bond, on account of the historical interest it has acquired. I am glad to say that the matter has been taken up with some enthusiasm by the press and public but whether anything will come of it in these bad times is more than I can say. At this luncheon the Judge-President, De Villiers, who like nearly all the high officials is, of course, of Dutch descent, proposed our healths and devoted some part of his speech to me. He talked with admiration of my work, but regretted that I had not always dealt too tenderly with 'the older section of the population'. In answering I remarked that we generally modified the hard and sharp views of youth as we grew older, a statement that was cheered. Still it has not satisfied some people to judge from a long letter I read in a local paper. These appear to overlook that in some books, such as *Swallow* and *Marie,* I have dealt with them very tenderly indeed. For the rest what is there that really should be retracted? *Cetywayo and His White Neighbours* is a true history, the Boers in *Jess* are true pictures of certain of their people at the period, the villain, who was drawn from life, is a true portrait of a certain sort of cross-bred man and as for Jess herself, they all love her, English and Dutch alike. Of this I had a proof when I addressed the agricultural congress on the following day. It was composed of delegates, many of whom were Dutch, indeed the president's speech of welcome to me was translated sentence by sentence. Yet when he spoke of *Jess,* for here she cannot even be kept out of agricultural topics, they *all* cheered alike. Moreover how about the terrible things that have been written of the English by Dutch people and their sympathisers?[13]

Close to The Palatial I was shewn Rider Haggard Street. It is somewhat in embryo at present but may become a fine thoroughfare if Pretoria continues to increase.[14] Also I saw in the museum the original deed of sale – of the ground on which the cottage stands – signed by Cochrane and myself. Another place I visited was the old cemetery,

Stephen Coan

The Ford family plot at the Old Cemetery in
Pretoria. The central memorial is to Johanna
Catherine Ford. The black gravestone behind it is
that of Haggard's child, Ethel Rider, by Mrs Ford.

now closed except to relatives of the deceased. Here I saw Oom Paul's
(Kruger) tomb which is massive but not ornamental, and others of those
whom I had known, some of them already neglected and in decay like
those who lie beneath.[15] It was an even sadder experience than that of
Jess's Cottage.

Also I was shewn the archives in the vaults of the fine new law
courts, many of them for the years 1878–79 in my writing or bearing
my signature. The son of my old friend Juta, who was high sheriff in
my time, is now the registrar but his office, and that of the master, both
of which I held, are separated.[16]

Mr. Justice Curlewis kindly motored me through the suburbs of Pretoria, which stretch for miles in all directions.[17] They are very pretty,
especially the country club and its neighbourhood, but I think too extensive. The new government buildings by Baker, standing on a koppie, are undoubtedly very fine, but the townspeople say that they are
too far off for convenience.[18] It is strange what a mania all young communities have for costly edifices.

Tuesday, 31 March

Some of us were motored to the further side of the Magaliesberg range[19] to see farms. Here we were shewn a wonderful example of what can be done with oranges *without* irrigation in this soil and climate. Mr. Hollard, the owner, will doubtless soon reap a rich reward of his enterprise. The trees look splendid, even after this long drought. Also we inspected the farm of Mr. Boswell, who has had a hard fight, his soil not being so favourable. He is a very nice fellow and hard-working. I hope he will succeed. A while ago he was bitten by a night adder on his bare foot.[20] His wife just saved his life by rubbing in permanganate of potash and giving him hot milk to drink till he was sick. I also visited, once again, the famous Wonderboom[21] whither we used to ride in the old days. It is one of the few things in Pretoria that does not seem to have changed. But the road there is better now.

That afternoon I attended the Administrator's [Rissik] garden party and reception given in our honour in the pretty park – new since my time. It was one of the most strenuous hour's of my life, since I had to talk to dozens of people who remembered me, or said they did, and to rack my brains to remember them. Among others I met a daughter of President Burgers and a grandson of Piet Joubert, also named Piet, to whom I spoke of their forebears.[22] I ended up by formally inspecting the boy scouts who were on duty. The scoutmaster told me that English and Dutch boys serve together and are the best of friends, which I rejoiced to hear. We dined that night with Mr. Justice Curlewis where I met the Administrator, and the Judge-President [De Villiers], after which I went to bed very tired.

Wednesday, 1 April

I attended the agricultural conference and found that I was expected to make a speech. This I did on South African agriculture and its possibilities, apparently much to the satisfaction of my audience who cheered vociferously and all rose up when I went away to see the zoo. A really wonderful place and admirably kept.

In the afternoon we left Pretoria, which is so changed that I do not think I want to see it again though my reception there was so kind. That night the whole commission partook of a farewell feast on the special train, after which we went to the Carlton Hotel.[23] Our rooms fronted on the street and the noise was fearful, especially that of the trams, so much so that I could scarcely sleep. Of Johannesburg itself I have little to say as I was hard at work during the two days of my stay and had no time to inspect mines and buildings. Nor indeed do these interest me who am essentially a *veld-ganger*.[24] It is a huge tumultuous city rather more evil and menacing than most and fearfully expensive to live, that is all.

At present the famous mines are giving out but others are believed to exist in the neighbourhood, if the investing public after their bitter experiences can be persuaded to put up the money to work them. Many of the 'magnates' are said to be going away which, like that of rats leaving a ship, I suppose is a bad sign. The labour population is very turbulent, which is scarcely to be wondered at as many only live for six or seven years underground. Such uncertainty would make anybody restless and dissatisfied. The most notable place I visited was the famous Rand Club[25] where I lunched. It was crowded with business men though times are bad.

Thursday, 2 April

I sat on a committee of the Royal Commission all day and in the evening attended a great dinner of 250 people, which was given us by the Chamber of Commerce. I could not escape speaking so held forth again on the great future of the land of South Africa and its supreme need of population. My remarks were listened to with much attention, indeed I think that even in Johannesburg people are waking up on this matter of the need of developing the agricultural resources of the country, as opposed to its temporary resources, the mines.

Friday, 3 April

After taking evidence on agricultural matters with Garnett all the morning I went to lunch with Julius Jeppe whom I used to know in our youth, at his house outside Johannesburg.[26] He reminded me of sundry incidents in the old days: how he served under me in the Pretoria Horse and used to bring my bathwater when we were out at Ferguson's watching the Boer camp.[27] How one day to the intense (and natural) indignation of old Von Levitzon, the postmaster, in his absence I broke into the post office through the window and abstracted my English letters which had arrived by the mail etc. etc. It was very pleasant to meet him again.

I sat again in the afternoon and on rising went to give evidence before a local commission appointed to consider what can be done with the poor whites, of whom there are so many in South Africa and especially in Johannesburg. I advocated settling them on the land according to the scheme I set out in my reports to the home government in 1905, where at any rate the children might grow up into useful citizens under charitable guidance.[28] I agreed that it might be most advisable to exclude all natives from such a settlement. So far as I could judge my views seemed to be held very worthy of consideration by the commission, who listened to them with much respect and rose in a body when I withdrew. This poor white question is one of the great problems of modern South Africa and is complicated by the presence of a vast native population which causes the white man to think it *infra dig* to do what he calls 'niggers' work'. I hope that my evidence may be useful, at any rate indirectly.

On my return to the Carlton Hotel about 5.15 I found the reception given in our honour still in progress. Here I added to the experiences of my life one of attempted blackmail. A hard-faced young man hanging about the door pounced upon me and informed me that he was the son of George Blomefield, alias George Mayes, the illegitimate child of old Col. Blomefield of Necton Hall, Norfolk. My father after Col. B's death persuaded old Miss Mason, his sister who inherited Necton, to make a settlement on him and have him educated; indeed to my father George B. owes everything. Subsequently when Cochrane and I started farming in Natal my father being anxious that G. Blomefield (as he was now called) should make a career in some country where his birth history was not known, arranged that he should enter into partnership with us. He did not prove a very good worker and on our return to England after the first Boer war the partnership wound up by mutual consent at Ditchingham. I think in 1882.[29]

My recollection is that in face of the losses we had all three sustained he had the best of the bargain. He then returned to Rooi Point, Newcastle, and I think rented our shares of that farm. Subsequently I made a present of my share in this property to my brother Jack,[30] who held it for a year or two and then thrust it back on my hands as he found it more trouble and expense than it was worth, I promising to pay him – Jack – 25 percent (I think) of anything that came from the property, which I did on its ultimate sale in or about 1895. What George Blomefield did or did not do during Jack's tenure of my share I cannot remember for certain, if indeed I ever heard all the details, but when I re-entered as a part proprietor I believe he had disposed of his interests to the late Gay Roberts (it appears that he is now an assayer at a mine in Barberton). About two years ago I received an insolent letter from Mrs. Blomefield beginning 'Dear Rider' (I had never seen her but once in my life), with a blackmailing note in it. (There was another letter which my wife opened during my absence in Egypt but which was lost in forwarding it to me in Italy. It was of like tenor). At Johannesburg, where this woman (of whom I have heard no good), is living apparently away from her husband, I received another insolent letter.

Under circumstances which I entered fully at the time in my rough notebook this young Blomefield, who apparently is an underground miner, proceeded with veiled menaces to demand that I should pay off a mortgage of £500 on some property this mother held at Pretoria or 'give them a farm'. I told him that if he or anybody belonging to him had any grievance the courts were open, and so we parted. The suggestion was of course that I of all people had perpetrated some fraud on G. Blomefield which I would pay to have hushed up. It was an attempt

at blackmail of a peculiarly disgraceful order when all my father's goodness to George Blomefield (from whom by the way I have heard nothing) is borne in mind, one that throws a lurid light on certain aspects of
human nature. I should not wonder however if it involves me in further trouble. I imagine that the young man came with the object of
making a scene at the public reception but that his courage failed him.

At this reception I met the children of old Pretoria friends – now
married with children of their own. After dinner I saw Louie and Lilias
off to Durban [en route to Eshowe] and started myself in the special
train with some of the others for Rhodesia.

Notes

1. Germiston, city close to Johannesburg, named after a farm near Glasgow,
    Scotland, the birthplace of the gold-mining pioneer John Jack. The largest
    railway junction in South Africa and site of the largest gold refinery in the
    world.
2. Pretoria, founded in 1855 by Marthinus Wessel Pretorius, the first pres-
    ident of the Transvaal Republic, and son of the Voortrekker leader, Andries
    Pretorius, after whom it is named. The capital of the Transvaal, in 1910 it
    became the administrative capital of the Union. Here the Commission ques-
    tioned 13 witnesses from Monday, 30 March to Wednesday, 1 April.
3. The Archbishop of Cape Town, William Marlborough Carter (1850–1941),
    was travelling with Haggard on the *Gaika*. He was Bishop of Zululand 1891–
    1901, Bishop of Pretoria 1902–08, Archbishop of Cape Town 1908–30. He
    married Hester Marion Rose in 1904. Although impressed at the reconcili-
    ation of the two white factions under the South Africa Act that led to Union,
    Carter was perturbed by the inadequate protection of non-white political
    rights. In 1929, at his last provincial synod, he was critical of racial matters
    being turned into political issues. He and his wife boarded the *Gaika* at
    Lourenço Marques, having travelled overland from Cape Town, on their way
    to visit the Diocese of Madagascar. Carter's verdict on Haggard: 'He is one of
    those very keen men who want to know about everything.' Quoted in O.J.
    Hogarth and R.L. White, *The Life of Archbishop Carter: Eton's Gift to South
    Africa*, England, 1952, p. 48. The Carter referred to as being killed by light-
    ning is not known. Bishop Carter had two brothers, one who predeceased
    him by a month and another who survived him.

    Haggard met Carter again during his visit to South Africa in 1916 and
    stayed at his residence, Bishopscourt. His diary entry dated 7 March records:
    'After trying to write some letters I returned to the Mt Nelson hotel where
    the Archbishop called for me & drove me out to this charming house
    where I found Mrs Carter, apparently very glad to see me, as I was glad to
    see her . . . After tea we walked up to the Botanical Gardens which are
    close by.'

    The entry dated 8 March records: 'While I was writing this diary last night about 11.30, the Archbishop appeared in his dressing gown to tell me that today being Ash Wednesday there was a celebration in his private chapel on the following morning. This I attended, one of a congregation of 3, His Grace, Mrs Carter and myself with the officiating chaplain. It is a nice little Chapel, small & plain but effective. After breakfast the A.B. & I had a long talk about various points of theology & the mystery of things in general. I said goodbye to him with much regret.' Cheyne Collection, Norfolk: 'War Diary of Sir Rider Haggard', pp. 307–8.

4.   *The Witch's Head* (London, 1884), Vol. 2, Chapter VIII, describes the arrival of Ernest Kershaw (Haggard's alter ego) and Mr Alston, a fictionalised version of Melmoth Osborn at Pretoria in 1877. They proceed to the market square (Church Square), which they find 'crowded with Boer wagons, whose owners had trekked in to celebrate their nachtmaal (communion), of which it is their habit, in company of with their wives and children, to participate four times a year'.

5.   'If it be any consolation to this great writer we may tell him that if the Dutch church – the disappearance of which from the Square he deplores – had not been pulled down, it would probably have fallen down and killed someone. Nor was it an act of vandalism by newcomers. Its removal had been decided by the Republican Government before the war.' From leading article, *Pretoria News,* 31 March 1914, in response to a speech given by Haggard.

6.   Haggard is not entirely correct. While it lost its status as the capital of a Crown colony, Pietermaritzburg remained the provincial capital of Natal.

7.   Johann Friedrich Bernhard Rissik (1857–1925), first Administrator of the Transvaal after Union. Born in the Netherlands he came with his parents to South Africa in May 1876 and they settled in Pretoria. He was appointed Surveyor-General of the Transvaal Republic in 1895 and Minister of Lands and Native Affairs in Louis Botha's cabinet 1907–10.

8.   'About a quarter of a mile from the outskirts of the camp stood a little house known, probably on account of its diminutive size, as "The Palatial" . . . (a) little tin-roofed cottage. It consisted of two rooms – a bedroom and a good-sized sitting room, in which stood a table and a few chairs, with a stable and a kitchen at the back.' H.R. Haggard, *Jess,* 1900 edition, p. 170. See Appendix Three.

9.   *Sluit,* Afrikaans word for a furrow for irrigation purposes or other water supply.

10. Blue gums, common name given to several members of the eucalyptus family introduced to South Africa from Australia. *Stoep,* Afrikaans for verandah in front of, or all around, a house.

11. 'Rider, at this time, had two very good horses, both stallions; one, Black Billy, had carried him valiantly through all the days of the Boer trouble. The second, Moresco, was a long, low chestnut, with high hip bones and a rather plain head. Originally he had been a racehorse down at the Cape, but an attack of horse sickness robbed him of his speed, and he was sold into the Transvaal as "salted", that is immune from horse sickness, and Rider bought him. He always said that those who love them have one horse and one dog in their lives who stand out far above all the others – Moresco's was Rider's horse.' L.R. Haggard, *The Cloak,* p. 83. While Haggard was in

England in 1880, Moresco, left in Cochrane's care at Hilldrop, was stolen. Some months later he reappeared 'a wretched-looking animal', recalled Haggard, who by then was back at Hilldrop. 'He was nothing but a skeleton, the hair was rubbed off him, and his back was covered with huge festering sores.' They did what they could for him but later, despite being "salted", Moresco contracted horse-sickness during an epidemic in the Newcastle area. 'We knew nothing of it till he was dying . . . In the middle of the night we were awakened by the sound of somebody banging on the back door of the house. It was Moresco. He had come down from the hillside, contrived to jump over the wall, dying though he was, and now with his head he was knocking on the door to call us to his assistance. We could do nothing for him.' Quoted from an unpublished article by Haggard dated 16 May 1893. Published as a privately printed pamphlet by Alfred Tella, *My Stallion Moresco*, McLean, Virginia, USA, 1998.

Ngama III (*c.*1837–1923), paramount chief of the Ngwato, allied himself with the British South Africa Company during the Ndebele War of 1893 and played a major role in the creation of the Bechuanaland Protectorate. He was the grandfather of Seretse Khama, first president of Botswana.

12. *Hesternae Rosae*, Latin for 'yesterday's roses'.
13. Jacob Abraham Jeremy (Jaap) De Villiers (1868–1932), Chief Justice, member of Louis Botha's cabinet 1907–10 as Attorney-General (Minister of Justice) and Minister of Mines. In 1910 he was appointed Judge-President of the Transvaal, and later Chief Justice of South Africa.

A long letter published in the *Pretoria News* on 1 April 1914, and signed by a 'Dutch Afrikander', responded to Haggard's speech and its reporting in the *Pretoria News* of 31 March 1914. The letter expressed outrage at 'the heinous literary diatribes against that "older generation" as a whole, of which Sir Rider had been successfully delivered since first he put his facile pen to paper in 1881!' The letter was highly critical of Haggard's depiction of the Boers in both factual works such as *Cetywayo and His White Neighbours* (London, 1882) ('one of the most scurrilous things ever written against your and my countrymen') and fiction such as *Jess* ('the embodiment of all the irreconcilable race hatred which its author felt towards what for some unscrutable reason he looked upon as the "degrading peace" of 1881'.)

The writer also rebutted Haggard's public statement that time softened one's views given in his speech at Pretoria, which was reported in the *Pretoria News*. On reading a serialisation of *Marie* (London, 1912) (in the Johannesburg *Star* in 1913) 'there was the same old "bastard" (cross-bred Englishman-Afrikander) stalking through these newly written pages of the popular English author, the same irreconcilable racialism, the same old . . . lies. That was little more than twelve months ago!'

This letter had a sequel in 1967. In March of that year it was announced that The Palatial would be demolished to make way for a block of flats. A number of people expressed the wish that it be preserved. H.M. Rex who was sympathetic to this was asked to prepare the April edition of *Pretoriana* as a 'special Haggard-house edition'. He recorded what happened in a pamphlet *Die Strydvraag oor Die Bewaring en Restourasie van Die*

Woonhuis van Henry Rider Haggard in Pretoria (Pretoria, 1967). (The Dispute over the Conservation and Restoration of the Dwelling-house of Henry Rider Haggard in Pretoria). Rex wrote that through the course of his research 'he became thoroughly acquainted with one of the most vitriolic Boer-haters that I ever came across in writing . . . I gradually became convinced that I would violate my conscience should I, as an Afrikaner, continue to assist in commemorating Rider Haggard, in Pretoria, the centre of Afrikanerdom. My sense of honour, as an Afrikaner, as a descendant of the Boers that Haggard slandered and as heir of their ideals, left me no other choice than to completely distance myself from any effort, in whatever form, of honouring Rider Haggard.'

Rex also reprinted the full text of the letter to the *Pretoria News* of 1 April 1914, revealing 'Dutch Afrikander' to be a pseudonym for the Afrikaner historian Gustav Preller (1875–1943). Following the letter Rex added this concluding paragraph. 'Today, after more than eighty years since his libellous writings saw the light of day, the Afrikaner, like any civilised person, has appreciation of Rider Haggard's literary abilities and his valuable descriptions of people, places and events in so far as they agree with the truth, but otherwise find his libellous and untrue sections of some of his writings so offensive and repugnant that he cannot assist in immortalising Rider Haggard's memory.'

Swallow (London, 1899) set against the backdrop of the Great Trek, and *Marie* featuring a young Allan Quatermain mixed up in Piet Retief's dealings with King Dingane, presents a more sympathetic picture of the Boers. *Cetywayo* is highly critical of the Boers in a manner distinctly racist.

The villain of *Jess* 'drawn from life' was G.H. Buskes, an advocate of the high court in Pretoria during the late 1870s. Buskes was later implicated in atrocities committed in the siege of Potchefstroom during the First Anglo-Boer War (1880–81) and detailed by Haggard in an appendix to *Cetywayo*. Buskes was the original of Frank Muller in *Jess*. 'He was a large and exceedingly handsome man, apparently about forty years old, with clear-cut features, cold, light-blue eyes, and a remarkable golden beard that hung down his chest. For a Boer he was rather smartly dressed in English-made tweed clothes, and tall riding boots,' p. 27 of *Jess* (1900 edition).

Harding, in a letter to his father, wrote: 'We had the usual scramble of evidence and entertainments for the 2° days we spent in Pretoria. Haggard was in his element, and made lots of speeches. Jess's cottage is in Pretoria. In one of his speeches he suggested that it might be bought up as a municipal – or even a national – possession. Not having read *Jess* I feel quite cold – nor did I notice a very strong feeling in the way of adopting the suggestion.' Constantine, *Dominions Diary*, p. 225.

14. Rider Haggard Street, small back street close to Pretoria station, not the 'fine thoroughfare' Haggard predicted.

15. Stephanus Johannes Paul Kruger (1825–1904), last President of the South African Republic. *Oom*, Afrikaans for uncle, often used as a term of affectionate respect for an older man.

The other graves 'of those whom I had known' included that of his child Ethel Rider and her mother Mrs Ford. Though not mentioned in the diary intended for publication, it is noted in NRO, MC 32/51: 'Rough Diary',

30 March 1914. 'Went graveyards w patience found graves surrounded by stone wall. Monument to A of weeping woman. Gate rotten. Some of the bulbs she planted still growing . . . 4 trees of cypress variety planted at corners'. On another page Haggard recorded the inscriptions: 'Ethel Rider B.16 Sept 79 D 5 Nov 79/Johanna Catherine Ford (born Lehmkuhl)/D. Aug 30 1885 in 31st year.' He also recorded in brief the verse on the bottom of the monument bearing the weeping woman: 'and I heard a voice fr heaven saying (indecipherable word) Blessed are in'. The graves can still be found in the Old Cemetery in Church Street, Pretoria. See Introduction, Note 35.

16.   C.J. Juta was Minister for War and a Member of the Executive Council of the Transvaal. He was appointed in March 1877 under the new constitution approved by the Volksraad on 7 March 1877. After annexation he became High Sheriff of the Transvaal.

17.   John Stephen Curlewis (1863–1940), Judge of the Provincial Division of the Transvaal Supreme Court, Chief Justice of the Union of South Africa in 1936. He was Acting Governor-General in 1933 and 1937.

18.   Sir Herbert Baker (1862–1946), architect, famous for his government buildings (with Edward Lutyens) in New Delhi, India. Designed South Africa House in London. The buildings referred to by Haggard are the Union Buildings built on Meintjeskop, Pretoria (1910–12).

19.   Magaliesberg, mountain range near Pretoria noted for its tobacco and fruit production. Haggard's nephew, Alfred Gerald Ansdell, a cyclist in the Scottish Horse, was killed in action at Naauwpoort in the Magaliesberg on 4 April 1901 during the Second Anglo-Boer War (1899–1902). Originally buried on the farm Cyferfontein, his remains were later exhumed and reburied at the cemetery in Krugersdorp where his name appears on the monument.

20.   Common night adder (*Causus rhombeatus*), adults average 40 to 60 cm (16 to 24 ins). A common snake in the eastern half of southern Africa. Light grey, olive or light to pinkish brown in colouring. Mainly docile and will move off if disturbed. Hunts at night, frequently venturing near or into dwellings. Relies on smell to locate its prey. Bites most commonly inflicted on bare feet. Poisonous but not deadly, the venom causes pain and swelling.

21.   Wonderboom, famous wild fig tree (*Ficus pretoriae*) on slopes of Wonderboom Ridge, north of Pretoria. It is thought to be 700 years old and now a national monument.

22.   Thomas Francis Burgers (1834–81). Nederduitse Gereformde minister and president of the Transvaal Republic at time of annexation in 1877. In 1858 he married Scot Mary Bryson (1836–1929). They had 10 children, two sons and eight daughters.

Petrus Jacobus (Piet) Joubert (1831–1900), farmer and politician, leader in the struggle to regain Transvaal's independence from Britain following annexation. He was a commandant-general in the Second Anglo-Boer War.

23.   Carlton Hotel, Johannesburg, founded by diamond magnate Barney Barnato (1832–97). 'The Carlton is a caravanserie of the approved London type – noisy, large and not too comfortable.' Constantine, *Dominions Diary*, p. 229.

Johannesburg mushroomed into existence following the discovery of gold in 1886. By 1914 it was the largest city in South Africa. The commission questioned 18 witnesses from Thursday, 2 April to Monday, 6 April. At the same time, a committee of the Commission, consisting of Haggard and Garnett, had been questioning eight further witnesses on April 2, 3 and 4. Most of the Commission members left for Cape Town on the evening of 6 April, followed on 9 April by Harding and the rest of the staff from where they disembarked for England. Thus ended the DRC's visit to South Africa during which they spent 26 days gathering evidence and questioning 141 witnesses. Haggard remained behind as he intended to visit Rhodesia and then Zululand. Apparently other commissioners had intended visiting Rhodesia but decided not to 'through fear of malaria'. Constantine, *Dominions Diary*, p. 232.

24.   *Veld-ganger*, Afrikaans for literally one who goes upon the veld.

25.   The Rand Club was established in 1887.

26.   Sir Julius Gottlieb Ferdinand Jeppe (1859–1929), Transvaal mining and property magnate, business associate of Abe Bailey. Born in Germany, he came to South Africa in 1870 with his parents and settled in Pretoria. Thomas Baines, Carl Mauch and other explorers were frequent visitors to the Jeppe home in Pretoria. At 17, Jeppe served on President T.F. Burgers's abortive commando against Sekukhune. He also served in the First Anglo-Boer War. See also Introduction, Note 35.

27.   In 1879 the Transvaal Boers threatened rebellion and Haggard, who had joined the Pretoria Horse, was 'sent out in command of six or eight picked men to an inn that I think was called Ferguson's' about 40 km (25 miles) from Pretoria to observe a Boer force. See H.R. Haggard, *The Days*, Vol. 1, pp. 126–31.

28.   The *Report on the Salvation Army Colonies* was published as an HMSO Blue Book, June 1905. A popular version was published as *The Poor and the Land* (London, 1905). See Introduction p. 19 *et. seq.*

29.   George Blomefield. An agreement dissolving the partnership was signed at Ditchingham by Haggard, Cochrane and Blomefield on 29 April 1883 (not 1882). Assets after liabilites, amounted to £250 4s. 6d., which was divided among the three signatories. See Introduction p. 12. In the original typescript the paragraphs relating the blackmail attempt have a line drawn through them. In the margin is pencilled the word 'OMIT!'.

30.   John George Haggard (1850–1908) always known as Jack. Invalided out of the Royal Navy in 1880, he subsequently came to South Africa in the hope of employment and visited his brother Rider at Hilldrop, Newcastle, in 1881. (See Introduction, p. 12) He subsequently embarked on a diplomatic career holding consular posts in Lamu, Madagascar, Malaga, Brest, Noumea and Trieste.

Chapter Six

Is it a white man's land?

After the Commission's formal business had ended, Haggard set off with three other DRC members to visit Southern Rhodesia, then adminis- tered by the British South Africa Company under a royal charter granted to Cecil Rhodes in October 1889. In the late 1890s the company divided Rhodesia into two equal-sized provinces – Mashonaland, home to the Shona, in the east, and Matabeleland, home to the Ndebele, in the west. The Ndebele (formerly rendered Matabele) traced their ori- gins back to Mzilikazi, who broke away from Shaka, the Zulu king, in 1822 and moved across the Drakensberg into what became the Orange Free State and Transvaal. There he came into contact with the north- ward movement of the Voortrekkers and, after defeats at Vegkop (1836) and Mosega (1837), retreated across the Limpopo River. Concessions granted in 1888 by Mzilikazi's son, King Lobengula, gave the Chartered Company access to the territories now known as Zimbabwe and Zam- bia. Haggard's brother, Alfred (1849–1916), also sought concessions from Lobengula at that time and helped to form the African Exploration Com- pany of which he became managing director. At the end of 1888 Alfred and his partner were denied access to Matabeleland by a party of Nde- bele, led or assisted by an agent of Rhodes. Alfred returned to Cape Town and was openly critical of Rhodes who, fearing a literary cam- paign against him by Rider, paid off the older Haggard with £2 400 worth of shares in the Central Search Association.[1] Southern Rhodesia became a Crown colony in 1922 after its white settlers voted not to join the Union of South Africa. From 1953 until its dissolution on 31 Decem- ber 1963, Southern Rhodesia was part of the Central African Federation with Northern Rhodesia and Nyasaland. When the latter two gained independence as Zambia and Malawi in 1964 it became known as Rho- desia. In November 1965 the government of Ian Smith declared its in- dependence from Britain (UDI) and in 1969 officially became a republic. A long-running civil war led to the ending of British sovereignty in December 1979 and majority rule for Zimbabwe.

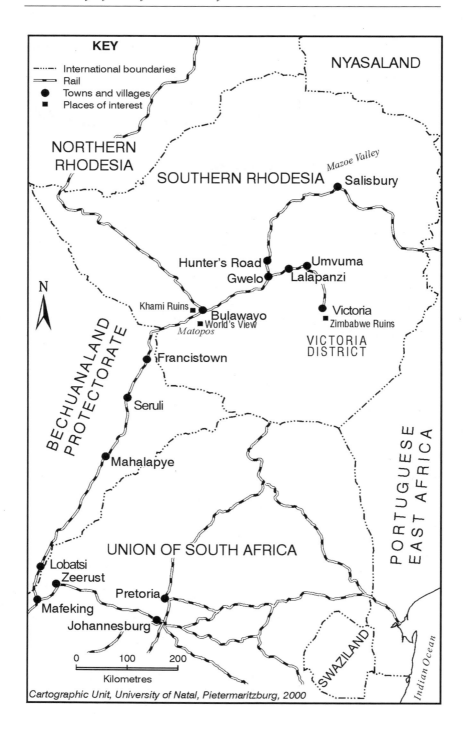

KEY
- ----- International boundaries
- ⫧ Rail
- ● Towns and villages
- ■ Places of interest

NYASALAND

NORTHERN RHODESIA

SOUTHERN RHODESIA

Mazoe Valley

Salisbury

Hunter's Road

Umvuma

Gwelo

Lalapanzi

Khami Ruins

Bulawayo

World's View

Matopos

Victoria

Zimbabwe Ruins

VICTORIA DISTRICT

N

BECHUANALAND PROTECTORATE

Francistown

Seruli

Mahalapye

PORTUGUESE EAST AFRICA

UNION OF SOUTH AFRICA

Lobatsi

Zeerust

Pretoria

Mafeking

Johannesburg

SWAZILAND

Indian Ocean

0   100   200
Kilometres

Cartographic Unit, University of Natal, Pietermaritzburg, 2000

Saturday, 4 April

I woke to find we were running through flat thornveld into the little town of Mafeking,[2] famous for its siege, a fairly flourishing place of the sort to all appearances. A while after we reached a place called Lobatsi among hills.[3] Here I spoke with a nice young Englishman who, I understood, manages a dairy which belongs to the Chartered Company, of which the produce is sold in Rhodesia. He told me, what indeed was obvious, that the drought was very severe. The normal rainfall is 20 inches. Last year there fell 13 and this year only four inches, with the result that the water in the boreholes is sinking. The cattle keep fairly well but give little milk and, of course, crops are wanting. Later we came to a village named Morwa where there is a large native kraal that overlooks a vast bush-clad plain. The black women and children flocked down to the train chattering and laughing in their merry fashion, hiding their faces too when Mr. Greene photographed them, an act they still hold to partake of witchcraft. Here Livingstone[4] had his mission station. I presume the low thatched and white-washed house among the kaffir huts is the one he occupied.

For most of the afternoon we ran on through thick thorn scrub, apparently unpeopled by man or beast. Then the veld changed to a park-like aspect diversified by quite large trees till we came to a railway settlement named Mahalapye in the Bechuanaland Protectorate.[5] Here an old lady shewed us her school, a tin-roofed building where, with the help of a grant from the Rhodesian government, she teaches 16 children, some of them 'off coloured', who in their leisure hours make pretty little objects with porcupine quills. These children, or their parents, pay a few shillings a month in fees, a family of them being charged 15s. the month. I walked to a little railed-in place where the dead are buried about the roots of a large thorn tree. One monument among the seven or eight is to a young Englishman who died of typhoid on service in the police, a second to another young Englishman who was accidentally shot, and so on. With such bones as these is the road of Empire paved. The mistress told me that there is a good deal of malaria here, especially at this season. She herself, poor woman, has recently spent three months in hospital for this cause.

We reached Seruli about 9 p.m. The stationmaster here says that on the previous day some native women went out to look for caterpillars to serve as food in the drought and met three lions, after which they gave up caterpillar hunting. Also a week or so since one of three white men who were employed on the railway got fever and began to drink. Ultimately he shot both of his companions and committed suicide, an incident that does not seem to have attracted any particular attention. Recently two natives here were encamped at night by a fire on the veld, one went to fetch more wood and a lion took him. He called to his companion (who tells the story) to bring a burning brand and drive off the lion, but the latter stayed where he was. Then the unhappy man described all that was happening to him in the darkness: 'Now he bites me here, now there. Now he has let me go, I am coming – Oh! now he has caught me again (evidently the lion was playing with him, as a cat does with a mouse). Now he is chewing me all over!' Then silence. The lion and his victim had departed never to be seen again. Surely the world is cruel in its ways. Seruli must be a lively place of residence.

Sunday, 5 April

Last night was terrifically hot in the train especially as it was necessary to shut the windows etc. to keep out the poisonous anopheles mosquitoes.[6] I should imagine that it must have been about 110F in my compartment where sleep was almost impossible under a mosquito net. Owing to the inefficiency of these nets some of us were badly bitten.

On arriving at Bulawayo[7] early I received a wire from Louie saying: 'We were not in accident. Both well.' Not until the following day could I find out anything about this accident. Then I learned that the train in which I had seen them off from Johannesburg had divided into two parts and that the second half had been involved in a severe smash with a goods train near Middelburg resulting in several deaths and many injured.[8] Apparently L. and L. were in the first part of the divided train, for which I thank God with all my heart.

At Bulawayo station Mr. Inskipp, the Chartered Company manager, came to meet me.[9] After consideration I made up my mind that I should learn more about Rhodesia by staying with him at Bulawayo than by journeying through this heat to the [Victoria] Falls. So I accepted his kind invitation and stayed. Motoring to his charming house three miles away I changed my clothes and went back to B. to attend the choral service in the cathedral, a fine stone building but rather narrow.[10] The view from the Inskipp's fine stoep is beautiful in its way, a vast bushclad plain where the silence is very soothing after the bustle of cities and the rattle of the train. The drought is very sharp, so much so that notwithstanding constant watering the fruit trees and flowers are dying in the garden. Want of water and of rainfall seems to be the curse of Bulawayo. About this house there is at present a perfect plague of butterflies and moths, the latter of which invade the house by scores after nightfall, many of the large hawk tribe.

Both the Inskipp's house and Government House, which stands within a quarter of a mile away, are built upon the site of Lobengula's great kraal Bulawayo (the Place of Slaughter), an ill-omened name that has been retained by the English town. I walked all over the site of the kraal, which must have measured more than a mile across, first visiting the tree under which Lobengula used to sit in council and to give judgement, that stands in the garden of Government House.[11] It is a particularly insignificant tree of the ilex [holly] tribe. Here no doubt he received my poor friends Patterson and Sargeaunt and here often the word of death has been uttered.[12] Near to stood the king's little house and by it the wagon in which he always slept. In front was the vast open space that was used as a parade ground and to kraal the cattle in times of danger, etc. All the bush has been cleared from this space in old days and the limits of the native town can be marked by the great circle where it grows in its primitive state. Into this bush were thrown the bodies of those executed by the king's command though it is said that some were cast to the crocodiles in the river beyond. On the further side of the open space I found the foundations and floors of many huts, all of which were burned by Lobengula when he fled before the advance of the English. Also I found the sites of several middens where the women threw ashes, etc. that still lie here in quantity. On the ground I picked up one of the smooth stones they used to pound up grain, worn with the pounding and marked by the fire. This I kept as a souvenir. All about too are the broken bones of cattle, eaten by the natives many years ago. Doubtless this poor savage king deserved his fate, yet it is difficult not to feel sorry for him, especially as he protected the white traders to the very last and when he could no longer do so sent to advise them of the fact, expressing the hope that their own people would treat them as well as he had done.

The manner of his destruction too was very sad. He wished to make submission and as earnest thereof sent £1 000 in gold and a letter by two *indunas*.[13] These men were frightened by the sight of the English column and hid till it had gone by. Then they emerged and gave the gold and the letter to two troopers who were riding behind. These wretches destroyed the letter and stole the gold thereby bringing about the death of Wilson and his companions near the Shangani River, also that of Lobengula and the break-up of his people. When the king found that his letter had been delivered with his present of gold to the English who returned no answer, his only course was to go on fighting. The thieves were found out and convicted but afterwards liberated on some legal technicality. I wonder whether they have imagination enough to understand how black is the shame they have brought upon the name of England.[14]

On this Sunday afternoon two ladies with their husbands, Mrs. Olive, the wife of the manager of the Land Bank, and Mrs. Papenfus, the wife of a large farmer of Dutch origin and sympathies, came to call on Mrs. Inskipp. With them I had some conversation. Neither of them gave a cheerful account of life at Bulawayo. Mrs. Olive, who is writing a Rhodesian novel for the Hodder & Stoughton competition in which I believe I am a judge,[15] said she was completing the work with two children delirious from malaria, and Mrs. Papenfus declaimed on the awful cost of living in Rhodesia where so much food is still imported and eggs, that the fowls produce scantily in this heat, have been known to cost 1/- ea., their normal price being five for that sum. Also they were eloquent on the subject of lack of water.

There is no doubt that most of Rhodesia is still more or less subject to malaria, though typhoid is a greater scourge. Both of these plagues, however, may be conquered in course of time. After all the country is vast and even on the higher lands almost semi-tropical in character. Indeed this saving altitude is not without its drawbacks since it causes many white women to suffer from heart and other troubles, my hostess Mrs. Inskipp among them. As regards its wild and still unsettled character I heard an amusing story. A tradesman from, I think, Nottingham, took it into his head that he would like to farm in Rhodesia. Out he came and drove from Gwelo to inspect what appeared a suitable estate.[16] Before it was reached, of a sudden he found himself in the midst of a herd of 14 elephants, which frightened him terribly. 'For God's sake, turn back,' he shouted to his conductor, 'I've seen enough of Rhodesia!' Presumably he is now reflecting on his adventures in Nottingham. Another old gentleman came out and was at once upset from a canoe on the edge of the Victoria Falls, down which he nearly vanished, but he accepted his experience in a more philosophical spirit.

Monday, 6 April

I was motored out by Mr. Jesser Coope, superintendent of the Chartered Company's farmlands in Southern Rhodesia, to see the Matopos and Rhodes's grave.[17] About a dozen miles from town after a journey through bushveld where I saw some cattle in good condition, we stopped at the farm known as Rhodes, which is rented from the trustees by Mr. F.A. Hull, a charming, hard-working and progressive agriculturist. We found him in his shirtsleeves engaged in 'dipping' his cattle, an operation that I was delighted to find an opportunity of witnessing. Mr Hull called to us to come to him as he dared not take his eyes off the business. The last time he did so, he explained, the kaffir broke the legs of two calves in five minutes. It was extraordinary to see these animals rush down the slope and plunge into the dip, which generally hid them head and all, with every symptom of delight. Do they know that the arsenical mixture rids them of the tormenting ticks, I wonder? Or are they merely anxious to get the job over? At any rate in they go one by one at such speed that the whole 500 of all sizes are put through in an hour, emerging dripping on the drying ground at the other end.

This dip contains 2 750 gallons of water. At each weekly dipping 750 gallons of water are added in which is mixed five gallons of Cooper's cattle dip that suffices to poison all the ticks but does not hurt the cattle.

Each dipping costs about 25s. Mr. Hull dips his horses as well as his cattle and since he began to do so three years ago has never lost a horse from sickness, though this disease used to sweep the district. His experience seems to controvert the view of those who declare that dipping is *not* a specific for horse-sickness. When the dipping was done I went to the fine farm buildings built at great cost by Rhodes and inspected the two imported Lincoln Red bulls and their progeny, very fine animals that are being crossed with the Afrikander cattle, an ancient breed with many merits. Thence we walked to the house built upon an eminence where two of Mr. Hull's children were playing on the stoep, one of whom, a little girl, has been suffering from some form of fever. Here we drank tea in a kind of large shed or summerhouse where Rhodes's body rested on the night before its burial. While we did so Mr. Hull detailed his woes to me. His black labourers cost him about £1 a month with food, but are he said utterly unreliable. The low lands of his great farm are supposed to be irrigated from the dam close by, which was constructed by Rhodes at a cost of £30 000. But this dam, though a fine work, is an expensive failure as it has only a catchment area of under 30 square miles, which in a dry climate is of course utterly insufficient. So but little land has received any benefit in this drought. As a result of the lack of rain, from 32 acres of maize sewn, Mr. Hull will not gather a single bag of mealies, or so he declared. Again the rape he has drilled to feed his ostriches (of which I noted about a score grazing on the lucerne patch) has not come up and the sunflowers are a fearful failure, scarcely a foot high. I only saw one miserable bloom upon the lot of them. On what then is he to feed his stock during the coming winter? It would seem as though ruin stared him in the face.

Moreover, his case is that of every other farmer in Matabeleland, or at any rate of most of them. One of these, a retired officer who has taken up citrus growing in the neighbourhood of Bulawayo, I passed upon the road. I am told he is very anxious for his young trees. The best information I obtained on the facts, however, came to me from a young doctor, named I think, Ackland, who was a contemporary at Barts [St Bartholomew's, a teaching hospital in London] of Tom Haggard and indeed a cousin of his through the Barkers.[18] He is a partner in a medical firm at Bulawayo and informed me that they had just sent out their bills, which had accumulated to 'thousands of pounds' but were getting scarcely anything in because none of their patients had any money owing to the three years of drought. 'Meanwhile,' he added pathetically, 'I have to live.' He said, moreover, that their case was that of every businessman and storekeeper in Bulawayo. All were giving credit because they must and none was being paid their debts. Something like ruin threatened the community owing to the lack of rain. Still it is a hopeful land although the climate does affect the nerves of many (I feel it myself) and all trust for better times. But when these come, if they do, how long will it take to pay the heaped up debts? Luckily Mashona-land seems to be better off.

From Mr. Hull's farm there is a good view of the stony range of the Matopos.[19] Wishing him farewell and better luck we drove on to these. Passing through a stone gateway presented by the late Mr. Beit,[20] which looks very incongruous in this wild place and will, I hope, be removed as the gates have been already, we entered some parklike lands where sundry trees have been planted by Rhodes's wish, none of which is doing very well. A few miles further on we left the motor and began our climb of the steep slopes of granite that form the hill, on the crest of which Rhodes is buried. It was a long trudge in that heat but at last we stood by the lizard-haunted grave; a slab of granite on which is the inscription 'Here rest the remains of Cecil John Rhodes'. (Personally I should have omitted 'the remains of'). I gazed on it sadly. The last time I was so near to this remarkable man was in a very different place, a sitting room in the Burlington Hotel in London. God rest him! This hill-top was named 'The World's View' by Rhodes but the prospect is curi-ous rather than grand. All round are the fantastic Matopos, the hard granite core or debris evidently of some earth plane or surface that was washed away millions of years ago. Brown shoulders of rock project, boulder is piled on boulder as though they had been the playthings of giant children. Really they tumbled thus when the softer strata or soil were washed away and so remained and will remain through uncounted ages till they too dissolve.

Mr. Coope, who was one of the pioneers and knew Rhodes in-timately (by the way it was he who blasted out his granite grave), told me under what circumstances he gave to this place its somewhat pre-tentious name. It was when he sat here almost at the end of his re-sources and credit after the Jameson Raid and well nigh hopeless of bringing the Matabele fighting to a successful issue, searching the sur-rounding koppies with his eyes as though he expected to find among their ancient stones some path of escape from his troubles, as in the end indeed he did. For it was on one of these koppies that finally he made peace with his savage enemies in a memorable interview. Knowing him as I did, and being able to enter more or less into his mind, I can quite understand what was passing there and how the name suggested itself to him. At the time those forbidding hills swarming with his foes were the world to him and the countless tumbled rocks represented all the difficulties in his path which he contemplated from this physical eminence, and from that other spiritual eminence of a towering ima-gination. Mr. Coope, a man of insight, informed me that he had good reason to believe that in his last years Rhodes regretted some of the avenues by which he mounted to success and fame.

Leaving the grave we went on to the Wilson Memorial, which stands near by, beneath which lie the bones of Wilson and his men removed hither from Zimbabwe. It is a fine thing and the bronze plaques are quite remarkably good. Still I do not think this is its place, it seems to jar upon the landscape like Beit's stone gateposts. I hope it may ultimately be moved to a more suitable situation. Rhodes wished this spot to be devoted to simple graves of notable men, not, I imagine, to costly memorials in bronze and marble. I find however that it was in accordance with his testamentary directions that the remains were moved hither from Zimbabwe, although Sir W. Milton and others thought this undesirable.[21]

On our way back Mr. Coope gave me an interesting account of his experiences as a pioneer and of the hardships which he and his companions underwent in those days, cutting a path through trackless wilds, being drowned in rains, parched, starved and racked with fever and dysentery. He says that they are nearly all dead now. Of the bravery of the Matabele he speaks in the highest terms, though they could not stand in the face of the machine guns. It seems that before they finally gave in it was touch and go with the Company's forces.

Tuesday, 7 April

Today I visited the museum guided by Mr. Molyneux and accompanied by Walter Scudamore,[22] who seems to be getting on to his satisfaction in his railway billet. Here there are some interesting relics from Zimbabwe, including the famous fragment of Nankin china on which Professor MacIver founded his theory, to my mind so very absurd, that this gigantic fortress and the other ruins were built by kaffirs in the middle ages.[23] How he can think so after seeing them I cannot imagine, especially as I remember that the Portuguese writers of three centuries ago say that the natives of that day asserted that they were the work of the Devil in unknown antiquity. At luncheon I met Mr. R.A. Fletcher, who may be called the head of the opposition to the Chartered Company regime and with him had an interesting talk.[24] He struck me as a perfectly honest if a rather narrow man with the face of one who is constitutionally 'agin the government'. He is in favour of paying out the company on fair terms and taking over the railways at cost, which seems to me scarcely just after the shareholders have borne all the risk. He would like a larger legislative council paving the way to responsible government as soon as the country is fit to bear the burden. His views have, however, met with heavy and recent defeat at the election that has just taken place, which in fact was a vote by the population against joining the Union and in favour of the continuance of company rule. At Mr. Inskipp's dinner to us before we left Bulawayo I sat next to Mr. Forbes, the distinguished leader of irregular troops and the present head of the legislative council.[25] From him and others I gathered that about one third of the population is anti-Chartered Company. This opposition is, however, split into three factions: (1) Those who wish that Rhodesia should join the Union; (2) Those who wish for immediate responsible government; and (3) Those who wish that Rhodesia should be declared a Crown colony. Whether in this last event the Colonial Office would do as much for the inhabitants as the company has done and is prepared to do under the draft Land Settlement Ordinance may well be doubted. Mr. Forbes, I should add, seems to doubt whether the ownership of the land does rest in the company, a matter which is to be decided by the Privy Council. Anyway he wants the matter authoritatively settled one way or the other.

In the afternoon I motored to the Khami ruins with Mr. Molyneux, who is of an antiquarian mind.[26] There are very remarkable relics of an unknown race, built on the tops of koppies in three or four different styles covering a large area of ground and protected on one side by the Khami River. I have no doubt myself that they were designed to protect the mouth of the valley and form one of a chain of fortresses and dwelling places occupied by a ruling race, probably of Semitic origin who for the purposes of gold-mining dwelt in the midst of a hostile population by which they were ultimately driven out or exterminated. These remains are well worth the trouble of a hot scramble but the visitor should beware of the snakes with which they swarm. The herring-bone stonework is very remarkable, also the state of preservation of the walls built without mortar of dressed granite blocks. They deserve thorough and complete excavation.

After Mr. Inskipp's dinner, at which all three of us made speeches [Haggard, Bowring and Campbell], we drove to the train and departed for Salisbury,[27] much pleased by our kind reception at Bulawayo. I forgot to say that in this town I had instances of the effect of romance on the minds of men. Thus Mr. Coope told me that it was my books which sent him to the interior of Africa. Also a young man in the post office, seeing my name on a telegram, told me it was I who had brought him from England to Rhodesia. In the same way a year or two ago in London one of our most famous archaeologists, who was then engaged in excavating the frontier cities of Palestine, told me that the reading of my *Cleopatra* had turned his feet into that path of life. I am glad to say he added that he had never regretted his choice.[28] Also I have heard of sundry other cases in connection with my works of fiction, so at least I have helped to populate the Empire!

On the whole I do not think I should care to live at Bulawayo. It is arid and expensive and the lack of water makes any system of drainage impossible, at any rate at present, which is a great drawback and causes sickness. Still there is a certain charm about the place and I shall never forget the view from the stoep of the Inskipp's house.

Wednesday, 8 April

This morning we passed the little town of Gwelo. Thence we went on through an eternal stretch of bushveld where tall grass grows between the trees. Neither here or in most of the districts of this vast Rhodesia does much use seem to be made of all this grass. It is neither mown nor fed, it just wastes by the million tons for lack of stock to eat it. Perhaps, however, this will be rectified in time as the country fills. But whence is there to come a population sufficient to occupy all this enormous land? It is a country for men with capital and of these a certain number are arriving. But that class after all is limited, for them there are many other colonies in competition with Rhodesia where no free land is given away as in the case of Canada. I am rather of opinion that, the cattle diseases having been conquered, Rhodesia's best future lies in the direction of stock-ranching after the example of the firm of Liebig, carried on by rich companies or individuals. At present it seems no place for the poor man, even if he would come. Also, although there are such enormous acreages of available land, the price of it is being run up to values that I think highly speculative. Holders who often obtained their great farms for little or nothing, under 'pioneer rights' or otherwise, now ask and sometimes (though not so often as is reported) get £2 the acre for these same farms, especially in the Mazoe Valley and other selected localities. Whether the purchasers will find them paying propositions at these prices remains to be seen. In this connection it must however be remembered that today the market is in fact local, therefore one which it will be easy to overstock, though in good years some mealies have been exported. If meat should all be raised in large quantities for the home market, freezing works will be necessary on the Argentine and New Zealand plan, which means large capital and a steady supply of sufficient beasts.

At a place we passed called Hunter's Road, elephants have of late been giving a good deal of trouble.[29] About 10 o'clock we came to a little township with many tin shanties clustered round the Globe and Phoenix mine, one of the most successful in Rhodesia, where so many have failed as the British investor knows to his cost.[30] Its belching iron chimneys are a great disfigurement to the veld.

For most of the afternoon we ran through flat bushveld on which grow big trees, some of them on antheaps large as cottages. I wonder how old those antheaps may be. Nearer to Salisbury the country becomes more open, with scrub of a smaller character. Here too are fine glades and sometimes we had views of enormous stretching plains of flat land. In this neighbourhood about 20 inches of rain have fallen during the season but a stationmaster told me that now the drought was beginning to make itself felt. Winding by some considerable hills we came to Salisbury about 7 in the evening where we were met by

Mr. Holland,[31] secretary to the Administrator, and taken to a dinner party at Government House where I spent the night as the guest of Sir William Milton. It is a charming house with a very wide verandah and large airy rooms built round a courtyard. The steel fabric was imported bodily from England, the concrete of which the walls are formed being made on the spot. I am told that it cost the British South Africa Company £30 000, an enormous sum when the amount of accommodation is considered and one which gives an idea of the cost of building in Rhodesia. The new hospital, a nice-looking building, is also said to have cost more than £30 000. Certainly the company is spending freely in the land but most of the money is paid away in wages, which are enormous, and thus circulates.

Salisbury is a thriving looking town with good shops and a cathedral in course of erection in stone. It is expensive as a visit to a chemist's shop will prove. To my surprise however, for a little snake-bite outfit containing powdered permanganate of potash and a lancet in a vulcanite case, I was only charged 2s. but perhaps this is considered a national necessity and priced in accordance with the demand. On the whole I liked Salisbury better than Bulawayo, though it is beginning to straggle over the surrounding veld in the same indeterminate way. Such is the fashion of most colonial towns, prompted to some extent by a natural desire on the part of their inhabitants to avoid payment of the city rates. The water here is said to be good but there is no drainage. The Administrator's dinner party was very smart and pleasant.

Thursday, 9 April

I went to see the agricultural laboratories and experimental farm station. Here many kinds of crops were being tested, among them a large indigenous bush known as Napier Fodder, which is said to make good food for cattle. The Australian Hunter River lucerne appears to be the best, but a tree lucerne which grows in bushes is also being tried. The lucerne was covered with butterflies and is much attacked by their caterpillars. In the same way the Indian dhal, which does well here and is cut green for fodder, is devoured by a terrible red beetle. It is a valuable crop because of the nitrogenous nodules on its roots and the natives eat its grain, which ripens somewhat unevenly. The castor-oil plants suffer much from a kind of borer and the leaves of the mangold plants were almost entirely devoured by grubs. Fifteen tons the acre seems to be an average crop, which is small. Wheats are being hybridised in search of rust-resisting varieties, the Victoria wheat and the Yellow Cross being so far the best in this respect, but Rhodesia is not proving a good wheat country and it is only grown as a winter crop under irrigation. The kaffir melons for dairy feeding and the large field radishes looked well. The baled hay of teff grass mixed with peas was very good, as was the veld hay, which cuts about two tons the acre, although the latter is rather coarse. The soil here is red and very deep. Its origin is the rock known as Epi-diorite. The average rainfall, short this year, is 31 inches.

Leaving the experimental crops, of which I have only mentioned some, we visited the laboratories. Here I was shewn a tsetse fly map shewing the distribution of that poisonous insect and many specimens of its different varieties that may be known by their sharp proboscis and crossed wings.[32] There is no doubt that these are nearly always associated with the large game, but fortunately they do little or no harm to men and donkeys. Also I inspected various kinds of soil in test tubes and methods of preserving wood from the attack of white ants. Altogether I thought this an excellent and well-managed institution but the impression I took away from it was that agricultural Rhodesia has many plagues to fight besides that of drought. Well it must be so in all new lands but I should not wonder if at the end as in the beginning cattle and mealies do not prove its best friends.

In the afternoon we were motored 30 miles out from Salisbury to the Mazoe Valley, one of the best farming districts in Rhodesia.[33] Our road ran through a beautiful country with many bush-clad hills which culminated in the Mazoe range and a mountain known as The Iron Mask, with brown precipitous cliffs. It was over this road that the Mazoe Patrol accomplished its famous rescue ride during the Matabele Rebellion in 1896, bringing back the women and children in a wagon, armoured with galvanised iron, from the little mine where they had taken refuge. It must have been a dreadful business as the natives potted at them all the way from the long tambouki grass and bushes in which they were hidden. I think that some of them were killed but their leader very deservedly was given the Victoria Cross. Surely this was deserved also by the two men who ventured across the valley from the mine to send the telephone message that brought help from Salisbury. They despatched the message but were killed on the return journey, and now my informant could not remember their names or one of them. Such is the way of the world. Death was the Victoria Cross of those brave men, and fame soon passes.[34] Thus I was told that only the other day, one of the most famous of the pioneer leaders, a man who had done great things, having fallen on bad times, came back to Salisbury and died in the hospital without being recognised by anybody.

In this fine Mazoe Valley great quantities of mealies are grown and up to £2 the acre is the price of the land. Also the company has a citrus farm that so far has not, I was told, been a great success as it has not sufficient water. There is now a gigantic scheme on foot to dam the whole valley of the Mazoe and put all the lower lands under irrigation. I saw the place and the business seems feasible but at what cost I do not know. As it is proposed to hold up two miles of water the retaining walls will need to be strong! The glory of Mazoe has departed since the railway left it on one side, its 'hotel' numbers few guests and the Jew owner has taken to cultivating mealies, or rather has hired a Christian to do so. It is a tiny collection of shanties, no more.

There are, I believe, only two white ladies in the place, Mrs. Drew, the wife of the native commissioner, and the matron of the hospital. They live close together but, they informed me, do not often meet because they are too busy for society. Mrs. Drew said she found the spot lonely as their mule, Jimmie, would not face motor cars and therefore she feared to go out driving. So she just remained at home with her husband and two little girls. I think that our visit made quite a pleasant change. Mr. Drew's office and courthouse is a queer place, a round native hut with a door to it and four black messengers in uniform lined up stiffly outside. His house is situated on an eminence 100 yards away and there he entertained us at tea in a summerhouse in the garden, which commands a fine view. It must be a strange solitary existence but not so much so as that of many officials in Rhodesia for is not the metropolis of Salisbury within 30 miles? Moreover there is a small mine in the neighbourhood which keeps on working though it pays no dividends, as happens in the case of many other Rhodesian mines, unless they are shut down altogether.

Before he came to Mazoe Mr. Drew filled a similar office for many years at Victoria near Zimbabwe. He told me that in the Devukwi district there he had seen the mummies of ancient chiefs kept in huts in almost inaccessible places, one mummy in each hut, seated doubled up on a framework. Whenever a new chief succeeds it is his sacred duty to rewrap these mummies as the Pharoahs rewrapped their predecessors. Only with great difficulty after many ceremonies did he succeed in inspecting these mysterious relics. A German missionary in that neighbourhood told him also that the natives reverenced the *scarabaeus* beetles. Now does not all this suggest some hereditary connection with Egypt? By the way, at Government House is a wooden image of a woman, about 18 inches high with a bit of cloth round the middle, which, as Cecil Rhodes remarked to Sir W. Milton, has 'an evil face, a very evil face'. This was the fetish of a certain female prophetess, an emissary from the Molimo or native High Magician, which was supposed to whisper to her the counsel of the power above, or below. The old prophetess was caught during the rebellion and hanged, but her counsellor remains upon the mantelpiece, doubtless still whispering its messages to nothingness in the night. Mr. Drew said that the number of farmers in the neighbourhood was increasing but that at present the market was purely local. I bade him farewell with regret.

Another place I saw at Salisbury was the Rhodesian Tobacco Warehouse, a venture of the Chartered Company, which next year is to be run in conjunction with a co-operative society. It is a large building in which new and costly machinery from the United States is being erected. The tobacco growers of the district send their crops here, which the warehouse grades, redries and bales. Last year they treated nearly 2° million pounds but this year the crop will be smaller owing to the drought. All this tobacco, which for the most part is consumed in South Africa, is of the virginian type and golden in colour. Last year the sales averaged 10∫d. the pound. This year as the quality is better, it should fetch 11°d. It is reckoned that South Africa cannot consume more than 3 million pounds so after that total output is reached it will be necessary to export. The difficulty for the farmers is to grow it cheaply enough to compete with America.

In the evening I bought a pair of canvas gaiters to protect my legs from the tormenting grass seeds and possible snakes at Zimbabwe and in Zululand, which cost 10s. 6d., and was interviewed by the local paper. Sir W. Milton and his secretary came to dinner on the train. It was our last meal together as Campbell, Bowring and Greene leave us here to catch their boat at Beira, a port on the Mozambique [then Portuguese East Africa] coast. At 10 o'clock I steamed off feeling rather lonely as I am now the sole survivor of the commission in these parts. It has been arranged that our train shall run over the unfinished line to Victoria, within 20 miles of Zimbabwe.[35]

Friday, 10 April

This morning we passed a place bearing the curious name – though one not unsuited to the climate – of Lalapanzi, which means 'lie down and sleep'.[36] Here is a little tin hotel with a tall stockade of timber at the back, built, I suppose, to keep out wild beasts. Personally I should like to see a wild beast since with the exception of three baboons my eyes have fallen on none in Rhodesia and, for the matter of that, of few birds either. The African sky seems strange with never a vulture in it even. Everything seems to have been killed out, mostly by the natives. Here too were six oxen drawing a sledge on which was a single sack of corn! About 1 o'clock we came to the little settlement of Umvuma where is a gold and copper mine with a really noble brick chimney.[37] I am told that it has been 'reconstructed' (I mean the mine not the chimney) more than once but that its shareholders are now animated by a sure and certain hope of large dividends. It is called the Falcon and is about to begin crushing. Here we were joined by the representative of Messrs. Pauling, the contractors for the extension of the line to Victoria 70 miles away, over which, although it is not open to traffic, they have kindly given us permission to run our special train.

All the afternoon we have been travelling over this line slowly as it is not yet settled and I write this within about a mile of Victoria where we must stop. As we went I saw standing among the trees two huge pointed rocks which look exactly like obelisks. What would not the Egyptians have given for them thus ready fashioned by the hand of Nature. The sunset on this wild veld was really beautiful and still more so the rising of the great moon at its full tonight. Its immense and shining orb seemed quite close to us as it came up behind a long line of tumbled koppies. In the foreground were the countless trees and in the distance a range of jagged hills that looked very black in colour, while on the desolate and measureless plain lay and changed a hundred hues of mingled light – purple, violet and rose. It was a sight to be remembered and alone worth all this long journey. Messrs. Pauling's engineer informed me that owing to its distance, 90 miles from Umvuma, not 50 people have visited Zimbabwe during the last two years and that most of these came from Victoria, which is but 17 miles away. We are the first travellers to reach that place by train, hitherto it has been necessary to make the journey by motor or mule wagon, a long and costly business.

Saturday, 11 April

This has been a hard but most interesting day. Before breakfast at about 7 a.m. we started in the government motor we had brought with us, and, as the train had stopped about 1° miles from Victoria, bumped across the veld to the road through the little township, the oldest I believe in Rhodesia. As we went a duiker buck sprung up in front of us and bounded away, the first I have seen for many a year. The road to Great Zimbabwe (Zimbabwe Makeru) runs 16 miles through bushclad valleys and between hills very beautiful to see.[38] Over it we rushed and rocked for an hour or more, passing numbers of nearly naked Mashonas armed with assegai and kerrie, who saluted us in the old fashion by raising the right arm. At length we came to the Zimbabwe Valley, which is surrounded by wild scenery compounded of hills, koppies and bushclad plains unlike any I have seen before. Here we pulled up at some glorified huts and little houses which constitute Mr. Mundell's hotel and were met by Mr. R.N. Hall, an old gentleman who has written a number of well-known works on Zimbabwe and the other ruins of Rhodesia, and recently, I am glad to say, has been appointed curator of this wonderful place.[39] Whilst waiting for breakfast to be cooked I walked with him to the crest of a neighbouring koppie on which the ground is being cleared to receive the foundations of the curator's house. Hence the view is really glorious. To the north is a great plain bounded by the Beza Hills, to the north-north-east Imjomi (the Hill of Birds); to the east, Zimbabwe Mount, on which stand the ruins known as the Acropolis, to the south-east, on flatter ground, the great grey circle of the Elliptical Temple, to the south appear broad brown granite slopes. Then (and these are naturally of interest to me) between south and east the two round hills that have been named Sheba's Breasts (the second pair I have seen in Southern Africa) after those described in my tale *King Solomon's Mines*. Down to the Sabi River, which runs far away from north-east to east, is the native path connecting a chain of ancient forts, which to my surprise Mr. Hall called Allan Quatermain's Road. Really there is no road and, in all probability, never has been one; the ancients, it is presumed, used men who walked in single file as their only beasts of burden. But the track is there, as it always has been, and by it they marched from the coast, brought up their goods and sent away their gold. Finally to the west, with one tall mountain in the centre, is the Refuri range (Refuri seems to mean 'highest hill among high hills'). I hope I have written these directions correctly. If not Mr. Hall is to blame as I had no compass with me.

Here I may say that I observe the *Guide to Great Zimbabwe* by Mr. Hall states in more than one place that 'Zimbabwe Hill provided the description of the residence of *She*, while the ruins in the valley contributed "the dead city" of the same romance' (p. 3). Again, 'Zimbabwe Hill provided the basis of the description of the residence of Mr. Rider Haggard's *She*' (p.23).[40] These and similar legends I have heard and read elsewhere, are quite apocryphal. When I wrote *She* and the other romances referred to, I had only heard in the vaguest way of the Zimbabwe Ruins and not at all of the famous caves in East Africa, which are also reported to have been her residence. These works were in the main dictated by my own imagination, stimulated only in the case of *K.S. Mines* by faint rumours I had heard during my residence in South Africa. In the instances of *She* and *Allan Quatermain*, indeed practically I had nothing to go on outside of my own inventive powers. Oddly enough Mr. Hall does not seem to be acquainted with the tale I did write about Zimbabwe, which is named *Elissa*.[41] I have rather forgotten it myself but shall re-read it now with great interest, if only to discover my own blunders.

After breakfast we visited the temple of this and the other ruins. I shall attempt no detailed descriptions as such are set out fully in sundry works, but content myself with a short summary of my private impressions. I may say at once that this place – and indeed all the other buildings – far surpassed my expectations. In its way, notwithstanding the wreck that has been wrought by time, by natives who have dwelt here for generations, and by explorers in search of treasure, it is unequalled. Who built all these huge walls of shaped granite stones? At least it must have been a skilled and mighty race who commanded labour without limit for scores or hundreds of years. And what exactly did this fane [temple] look like when in its perfect glory? For my part I believe that most of the puzzling walls and enclosures within are of later date, that in the beginning the place was of a grand simplicity, that most of its 300 feet of length by 200 feet or so of breadth was empty, with the platform, the shrine and the symbolical cone with its veils of wall standing more or less in solitude to the south. Of course, however, this conjecture may be quite wrong. I was much puzzled by the little cone, of only a few feet in height, which stands quite close to its big brother, apparently without object or significance. It interested me much, therefore, when in answer to my question Mr. Hall said that he believed it was no part of the original sacerdotal plan but had been built by unknown hands out of the stones that have fallen from the top of the great cone. In support of this theory he advanced various arguments, such as the shape of the component stones, the fact that those fallen are wanting, and that the total number in the small cone would just suffice to complete the broken large cone and bring it to its original height. The two parts of the temple that impressed me most were the parallel passage between the outer and the inner wall of over 200 feet in length, and appearance of the eastern wall from without the temple. About this narrow passage there is a kind of eerie solemnity which reminded me of somewhat similar places in the Egyptian temples. Well can I imagine the priests of some dark and bloody ritual creeping down its gloomy and narrow depth, thrusting or bearing between them the human being destined to the sacrifice. In the same way the aspect of the towering outer wall, with its effective chevron pattern, is grand in its simple dignity.

At one of the entrances, I think that to the north-west, we found Mr. Wallace, a young farmer of the neighbourhood, and a very charming person, engaged in the task of rebuilding the tumbled gateway with the assistance of a gang of naked natives. Really his work is very creditable (he has already completed one gateway) but I will not flatter him by saying that it altogether equals that of the ancients. There was something amusing too in an English farmer eking out the problematical profits of the local agriculture by taking a contract at £20 a month to restore a Sabaean or Phoenician temple, and I may say that he quite saw the joke of it himself. Well, he might be worse employed for this temple needs a great deal of *judicious* restoration in the way of replacing fallen stones and walls overthrown by treasure-seekers, etc. Also it needs *systematic* excavation and the clearing away of some more of the trees which stand too near the walls. In it alone there is work for half a lifetime. And of the scores of ruins without, what is to be said? Many of them have as yet not even been cleared of the encumbering and destroying brush and creepers. To put them all in order, to excavate them, to build up the broken walls would occupy 100 men for many, many years. How any antiquarian can have suggested that all these buildings were erected by African natives in the Middle Ages passes my comprehension. Surely he must have but a slight acquaintance with kaffir races. Further, if the fragments of Nankin china are relied on as a proof, it might as well be argued that the soda water bottle, which was

Bryan Hall

Haggard (third from left) *at the Zimbabwe Ruins.*
(Lilias Rider Haggard's photograph album)

found *beneath* the said fragments, demonstrated that this temple was erected by English pioneers in the nineteenth century. But I will not enter on that old controversy, which to my mind has been finally decided against the Nankin-China party by my late friend Theodore Bent, Hall and others.[42] Talking of arguments, I forgot to state that Mr. Hall seemed a little aggrieved with me because I, he said, was responsible for various false ideas about Zimbabwe. He said that once he made a practice of sitting on the top of the great cone, reading my stories, noting their every *word*. I tried to explain to him the differences between romance and history of fact. *K.S. Mines* is one thing and *Rural England*[43] another, to take examples which owe their origin to a single intelligence; also, as I have stated above, with the exception of *Elissa,* which he has not read, I never wrote of Zimbabwe, but rather of a land where the ruins were built by the fairies of imagination.

Leaving the temple we visited a selection of the numberless ruins without. What were they all: dwellings of priests, storehouses, *¿Quien sabe?* [Spanish: Who knows?]. A fresh discovery has recently been made in a valley some miles away with monoliths in situ but this is being kept secret for the present lest tourists should break in and steal; also break up and destroy. Once upon a time this must have been a great city and doubtless all the valleys round were cultivated to provide its inhabitants with food. Indeed a farmer I met averred that many of them have been worked out and made infertile by these same ancients who ruined the land by long-continued cultivation without refreshing it with manure. Just so have they worked out many of the mines, at any rate down to water level. Of these I think there are few at which the same people who built Zimbabwe have not tried their hand, for the most part not in vain. Tens of millions worth of gold did they with their primitive methods take from the reefs of Rhodesia, doubtless by the aid of forced labour as the slavepits of Inyanga tell us.[44] That is what makes prospecting in Rhodesia so comparatively easy. It is, I believe, called 'blanket prospecting' from the circumstance that the prospector calls upon the natives in any given district and promises them blankets if they will reveal to him the whereabouts of old workings.

Bryan Hall

Haggard (right) *with Richard Nicklin Hall who showed him around the Zimbabwe Ruins.*
(Lilias Rider Haggard's photograph album)

When we had visited as many of the ruins as our time and strength would allow, we trudged back through the heat to lunch at the hotel. Here I may state that it knows how to be hot in this low-lying, shut-in valley especially in this year of drought. Also it is not precisely a health resort. Our landlord, I am told, has suffered from blackwater here. Two settlers who went to look at a farm not far off the other day both returned with blackwater from which they very nearly died and many people in this neighbourhood, including Mr. Hall, think it desirable to take five grains of quinine daily throughout the summer months. Others, however, scorn such precautions though there be few nowadays who reject mosquito nets.

Having rested till 3 o'clock and drunk everything we could get, we started forth again to climb the Acropolis, the only lady with us electing to remain behind. There were some doubts as to whether we should not suggest to Mr. Hall that he should not accompany us, both because of his age and of a recent severe illness from which he has suffered. When he reached the koppie we found how unnecessary was our solicitude. Rejecting the easier, recently cleared road, he insisted on our following one which he declared was 'more interesting'. It proved to be a very good imitation of a precipice. Up he scrambled now over boulders and ancient walls, now through scrub that forcibly suggested snakes, plunging at last into a narrow darksome cleft which ran skywards through two cyclopean masses of granite. Probably in remote ages it was one mass that had split asunder, separating by 18 inches or so, which width was that of the path. Halfway up this impossible place he turned to beckon to us hesitating weaklings who crawled behind and instantly there flashed into my mind the picture of old Gagool in *K.S. Mines*. In just such physically formidable and spiritually haunted surroundings did she evince a supernatural activity and turn to beckon to those whom she was guiding. Indeed in that gloom our learned conductor looked very like Gagool, seeing that he too is aged, shrunken and quite bald.[45] The resemblance was so ridiculously accurate that I burst out laughing and nearly came to grief, to say nothing of stinging myself with a peculiarly deadly kind of nettle that grows upon this hill.

This reminds me that the vegetation of the place is most interesting, some of it evidently being descended from trees and plants introduced by the ancients. Thus their fig trees have degenerated and now flourish wild, and the vines from which they gathered grapes now crawl attenuated and small-leaved about the ruins of their homes. Whether the hard-skinned fruit known as the kaffir orange, or rather its prototype, was introduced by them I do not know. If, as I am told, it is a true citrus, it would be worth while making use of the stock as a parent for oranges planted in dry places.[46]

At length the 300 feet were accomplished and we reached the summit of the koppie, in doing so passing over many walled terraces on which I suppose the ancients built their houses. It is indeed an extraordinary place. From below it does not seem so very large but here one sees its true extent. Perhaps it may best be described as a precipitous hill on the crest of which are scattered enormous masses of water-worn granite, some of which must weigh thousands of tons. In between these masses, round them, over them, run the walls of the ancients. Here are the remains of temples, courts, platforms, passages, balconies, smelting furnaces, treasuries, forts, guardrooms, monoliths, sundials and I know not what beside. To me, the plan of this dizzy place was impossible to discover. Soon indeed I gave it up and contented myself with allowing its atmosphere to flow into my mind as I crept and jumped after our guide, who leapt from wall to tottering wall across caverns and trenches with all the sure-footedness of a rock-rabbit, or swung himself round granite points projecting over space with the ease and certainty of a baboon. Truly his foot was on his native heath and it would not surprise me to learn that he could thread his beloved ruins in the dark when, by the way, no native will approach them. It is, I think a very strange atmosphere, almost uncanny indeed. I do not wonder that the kaffirs flee these spots; when once the sun is down though, if fortified with quinine and a really good mosquito net, I think that I should like to sleep in them for so perhaps their true past would come back to me.

The view from various sites was superb. How often must it have been studied by Sabaean eyes (if they were Sabaean) when ceremony and sacrifice to Bel or Ashtoreth were toward the temple that lies like an amphitheatre far beneath us and all the enormous plain between the guarded hills was green with crops through which the slave gangs trudged beneath the overseers' lash, bearing from the distant mines their allotted weight of ore. (Think of it, all these hundreds of thousands of tons of dressed stone whereof this fortress was constructed were carried up that terrible path upon the shoulders of those poor slaves!). But perhaps the mighty granite boulders moved me more even than those prospects. There they are as they were millions of years before the ancients came and built walls over or around their bulk, as the ants here build around a tree. There too they will be millions of years after I and all my race have ceased to be – if we ever cease to be. Oh! if only they could speak, those stones, and tell us of the feet that have pressed them, of the hands that have rested on them, of the tears and blood that have dried upon them, of the drunken laughter and the sighs of passion that they have heard, they who stand there today, so solemn and so lovely, just the same as they always were. No, not quite, for a portion of one of them has split off within the last few centuries, and swept away a great breadth of the human handiwork beneath. And if they could tell us of the last scene of this incident in their endless epochs, when the men and women who crawled about them and dwelt in these shadows, eating their food and melting their gold for a brief thousand years or so, being born and joining and dying, at length passed away and gave back their silence to them – the eternal rocks. How did it come? As the scattered gold and broken vessels of worship suggest – was it sudden? Did the fierce Bantu hordes, flowing in thousands from the north many centuries ago, and aided perhaps by treachery from within, storm up those terrible pathways and put to the assegai the proud overlords who dwelt within, dragging away the women and the children that they in their turn might drink the cup of slaves? Or was starvation the general to whom they were forced to bow? Were they cut off from the water which, as we can see today, they dammed up in the river below within the outer wall of defence. (There is the pool, and there, not far away, the bubbling spring that supplied the temple. I visited it, it is half choked with one of the monoliths, made some use of by a treasure hunter, Sir John Willoughby I was informed, in washing the debris for fallen gold.)[47]

Let the clairvoyants of Europe come here and answer these questions and I will believe in them perhaps! The clairvoyants are and will be dumb, but if only the graveyards of these people can be found, then we shall learn something. They must be somewhere, those well-filled cemeteries, for assuredly the death rate among the ancients cannot have been light and a people so developed would never have thrown their dead to the vultures, which still hang above Zimbabwe. But where are they? As yet no man knows or even guesses. At last we scrambled down from this koppie, storied in every sense of the word, as we had scrambled up but by an easier road, passing on our way a wonderful passage defended by walls built out on either side at a distance of each few feet, so that he who won past one guard must fall by the spear of the next. Reaching the plain below we paused a while to examine the system of the ancient water supply and then drove past the mound where the bones of Wilson and his brave men once were buried, in whisky boxes some of them, Mr. Hall said, till they were moved to the Matopos, to the temple spring that I have mentioned. Also the place was pointed out to me where Theodore Bent had his camp, the site of which is marked by a growth of castor-oil bushes. So at last we came back to the hotel to tea of which I, for one, drank a great deal for the climate of Zimbabwe is extraordinarily hot and exhausting.

At the inn, which consisted of some large kaffir huts, I had a very interesting conversation with Mr. Wallace who, with a partner, owns an 8 000-acre ranch in this neighbourhood and from him at first hand obtained the views of a bona fide Rhodesian settler of the best type. His account of the situation was not altogether encouraging, though he said (and I believe him) that he tried to look at the bright side of things. First he went to Canada (which he now appears to regret having left). Then he came to Rhodesia and to gain experience of the country enlisted in the mounted police, rising to the rank of sergeant. Unfortunately, he and his partner took up this land from the Chartered Company on the usual terms, viz. that the purchase price is to be paid after a lapse of five or, if an extension is obtained, of 10 years, interest only on the capital sum being charged during this period of grace. The cost of the land is, I gathered, 6s. 3d. the acre, which taking everything into consideration, is, I should say, quite enough for it, although this particular stretch is well watered. Also he has to pay £75 for the survey fee, which, as the work only occupied two days, is presumably also enough. At any rate he thinks so. The land is suitable for cattle, which even if no sickness or accidents occur, take a long while to breed up, and probably I am right in concluding that Mr. Wallace and his partner, after investing in a nucleus stock, are not overburdened with spare capital, which perhaps accounts for his antiquarian labours at the Temple.

Speaking generally, he said that he was doubtful of the future of Rhodesia, of which the suitability to white folk had yet to be proved. It was enervating and very hot for much of the year and did not, as a rule, agree with white women, many of whom went physically wrong in one way or another. Children also suffered in various respects. Moreover there was still a good deal of malaria and blackwater fever. The presence of the native population, he thought, was not an unmixed blessing, as it lessened self-reliance in the whites and in the case of young men, exposed them to moral dangers. Further, the great expense of living, and building, the high railway rates and the lack of any but local markets, which were easily gorged, were adverse factors that had to be taken into account. That the farmers were not doing too well even where there had been sufficient rainfall, was, he pointed out, obvious from the fact that so many of them tried to add to their incomes by outside means, such as transport riding, driving motor cars for hire, etc. Finally he declared that, after a fair trial of it, he could not conscientiously recommend any young Englishman to settle in Rhodesia and further that he thought the price to which the company was running up land was altogether unjustified by the net returns that could be got out of the soil. Such were his views, very modestly and quietly expressed, but to them he added the hope that things might turn out better than he saw any present reason to expect.

That evening another farmer, Mr. Williams, dined with us on the train. His position evidently is very different to that of Mr. Wallace. Once he was a native commissioner here, a fact, he explained, that gives him command of any amount of labour, since in the eyes of these raw black people he is a great chief. Moreover, he likes them and they like him. He holds large areas of land and (I am told), owns 3 000 cattle in which he deals with the natives and others. Also he is attached to Rhodesia where he has spent most of his life and, personally, he and his family have remained healthy in the climate. Yet on many points he corroborated Mr. Wallace, saying that to get on most farmers must do something besides farming, which was why he dealt in cattle. He too complained bitterly of the speculative values which were being put upon Rhodesian land, especially by the Chartered Company. He stated that one of the directors, whom he saw quite lately, told him straight out that they were a commercial company and as they found that a market in farms had arisen they intended to make the best of it in the interest of their shareholders, which after all is a natural position. He thought however that the land would not pay at the prices now demanded. At the same time nothing would induce him to farm in a country like Canada, where a man's 'hands' considered themselves as good or better than their master, and where often enough that master had to chop his own wood, draw his own water; where too his wife must generally cook not only the food of her family but that of the said 'hands' as well. Rhodesia was more comfortable in all these respects and therefore good enough for him notwithstanding the narrow markets and the high railway rates. He confirmed, however, what Mr. Wallace told me that a year or two ago mealies had actually been thrown away by the roadside because it would neither pay to drag them on or to bring them back to the farm. In this respect things would be better now that the railway had reached Victoria. Of the fever he made light, saying he only got a little when he went on trek in the veld. Generally it resulted from stupidity and neglect of ordinary sanitary precautions and mosquito nets. I gathered that he saw no sign of any great immediate prosperity for agricultural Rhodesia.

Mr. Williams also gave me some interesting information about the native mummies mentioned by Mr. Drew. He says that a tribe called the Duma, which is scattered among other tribes, follow, or till recently followed, this practice in the case of their chiefs. A man called Malindi, which is an hereditary title, descending through all his kin, alone carries out these dessicating operations, just as happened in Egypt in the case of the professional embalmers (*vide* Herodotus).[48] Mr. Williams (who stated he was only allowed to see the mummies after the performance of religious ceremonies and the raising of many difficulties, and could never have done so at all but for his official position) promised to collect more information on the point and let me have it in writing.

I cannot refrain from attempting a short description of another sunset which I saw as we returned from Zimbabwe. As soon as the red hot ball of the sun went down great, fan-like rays of light shot upwards across the western heavens. Then came a glorious glow in which presently appeared a single star hanging like a celestial lamp. A few minutes later the full moon appeared above the crest of the Zimbabwe hills illumining all the wild veld, which it seemed to plate with silver. To complete the splendid picture, far away to the north some black and ominous clouds became alive with the vast and slow pulsations of intermittent lightning.

Our chauffeur brought us home at an alarming rate over that very elementary road in spite of all remonstrations. While I wondered if he feared either lions or anopheles mosquitoes the true reason became obvious – his lamps were out of order. Our last two miles over the bush-veld without any road at all, which we had to cross to reach the special train that could approach no nearer to Victoria on that unfinished line, were quite an interesting experience in locomotion. Once we got wrong but steering by the lights in the carriages finally fetched up without falling into a donga or other disaster. This is the second time that I have found myself in an unlighted motor on the veld within the last six weeks. Lamps, or rather the cleaning of them, seem to be beneath the notice of the average white chauffeur. It is fortunate that I vetoed a suggestion that we should wait *at* Zimbabwe to see the moon rise over the ruins.

Sunday, 12 April

This morning (Easter Sunday), after an appalling hot night, we started for Bulawayo, the train arriving at Umvuma, where as I have said there is a mine chimney set upon a hill that would do credit to Birmingham, but (I was told) no church, about 1 o'clock. Thence we proceeded to Gwelo, which we reached in time to have a walk before dark. It is a quaint little town with a few nice houses, which suggest that there must be a mine in the neighbourhood, a public park and a monument to those who fell in that neighbourhood during the Matabele Rebellion of 1896, or were massacred, perhaps 50 names in all. Most of them were massacred. It is terrible to think of those poor men, cut off in lonely places and put to the assegai, some of them after a desperate and unavailing resistance and some of them in their sleep. Such, but too often, has been the fate of British 'pioneers' in savage wilds and, after all, it must be remembered that there is something to be said for the Matabele whose country had been taken from them. Well, by conquest they took and by conquest it was taken from them, since it has been decreed that this world and its dominion is to the strong man armed. Conquest, conquest, conquest! that is history, especially in the blood-stained land of Africa. Perhaps one day their turn will come again, either with steel and bullet, or more probably by mere weight of numbers and the ballot box.

At Gwelo we spent the first half of another baking night since the threatening storm refused to burst, made more restless by the continual shunting of our carriages. At last about 1 o'clock in the morning we departed.

Monday, 13 April

We reached Bulawayo at 6.30 in the morning. Here practically ended my Rhodesian tour. In the course of it I have covered a good deal of ground and managed to talk with many representative people. What are my impressions of the country which I came forth for to see? The first is that of its vastness. In every direction it seems to stretch on for ever. The second is its semi-tropical nature, for even now in the autumn the heat is great. Is it a white man's land? In parts yes, or so I suppose. In other and larger parts I should be inclined to answer 'no'. At any rate I should not wish to take the responsibility of trying to bring up a family in them. Nor, with all South Africa to choose from, would I select Rhodesia as a dwelling-place. It is very far away and has no ports of its own. Its rainfall is most uncertain in many parts, some think, decreasing. The land is certainly no better than in sundry other sections of South Africa, indeed on the whole I think it worse. For that portion of it which is rich almost as high a price is asked as in Natal, or say on the flat and accessible coast near East London. Living is very expensive, so are building and house rents. Much of the food consumed is, and for a long while is likely to continue to be, imported. The towns are as yet undrained and fever and typhoid are still prevalent. Some of these disabilities will lessen or vanish with time, but meanwhile Rhodesia is in competition with other lands where either they do not exist or are present in a much modified degree. A great population might cure many of them but even if this were available and prepared to settle here, it is essentially a country for the man with capital who is a *rara avis* [Latin: rare bird].

My own idea is that the agricultural future of Rhodesia lies in the direction of cattle ranching conducted on a large scale by companies or individuals, combined in certain districts, with the growing of maize. Great discoveries of gold mines might change all this and perhaps will do so, but up to the present I imagine that more precious metal has gone into the ground in Rhodesia than has been taken out of it in profit – that is in our time. With all its drawbacks it is a country of great charm and one that I am very glad to have visited. Good luck to it and to its plucky and English-hearted inhabitants. Still, I misdoubt me of that good luck, why I cannot say, but I think that not yet will kind Fortune set her crown on Rhodesia's sun-scorched brow.

Tuesday, 14 April

Yesterday afternoon we ran into a terrible thunderstorm, such as I have not seen for many years, that no doubt marked the culmination of the long-continued heat. The lightning was of the true African type, jagged and savage, like to the tongues of fiery serpents. In the end there came two fearsome flashes, followed instantly by ear-splitting crashes of thunder. The first of these flashes struck a tree within 20 feet of our coach. Mr. Pearce and the head steward both saw the tree fall and *vanish* in a cloud of dust, caused no doubt by the lightning striking the dry earth around its roots. A near thing! During this storm I saw a good example of how the water runs off the baked veld after a long drought. It did not sink in, it lay there to the depth of an inch or more like fluid on a dish and rushed away by every possible channel in a foaming torrent.

The sunset that followed was very magnificent but of a different type to those I have described. In the west appeared a double rainbow passing in and out of the sullen clouds like gorgeous braids through blackest cloth. In the east the sun sank, a furious eye of fire. Where it had been was seen a lake of pale green light, while above the black heavens were lined and splotched with blood-red masses of glory indescribable.

At the stations on our route Bechuanans appeared with native goods for sale, wire bracelets, copper-bound fly-whisks and sticks, effigies of game fashioned in wood and adorned with poker-work, karosses, etc. All are very cleverly made and those who fashion them might, I imagine, be trained to considerable proficiency in art.

Notes

1. 'Some years ago before . . . my brother Alfred conceived the plan of obtaining some great concession of land and minerals from Lobengula. He was, I recollect, angry with me because I would not enter into his scheme with enthusiasm, and I think has never quite forgiven me my backwardness. But I knew a good deal about the Matabele; also I held that Lobengula would never grant him what he wanted unless it was wrung from him by force of arms. Indeed I am convinced to this day that no one except Cecil Rhodes, with his vast command of money, could have dispossessed this tyrant and annexed those great territories.' H.R. Haggard, *The Days*, Vol. 2, p. 115. See also Manthorpe, *Children of the Empire*, pp. 158–62 and Robert I. Rotberg, *The Founder: Cecil Rhodes and the Pursuit of Power*, Oxford, 1988, p. 277.
2. Mafeking, corrupted form of Mafikeng (to which it has now reverted), originally a homestead of the Barolong people who gave it the name meaning 'among the stones'. It came under European settlement in 1884. Until 1961 it was the administrative capital of the Bechuanaland Protectorate, the only capital in the world outside the country it governed.
3. Lobatse, established by the British South Africa Company in the early twentieth century. Its name comes from Tswana word meaning 'lumps of wood', referring to hills in the area.
4. David Livingstone (1813–73), explorer and missionary.
5. Bechuanaland Protectorate. To prevent the Transvaal linking up with German South-West Africa, the British annexed this territory occupied by Tswana and Sotho-speaking peoples in 1885 as a Crown colony. The region south of the Molopo was incorporated into the Cape Colony in 1895, thereafter becoming part of the Union of South Africa. The area north of

the Molopo, the Bechuanaland Protectorate, remained a High Commission territory until it gained independence as Botswana in 1966.

Mahalapye, a village. Its name is thought to be Twsana in origin and to refer to impala.

6. There are several varieties of anopheline mosquito that transmit malaria. In its most severe forms this disease can damage the brain (cerebral malaria) or the kidneys (blackwater fever). According to Harding 'a good many of the original party on the *Kinfauns* – having planned to go up to the Victoria Falls (had) forgone the trip through fear of malaria.' Constantine, *Dominions Diary*, p. 232.

7. Bulawayo, capital of Matabeleland, second largest city in Southern Rhodesia (now Zimbabwe) built on the site of Lobengula's royal homestead. The name means 'place of slaughter' and commemorates a battle fought by Lobengula to assert his right to be king of the Ndebele.

8. The 6.50 p.m. mail train from Pretoria to Durban ran in two parts on 3 April 1914. According to a statement issued by the railway authorities and published in the *Pretoria News* of 4 April, the 'second train, containing the second- and third-class passengers, was run into at Kraal Siding by a goods train. Next to the engine was the Volksrust coach, and this was followed by the Pretoria coach. These were telescoped and three children were unfortunately killed while several passengers were injured.' Louie and Lilias boarded the separate, first part of the train at Johannesburg.

9. Frank Warren Inskipp, Chartered Company (British South Africa Company) manager.

10. St John's cathedral, Bulawayo, in the Anglican diocese of Matabeleland, is a fine stone building of reddish hue and exceedingly narrow width. The congregation was founded in 1898 but the cathedral was only built in 1913.

11. The main trunk of the 'Indaba Tree' is housed in Bulawayo Natural History Museum and is about 4 m (13 ft) high. Its species is given as *Pappae capensis/Isoqoqwane/Chitununu*. The exhibit has the following annotation: 'This is the main trunk of the tree under which Lobengula conducted business during his occupation of the Royal Palace (*esigolweni sako Bulawayo*) on the site now occupied by the State House. The tree collapsed during a rainstorm in February 1984 when it was over 200 years old. A new generation of saplings has sprung up from its roots and are also protected by Natural Museums and Monuments of Zimbabwe.'

12. Lobengula (*c.*1830–94), son of Mzilikazi and king of the Ndebele. The deaths of Haggard's friends, Captain Robert Patterson and John Sargeaunt, is the only known case when whites came to harm. It is thought Lobengula felt threatened by Patterson's mention of the 1872 invasion by supporters of Nkulumane, another son of Mzilikazi and potential heir. See Haggard's account of the incident 'The Patterson Embassy to Lobengula' in Wills and Collingridge, *Downfall of Lobengula*, 1971, p. 227. Haggard joined William Wills as a partner in publishing *The African Review* and other business ventures. See Introduction p. 17. See also Tim Couzens, *A Tale of Two Mysteries: The Patterson Embassy to King Lobengula*, Vol. 2, No.1, Johannesburg, 1995, p. 33.

13. *Indunas*, headmen, chiefs.

14.   Allan Wilson (1856–93). During the 1893 Ndebele War a small force com-
      manded by Major Allan Wilson in pursuit of King Lobengula was sur-
      rounded by the Ndebele and destroyed. Two troopers of the Bechuanaland
      Border Police, James Wilson and William Charles Daniel, were later con-
      victed of the theft of the gold and sentenced to 14 years hard labour. Two
      years later the conviction against Wilson was set aside. Daniel served only
      three months, an appeal court finding the evidence against him insuffi-
      cient.

15.   Mrs Olive's husband was William Olive, previously a South African govern-
      ment service accountant who later became accountant to the Bechuana-
      land Railway Company. The Hodder and Stoughton competition was won
      by Horace Rose (1876–1965) with his book *Golden Glory* (London, 1915).
      Rose was editor of the *Natal Witness* 1904–25.

16.   Gwelo, founded as a camp in 1894 and used as a camp for settlers during
      the Ndebele Rebellion of 1896.

17.   Matopos and Rhodes's grave see p. 148 and Note 19.

18.   Thomas Barker Haggard (1874–1925), the son of Haggard's brother Bazett
      (1847–99) who married Julia Barker (1853–?). Thomas married Hag-
      gard's eldest daughter, Angela, in 1907.

19.   Matopos, an 80-km (50-mile) range of granite hills with striking bare
      granite domes. The name derives from the Ndebele king, Mzilikazi, who
      described the hills as looking like an assembly of the elders of the people
      and called them *the amaTobos*, – 'the bald heads'. This was corrupted by
      Europeans to Matopos. See Terence Ranger, *Voices from the Rocks: Na-
      ture, Culture and History in the Matopos Hills of Zimbabwe*, Oxford, 1999.
          During the Ndebele Rebellion of 1896 military operations proved diffi-
      cult and so Rhodes adopted a diplomatic approach to bring about an end to
      the fighting. He camped in the hills among the Ndebele and held a series of
      four *indabas* that led to peace. Rhodes bought a large estate at the edge of
      the hills and is buried in the Matopos on the hill Malindidzimu (renamed
      World's View) at an elevation of 1 400 m (4 500 ft).
          Sir Leander Starr Jameson and Sir Charles Coghlan (first Prime Minis-
      ter of [Southern] Rhodesia) are buried nearby, as are Major Allan Wilson
      and the men of the Shangani Patrol.

20.   Alfred Beit (1853–1906), mining magnate and associate of Cecil Rhodes.

21.   Sir William Henry Milton (1854–1930), South African civil servant, be-
      came private secretary to Cecil Rhodes in 1891 who was then Prime Min-
      ister of the Cape Colony. He was transferred to Southern Rhodesia in
      1896; appointed Administrator of Southern Rhodesia in 1901; and retired
      in 1914.

22.   A.J.C. Molyneux, staff officer in 1893 war against Lobengula, founded the
      Rhodesia Scientific Association; author of papers on geology and geo-
      graphy of Rhodesia. He was a trustee of the Rhodesian Museum in
      Bulawayo and curator at the time of Haggard's visit.
          Walter Scudamore was from Norfolk and a friend of the Haggard
      family.

23.   David Randall-MacIver (1873–1945), the first trained archaeologist to
      excavate at Great Zimbabwe in 1905. He published his results in *Mediaeval
      Rhodesia* (London, 1906), concluding that the ruins were of purely

African origin and were constructed after 1300 AD. While fellow professionals accepted his findings, the settler community was outraged. See Peter Garlake, *Great Zimbabwe*, London, 1972. Haggard's musings on the origins of Great Zimbabwe during the course of this chapter are romantic but wrong.

24. Robert Alexander Fletcher, farmer and politician, campaigner for responsible government and president of the Rhodesian Agricultural Union. 'A forceful but wayward man he later resigned from the association.' See L.H. Gann, *A History of Southern Rhodesia: Early Days to 1934*, London, 1965.

25. Haggard has confused Patrick William Forbes (1861–1923) with Gordon Forbes, who was elected to the Legislative Council, along with Robert Alexander Fletcher, in 1908. Patrick William Forbes, 'the distinguished leader of irregular troops' during the Ndebele War, commanded the Salisbury Column through two major battles and the occupation of Bulawayo. He then led a column in pursuit of Lobengula. He returned to England in 1902.

26. Khami Ruins, 20 km (12 miles) west of Bulawayo, a complex of 10 distinct ruins spread over a large area dated to the seventeenth century. The main structure, known as the Hill Ruin, stands on a hill surrounded by tiered retaining walls.

27. Salisbury, now Harare, capital city of Zimbabwe, was founded by the Pioneer Column in 1890 and named after Lord Salisbury, British Prime Minister at the time. The current name is derived from Neharare, a chief said to be buried on Neharare Chikomo, the hillock of Neharare.

28. This was possibly the Egyptologist Walter B. Emery, who claimed his interest in Egypt was inspired by reading Haggard's adventure stories at the age of 13. See Shirley M. Addy, *Rider Haggard and Egypt*, Lancashire, 1998, p. 134 and H. Rider Haggard, *Cleopatra*, London, 1889.

29. Hunter's Road, route favoured for years by European hunters, traders and travellers and the name subsequently given to the village where the route crossed the road and railway between Bulawayo and Salisbury.

30. The Globe and Phoenix Mine, third largest gold mine in the country, near the town of Que Que, now Kwekwe.

31. Arthur Herbert Holland, South African civil servant transferred to Rhodesian Civil Service in 1897. Appointed private secretary to Sir William Milton in 1900.

32. Tsetse fly, blood-feeding insect (genus *Glossina*), several varieties of which transmit trypanosome parasites that cause the disease trypanosomiasis in animals and humans popularly known as sleeping sickness.

33. Mazoe, corruption of Mazowe, meaning 'place of the elephants' and now called Mazowe. The centre of the valley is bordered by the Iron Mask range.

34. During the rebellion a number of settlers were cut off at the Alice mine, 43 km (27 miles) from Salisbury. They made their escape in a wagonette covered with sheets of iron. The two men who sent the message were John Lionel Blakiston and T.C. Routledge. Captain Randolph Crosby Nesbitt was awarded the Victoria Cross for his role in the rescue.

35. Victoria, district of which Victoria is the main centre and named in honour of Queen Victoria by the Pioneer Column. Victoria is the oldest European settlement in Zimbabwe. It is now called Masvingo.

36. Lalapanzi, village on the branch line from Gwelo to Victoria. The name

derives from *lala* (lying) and *panzi* (down). There was once a marsh in the area where the oxen drawing wagons sank down to their bellies and looked as if they were lying down.

37. Umvuma, established in 1902, town on the branch line from Gwelo to Victoria. It was expanded greatly from 1912–24 when the Falcon mine was operating, the largest copper mine in Rhodesia.

38. 'Natives name this place Makeru Zimbabwe', NRO, MC 32/51: 'Rough Diary', n.d.

39. Richard Nicklin Hall (1853–1914), lawyer, archaeologist and journalist, went to Southern Rhodesia in 1897. He was editor of the *Matabele Times and Mining Journal* and *Rhodesian Journal*. He was engaged by Cecil Rhodes in 1900 to explore the Zimbabwe Ruins and was made Curator of Great Zimbabwe 1902–04. He was the author of *Ancient Ruins of Rhodesia* (with W.G. Neal, 1902) and *Great Zimbabwe* (1905). He was removed from his post by the administration which brought in Randall-MacIver to conduct proper excavations and who proved the ruins were of African origin. This led to angry debate with Hall who published his rebuttal of Randall-MacIver in *Prehistoric Rhodesia* (1909). The settler community took the side of Hall and it is presumably due to pressure from that quarter that he was reappointed site curator. In the original typescript is pencilled: 'Mr Hall died about a month ago H.R.H. 23/1/15'. Hall died on 18 November 1914.

40. Quotes taken from *Guide to Great Zimbabwe*, Bulawayo (no dates). Similar observations by Richard Nicklin Hall are to be found in *Guide to Rhodesia for the use of Tourists and Settlers*, Salisbury, 1914, p. 287:

> Great Zimbabwe. Ruins are the remains of an old city, at various times the home of enormous populations. Over the region hangs a veil of the intensest mystery. Evidences point to Great Zimbabwe being the work of a pre-historic and long-forgotten people. Sir Rider Haggard, in *Allan Quartermain* (sic), *The Dawn* (sic) and in *King Solomon's Mines*, has woven over the Zimbabwe country the webs of most interesting and exciting romance; and Zimbabwe Hill provided the description of the residence of *She*, while the ruins in the valley are 'the dead city' in the same romance.

While visiting the ruins, Haggard took the opportunity to recite Andrew Lang's poem 'Zimbabwe' (from *New Collected Rhymes*, London, 1905) – 'a poem he once wrote at my request for a paper in which I was interested'. See H.R. Haggard, *The Days*. Vol. 1, p. 243. A photograph of Haggard reciting the poem can be found in Hedley A. Chilvers, *The Seven Wonders of Southern Africa*, Johannesburg, 1929, p. 316. The same work also credits the ruins as the inspiration for *She*.
These are the words of Andrew Lang's poem that moved Haggard to recitation:

> *Into the darkness whence they came,*
> *They passed, their country knoweth none,*
> *They and their gods without a name*

Partake the same oblivion.
Their work they did, their work is done,
Whose gold it may be, shone like fire
About the brows of Solomon,
And in the House of God's Desire.

Hence came the altar all of gold,
The hinges of the Holy Place,
The censer with the fragrance rolled
Skyward to seek Jehovah's face;
The golden Ark that did encase
The Law within Jerusalem,
The lilies and the rings to grace
The High Priest's robe and diadem.

The pestilence, the desert spear,
Salute them; they passed, with none to tell
The names of them who laboured here:
Stark walls and crumbling crucible,
Strait gates, and graves, and ruined well,
Abide, dumb monuments of old,
We know but that men fought and fell,
Like us, like us, for love of Gold.

41. 'Elissa' published in *Black Heart and White Heart and Other Stories,* London, 1900. The novella uses a fictional romance to support the theory that the Phoenicians built Great Zimbabwe. For the origins of *King Solomon's Mines* see Norman Etherington, 'South African Origins of Rider Haggard's Early Romances', *Notes and Queries,* October 1977; Couzens, *Tale of Two Mysteries* and Henry Rider Haggard, 'The Real King Solomon's Mines', *Cassell's Magazine,* June 1907.

42. J. Theodore Bent (1852–97), antiquarian and traveller invited by Cecil Rhodes to explore the Zimbabwe Ruins. He was the author of *Ruined Cities of Mashonaland* (London, 1892). Oddly Haggard does not mention by name Alexander Wilmot (1836–1923). Haggard wrote the introduction to Wilmot's *Monomatapa* (London, 1896). Wilmot was living in Cape Town at the time of Haggard's visit.

43. *Rural England* (London, 1902), Haggard's non-fiction work dealing with the state of British agriculture. See Introduction, p. 18 *et seq.*

44. The 'slave pits of Inyanga' were more probably used to house pigs and goats and not slaves. They are more correctly referred to as stone-lined pits and are a characteristic of the Eastern Highlands, especially within the Inyanga Ruins where thousands of such structures have been found. 'The pits are typically circular, with stone-lined floors about six metres in diameter, with stone walls two to three metres in height' – R. Kent Rasmussen, *Historical Dictionary of Rhodesia/Zimbabwe,* New Jersey and London, 1979, p. 314. Cecil Rhodes is said to have coined the term 'slave pits'.

45. At the climax of *King Solomon's Mines* the ancient witch-doctress Gagool a, 'wizened monkey-like figure', leads Allan Quatermain and his party to

the burial chamber of kings 'The Place of Death' and Solomon's treasure chamber. See H.R. Haggard, *King Solomon's Mines,* Oxford and New York, 1992,   p. 260 *et seq.*

46.   Kaffir orange, *Strychnos spinosa,* a member of the Strychnaceae family. A small tree or shrub that bears a fruit the size of an orange. Not a true citrus but the custard-like pulp is edible.

47.   Sir John Willoughby (1859–1918), soldier and financier who 'recklessly excavated the Zimbabwe Ruins' (Rasmussen, *Historical Dictionary,* p. 349) in 1891; served in 1893 Ndebele War and later served as military commander of the Jameson Raid (1895), subsequently spending 15 months in prison.

48.   The Duma, 'branch of the Karanga cluster of Shona, with unclear connections with the Rozvi. A belt of Duma communities has occupied the region between present Fort Victoria and Chipinga since at least the mid-nineteenth century.' Rasmussen, *Historical Dictionary,* p. 79.

   See Herodotus (Walter Blanco, tr.). *The Histories,* Book 2.86, New York, 1992, p. 99.

Chapter Seven

Four hundred miles through Zululand

ৡৡৡৡৡ

Haggard continued his tour with a much-anticipated trip to Zululand. Though the setting for several of his novels, this was his first visit. He had developed a regard and sympathy for the Zulu[1] – which is charac- terised in his novels and journalism. Haggard had wanted to make the trip in an ox-drawn wagonette, his mode of transport when travelling in the 1870s with Shepstone, but it had proved impossible to find such a vehicle. The major part of his travels through Zululand were made in an American-made Overland motor car. The five-strong party included his old servant Mazooku and the historian and former civil servant James Stuart. They covered 400 miles (644 km) in a week, many on roads little better than rough tracks.

Wednesday, 15 April

Last night was not so stifling and this morning we woke up in cool and refreshing air. I write this near to Zeerust – remarkable for a Dutch church of peculiar hideousness – where trees grow scattered singly on the round hillsides like hairs upon a negro's chin.[2] We are running an hour late owing to delay at Mafeking but shall, I hope, catch the Durban mail at Johannesburg. By the way, Sir W. Milton told me that it would have been easy for the Rhodesian forces to have relieved Mafeking at any time during the famous siege. This however, he said, was not allowed by the generals below; they knew that the town had sufficient food and was in little danger of capture and therefore left it to distract and weaken the Boer commandos. It was a part of our plan of campaign to do so.

Heavens! how this train shakes, owing I suppose to the iron sleepers used to avert the attack of white ants, and the narrow gauge. The adop- tion of a 3 foot 6 inch gauge throughout South Africa is now recognised to have been a fatal error. It means, in addition to other disadvantages,

PORTUGUESE
EAST
AFRICA

Transvaal

SWAZILAND

Pongola

Khambula

Newcastle

Ingome Forest

Nongoma

White Umfolozi

Ceza Mountain   Ivuna

Talana

Dundee

Glencoe

Nqutu

Mahlabatini

Black Umfolozi   Hlabisa

St Augustines

Isandhlwana

Italeni   Ulundi

Somkeli

Rorke's Drift   *Malagati Hills*

† Piet Retief's Grave

Ladysmith

Umgundundhlovu

Emakhosini

Umfolozi

Empandhleni
Mome Gorge

Melmoth

Umfule

Umbonambi

Colenso

Tugela

Inkandhla Forest

Umhlatuze

Eshowe

Richards Bay

Gingindhlovu

Amatikulu

Natal

Indian Ocean

Stanger

Pietermaritzburg

N

Phoenix

Pinetown

Marrianhil   **Durban**

Isipingo

KEY

▬ ▪ ▪ ▪ ▪	International boundaries
▬ ▪ ▬ ▪ ▬	Regional boundaries
▬▬▬	Rail
———	River and coast
●	Towns and villages
⤫	Battles
†	Grave
■	Places of interest

Cape

0	50	100

Kilometres

Cartographic Unit, University of Natal, Pietermaritzburg, 2000

that it will never be safe to run trains at speed, which implies loss of time and money.[3]

The train was held up for us at Jo'burg, so that I had just time to get into it and shut the cabin door as a crowd had collected outside staring at me as though I were a strange animal. Here I bade goodbye to Frank Robb and Pearce, both of whom had been very kind to me.[4]

Thursday, 16 April

I looked through the early-morning mists at Hilldrop amid its trees on the koppie's flank, I daresay for the last time. At Maritzburg, Mr. Stuart met me and we proceeded through a bad thunderstorm to Durban.[5] Four inches of rain fell in an hour or two so that the train had to crawl into Durban station through 18 inches of water. At the Marine Hotel I found Louie and Lilias well. They had a poor time at Eshowe on account of the persistent rain.

This morning I wrote a long letter to R.F. Morcom & Co. as to the Blomefield business.[6] In the afternoon Louie and I took the tram round Durban to see the Berea. Allan Quatermain would not know it again![7] The changes in the town are wonderful – many costly public buildings erected. I think the money would have been better spent on developing the already excellent port. As I told an interviewer in the evening, Durban harbour and the coalfields are to my mind the great assets left to Natal now that union has taken away her separate dignity and importance. Indeed they are her commercial life.

Friday, 17 April

Today Lilias, Dorothy Scudamore[8] and I were taken by Mr. Stuart to see a war dance at a place called Isipingo, about 15 miles from Durban. After we left the high road the motor stuck and had to be hauled back by oxen. We walked on but the weather was so hot and the place so far away that in the end, fearing that Lilias would be tired out, I suggested that the dance should come to us instead of our going to the dance. This was done and after a delightful picnic beneath a tree we went to a kraal where presently the dancers, male and female, arrived in all their finery. They made a good show considering their numbers, but the general effect was a little marred by the difficulty of persuading them to abandon their umbrellas to which they clung as their forefathers might have done to a favourite assegai. Umbrellas do not go well with shiny naked skins, beads, saccaboola plumes[9] and mottled oxhide shields. However, everything went off well and I made the young women a little present and a speech and we parted the best of friends. I was so sorry that Louie could not come but she was unwell that morning.

Bryan Hall

A page from Lilias Rider Haggard's photograph album. These photographs probably depict the dance at Isipingo.

Saturday, 18 April

This morning I bid farewell to dear L. and L. and departed for Zululand by an early train. They go on board the *Briton* tomorrow to sail for the Cape and England.[10] I feel somewhat sad at parting with them but please God we shall meet again in safety. The journey to Gingindhlovu, where Cetywayo had one of his kraals and there was a fight in the Zulu War, is hot and wearisome but the country through which we passed was very pretty.[11] Also it was enlivened by the conversation of Mr. Maydon, an ex-Minister for Railways in Natal and a most intelligent gentleman of great colonial experience.[12] He told me many incidents of the Boer war in which he served, every one of them sadder – and more discreditable to our generals in that unlucky business – than the last.

We passed a great deal of sugar cane both before and after crossing the Tugela. An average crop of cane here seems to be about 1° tons the acre, rising on certain estates to three tons. The Uba cane is the variety planted as that is said to be the only sort in this country that will ratoon well, i.e. throw up shoots from the root for succeeding crops. Its disadvantage is that it is very hard to crush. As yet the land is not manured as a rule but soon this must be done. South Africa, up to the present has not produced enough sugar for her own needs, when she grows a surplus she will come into competition with the other sugar-producing countries. This will be the test of the suitability of her somewhat patchy soil and erratic climate to sugar growing on a large scale. Meanwhile a good deal of money has been made out of the plantations, especially by those who have purchased the raw land for a song (payable in many verses, i.e. over a long term of years) from government, put it under crop and sold it for £6 or £7 the acre.

On our journey we passed several places of interest, among them a spot called Phoenix where lives the Rev. John Dube, a native clergyman of very progressive mind. I understand that he edits a paper and runs a school entirely at his own expense. I should much have liked to meet him though I am told he is looked on with suspicion by what I may call the ultra 'white' party.[13] Another historic spot is the long black ridge in the distance towards the coast. Here was fought the terrible battle of Indondakasuka in 1856 which I have tried to describe in *Child of Storm* when Cetywayo conquered his brother Umbelazi with great slaughter.[14] The battlefield seems to have stretched over an area of several miles and the awful flight to the flooded Tugela took place down a spur of the hill. Also I saw above the little town of Stanger where once stood the royal kraal, Duguza, the place marked by some trees where lie the bones of the mighty Chaka whose death at this very spot I have written of in *Nada the Lily*.[15] So little regard have the local inhabitants for his story that some while ago a shanty was actually about to be erected on the exact site of the grave. Luckily, however, this was stopped in time. We crossed the Tugela, a wide river, muddy and rushing after the recent rains, by the long iron bridge which is built above the old ford and travelled over rolling veld to the Amatikulu river in the neighbourhood of which much sugar cane is grown. Thence we came to Gingindhlovu, the site of another royal kraal, now a little settlement with an hotel at which we lunched on bread and cheese and beer. This done we motored on an excellent road past the place where one of the battles was fought in the Zulu War and Cetywayo had a kraal, of which a travelling native shewed us the site.

The country here and right up to the hot but beautifully situated town of Eshowe 16 miles away is really lovely, with many grass-clothed hills. At Eshowe after despatching a weekend cable to England detailing our movements I went up to the Residency where I was kindly received by my hosts, Mr. and Mrs. Gibson,[16] who are just settling themselves in the house and enduring many things at the hands of native servants. This place, which has large gardens planted with various trees, was built and laid out by my old friend Sir Melmoth Osborn, who lived in it for five years before his retirement. Afterwards another old friend, Sir Marshall Clarke, occupied it, subsequent to whom came Sir Charles Saunders and others I do not know.[17]

Both Osborn and Clarke are dead, so is Jack Osborn the son of the former who, for a while was once my ward. He, his sister, Mrs. Hignett (the wife of the magistrate here, tells me) breathed his last in this house, perhaps in this very bedroom in which I write. In truth it almost seems as though I felt them about me now. If so I hope they are aware of the true affection with which I am thinking of them.[18]

Stuart dined here that night and the arguments between him and Mr. Gibson on obscure points of Zulu history were prolonged and at times rather hot. Rival experts are always apt to grow fierce about their own subjects, especially when both have written books thereon.

Sunday, 19 April

Today I attended service twice in the neat little church of Eshowe. In the morning the office was taken by a lay reader and there was practically no congregation. In the evening the Bishop of Zululand (Vyvyan) officiated, assisted by the vicar and the place was crowded.[19] One young lady was confirmed all by herself, and the bishop preached on the local desecration of Sunday by the continual playing of golf, tennis, etc., which it seems has become almost a vice in South Africa, tacking into his dissertation a few remarks about the future state of man. It appears that he and I ate our dinners together at Lincoln's Inn, after which he became a bishop and I a writer and other things. I believe that he is a very able and energetic shepherd of his motley flock. At the station he has built he is doing his best to teach the Zulus agriculture – a good worker indeed.

I forgot to say that I found old Mazooku waiting for me here. When I woke up next morning there he was laying out my things just as he used to do nearly 40 years ago; indeed I caught him in the act of consigning my wretched false teeth to everlasting oblivion. These he did not know the use of or recognise! It was as though all the intervening years had faded away and we were young again.

Monday, 20 April

This morning Stuart and I walked through the heat to the kraal not far away that is (or was) called Jazi, which means, they told us, 'Finished', or 'Finished with joy'.[20] Two or three huts and in front of them a patch of kaffir corn. In the centre of this patch, whither I was led by a native who once inhabited Jazi, the corn grows weakly. Once there was a large hut here and in that hut at the very spot on which I stood to the left of the entrance died our old enemy (or friend?) Cetywayo, the last King of Zululand – poisoned. (I have Osborn's letter written to me just after he had viewed the body).[21] We tried to extract details of his end from one of the men who guided us who is named Umnikwa, but he would not speak of the matter freely, especially in the presence of Mazooku.[22] He said, however, that he thought the king was killed with strychnine and that he was ill three days – which suggests some native poison rather than strychnine; also that there was nothing in the tale of the water being doctored. Who did the deed? Dabuko his brother, who was with him when he died, or Usibepu his enemy, or one of his women, or some witch-doctor?[23] No one knows or will ever know (at least no one will tell, least of all that quiet, secret-faced native. He had become useless and was put out of the way – by someone). The rest is darkness. Well may that kraal have been named 'Finished' (because a chief named Umfokaki or 'Stranger' who married Cetywayo's sister, was killed here by his brother Gundane, which means 'The Rat'). The situation of this ruined kraal is very beautiful, commanding a fine view of many surrounding hills and of the wide plain stretching towards the sea. Once it numbered about 50 huts.

This afternoon I went to Mr. Gibson's office and inspected a large map of Zululand. So far as I could make out about two thirds of the country as I knew it in 1875 has since that date been appropriated by Boers and other white men. If this goes on what is to become of the poor Zulus. And what will happen if they are continually crowded together. I imagine that which happens to a thin glass bottle when compressed air or water is driven into it. Truly their case is sad and they have been ill-treated. First, an unnecessary war in which 10 000 were killed, then all the subsequent troubles. And now so I hear from Gibson and on every side, notably from Mr. Parkins the editor of a little local paper, degradation largely brought about by contact with whites. Many of these white men, he and others declare, live with native girls, whom and whose children afterwards they subsequently desert. Miscegenation is going on everywhere and the only education is that given by the mission schools which are, however, aided by government that gives a capitation grant. Frequently too the natives are badly treated by white men. Mazooku's story is a case in point.

This afternoon we drove in a motor round Eshowe. The country is beautiful especially towards the hills on which stands the township of Melmoth.[24]

Tuesday, 21 April

I wrote letters this morning. In the afternoon there was an excitement about snakes. The policeman working in this garden with convicts had killed two, a puff adder and another, and a great green mamba had taken refuge in an aloe-like tree.[25] We fired the dead leaves on this and another similar tree but did not find the mamba. However, another brown snake came out which Stuart (very rashly) jumped on and killed. The place swarms with these poisonous creatures.

After the snake hunt we went to the war dance which was attended by all the population of Eshowe and many natives. Perhaps 200 danced, men and women, but the thing, except for a girls' dance, had not the fire of that I saw nearly 40 years ago, which I described in *A Zulu War Dance*, the first thing I ever wrote.[26] The pervading umbrellas marked the change. Old things are dying out and new ones draw near. It is a tie of transition and therefore a bad time. Still I enjoyed the dance though the sun was terribly hot and the dresses, or in the case of the women, the lack of them, were appropriate and striking, as were the swelling chants and the advance and retreat of the lines of dancing men and women.[27]

Wednesday, 22 April

Today we departed on our tour. On our way to Gingindhlovu (where the thermometer stood at 104 in the shade yesterday and it was almost equally hot today) we stopped while Stuart took a photo of the graves of those who fell in the battle here during the Zulu War. The spot which is by the roadside is surrounded by long grass and looks rather desolate. On our way Gibson and Stuart gave me details of the strange disease called *Mandiki*, which was epidemic about 1886 and is believed still to be prevalent.[28] It appears to be of an hysterical character: the patient (generally a young woman) becomes rigid, hears voices, sees visions and can only be cured by one who has herself recovered from the sickness. I should like to know more of this. Apparently only natives are affected who believe themselves to be haunted by the spirit of an ancestor. I suppose that the kaffirs chose these very hot situations for their royal kraals because of their dread of the cold and above all of the frost upon the healthier high veld, which are formidable to a very lightly clothed people. At any rate they all seem to occupy low-lying unwholesome sites.

Departing with gratitude from the burning Gingindhlovu, whither Mazooku had walked forward at dawn, we travelled for the next five hours over the 80 miles between that place to Somkeli.[29] At first we ran by wooded sand dunes bordering the sea. Then about Umhlatuze came vast rather sandy plains, through which runs the river edged with dark-green bush.[30] In the bay here is a possible site for a harbour. I know not of what character.[31] On all these vast plains practically no cattle were visible and very few huts. The former have been swept away by the disease of recent years and the latter have followed them, or perhaps in some cases been turned off by the sugar planters. So it comes about that enormous acreages of excellent grazing stand useless, to be devoured presently by the grass fires. Only by journeying through the country can one understand how terrible were the ravages of pleuro-pneumonia and East Coast Fever[32] among its herds. These slew by the ten thousand, leaving but a pitiful remnant of horned beasts. Now that dipping has come into use, the stock are breeding up again but it will be years before they can stand at their old numbers. One of the results of this crushing misfortune has been the deprivation of the native children of milk, with the natural result of a largely increased infant mortality. Further on we reached the wide and placid Enseleni River, one of the finest I have seen, which pursues its winding course through a very pretty landscape. In the swamps here are many beds of the tall and graceful papyrus, just now in their full beauty. After passing Umbonambi, where Bishop Schreuder established one of the first missions in Zululand,[33] and a large vlei or lake, we came to the Umfolozi River, which pursues its course to the sea through vast untenanted plains.[34]

About half an hour after dark we arrived at Somkeli, the terminus of the line, and put up at an hotel of which I may say that it was the dirtiest in which I ever slept.[35] I am glad that I did not examine the bed until searching for something on the following morning. However it had a tattered mosquito curtain, which I mended to the best of my ability with safety pins, toothpicks and matches, to keep out the dreaded anopheles mosquitoes.

Here we found our motor waiting for us, driven oddly enough by a young fellow of the name of Edwards, the grandson of old Marsdon, the miller at Bungay [Suffolk] where he was born. He is a nice young man and seems to be getting on well in South Africa.[36]

Thursday, 23 April

About 9 o'clock we packed ourselves (including Mazooku) and our belongings into the motor and started for Hlabisa, about 20 miles away. Our road ran through beautiful but unhealthy country where tsetse fly is so prevalent that it is difficult to keep cattle. It has occurred to someone in authority to cut down the beautiful thorn trees on either side of the road, the suggestion being that the tsetse sits on these and pounces upon the oxen and horses that pass beneath. Whether it is founded on fact remains to be seen but meanwhile the trees are gone and the road is disfigured. The truth is that there is much big game in this neighbourhood and where game is in low country there is tsetse fly. The local superstition is that it accompanies certain species, I believe that koodoo [kudu] and buffalo are supposed to be the principal sinners, but this is probably apocryphal.

On our way we ran over a puff adder which was stretched out sunning itself on the road. Unfortunately the wheel only went over its tail, for looking round I saw it painfully wriggling itself into the scrub. We stopped and went to look for it, but the bush was too thick to attempt this with safety, so we left the horrid reptile, which I trust died. Certain snakes, especially puff adders, have this dangerous habit of lying upon paths for warmth, particularly just after sundown when they are most difficult to see. I asked Mazooku if he would like to learn to drive a motor. 'Ka' (no) he answered, 'too many weeds have grown up in my brain, Inkosi,' by which, of course, he meant that he was becoming old and stupid.[37]

We reached Hlabisa about midday, where we were received by Mr. Harrington, the magistrate.[38] In his office hung a map of the district from which I made out that in it 600 000-odd acres are what are called Crown lands, i.e. occupied, or to be occupied, by white men, while 334 000 acres are native reserve. The white population, I was told, is about 100, and the native population about 16 000, yet the whites are supposed to require twice as much land as the natives! This is typical of what is going on all over South Africa. The low-lying lands on which sugar will grow is valued at about £4 the acre and the top lands at about 10s. the acre. Mr. Harrington says that fever is bad in all this district.

At the *indaba* here were gathered about 50 chiefs and headmen come together to greet Mr. Gibson.[39] They were a wonderfully fine-looking set of Zulus of all shades of colour, from jet black to light yellow. Indeed one chief of high blood, whose name, I think is Untangweni is of the hue of copper mixed with tin and his daughters I am informed are almost white.[40] Yet they have none of our blood in them, being of pure Zulu descent. The family throws back to some remote Arab ancestor, that is all. Not everyone of them however, from his brother, who sits beside him in the simplicity of a moocha and a necklace, is of the colour of coal. Near to these two squats a man whose skin is almost grey and there are others of intermediate shades. If we could see their progenitors of thousands or tens of thousands of years ago we might understand these variations. Doubtless, like our own their blood is very mixed. This Untangweni, for instance, might be and possibly is descended in a direct line from those fair-haired, red-skinned proto-Egyptians whose dessicated bodies have been discovered lately lying under slabs of stone upon the banks of Nile.

Mr. Gibson, who on appearing has been greeted with the royal salute of *Bayete*, given to him as the representative of the king, takes his seat and the *indaba* begins.[41] Compliments are interchanged and then come the complaints. Untaminedwa and two others complain of the 'alteration of boundaries', i.e. of encroachments and the laying out of farms on their lands. Others complain of the spread of *nagani*, i.e. of the tsetse-fly sickness,[42] others of the new land law which prevents them from living on farms unless they pay rent in labour, others that they may not kill the game as the white man does. But there is nothing rude or clamorous about this, all is done decently and in quiet; the chiefs speaking in order of seniority and never interrupting each other. Here is a sample of the talk.

> *A chief*: 'We have long made representations but we get no redress. Why does not the government help us? Our cattle will be swept off.'

Another (who wears a necklace of leopard claws): 'We are always making complaints without result. We black people are forced to eat the soil.'

Another: 'We have to pay taxes with cattle, yet we lose them through sickness because you will not protect us. If we could, we would bring a law-suit against the Bucks. You defeated us but you are not ruling as you should do.'

Another (gracefully draped in what looks like a bath-towel): 'Bucks do not pay taxes; we submit, Lord, that you are not governing as rightly, The waterbuck, koodoo and zebras are eating our crops. We die as we make our plaint!'

Another: 'What is the use of dipping cattle when the game remains undipped?'

Another: 'We are rejoiced to see you, Father, but we can assure you that our grievances are countless.'

To all of which Mr. Gibson replies most sympathetically, his remarks being punctuated with exclamations of respectful assent. So, in the end, after he has promised to represent their troubles in the proper quarter, whatever that may be, the meeting breaks up, apparently in a very good humour and we depart amidst a volley of salutes.

We lunched at a little store, of which – to judge by the number about on shelves – the owner, who gave me a fine iguana skin,[43] is a great reader of novels. Indeed these were everywhere, notably on a deal shelf over his bed on which stood two ends of candle. 'One must do something in a place like this,' he explained to me with a rather melancholy smile. Indeed the lot of a cultured man in the wilds of Zululand must have its distressing side, especially if he be but a little kaffir trader. After lunch we motored a good many miles to another store kept by an old inhabitant of Zululand of the name of Dore,[44] where, while I drank tea, I occupied myself in correcting an infamously printed extract from one of my books, which was pointed out to me in a collection of snippets from English writers, done in many volumes.

Here more chiefs and headmen were waiting to see the commissioner. One of these, a rather small man named Funwayo, performed a great if not an unequalled feat not long ago by killing two lions with two successive stabs of the assegai. The first lion he saw lying in the grass and threw an assegai at it which reached the heart. Then another charged him and this he met upon the point of his second assegai, killing it outright. He spoke of the adventure in a most modest way. A day or two later at Mahlabitini, the magistrate, Mr. Graham, shewed me the skull of a leopard which a native there had also killed with an assegai.[45] Its mate he engaged and despatched immediately afterwards with a kerrie. Certainly these Zulus are brave men.

Leaving Mr. Dore's place we travelled on over a bad road, very steep in places and always running uphill, to Nongoma, 20 miles away. As we went we saw that a great thunderstorm was in progress both to our right and behind us where it poured. Fortunately we only came in for the tail of it both as regards rain and lightning for which we were thankful. It is not pleasant to travel in a motor through the heart of such a tempest over these vast treeless hillsides where the vehicle, with all its ironwork, becomes a mark for the flashes to aim at. I remember Sir Melmoth Osborn telling me that he was riding just behind a wagon full of Boers under such circumstances. There came a blaze of lightning and it stopped. He went up to it and found that of those who had crowded beneath the tent to shelter from the rain seven were dead!

At length, thoroughly tired, we reached Nongoma on its healthy hilltops.[46] Here, about 2 500 feet above the sea, the climate is indeed different from that of the hot and fever-stricken Somkeli, and indeed of Gingindhlovu, both of which are little removed from ocean level. Thus whereas on the previous day the thermometer at the latter place as I have said stood at about 100F, here at Nongoma, when I rose next morning, it only marked one half that total, viz: 50F. It is these tremendous variations in temperature that makes travelling in Zululand and some other parts of South Africa so trying and dangerous. One day you gasp and sweat in shirtsleeves, the next, especially after a storm, you must pile on wool waistcoats and cloaks or, if these are lacking, be prepared for evil consequences.

At Nongoma we put up at a store (combined with a kind of hotel as is common in these parts) kept by Mr. Adams, a very clean and comfortable place. Mr. Adams's late father, who also was a storekeeper and a much-respected man, accompanied Livingstone on some of his expeditions.[47] His son told me two stories which he had from him. One day in Panda's [Mpande] time, he passed the Nonela rock on the White Umfolozi River which was a favourite place of execution under the Zulu kings. Here he was horrified to see two young women, daughters of Panda he was informed, whose eyes had been gouged out, dragged to the top of the cliff and thrown living to the crocodiles in the pool below. Their offence was either witchcraft or some moral slip. I wonder if they were really Panda's daughters. If so, remembering his kindly nature, I think that this barbarous act must have been the work of Cetywayo, his son. It was Cetywayo who, after the battle of Indondakasuka, caused the beautiful Nomantshali, the favourite wife of his father Panda, to be dragged out and killed with her son before her husband's eyes, if I remember right on a charge of witchcraft.[48] Old Mr. Adams's second story was that he climbed a certain very sharp pointed hill (which I saw next day) and found Zulu smiths at work there who fled at his approach. By the primitive furnace were two large pots which he had the curiosity to examine. They were full of human bones and flesh which were being used in the smelting of the iron. Whether this was because the ingredients of man's body were supposed to give a better temper to the blades of assegais, or for magical reasons, remains obscure. I have however since been informed that dipping them in human blood was supposed to improve the steel.

Next morning on our way to the *indaba* at the courthouse, Mr. Gibson who, years ago, was magistrate here, shewed me the site of the battle between Dinizulu, Cetywayo's son who died a year or two ago, and Usibepu. It took place on the slopes of the hill called Undunu, on which grows much low bush, that is opposite to Nongoma, but separated from it by a broad gulley and a swamp.[49] Usibepu had only five or six hundred men, Dinizulu quite 4 000 so the issue may be guessed. Dinizulu's *impi* as usual threw out wings or horns wrapping Usibepu round. For a while the fighting was fierce, then the overpowered Usibepu fled leaving sone 200 dead upon the field. When Mr. Gibson came to the magistracy the place was still white with skeletons, of which some doubtless still lie in the bush.

Sir Rider Haggard.

MR. GIBSON INTERVIEWING CHIEF MPIKANINA AND OTHER CHIEFS, WITH THEIR FOLLOWERS, AT NONGOURA MAGISTRACY, SIR. RIDER HAGGARD, CAPTAIN MATRAVERS, AND MR. TRITTON BEING ALSO PRESENT.

Bodleian Library, University of Oxford

'Mr. Gibson interviewing Chief Mpikanina and other chiefs with their followers at Nongoura [Nongoma] magistracy, Sir. Rider Haggard, Captain Matravers, and Mr. Tritton being also present.' (Windsor Magazine)

Left to right: *Tritton, Matravers, Gibson, Haggard and uMpikanina. Edgerton Isaac Tritton was a clerk of the court at Ndedwe.*

From the courthouse, which we reached after inspecting the site of the British fort that was under the command of the late Jack Osborn who once was my ward, the view is very fine. In the distance appears a remarkable square-topped mountain called *The Seat of King*s in its Zulu name. On another mountain about 20 miles away to the west, or rather on its crest and further slope is the beautiful Ingomi Forest where Cetywayo was finally ran down and caught after the Zulu War.[50] Nearby it is the famous Ceza stronghold, which I could see is a flat plain on a hilltop surrounded by a belt of almost impassable bush.[51] It was from this natural forest that Dinizulu made his long night march to attack Usibepu. To the far north appears the distant ranges of Swaziland and away on the south bank of the Pongola the needle-pointed mountain Uva (or is it called Magundu?), where Nongalazi, Panda's general, defeated King Dingaan.[52] The Boers claim a share in this victory but as a fact they were 60 miles away from the place of battle. Then there is the ridge of Xedeni, which we passed on the road from Hlabisa, where once dwelt Panda's brother Unzibe.[53] To his spirit (after his death) Panda married a wife or wives.[54] Of this mysterious union was born the great chief Uhamu or Oham, who was a notable figure in my early days in South Africa.[55] I remember that it was said of him that he wished to become a Christian but refused to do so when he was told that he must put away all his wives save one: 'How can I turn off those who have been the companions of my life?' he queried. It would have been interesting to hear from him his own views of his supernatural parentage. Perhaps Panda himself was the father. At any rate the story shews what strange beliefs the Zulus hold of things beyond those tangible on the earth, although they are supposed by ignorant persons to have 'no religion'.

Another instance of this is their curious faith that the spirit of an ancestor can be 'moved'. Thus the spirit of Chaka was formally 'moved' from Stanger where he was murdered, where to I do not remember. Mr. Gibson told me also that a man driving a cow once applied to him in the most matter of fact way for a pass that he might go to some distant place 'to move his father's spirit'. What part was played in the ceremony by the cow I do not know but probably it was sacrificed.[56]

At the Nongoma *indaba* I made the acquaintance of Umpikanina, a grandson of Panda and son of Ziwedu, Cetywayo's brother.[57] He is a fine-looking man, very like the rest of his royal race. He sat in front of all the other chiefs by virtue of his rank and was clothed in a military helmet and mackintosh cloak. He wore no ring upon his head, either because he was not old enough or because it would get in the way of the helmet.[58] Some of the chiefs present had fine faces and the attire of one young man who wore a leopard skin band or turban on his head, of which the ends hung down upon his breast, was very striking. Here there was not so much complaint about the depredations of big game, but more of the taking away of ancestral lands. Said one old chief: 'If you can exercise any power as to these lands which have been given away to the white men, you would indeed be ruling us for our good.' From one of these chiefs I purchased the most beautiful and curiously cut kerrie that I have ever seen. It is made of red ivory wood,[59] bound about at intervals with copper wire.

After the *indaba* we bade farewell to the officials, Lt. Matravers and others, in weather so cold that the natives were shivering, and started cheerfully for Mahlabatini 30 miles away. (If we had known the kind of road that lay before us we should have been less lighthearted!) Shortly after leaving Nongoma we passed the spot where Dingiswayo the Wanderer, who befriended Chaka, was killed (some say by his own request) after he was taken prisoner by Zweeti.[60] Then we travelled downhill to the Imbekamuzi (which means 'Watch the Kraal') valley that is I suppose one of the most unhealthy in all Zululand.[61] Also it is full of big game and tsetse flies. So deadly is this place to natives who settled here and planted crops they have been known to go away and leave them unreaped because they found that most of them were dying of fever. Along all those miles of dreadful road, if road it could be called, we met no one and saw no sign of man, while the track itself was often quite hidden by a growth of tall grass – so little is it used. The bush here also is the densest I have seen in Zululand, in places it reminded me of that of New Zealand. Yet that silent sleeping valley shimmering with hot air surrounded by tall hills and to all appearance lifeless (since at this time of day the great antelopes lie hidden) has a wonderful beauty of its own. It is a death-like beauty however. Had I not been told it, I should have known that this place was fatal to man. No wonder that the Zulus declare that it is haunted. Through the deep sand we struggled – and over the muddy spruits and dongas which had any rain fallen would have been utterly impassable, till presently by one of the worst we found what I least expected to see in such a spot, a Ford motor car, broken-axled and abandoned. It seems that it has been there for weeks and there I should imagine it is likely to remain.

At length we lurched and wallowed out of the place onto higher and healthier ground where it was no longer necessary to watch one's hands lest they should be bitten by tsetse or poisonous mosquitoes. But now we came into other troubles. On this side of Mahlabatini is a most fearsome hill on which presently we stuck. We got out and pushed till our hearts nearly burst; we took off and carried the luggage, we did everything that men could do, but it was no use. So steep was the track that the petrol could not get to the engine. Finally after over an hour of it, with the help of some native boys, foot by foot we did get the car up *backwards,* propping it with stone every few yards to prevent it running down again. After this our path was by comparison easy and, to our great gratitude, the motor, which was strained, crawled up to Mahlabatini before dark.[62]

This place where we slept at a store not too well supplied with eatables, stands high and was very cold. It is a beautiful situation but has no water, except what is collected from the roofs of the three or four dwellings that constitute the 'township'. We dined that night with Mr. Graham, the magistrate, and his wife, a large and most grateful wood fire burning on the hearth. Amongst other things he told me that the country round was full of game and that there was said to be a white rhinoceros in the neighbourhood, one of the survivors of a species that is almost extinct.[63]

Saturday, 25 April

We started fairly early on our longest day's journey, I leaving a telegram of farewell to be sent to L. at Cape Town, who was sailing that day by the *Briton* for home. I wonder if it ever reached her. An hour or so later we came to the battlefield of Ulundi on the left of the road, near to the Norwegian Mission Station, passing the spot where our friend and ally, King Panda, was buried. His grave was robbed by British soldiers and it is said that his skull is now at Netley Hospital. To my mind it was a shameful act, especially as the burying places of their kings are very sacred to the Zulus.[64]

Being doubtful as to the exact site of the battle we sent Mazooku to inquire at a neighbouring kraal. Presently he returned with an old Zulu named Simpofu, who by good luck had fought in it and was able to tell us everything.[65] He guided us across the flat, open veld to a spot where there is the remains of an earthen entrenchment thrown up by our troops. Here too is the little graveyard with 12 iron crosses which stand above those who fell in the fight. These crosses were, I believe, repaired and set straight a few years ago by some officer who chanced to be in Zululand. The place is surrounded by a ditch and wire fence. It is somewhat smothered with grass, amongst which still grow two geranium bushes, planted I know not when but probably shortly after the interment took place. Not far away is another spot of which the centre has sunk in. This may have been a gun platform, or more likely – from the hollow in its middle – those Zulus who fell near the entrenchment were here collected and thrown into a pit.

All about the square rusted bully beef tins and Martini cartridge cases still lie in numbers. Soon I collected a pocket full of these cartridges. The odd thing is that every one of them is flattened, I suppose by the trampling of cattle during the last five and thirty years. Standing by the graves, the old Zulu, Simpofu, who fought that day in the ranks of the Ingobamakosi Regiment,[66] shewed us all the plan of the battle which, for the Zulus, was from the first a most impossible adventure, seeing that they must advance over an open plain against an army behind an entrenchment and armed with breechloaders. What kind of courage

SIR RIDER HAGGARD, IN 1914, VISITING THE GRAVES OF SOLDIERS WHO FELL AT ULUNDI, NEAR WHITE UMFOLOSI RIVER, IN 1879.
The native in the foreground took part in that battle.

'Sir Rider Haggard, in 1914, visiting the graves of soldiers who fell at Ulundi,
near White Umfolosi River in 1879. The native in the foreground
took part in that battle.' (Windsor Magazine)

Simpofu in the foreground, Haggard on the right.

must these people possess that it enabled them to persist in the attack
until – well until they or many of them died. Simpofu told us that the
only Zulu wounded attended to were those who chanced to be found by
relatives who lived in the neighbourhood. The rest died where they
fell. How did they die? Imagine it! Many of them, however, lived through
wounds that would have killed Europeans. Thus Simpofu pointed to a
scar on his neck and another beneath the shoulder, the bullet having
travelled right through him. He received it at Kambula evidently fired
from above, yet he was able to travel 200 miles or so and a while later
to fight again at Ulundi.[67]

This great hill-surrounded plain of Ulundi is the cradle of the Zulu
race. On the ridge to the west stood the Nobamba kraal where lived
Jama and Senzangacona.[68] On the slope to the north-east, Cetywayo
had his kraals, while more to the right stood that of Ulundi. Close by,
nearer to the White Umfolozi, was Panda's dwelling place, Nodwengu,
which was, apparently, still standing at the time of the battle.[69] It is
indeed a historical district. We asked Simpofu what had become of the
remains of his people as we saw no skeletons lying about the veld. He

replied: 'The white men came and took them (the skeletons) away in wagons.' Mr. Gibson says also that he remembers seeing piles of bones lying at a store in this neighbourhood, so I suppose that the end of the mortal part of those Zulus was to be ground into bone-dust for manure. I forget what exact number fell at Ulundi but I believe it was reckoned that we killed over 10 000 of them during the war.[70]

Leaving Ulundi we went on to the White Umfolozi at which we rushed hoping to get through it as easily as we had done in the case of the Black Umfolozi. But it was not to be for in the centre of the stream we stuck fast. Mr. Gibson jumped out and wet his legs. Stuart took his boots off and began to photograph. I sat where I was until the oxen which, by forethought, we had provided for this emergency arrived and quietly hauled the motor out. It is a beautiful spot but like so many others in Zululand it has its melancholy history for there to my right, about 400 yards away, frowned the cliff over which Mr. Adams saw the two blinded girls thrown in Panda's time. It is said to have been a fa-vourite place of execution so I suppose that very many poor human creatures have here looked their last upon the light as their bodies hurtled down those striated rocks to the alligator-haunted pool below.[71] The view of it however is better from the farther side of the river, near to the telegraph pole by which Mr. Stainbank was murdered at the commencement of the 1906 rebellion. It is a wild and lonely place and the hilltops, covered with tall scattered aloes, look from a distance like an *impi* rushing to attack.[72]

About midday we reached the spot where horses were waiting to carry us to the site of Dingaan's old kraal Umgungundhlovu, now a farm called by the cheerful name of Moord-Plaats (Place of Murder), where resides an Englishman named Davis.[73] Here we lunched off bread and a tin of potted meat in company of the magistrate of the district, Mr. Kinsman.[74] Then I mounted upon a wooden and not too sure-footed animal (it was the first time I had ridden for many years)[75] and we set out. Our road ran through bushveld in which are buck and many part-ridges, over some steep and swampy dongas and streams and past a small Boer stead where a few ostriches were kept. At length after we had traversed some seven miles of this rough country in about an hour, we came to the famous and very seldom visited Hill of Slaughter, known as *Kwa Matiwane* (at, or the place of, Matiwane) from an unfortunate chief who threw himself on the mercy of Dingaan and in return was here massacred. Hence by a kind of metaphor *Kwa Matiwane* among the Zulus signifies the Gates of Death through which there is no return. It is also called Hloma Amabutu. It and the Umgungundhlovu kraal are situated in the Makosini or 'Place of Chiefs' (see *Marie*) district where are interred all the ancestors of the Zulu royal house.[76] To this neigh-bourhood not long ago Dinizulu, Cetywayo's son was borne to burial, but Cetywayo himself lies in the neighbourhood of the Nkandhla for-est, on the river side that looks towards Natal.[77]

This hateful hill, where thousands have given up their breath in agony, is a stony ridge of perhaps 400 yards in length, with occasional eminences of rock and some small hollows. Coarse grass grows between the stones and all about are aloe-like plants, euphorbias and twisting stunted trees set sparsely. I know not why but the place has an evil air and gives the impression of being horror-haunted. (On the whole my description of it in *Marie* is not inaccurate, but speaking from memory I made the hill too steep.) A ravine deep and rocky enough to make it necessary to lead horses over it, separates it from the site of Dingaan's great kraal, of which the cattle enclosure has now been planted with corn on account of the richness of the soil. (Will the inhabitants of South Africa never learn to respect their historical places?) This kraal is situated in the fork of the Umkumbane and Unzololo streams, one of which, I think the Umkumbane, runs down the ravine. At the head of the kraal to the west is a mound or koppie on the slopes of which stood the *Isigodhlo* or royal harem and Dingaan's own hut.[78] Here many of the cooking hearths are still in place though the huts that covered them were burned by Dingaan when he fled before the Boers in December 1838, 10 months after the massacre of Retief and his party (100 souls in all counting the 30 servants), on 6 February.[79] The main gateway of the kraal to the east is marked by two large euphorbia or milk trees, which I saw growing there, beneath one of which Senzangacona's ancestor Nkosinzulu is said to be buried.[80] These, however, are not the identical milk trees under which Retief's people tied up their 200 horses when they went in to bid farewell to the king on that fatal morning, but others which have sprung from the same roots as, I noted, is the case with the olives at Gethsemane.[81] When Mr. Gibson first saw this place 20 years ago he tells me that one of the veritable trees was still standing, very grey and ancient but since then it has fallen.

It was through this gate that the Boers were dragged out to slaughter, those of them at least who still had any life in them, for whether they were dead or only stunned is now not known. Living or dead, or both together, they were hauled across the Umkumbane rivulet and up these stony slopes where their necks were twisted and (according to certain accounts) the barbarity of impalement was inflicted on some of them. Here I may state that only just before I left England, General Owen, a nephew of Mr. Owen, the missionary who was living at Umgungundhlovu at the time, having by chance read *Marie*, kindly sent me his uncle's original diary.[82] From it I gathered the impression that the Boers were hauled *living* to the place of death. I should add, however, that to the best of my recollection Mr. Owen could not bring himself to look upon the hideous scene with his own eyes. He relied, I think, upon the reports of his native servant who from time to time informed him of what was taking place without. Still this diary is a document of the most poignant historical interest and I hope that General Owen will take my advice and present it to some museum. Where did the Rev. Mr. Owen's huts stand? Studying the landscape *in situ* I came to the conclusion that it must have been almost upon the site of the little dwelling of the present owner of the farm Moord-Plaats. Thence he, or his servant, could very well see the Boers dragged from the gate of the kraal close by and across the gully below to the slopes of *Kwa Matiwane* opposite. Evidently he had his abode at a spot which commanded this hill since, unless I am mistaken, he mentions other events that he saw in progress on it in the pages of his diary. I regret greatly that lack of time made it impossible for me to cross the Umkumbane stream and visit the actual site of the great kraal, of which however we had a most excellent view from the opposing ridge.

I will now describe what we saw upon this place, one that I can never forget while memory remains to me. On our arrival Mr. Gibson, who had visited the hill twice before, once some 20 years ago and once in 1911, began to hunt for the pile of stones which is said to – and in all probability does – mark the spot where his Boer compatriots in 1838 burned the remains of Retief and most of his companions. On the occasion of Mr Gibson's first inspection a Boer who was staying in the house where we saw the ostriches, who, for a wonder, had some historical knowledge, a very rare thing among his countrymen, told him (Mr. Gibson) that wherever they found a skeleton the Boers erected a little pile of stones to illustrate and commemorate the fact. Knowing the careless habits of this people, also the hurry they were in being at the time engaged in active war, this struck me as a very unlikely story. Still, there scattered about on the hill over a distance of several hundred yards, undoubtedly were the stone heaps of which the Boer, whose name Mr. Gibson forgets, had spoken to him.

To return, for a long while we could not find the grave of Retief nor could two stupid kaffirs whom we summoned from a neighbouring hut give us any assistance. They were 'farm kaffirs' who said that they had been there only a few years and knew nothing of the traditions of the place. Or if they knew, being ignorant of who we might be and therefore suspicious, they would not say anything. Ultimately however we did discover and photograph the grave, a pile of little stones about 8 feet in length set among a rough growth of trees.

Meanwhile, or rather immediately afterwards, while I was riding about the hill hoping to find some relics of the massacre (when he was there first Mr. Gibson picked up a broken coffee bowl such as the trek Boers carried in their haversacks, which he has now lost), I made a very strange discovery. One of the cairns that I have mentioned had been torn open by man or beast and there all about were scattered human bones. Now the truth became evident. The Boers had not erected these piles to commemorate the spots where they found the skeletons, they had dragged together the skeletons in or near to the places where they found them and heaped the stones over them. Doubt-less most of these are in the largest grave, because there they lay thick-est, but others are interred here and there wherever they were found. What we saw before us, and photographed, were the mortal remains of some of Retief's people and, for aught I know, of Retief himself. A little hollow a few inches deep had been scratched in the stony soil for I saw bones sticking out of it, including the base of a skull. Probably this was done with the hand or pocket knives, as it is not likely that the burying party had spades with them on their horses. The remains that were nearest were then thrust into the hollow, the excavated soil replaced and some of the stones which lay around in such plenty piled over the place to keep away the hyenas. That was all. To judge by the number of leg bones I should say that this particular cairn covered about three bodies.

Evidently what happened was this. A number of warriors from the young regiment who did the killing with *sticks* that, according to the evidence given to Mr. Stuart by an old Zulu who took part in it, were, for some hidden reason, cut for this special purpose, threw themselves on an individual Boer and having overcome or stunned the man, dragged him as ants drag a beetle, down the kraal, out of the gate, across the donga to the appointed place of execution. Probably this was on the highest part of the ridge by a certain little rocky eminence. But some groups who had to deal with a heavy or a struggling man grew tired and finished the business before they reached there; some who dealt with a lighter or a senseless man went further in their dreadful zeal. Also the one or two thousand employed needed elbow room for their task; they could not all crowd together. Thus it came about that after it was over the dead were very scattered. When the Boer com-mando arrived 10 months later, there they found them undisturbed since, after he had ripped his enemy open, the Zulu does not like to touch his body and indeed must go through a cleansing ceremony.[83] There too they burned them as reverently as circumstances would al-low, for it must be remembered they had no stretchers or other means of carrying them and the bones would still have been unpleasant to handle. So it came about that after a lapse of 76 years actually we looked upon the mortal remains of these murdered men. It was a strange thing to see.

Doubtless if we had found time we could have discovered more for save a few wandering kaffirs no one visits this ill-omened Golgotha and the probability is that articles from the pockets of the Boers still lie about. But as we must complete our journey in daylight this was lacking to us. So we turned our horses' heads and went away, guided by one of the stupid kaffirs who presently deserted us. As we wandered over the veld and uncertain footpaths (how I wonder does that farmer ever get his produce to a market!) I reconstructed in my mind some of the fierce and terrible scenes connected with the kraal Umgungundhlovu. Particularly did I picture the poor folk who, time and time again, had trodden these very paths at the summons of the King well knowing that they went to look their last at the light upon the stony crest of the hill of Matiwane. I forgot to say that among the bushes I found another skull. It *may* have been that of one of the lads who accompanied Retief's party, but from its appearance I judged that it had belonged to a wo- man. One of Dingaan's countless victims, butchered on this place.

On regaining the motor we immediately began to climb some terrible slopes (on one of which we stuck) and gained the vast expanse of swelling green hills, known as Proviso B, being part of the 270 000 acres out of which the Boers jockeyed the Zulus by virtue of a vague agreement with Dinizulu.[84] It is a glorious country, high and healthy with deep and wooded ravines between the hills. In one of these Stuart nearly came to his end some years ago. He lost his way in rain and storm and wandered on through the darkness till his horse pulled up and snorted. Wisely he stopped where he was till daylight when he found himself on a little spit of land with sheer gulfs to the right and left.

After crossing the Umfuli river without accident we branched off across the veld to the right and struck the new road, which runs past Sir Charles Saunders's place from Melmoth. This settlement we lacked time to visit although some chiefs were waiting for Mr. Gibson there. Passing a good many plantations of the monotonous black wattle trees, which somehow look artificial and out of place on these vast, dome-like high- lands, we arrived just as darkness fell at Sir Charles's charming house, Imfulazane, where we received the warmest of welcomes and what we needed much after our exhausting day – something to drink. It seemed strange to reach this refined, English home in the heart of Zululand. Formerly Sir Charles was the British Resident in Zululand in succession I think to Sir Marshall Clarke.[85] On retiring he took over this farm from a son by his first marriage and is now working it with great vigour. I think however that it is rather late in life for a man to enter upon what must be an arduous and costly agricultural enterprise. He is now engaged in growing mealies and breeding up a herd of cattle, which by the aid of constant dipping (every three days I think) do ex- tremely well here. The black wattle, which were planted by the first owner of the land and by Sir Charles's son, he finds more of a nuisance than anything else; indeed he has recently burnt out 200 acres of them which occupied some of the best grazing land.[86] Here, 70 or 80 miles from a railway, the bark is useless because of the cost of transport and still more is this so in the case of the trunks that otherwise are valuable as props in the Johannesburg mines. Even in more accessible situations the black wattle industry has received a formidable check owing to the fall in the price of bark to about half its former value. By the way, the monks at Mariannhill at Pinetown in Natal, told me that they found the bark of the mimosa more effective for tanning than that of the wattle.

At this place the air was so sharp that good fires both in the drawing and my bedroom were very welcome. More than 20 years ago, when he was staying at Ditchingham, Sir Melmoth Osborn told me of a wonderful *yellow* Imatophyllum of which a single plant only had been discovered in the forest at Eshowe. Of this rarity he promised to send me a root and in due course did so – indeed I have it still at home. But, when it flowered it turned out to be of the ordinary red variety. Clearly some mistake had been made. At the Saunders' by a mere accident I discovered the original plant moved here from the Residency at Eshowe. Now I have two roots of it in my holdall which, I hope, will survive the journey. A piece of it has been sent to Kew and named, I think, *Imatophyllum Sulphurea*.[87]

I had an interesting conversation with Sir Charles about the Zulus, a race in which he takes the deepest and most sympathetic interest. He spoke feelingly of the harsh treatment they have received and are receiving and declared that 'constant pin-pricks', such as land-snatching and the poll tax were the direct cause of the 1906 'rebellion'. He added that this was suppressed with great cruelty notably in the last affair in the Insimba Valley – Mome I think the place was called, where all quarter seems to have been refused even to those who threw down their arms and pleaded for mercy, as did the old chief Mehlokazulu, who held up his hands and said 'please' before they shot him. In that fight, if so it can be called, 547 Zulus were slain and one white man received a scratch on the wrist (see *The Natal Rebellion* by Capt. Bosman), somewhat significant figures. (Unofficial estimates, probably exaggerated, put the number of Zulus shot in this one affair at 3 000!)[88] Some natives, I am told, were finished who had taken refuge in caves and up trees. Well, cruelty bred of fear, is no new story in South Africa. The white man neglects or oppresses the native and slights his needs until something happens; then in a panic he sets to work and butchers him.

Sir Charles said that the Zulus have a great thirst for education. Even the raw 'house boys' will pay 1s. a month out of their small wages to be taught at an evening school. (I remember that Mrs. Gibson gave me identical information on this point.) He added: 'They cannot be kept back.' Yet, as he pointed out, the missionaries, whatever their mistakes, were the only people who did anything to satisfy this thirst for learning. Poor natives! Sir Charles is of the opinion that the Zulus should be given representation on some local council in which they could express their views and help to manage their own affairs. At present they were at a loose end, indeed in complete confusion. 'It is impossible that they should be perpetually suppressed: something *must* be done,' he concluded.

THE CAR HAD STUCK FAST IN MHLATIEZE RIVER, WHEN SIKOUYANA AND HIS DAUGHTER NOMBI, DRESSED AS A ZULU DIVINER, CAME TO HELP TO EXTRICATE IT

'The car had stuck fast in Mhlatieze [Mhlatuze] River, when Sikouyana [Sikonyana] and his daughter Nombi, dressed as a Zulu diviner, came to help to extricate it.' (Windsor Magazine)

From left: *Haggard, Sikonyana and Nombi.*

Sunday, 26 April

After luncheon we bade farewell to our kind hosts and started for Empandhleni, 30 miles or so away. In due course we reached the Umhlatuze River, which looked formidable enough, even now when the water is low. We charged at the ford – there was nothing else to do and presently stuck fast right in the middle of the river. Moreover, the water got to the baggage, utterly soaking poor Stuart's belongings but only damping mine. At this juncture who should appear but a pretty young witch-doctress in full professional array with the regulation bladders in her hair, etc. She was accompanied by her father, a wizened old fellow and one of two other people. I told her that she was very pretty, which seemed to please her enormously notwithstanding her spiritual attainments, for she smiled, nodded and even seemed to blush beneath her light copper-hued skin. Proceeding to the further bank she sat down and apparently began a course of incantations on our behalf, swaying herself to and fro. Meanwhile, her parent and the others rendered us mundane assistance by dragging at the wheels. The end of it was that after prolonged and arduous efforts and the removal of all the luggage, I steering and everybody else pushing, we did get through that dreadful river. I pointed out to Stuart, as we emptied the water from his bag, that mine remained dry, although it was as deep or deeper in the stream, because *I* had told Miss Nombé (that was her name) that she was beautiful whereas he had done nothing of the sort. Therefore, she had brought her Lord of the Spirits to my particular assistance and incidentally rescued the motor from its very awkward predicament; an explanation of our escape from a night on the banks of the Umhlatuze that made everybody laugh. Indeed the good effect of this young lady's magical implorations followed us for some way, since they enabled us to surmount the hills and with only one electrical starting gear put out of action, and though with difficulty before dark and without further mischance to reach the store where we slept at Empandhleni.[89]

Monday, 27 April

The view from this place as I studied it in the clear light the following morning, one of the most perfect that can be conceived, was very fine, stretching as it does to the range of mountains beyond which lie the Inkandhla forest. Near to our inn is buried Sigananda, who died not long ago. This old, old Zulu, the chief who fought in Chaka's battles and was present at the massacre of Retief, the details of which he described to Stuart, ruled over all this 'war'. It was he who, as I saw some years ago in a London paper, declared that much of what I wrote in *Nada the Lily* was quite true. He was noted for his skill as a worker in metals.[90]

Here there was an *indaba* at which 70 or 80 chiefs and their *indunas* were present. Mr. Gibson introduced me to them, saying: 'The *Inkoosi* is going through the land with his heart. He who is very well known across the seas, does not come as an official but because he has a love of you and your country' etc. etc. etc. As it was expected that I should speak I answered, Stuart rendering my words, to the effect that it was true I had spent my youth in this country, when I was as the child of Sompseu (Sir T. Shepstone) and of Mali-mati (Sir M. Osborn), their late heads and chiefs.[91] That then I had heard all their history from the lips of those Great Ones and had learned to love them with a love, that although since those days I had wandered far across the black seas and up and down the earth, I had never forgotten through the falling years. That I had written of them in books and striven to make their name known about the world. That I wished, now that I was grown old, to look once more upon the faces of the Zulus, though most of them were not the same who breathed beneath the heavens when I was young. They had 'gone down' but these their children remained. That, as the *Inkoosi* had said, although the King [George V] had sent me to this country, I did not visit them as an official but as their friend with my heart, that I might see them with my eyes and hear their thoughts and help them in anyway I could. That I knew they had gone through many troubles of which this was not the hour to speak, but that I hoped the storm clouds had broken and that in the time unborn the good sun of peace, happiness and plenty would shine upon them from day to day and year to year.

This little address, which necessarily must be somewhat diplomatic in tone since there was so much of which I could not speak save by allusion, was received by the audience with a chorus of *Inkoos! Inkoos y umcool! Inkoos y pagate!* (Chief! Great Chief! Chief from of old!)[92] and acknowledged by several of the principal men. Then one of them said that they would wish to know by what name they must remember me. Stuart told them 'Sir Rider Haggard' but at this they shook their heads and smiled, saying that their 'tongues could not go round' those words – was there no other name? He answered, Yes. In the land years ago I had been called *Lundanda,* or, with my title of praise, *Lundanda u Ndand Okalweni* (The tall one who walks on the mountain tops). Possibly this means 'with his head in the air' or 'absent-mindedly'. 'Ah!' they answered, '*now* we hear, *now* we understand, *now* we shall never forget.'[93] Then one of them added that they were indeed glad to see a chief who had always been and who remained their friend. 'It is good and fitting that they should find friends among the people to whom we have given our loyalty.'

It was a very pleasant episode, and touching in its way. Poor folk, they do indeed need friends who understand them, their history and their aspirations. Would that I could do more for them. As one of them, an old chief who wore bladders in his hair as a sign of rank, said: 'We are orphans left to wander alone by our fathers. Now we owe our life to the fact that England is.'

After the *indaba* we went to drink a cup of tea with Mr. Jackson, the magistrate, and his wife.[94] Their house is very pretty with a wide avenue of gums leading up to it, which were planted by the late Arthur Shepstone, Sir T's son, one of the family whom I never met.[95] In it are many interesting Zulu curiosities. Mr. Jackson had been reading *Child of Storm* and would scarcely believe that Zululand was not familiar ground to me.

Shortly after leaving Empandhleni (which means The Bald-headed Man), we passed the valley where Piet Uys was killed years ago and came to another horrible hill called The Itala.[96] Here we stuck again and went through the usual performances, but by the help of a brawny mounted policeman whom we met, at last crawled to the top. We lunched in the veld upon some food we had brought with us – a very enjoyable meal – and started on over bad roads but more level country for Isandhlwana. By the way, Mr. Gibson declares that this name means 'Like a little house'; Stuart, on the contrary, says that the true inter-

Cheyne Collection

Zulu woman and girl bird scarers – a photograph
taken by James Stuart.

pretation thereof is 'the second stomach of an ox'. When such learned doctors disagree, as they did with vigour, I may be pardoned if I cling to the old rendering 'the place of the little hand'. Certainly it is not in the least like either a little house or an ox's stomach; whereas it has *some* similitude to an arm with a clenched fist at its end.[97]

As we went we saw a pretty sight, a native girl standing on the roof of a small hut-like erection with a naked child on either side of her engaged in protecting a crop of *mabele* or kaffir corn from the attacks of birds.[98] Stuart went to photograph them with the Kodak. The moment she saw this instrument levelled at her the girl, mistaking it for a pistol with which she was about to be shot, bundled off her stand with wonderful rapidity as a sleeping buck leaps from a rock when disturbed, and ran. One of the children accompanied her but the other stood like a stone. I think that this little girl who thus resisted the contagion of sudden panic will grow into a woman of strong character. The end of it was that they were persuaded to come back and be photographed and very pretty the picture is. It might serve as a model for a group of statuary. Archbishop Carter,[99] to whom I shewed it, said it should be enlarged and placed in the Cape Town museum.

At length the strange, abrupt, lion-like mount of Isandlwana appeared before us, standing solitary and, in a way, terrible upon the plain; its sheer brown cliffs of rock rising like the walls of some cyclopean fortress. Between it and another low and stony hill there lies a nek of some 500 yards in width. All about this nek stand monuments and little cairns built of rough stones marking where the bones of the dead were buried when our forces returned to Isandhlwana in 1880, a year or so after the disaster.

Viewed from this nek the whole plan of the battle becomes clear. The right wing of the great Zulu impi, which was under the command of the *Induna* Untshingwayo, coming along the ridge of the Nqutu mountains (the plain of Isandhlwana lies in a ring of hills), executed a flanking movement both in front and at the back of Isandhlwana mount, while the left wing or horn was carrying out a similar movement to our right towards the terraced Malagati hills.[100] As these terrible horns closed in while the chest of the Zulu army was waiting to deliver the main attack those who were left of our men became aware that the net of steel was closing round them and fled, or attempted to fly. The course of their route is marked by more stone cairns piled over their bones, many of which I saw on the following day, similar to but much larger than those erected over the remains of Retief's men.

Few relics are left of the struggle now after the lapse of 35 years, some broken medicine bottles, a good many fragments of bully-beef tins, pieces of the bones of men and animals, that is all. Also we picked up the remnants of two Martini cartridges; the one I found on the nek had not been fired, probably it came from the pouch of some slain soldier, a slate pencil and such sundries. Mr. Parr,[101] however, the owner of the store where we slept, gave me a number of cartridge cases and the head of one of Durnford's rockets. He has another rocket dug out of the bank of a donga near the store, which is still unexploded. This is valuable in its way, as from the place of its discovery it shews that the rocket battery, of the history of the destruction of which nothing is known (its remains were found behind an isolated round koppie in front and to the left of the nek), must have fired some shots at the chest of the impi.

It was sad for me to stand by the piles of stones which cover all that is left of so many whom once I knew; Durnford and Pulleine and many other officers of the 24th, George Shepstone and the rest. Coghill I knew also very well but he died with Melville by the river bank.[102] It makes me feel too how old I have become for few others whom I meet today can remember them, not even Mr. Gibson. We walked back towards the store past the little graveyard where I see that Hitchcock, the first husband of Osborn's daughter, is buried with a few others whom it was possible to identify, and across the dongas and the rough ground about them.[103]

When I had gone some way I turned and looked back at this lonesome, formidable hill standing there, a fit monument for the multitude of dead; immemorially ancient, stern and grand. The twilight was closing in, the sky was red, fading into grey. Over that savage crest trembled one star. Heaven's own ornament; near to it gleamed the faint but luminous bow of the new-born moon, that same young moon which once hung above the slain upon this forsaken field of blood. I walked a while picking my way over the stony ridge and dongas where the last stand was made against a roaring flood of foes and again looked back. Now the stark mount had become very black and solemn, the trembling star had sunk or vanished and of the following crescent of the young moon but one horn appeared above the hill. It looked like a plume of faint, unearthly fire burning upon Isandhlwana's rocky brow. This must be a quiet place for man's eternal sleep. But the scene which went before that sleep!

Tuesday, 28 April

In the morning we followed the path of the routed towards Fugitive's Drift. At first the cairns are many but by degrees they cease. All were

'Isandhlwana, with monument to the 24th Regiment. Sir Rider Haggard and Mr. Gibson in the foreground, a few weeks after the completion of the memorial.' (Windsor Magazine)

The monument to the 1st and 2nd batallion of the 24th Regiment (South Wales Borderers) killed in action at the battle of Isandlwana and the defence of Rorke's Drift was unveiled on 6 March 1914.

slain by now save those who were marked for another space of life. But even today I can scarcely bear to think of those last incidents of a mighty tragedy of which I heard so much when I was young, and will write of them no more. They are forgotten among men. Peace to the brave, white and black together, for be it remembered our men did not die alone. 'Is this a victory of which you tell me?' asked Cetywayo, as he surveyed his thinned regiments, 'Wow! I name it defeat.'[104]

Rorke's Drift I saw also, but from a little distance. There stands the place upon the slope of the hill above the Buffalo River and about it the tall gums and beyond the plain the Mankamani Range and the great mass of Sibindi.[105] Never will these see such another sight. Surely some merciful power must have put it into the hearts of those Zulus who had not tasted their share of battle to attempt this mad adventure against walls, instead of waiting for the return of Chelmsford and his companies.

On our way to the Nqutu magistracy Mazooku, on being questioned, said he quite well remembered the old Hottentot washerwoman telling me of the disaster at Isandhlwana at Pretoria, 200 miles away, on the morning after its occurrence.[106] He even recalled what horse I had saddled to ride down to the government offices and repeat to Osborn what I had heard, viz: 'Black Billy'.[107] He said that he asked the old vrouw how she learned the news so quick, and she replied that 'somebody told her'. We could get no more out of him on this point, for if he knew he would not reveal it. Natives are very shy of speaking of anything they know to partake of the nature of mystical national lore, especially before men in high official position like Gibson. While I am on this point I may mention that the Archbishop of Cape Town (Carter), with whom I am travelling on the *Gaika* while I write up these notes, tells me that Canon Mullins, who died last year, assured him that *he* heard of this catastrophe through his natives at Grahamstown in the Cape Colony many hundreds of miles away, also on the morning after it happened.[108] In the absence of telegraphs or of any means of conveying information, especially over high veld where it cannot be called from hill to hill, there seems to be but one possible explanation of this phenomenon, viz. the existence of some unascertained telepathic power among these people, of which the witch-doctors are the chief possessors. Too many instances of such happenings have been recorded to admit of their being set down to chance or coincidence. In the same way the Archbishop, shut up in Zululand, learned of all the important events of the Boer war through the natives, almost simultaneously with their occurrence, but could never trace how the news arrived.

Talking of such hidden arts Mazooku, apropos of the pretty witch-doctress Nombé, gave me an account of how such people came to take to the business and of the fashion of their initiation. It is worth recording. First, the man or woman, who is generally young at the time, falls into vague ill-health which may continue for a year. This may happen, however, at any age, but for the most part overtakes girls about the time of puberty. Ultimately the sickness settles in the shoulders, whereon the patient is taken to some experienced witch-doctor who decides whether the ailment is of a normal nature or is due to the workings or inspiration of the spirits. If he alleges the latter to be the cause, probably the parents or friends take the patient to one or more doctors living at a distance who know nothing of the family. Should these confirm the first diagnosis, the neophyte is put on a course of purges etc. known as *black* medicine. After this follows a second course of *white* medicine, which may continue for a whole year. It is made by heating up certain herbs until they froth, and its effect is to make the patient sick. Also it does other things for he (or she) begins to dream and 'multitudes' of spirits visit him in his sleep and talk to him. Some of these are the shadows of living people; some the shades of ancestors and others.

By degrees the neophyte acquires the power of divination. First he is tried with small matters and if he succeeds, with those of more importance. If he fails he must go through another course of the potent white medicine and if he fails again he is rejected from the ranks of the profession. Also the training sometimes involves long and solitary sojourn in the bush. In the old days the neophyte used to run to a river and dive into a deep pool whence he emerged covered with white mud and holding in his hand a lizard or, more commonly, a snake. One doctor told Mr. Gibson that he came up from the water with a boa-constrictor coiled round him. This snake, I understood, was his 'familiar', which had assumed that form.[109]

Such was Mazooku's story of the mode of initiation but when we questioned him on deeper matters, such as the nature of the spirits and the real extent of the powers of the witch-doctors, he professed ignorance. It struck me that he did not think these questions for open discussion. It will be observed, and this was confirmed by both Gibson and Stuart, that the initiate has no choice in the matter of his mystic trade; if he is 'called' he must come. There is no doubt that the general belief in the powers of these 'doctors' is still wide and deep, also that they credit them themselves. In practice they are very similar to the 'mediums' with whom we are familiar in civilised countries. Nowadays, however, they can no longer bring people to their death on the charge of working witchcraft.

Not very far from Rorke's Drift we stopped awhile to visit the famous mission station of St. Augustine. Unfortunately Archdeacon Johnson was out but his able and energetic wife showed us the school where about 200 native scholars are educated and the really wonderful stone church, built almost entirely by native labour, which will accommodate as many as 2 000 worshippers. It is a great achievement and the mission is doing very good work.[110]

Thence we travelled on over horrible sandy tracks on which we bent our steering gear, to the Nqutu magistracy where we were received by the magistrate, Mr. Farrer.[111] Here there was another large *indaba* at which many chiefs were present with their followers. Again I was called upon to address them which I did in a somewhat similar speech to that which I made on the former occasion. When I had finished one of the audience answered that I did well to allude to their sorrows as these were countless as the leaves – that they were endless, to which I answered that the morning always followed the night however black that night might be. Then he proceeded to set them out in some detail.

Among those present was Manzolwandhle whose name means 'Water of the Sea'. He is the son of the late King Cetywayo, either posthumous or born shortly before his father's death, and received this name because he was conceived after Cetywayo had crossed the ocean during his period of exile.[112] He is a fine open-faced man, still young, and by most believed to be the rightful heir to the House of Senzangacona inasmuch as he was born of the head wife, whereas Dinizulu, whose son Solomon has now been recognised, is alleged to have been the child of a concubine.[113] In appearance he is extremely like Cetywayo and indeed to all of the royal family. He is suspected of entertaining ambitions such as would be not unnatural in his present case and it is darkly hinted that a mysterious murder, complicated with the disappearance of the body, which has taken place in his kraal, may possibly have been connected with the manufacture of *mouti* or medicine, romantically designed to bring these to a prosperous issue.

However this may be, he is a very taking personality and to all appearance quite civilized in his military costume. By virtue of his high rank Manzolwandhle took the lead at this *indaba*, sitting in advance of the others. For a while he listened to the grumbles I have mentioned. Then at last he broke out. 'Who are you?' he asked, 'that you throw up all this froth? What kind of breeding have you that you sing so loud a song about the words of the *Inkoosi Lundanda*? Surely you are a low fellow. Do you not know that when the *Inkoosi* speaks it is your part to listen and be grateful, not to weep and whine and make comments upon the acceptable words that he has been pleased to say to us? Be silent,' he ended sharply, whereupon the unlucky Jeremiah collapsed.

Afterwards I told Manzolwandhle how glad I was to meet him, which seemed to please him very much, if I might judge from his face and the warmth of his salute. I do not pay much attention to such matters as a rule, but I must say I thought it interesting to be addressed as 'Father' and 'Chief from the dead days' by the head of the race of Zulu and Senzangacona.

At this talk one old boy amused me very much. He was complaining of the degeneracy of the younger generation of Zulus and of their aping the ways of the English. 'They try to be white,' he concluded, 'but white they will never be. Black they were born and black they must remain until they die.'

I observed a very pleasant-looking headman of about 50 years of age who was present, dressed in European clothes, on whose breast was pinned the Rebellion Medal, a rare distinction of which only 20 or 30 were issued to those who did notable service in 1906.[114] His name, I ascertained, is Tshetsha, son of Nongamulana, who was one of the principal native attendants of my late chief, Sir T. Shepstone. This Tshetsha served as a British scout during the Boer war and in a like capacity during the Rebellion. What particularly attracted my attention to him was that round his neck he wore the ancient necklace called *Iziqu*, an article of which I greatly coveted a genuine specimen that is almost impossible to obtain as the owner of an *Iziqu* will rarely part with it and the article is always buried on him.

The *Iziqu*, I should record, can only be worn by a warrior who has killed an enemy in battle and when they came into use is not known, certainly it was before the time of Chaka. They must be made of willow wood cut in little dies, burnt at the ends and threaded on a string. (There is another form of *Iziqu*, which is made of round pieces of thorn wood with the horn of a ram at either end.) In the old time after a battle, those who had slain foes were separated for some days from other men to undergo the cleansing rites, when they went by the name of *Amaqawe* (i.e. heroes) or of *Izinqwelara*. On this occasion they must wear some article that was on the person of the slain man. Then it was that the *Iziqu* was assumed, probably at the *Xoxa-impi* or public discussion of the victory in the presence of the king, when all who had distinguished themselves in the fight were pointed out.[115] Now anybody may assume the *Iziqu* without fear of consequences but if he does so lacking the qualification he still exposes himself to the contempt of society and more particularly to the mockery of women. Thus Dinizulu wore the *Iziqu* because he is said to have killed a little boy as he was creeping out of a hut, but it does not seem to have redounded to his credit.

To return, by what arts I know not, Stuart succeeded in persuading Tshetsha to part with his *Iziqu* on my behalf in return for a present and that relic now reposes not on my neck but in my collar-box. It appears that the amiable-aired Tshetsha has killed seven men in battle on various occasions in his warlike life, two of them (who these were he did not seem inclined to reveal) during the Boer War.

On obtaining the thing I noticed at once that the willow wood blocks are divided by seven short pieces of stick, which no doubt commemorate the seven dead, also that these white sticks are set at irregular intervals in the necklace that perhaps indicate the length of time which elapsed between the fall of each of them. There are too further mysterious knobs and excrescences that may or may not denote the wounding of more foes. Altogether it is a scarce curiosity and valuable because of its ascertained pedigree. That Tshetsha could have been persuaded to part with it is strange and contrary to custom but perhaps he did so out of compliment to myself.

These *Iziqu* which answer, more or less, to our Victoria Cross, have exercised a very evil influence in the past. Sobuza, the old warrior of Chaka's time, told Mr. Gibson that in those days they used to watch for smoke to rise and shew them where people lived and then rush down and kill them. When asked why they were so cruel he answered but one emphatic word, *Iziqu*!

On that same day the landlord of the Masonic hotel at Dundee presented me with the half of an ancient copper neck-ring. Originally this ring was given by old Mehlokazulu, who was killed – or executed – in the 1906 rebellion, to the great hunter Gordon Cumming.[116] Mehlokazulu told Cumming that it had last been worn by one of his wives. Also he said that before this it had been buried with others by the order of Chaka because the heavy weight of them blistered the necks of the women and the copper poisoned the open wounds. Others say however that it was the armlets, that I think were called *Inxota*, which were so buried, whereas Stuart declares that the story refers to certain unknown ornaments of some metal like silver.[117] All that appears to be certain is that the poor men who carried out the interment of the articles were afterwards killed so that none might know where these were hid. These rings, of which I have another perfect specimen given to me by Stuart, were called *Umnaka* and have certainly not been worn since Dingaan's day.[118] They must weigh 2 pounds and were made of metal, which the Zulus purchased from the Portuguese. The custom was for Chaka and Dingaan to issue them to be worn as distinctive ornaments by the members of their harems. They were not however buried with their owners, perhaps because of their value, but like the native iron hoes passed on to descendants.

Speaking of neck ornaments I saw a Basutu woman near Rorke's Drift who wore a great disk of flat copper as large as a soup plate. These disks they assume when they marry but how they manage to sleep in an extra sized halo moved down onto their shoulders, remains a mystery. One thing is certain, once on it cannot come off again.

After the conclusion of our Nqutu *indaba* we lunched with Mr. and Mrs. Farrer, who have an excellent house here. This pleasant meal concluded we entered our motor for the last time and trekked on over a wide, open country where, by contrast, the roads seemed almost heavenly, to the little town of Dundee in Natal, which we reached before nightfall.[119] So ended my journey of over 400 miles through Zululand. It was accomplished without any serious accident, for which we might well be thankful considering the conditions of the country and the awful tracks we negotiated. Twice or thrice, however, I was thrown heavily against the wood bars of the top of the machine hurting my head and on one occasion somewhat straining my neck. On the whole this was one of the most interesting journeys out of the many I have made in various lands in the course of my life. We saw, if not everything (for instance we were obliged to miss out the Inkandhla forest), at least a great area of Zululand, as that country used to be in my youth, before the Boers and other white men had bitten off such vast districts.

I was particularly fortunate also in having the companionship of Messrs. Gibson and Stuart, who I suppose are, with Sir Charles Saunders and Archdeacon Johnson, the greatest living experts in the Zulu history and language. From them I heard all sorts of things which would never come to the ears of the ordinary traveller. Also I was present at four large *indabas* with chiefs and their principal attendants, two of which I addressed myself. Thus I attained to an insight into the state of the land and of its inhabitants that might have been lacking to me after a much longer stay under other conditions. Indeed the traveller in Zululand who is not really familiar with the language would be practically helpless and would acquire little trustworthy information. It is no place for the Cook's tourist and, except for the very strong, the journeying is extremely rough. I am surprised that I stood it so well and unless I had plenty of time at my disposal I should not care to face it again. Very glad am I that I managed to do so under such favourable auspices before advancing age and physical weaknesses made the venture impossible. At any rate my mind remains as strong as ever it was and I am still able to observe and to collect and remember information. Only at my time of life I do not know that there is great use in collecting more knowledge when already I have so much about various lands and matters. Ere long it must be spilt upon the sands of time, this vessel of the water of learning painfully collected drop by drop throughout the years, unless indeed we take our garnered experience with us to whatever place we go. I hope this may be so; otherwise there is great waste in the world.

How few people, even in South Africa, know anything about the Zulus, their conditions, history and aspirations. I believe that one might count them upon the fingers of one's hands. To 99 out of 100 a native is just a native, a person from whom land may be filched on one pretext and another, or labour and taxes extracted, and who, if he resists the process or makes himself otherwise inconvenient, may be shot with a clear conscience. The rest is darkness so far as they are concerned; with it they cannot be troubled. '*Tshetsha Umfan* (make haste boy),[120] go bring my horse, go hoe my corn, go pay your tax in malt or meal – or see, here are whips and rifles.' That is the dominant note of the time to which we white people have too often sought to teach the black the way to dance! But of all this I hope to write in due course, and fortunately everybody does not think or react in such a fashion.

At Dundee we saw the Talana mountain where the fight, the first of the war, I think, took place between the English and the Boers; an old resident who was here at the time explaining the details of the action to us and pointing out the trees in which General Penn Symons was mortally wounded and the wall that was lined by the British troops before the advance up the hill. Afterwards, as I knew I should have no other opportunity, by the light of the moon I visited the little strip of ground (it is not the usual graveyard) where the Boers allowed Sir W. Penn Symons and some other officers to be buried during their occupation of Dundee, which we evacuated after the battle. So seen it looked very peaceful but very sad. The place seems to be well-kept and the headstones are in good order and easily read.[121]

Wednesday, 29 April

We left Dundee early in the morning and caught the Durban mail at Glencoe.[122] At Maritzburg station I said goodbye to Mazooku whom, I suppose, I shall never see again. The night before at Dundee, with the kind aid of Stuart, I had settled up his rather complicated business affairs. He used to be well-to-do, but the East Coast Fever had killed his cattle.[123] Then he got into a lawsuit with a white man who forbade him to grow crops on the land he hired. He won the lawsuit but took no advantage for when he had planted his crops and they were growing the white man turned his cattle in and destroyed them all. Then came worse trouble. Another native wanted to marry his daughter and paid him £10 as a propitiatory gift, or on account of *lobola,* which, being pushed, Mazooku spent.[124] But *souvent femme varie.*[125] Ultimately (as I gathered) Miss Mazooku would have no more of her suitor, who promptly sued for the return of the £10, and under the peculiar law prevalent in Natal got an order made on her father in default of satisfying which he was now in danger of being sent to prison. (I think it is a very bad ordnance which allows the *lobola* or marriage gift to be discharged in money instead of cattle which were settled on the girl, as was formerly done.) The upshot of it was that I had to discharge the obligation so I suppose that in native eyes, Miss Mazooku is *lobola*'d to me! Now everybody is happy, the rejected has got back his cash, Mazooku is freed from terror of the *tronk,* as prison is, or used to be, called,[126] and the young lady need no longer hesitate between sacrificing her personal predilictions and consigning her impecunious parent to durance vile. It is not often that so much good can be done with £10.

Poor old Mazooku. His last salute to me of *'Inkoos! Baba!'* (Chief! Father!)[127] was given in a somewhat quavering voice for I believe he loves me dearly, and the appearance of an angel from above, or the spirits of all his ancestors, could not have been more welcome to him than mine in Natal at this critical juncture of his affairs. Well, he served me faithfully for years and once he saved my life so I should not grudge him a matter of under £20 in all. Nor do I indeed. I felt very sad as I watched him disappear with his bundle in that crowded station – good fortune go with him! He proved a perfect treasure on our Zululand journey. Stuart is kindly going to try to arrange a new home for him on the corporation lands of Maritzburg, far from his persecuting white man, where I hope he will grow old and die in peace. Whoever forgets me I am sure that Mazooku never will in whatever land memory remains to him.[128]

Notes

1. The Zulu emerged as a powerful nation state under King Shaka (c.1787–1829) in the 1820s. After his assassination in 1828 he was succeeded by his brother Dingane. Threatened by Voortrekker incursion and settlement, Dingane (1795–1840) killed a trekker group led by Piet Retief at uMgungundlovu (6 February 1838). The Zulu army was defeated by the trekkers at the Battle of the Ncome or Blood River (16 December 1838) and Dingane was subsequently deposed by his half-brother Mpande (1798–1872) in alliance with the trekkers. It was agreed the Zulus would control the area north of the Thukela River. After the British annexation of Natal in 1843, the Zulu kingdom was recognised as an independent state north of the river. A dispute over the succession to the throne led to civil war in 1856 between Mpande's favoured son, Mbuyazi, and another son, Cetshwayo (c.1826–84). The succession was decided in Cetshwayo's favour after the death of Mbuyazi at the battle of Ndondakusuka in 1856.

    By the late 1870s the militarily powerful Zulu kingdom was seen as a threat by both Boers and British, with the latter perceiving it as an obstacle to confederation. In January 1879, an ultimatum to the Zulus from Sir Bartle Frere, the British High Commissioner, finally precipitated war. After the Zulus won a devastating victory over the British at Isandlwana (22 January 1879) – followed on the same day by the famous British defence of Rorke's Drift – the tide turned against them and they were finally defeated at the battle of Ulundi (4 July 1879). Cetshwayo was deposed and sent to Cape Town. Sir Garnet Wolseley, advised among others by John Shepstone and Theophilus Shepstone, devised a settlement of the country, dividing it into 13 chiefdoms. It was a recipe for disaster. After much conflict and civil war, Zululand was partitioned into three areas in 1883. Cetshwayo was permitted to return to rule his original kingdom but, following the destruction of his capital by the forces of his rival Zibhebhu (c.1841–1904), he took refuge under British protection in Eshowe where he died in suspicious circumstances in 1884.

    His son Dinuzulu (c.1870–1913) took up the cause against Zibhebhu, enlisting Boer help in exchange for land. In 1887 Britain annexed Zululand to forestall the Boers of the New Republic pushing to the coast. Dinuzulu rebelled in 1888 against the new British administration of the colony of

Zululand. Arrested and tried on a charge of high treason, he was exiled to the island of St Helena. In 1897 Zululand was incorporated into Natal. In 1898 Dinuzulu was allowed to return as a minor chief but sought recognition as king. For his perceived role in the Bhambatha Rebellion of 1906 he was sentenced to four years imprisonment. For further information see Richard Cope, *Ploughshare of War: The Origins of the Anglo-Zulu War*, Pietermaritzburg, 1999; Guy, *The Destruction*; John Laband, *Rope of Sand: The Rise and Fall of the Zulu Kingdom in the Nineteenth Century*, Johannesburg, 1995. While Donald Morris's *The Washing of the Spears: A History of the Rise of the Zulu Nation under Shaka and its fall in the Zulu War of 1879*, London, 1966, remains the most popular available account of the Anglo-Zulu War, it has been superseded by subsequent research. See instead Andrew Duminy and Charles Ballard (eds), *The Anglo-Zulu War: New Perspectives*, Pietermaritzburg, 1981; Ian Knight, *Brave Men's Blood*, London, 1990, and *Zulu: The Battles of Isandlwana and Rorke's Drift, 22/23rd January 1879*, London, 1992; John Laband and Paul Thompson, *Kingdom and Colony at War: Sixteen Studies on the Anglo-Zulu War of 1879*, Pietermaritzburg, 1990; John Laband and Paul Thompson, *The Illustrated Guide to the Anglo-Zulu War*, Pietermaritzburg, 2000.

2. Zeerust, established 1864 by Casper Coetzee who commissioned a fort and a church to be built on his farm. He died before they were completed and was buried there, hence the name Coetzee's Rest or Zeerust. The principal town of the Marico district featured in the works of Herman Charles Bosman.

3. Travellers used to the comfort and higher speeds of European rail travel often expressed similar frustrations to Haggard. Railway construction began in South Africa in 1859 and by 1914 there were 14 400 km (8 948 miles) of track, mainly of the 3 ft 6 in. gauge. The top speed possible on this gauge was 50 to 80 kph (30 to 50 mph). Colonial authorities had decided the 3 ft 6 in. gauge was the most economical – narrower curves could be built with this gauge – considering the South African topography. Modern technology has solved the speed problem.

4. Frank Robb and H. Pearce, South African members of the DRC staff.

5. Durban, South Africa's principal port, established in 1824 as a trading station called Port Natal by Henry Fynn and Lieutenant Francis Farewell. It was formally established as D'Urban in 1835 on land ceded by Shaka and named after Sir Benjamin D'Urban (1777–1849), Governor of the Cape 1834–38. It was known as D'Urban until about 1870.

6. This line is pencilled through in the original typescript. See also Chapter Five, p. 134 and Note 29.

7. The Berea, a long ridge overlooking the city and harbour. In 1835, the missionary Captain Allen Gardiner (1794–1851) established a mission on the northern end and named it after the place mentioned in the Acts of the Apostles, 17: 10 and 11, which records St Paul's rejection by the Thessalonians and his arrival at Berea in Macedonia, where the people had listened to him 'with all readiness of mind'. Haggard's fictional hero Allan Quatermain had a house on the Berea. In an interview with the *Natal Mercury* (18 April 1914), Haggard recalled the Berea of the 1870s: 'there were only a few scattered houses in pretty wildish sort of gardens, so much so that when I wrote those romances I made Allan Quatermain have his home on

the Berea. Now if the old hunter came to life he would hardly know the Berea, from what I saw of it yesterday.'

8. Dorothy Scudamore, a friend of the Haggard family from Norfolk.

9. Saccaboola plumes, the tail feathers from the male Longtailed Widow. The male in breeding plumage has extremely long (up to 40 cm or 16 in.) floppy tail feathers. The Zulu name for the bird is *iSakabuli,* which has become corrupted as saccaboola or saccabula.

10. The *Briton* (10 248 tons) was a Union-Castle steamer, the third ship to bear this name, and then the largest sailing between two ports in the British Empire. It entered service in 1897 and was sold to Italian shipbreakers in 1926.

11. Gingindlovu, site of military homestead, means place of the big elephant or swallower of the elephant in Zulu. It was the site of a battle during the Anglo-Zulu War, 2 April 1879.

12. John George Maydon (1857–1919), Natal businessman and politician, who assumed control of Natal's Railways and Harbours Department in 1904 and was responsible for enlarging Durban harbour. He volunteered for the Second Anglo-Boer War (1899–1902) but was not accepted and became a war correspondent for the London *Daily News.* He was with Lord Methuen and General John French at the relief of Kimberley and also present at the surrender of General P.A. Cronje at Paardeberg and the fall of Bloemfontein.

13. Phoenix, 18 km (11 miles) north of Durban, and site of a mission founded in 1858 by Daniel Lindley (1801–80), an American missionary. Mohandas Gandhi (1869–1948) established a farm settlement there in 1893.

    John Langalibalele Dube (1871–1946), educationist, journalist, politician and first president of the African National Congress. He was educated at the American Board Mission at Amanzimtoti, and subsequently at Oberlin College, Ohio, US, from 1898. He was later ordained as minister of the Congregational (American Board Mission) Church. During his stay in the US he was much influenced by Booker T. Washington. When he returned to Natal he unsuccessfully attempted to set up an industrial college along similar lines to Washington's Tuskegee model. He returned to the US on a fund-raising tour, which enabled him to build the Ohlange Institute. In 1904 he founded the newspaper *Ilange lase Natal,* which he edited until 1934. In 1909 he participated in the Bloemfontein conference of African leaders debating the South Africa Bill of 1909. He was a member of the Natal Native Congress, which affiliated to the South African Native National Congress in January 1912. This is considered the founding moment of the African National Congress (the name adopted in 1923) of which Dube was the first president 1912–17. In 1914 he led a Congress deputation to London to protest the Native Land Act (1913). Haggard met and interviewed Dube when he returned to Durban. See Chapter Eight, p. 227.

14. Battle of Ndondakasuka, 2 December 1856, between the forces of Cetshwayo and Mbuyazi, rival sons of Mpande. See H.R. Haggard, *Child of Storm* (London, 1913), Chapter 13, 'Umbelazi the Fallen'. Haggard made use of Melmoth Osborn's eyewitness account of the battle.

15. Stanger, established in 1873 and named after William Stanger (1811–54), first Surveyor-General of Natal. The Zulu name is kwaDukuza, meaning

'secret place' or 'place of concealment'. It is the site of the homestead of King Shaka established in 1826. It was renamed Dukuza in 1998. See H.R. Haggard, *Nada the Lily*, Chapter 21, 'The Death of Chaka'.

16. Eshowe was originally a Norwegian mission station. The name is possibly derived from Zulu word meaning 'wind in the trees' or 'windy place'. It could also be from the name of a species of tree that grew in the area and was used in the preparation of hides as the smell kept dogs away. A British force was besieged there during the Anglo-Zulu War (1879). After the annexation of Zululand (1887) it was selected as the seat of the resident commissioner and chief magistrate.

James Young Gibson (1857–1935), civil servant and magistrate, author of *The Story of the Zulus*, London,1903. His wife was Harriette Augusta (d.1927). He was appointed District Native Commissioner at Eshowe just prior to Haggard's visit.

17. Sir Marshall Clarke (1841–1909), soldier and administrator, ADC to Theophilus Shepstone at time of annexation of Transvaal in 1877; Administrator of Basutoland; Resident Commissioner and Chief Magistrate of Zululand, 1893–98; Imperial Resident Commissioner of Southern Rhodesia, 1899–1905.

Sir Charles James Renault Saunders (1857–1931), civil servant, Magistrate at Eshowe 1888–95, Chief Magistrate and Civil Commissioner for Zululand 1897 at the time of incorporation of Zululand into Natal. 'In 1902 he was made colonial representative on the Zululand Lands Delimitation Commission, which had been set up to determine land ownership and use in Zululand. As a result of the commission's report, certain areas were set aside for Zulu occupation, and the remainder, especially the rich coastal sugar lands, were opened up for white settlement. For these and other services he was made a KCMG in 1906.' Beyers and Basson, *South African Biography*, Vol. IV, Durban, 1987, p. 535.

18. Jack Osborn, son of Sir Melmoth, accompanied Haggard when he returned to England in 1879. 'I have come out in a new character viz. that of a guardian. I have got a youngster of 16 in tow, the son of my friend Osborn. I have got to put him to school in England. I think I shall send him to Graham (Haggard's former tutor. See Introduction, p. 4). Will you allow me to bring him down home for a little while when I arrive, for I shan't know what to on earth to do with him and the poor boy doesn't know a soul in England.' Cheyne Collection, Norfolk: Haggard letter to his father, 3 July 1879.

Charles Francis Hignett (1866–1940), appointed magistrate at Eshowe, May 1912. His wife was Alice Mary née Osborn (d.1925).

19. Wilmot Lushington Vyvyan (1861–1937), who succeeded Carter (see Chapter Five, Note 3) as Anglican Bishop of Zululand in 1903. He originally embarked on a legal career and was admitted to Lincoln's Inn in May 1883. While reading law he became interested in missionary work among the London poor and in 1887 began studying for the ministry.

20. KwaGqikazi in Zulu means 'finished' or 'finished with joy'. The name of this homestead provided Haggard with the title for his final volume of the Zulu trilogy, *Finished*, which was dedicated to Theodore Roosevelt. *Finished* incorporates several aspects of Haggard's tour through Zululand. In the introduction he records how he 'took the opportunity to travel through

Zululand, in order to refresh his knowledge of its people, their customs, their mysteries, and better prepare himself for the writing of this book'. See H.R. Haggard, *Finished*, London, 1962 edition, p. xi.

21. Cetshwayo died on 8 February 1884 at about 2.30 a.m. after having eaten. His family refused a post-mortem and a military medical officer who examined the body declared Cetshwayo had died of a heart attack. However, the case for him being poisoned is a strong one. See Laband, *Rope of Sand*, p. 367, and Guy, *The Destruction*, pp. 207–9. Osborn's letter to Haggard appears to be no longer extant. Haggard gives an account of Cetshwayo's death based on Osborn's testimony in the Introduction to the 1888 edition of *Cetywayo* (pp. 28–9). He concludes: 'Altogether it is my firm belief, gathered from information which I have received, that Cetywayo died by poison, a fact which I believe is not now disputed by those who are in the best position to know the truth.'

22. A character named Umnikwa guides Allan Quatermain to kwaGqikazi and relates the history of the homestead as given by Haggard in the diary. See H.R. Haggard, *Finished*, 1962 edition, p. 297.

23. Ndabuko, son of King Mpande, full brother to King Cetshwayo and later guardian of Dinuzulu.

   Usibepu is Zibhebhu kaMaphitha (*c.*1841–1904), chief of the Mandlakazi, who was appointed one of Wolseley's 13 chiefs in 1879. He was the leader of the opposition to the Zulu royal family and their supporters.

24. Melmoth, established in 1879, takes its name from Sir Melmoth Osborn, British Resident of Zululand in 1879.

25. Puff adder (*Bitis arietans arietans*), the most widespread poisonous snake in southern Africa. Adults grow to an average 90 cm (35 in.). Yellow to light brown or grey with distinctive chevron marking along the back, they rely on camouflage and immobility to escape detection. Most people are bitten when they tread on or close to the snake.

   Green mamba (*Dendroapsis angusticeps*), grows to average length of 1,8 m (1.9 yds). Usually a bright emerald green, it is shy and strictly arboreal. It is found in the forested coastal belt of KwaZulu-Natal northwards into Mozambique and eastern Zimbabwe. It is not as poisonous as the black mamba, but still dangerous.

26. 'A Zulu War Dance', *The Gentleman's Magazine*, July 1887. See Introduction, p. 6. In his diary James Stuart notes: 'Zulu dance on Golf ground – began 2.30 pm. As Chief Ntshingwayo was seriously ill, only members of Mpungose tribe (chief Mbango) could take part. There were about 400 of these, counting women and girls. For most part they were well dressed. A few women, however, had brought umbrellas . . . Dance lasted until about 5. A scorching afternoon. Many Eshowe residents attended.' Norfolk Record Office, MC 32/53: James Stuart, 'Diary – Zululand Trip', p.1.

27. The dance was hosted by Harcourt Tyrell, a Native Affairs Department official. His daughter, Barbara, who later became prominent as an ethnological artist, was present and recalled the event in her autobiography. 'Adults were seated in deck chairs facing the dancing area, VIPs in the front row; the shadowy figure of the Great Man, Haggard . . . The scorching Zululand sun beat down and up again from hot earth, baking us in our unaccustomed, uncomfortable, starched white "best" . . . A dance of brown

people watched by white people, of almost unclad people and heavily overclad people. High-stepping, stamping, chanting, girls of the front ranks in high-pitched song, shining bodies in beads only; deeper song from men at the back with shields and tall plumes. Old women scuttling along the line of girls, between them and the audience, mopping the girlish brows, cleansing the air with whirling switches . . . Ululating, that strange and exciting sound. Ropes of beadwork tossing wildly around brown bodies, and ostrich feathers against blue sky. A dance of praise for the honoured visitor.' Barbara Tyrell, *Her African Quest*, Cape Town, 1996, pp. 2–3.

28. Mandiki, *amandiki* in Zulu, persons suffering from hysterical disease.
29. Somkhele, named after the Zulu chief Somkhele of the Mkhwanazi clan, a nephew of King Mpande. Discovery of coal in the area in the 1890s led to brief influx into the area. Mining had ceased by 1926.
30. Mhlatuze River, in Zulu 'the forceful'. It enters the Indian Ocean at Richards Bay, named after Sir Frederick Richards, commander of the British naval forces assisting the land forces during the Anglo-Zulu War (1879).
31. Haggard was correct. In the 1960s the bay, known as Richards Bay, was developed as a seaport to handle coal and other exports brought in by bulk carriers and supertankers.
32. See Chapter Four, Note 34.
33. Umbonambi now Kwa-Mbonambi, the name derives from the Mbonambi people who lived there and means 'place of ill omen'. Hans Paludan Smith Schreuder (1816–82) was the first missionary of the Norwegian Mission Church (the missionary arm of the Lutheran Church) to come to Zululand, arriving in 1843. But after making no headway among the Zulus went to China. He was even less successful there and returned to Zululand in 1847. He set up several mission stations in the 1850s and 1860s; the last of these was Umbonambi in 1869.
34. Umfolozi, Mfolozi, formed by Black and White Mfolozi Rivers. From Zulu meaning either 'river of fibre', referring to wild fig trees, the bark of which was used for sewing-fibre, or 'erratic one', a reference to its meandering course. Also 'river of reeds'.
35. 'The journey in parts, especially about Enseleni, was very picturesque. Owing to absence of game and birds, much of the country was uninteresting. Put up at Redgrove's Hotel, one of the poorest places imaginable. Masuku, who walked from Eshowe to Gingindhlovu, joined train and came with us to Somkele. ' NRO, MC 32/53: 'Diary – Zululand Trip', p. 3.
36. Bungay, Suffolk, is close to Ditchingham, Haggard's home. The car, hired from Berea Livery and Bait Stables in Durban, was an Overland, an American car manufactured by Willys-Overland Motor Company in Toledo, Ohio. At one stage the company's cars were second only to Ford in popularity. The driver was H.M. Edwards. See also Note 119 and Chapter 4, Note 37.
37. Ka, *cha* or *qha*, Zulu for 'no'. *Inkosi*, a Zulu chief.
38. Hlabisa, name of a Zulu clan in the area. Albert Edward Harrington (1867–1961), appointed magistrate (October 1906) at Hlabisa.
39. *Indaba*, Zulu for meeting, conference, gathering.
40. 'Ntangwini, son of Maganda (Chief Somkhele's father). He was tall, say 6ft 1in, aged about 60, and had a headring. Was accompanied by his brother Mkambi, who, however, was of normal, dark colour. Mkambi and Ntang-

wini were by different mothers – same father.' NRO, MC 32/53: 'Diary – Zululand Trip', p. 3.

41. Bayete, *Bayethe*, Zulu for the royal salute.

42. Nagani, or today more commonly throughout Africa nagana, from the Zulu word *unakane*. Animal trypanosomiasis or sleeping sickness, an endemic parasitic disease transmitted among animals by the tsetse fly.

43. No species of iguana occurs in South Africa. The skin would have been that of one of the two species of monitor lizard that are found in South Africa and commonly known as leguaans. The rock or white-throated monitor (*veranus exanthematicus*) grows to a maximum length of 1.1 m (3 ft 8 in.) Haggard's 'fine iguana skin' most likely belonged to the Nile or water monitor (*varanus nilotis*) which grows to 1.4 m (4 ft 6 in.).

44. William Walter Dore (1842–1918), born on the Isle of Wight, England, and came to South Africa with his parents. His establishment at Xedeni, Hlabisa, consisted of a brick store and two wood and iron buildings.

45. Arthur Dicks Graham, appointed magistrate at Mahlabatini, August 1909.

46. Nongoma, formerly Ndwandwe after the clan that lived there but later changed to name of chief's principal homestead. The name is thought to be from KwaNongoma meaning 'place of the divine'. It is the site of the Battle of Ivuna, 23 June 1888, between Dinuzulu and Zibhebhu.

47. Charles Frederick Adams (1874–1942), storekeeper, auctioneer and farmer. His father was a 'cockney labourer', whose official title was 'agriculturalist' on the Universities Mission to Central Africa in 1861. See Tim Jeal, *Livingstone*, London, 1973, p. 236.

48. Despite his defeat of Mbuyazi in 1856 'Cetshwayo's recurrent nightmare that a new rival might yet emerge to challenge his hard-won position as heir was given uncomfortable reality by Mpande's growing favour for Mthonga, his son by a beloved junior wife, Nomantshali.' See Laband, *Rope of Sand*, pp. 151–2 for an account of Nomantshali's death.

49. Ndunu. The Battle of Ivuna, 23 June 1888. See Laband, *Rope of Sand*, p. 407 *et seq*.

50. Ngome forest, one of the largest indigenous forests in Zululand. The name means 'precipitous heights'. After the defeat of the Zulu army at Ulundi on 4 July 1879, and the destruction of oNdini, the royal homestead, Cetshwayo became a refugee in his own country. He was captured in the Ngome forest on 28 August 1879.

51. Ceza mountain, a traditional place of refuge for the uSuthu clan and the site of a skirmish between Dinuzulu and a colonial force on 26 April 1888. In *Finished*, Ceza mountain is the location for the Black Kloof, home of the 'great wizard Zikali, known throughout the land for longer than any man could remember as "Opener of Roads", a title that referred to his powers of spiritual vision, also as the "thing-that-should-never-have-been-born", a name given him by Chaka, the first and greatest of the Zulu kings, because of his deformity'. See H.R. Haggard, *Finished*, pp. 137 and 139.

52. Nongalaza kaNondela, Mpande's commander at Battle of Maqongqo hills (1840) near the Mkhuze River, north of Nongoma.

53. Nzibe kaSenzangakhona, a younger brother of Mpande. He died of malaria in 1828.

54. A reference to the custom of 'raising seed' for a deceased brother who has no issue. The Zulus followed the custom of levirate, marrying the widow(s)

of their deceased brother (usually only if he had no children of his own). The children born of this union were known as the children of the deceased.

55. Oham or Uham. Hamu was the genealogical son of Nzibe kaSenzanga-khona and the biological son of Mpande. Opposed to Cetshwayo, he defected to the British during the Anglo-Zulu War (1879). He was appointed a chief in the Wolseley settlement.

56. 'Moving the spirit', a reference to the *ukubuyisa* ('bringing back') ceremony held a year after the death of a head of a family homestead. A beast is slaughtered to call the spirit from its wanderings and to 'bring it back' to the family homestead, where it should 'settle down'. In the unlikely event of a homestead having to be moved (eg. after various disasters, such as fire, multiple deaths from illness, etc), then the spirits of the ancestors must also be 'moved', i.e. called to the new home. In the modern context, if a person decides to make the family homestead in a town instead of the traditional homestead in the country, they should signal this to the ancestral spirits by slaughtering a beast in the new place to call the ancestors there.

57. Umpikanina, a grandson of Mpande and son of Ziwedu, Cetshwayo's half-brother. An uSuthu leader, he was placed under Zibhebhu in the 1879 settlement of Zululand.

58. Zulu head ring, *isicoco,* ring of fibre and gum bound into the hair on top of the head as the mark of a mature married man.

59. Red ivory, the popular name for *Berchemia zeyheri*. The heartwood fades from a pink to a deep red after cutting and is much prized for carving into ornaments and curios. Only Zulu chiefs were allowed to carry knobkerries made from the wood.

60. Dingiswayo (*c.*1770–1818), chief of the Mthethwa. He sheltered Shaka and his mother Nandi. After Dingiswayo was captured and killed by Zwide, chief of the Ndwandwe, Shaka defeated Zwide at Hlabisa.

61. Imbekamuzi, meaning 'watch the kraal'. Now *uMbhekamuzi*. '. . . we tramped for miles through the terrible Bekameezi Valley, a hot and desolate place which the Zulus swear is haunted. So unhealthy is this valley, which is the home of large game, that whole kraals-full of people who have tried to cultivate the rich land, have died in it of fever, or fled away, leaving their crops unreaped. Now no man dwells there. After this we climbed a terrible mount to the high land of Mahlabatini.' See H.R. Haggard, *Finished*, p. 160.

62. Mahlabatini in Zulu means 'country of the white sandy soil'. It is the site of magistracy of the Mahlabatini district.

63. Two species of rhinoceros occur in southern Africa, the white or square-lipped and the black hook-lipped. The name white is derived from the Dutch 'wydt', referring not to its colour but the width of its mouth.

64. In a standard British square action, Lord Chelmsford defeated the Zulu army at Ulundi, 4 July 1879. The British casualties were 13 dead and 69 wounded; the Zulu losses are estimated to have been around 1 500.

    In *Cetshwayo's Dutchman: Being the Private Journal of a White Trader in Zululand during the British Invasion,* (1880) by Cornelius Vijn, and translated with notes by Bishop J.W. Colenso, there is an account of the disinterment of Mpande's remains. However, another account is included stating the grave was not interfered with. See pp. 86–8. During 1880 there was some debate on the matter, reflected in the columns of the *Natal Witness*. The 'white chief of the Zulus', John Dunn (1836–95), who is mentioned as being involved in the exhumation recounted in *Cetshwayo's Dutchman*, wrote an outraged letter, published on 5 August, offering £100 'if anyone can prove I was connected with the exhuming of the body of the late King Panda'. The editor responded, saying that judging from Dunn's letter the grave had been rifled, even if Dunn had nothing to do with it.

The 18 December edition of the *Natal Witness* records the answer to a question asked in the Natal Legislative Assembly as to whether or not the grave had been rifled. In answer 'the Colonial Secretary stated that his attention was drawn to the matter by the Bishop of Natal and he did what he could to help His Lordship in his researches but with little result. He (the Colonial Secretary) could not assert that the grave had not been rifled, nor on the other hand could he say that it had not. His own impression was that the grave had been disturbed, but not by any officer of Her Majesty's service, but probably by some small party moved more by curiosity than anything else.'

The Royal Victorian Hospital at Netley, Hampshire, a military hospital.

65. Simpofu's name is given to a minor character, killed by Allan Quatermain at the battle of Isandlwana, in H.R. Haggard, *Finished*, pp. 223–4.

'A Native headringed man Simpofu, whose kraal is on the spot, gave a lot of useful information about the battle, in which he himself had taken part, though barely 3 mo. before it was fought he had been shot through neck and shoulder at battle of Kambula in the north west of Zululand.' NRO, MC 32/53: 'Diary – Zululand Trip', p. 4.

66. iNgobamakhosi *ibutho* (regiment) 'the humblers of kings', formed *c.*1872 from youths born *c.*1853.

67. The battle of Khambula, 29 March 1879. The Zulus attacked uphill against a laagered position. British casualities were 29 dead and 54 wounded. The Zulus lost an estimated 2 000 men.

68. Senzangakhona (*c.*1757–1816), son of Jama, chief of the Zulu clan. Jama was a descendant of Zulu Nkosinzulu from whom the Zulus supposedly take their name. Senzangakhona succeeded his father in about 1781 and it was under Senzangakhona that the Zulus first rose from obscurity. The Nobamba homestead in the emaKhosini Valley founded by Jama, the grand-father of Shaka, was re-established by Dinuzulu. On his death he asked to be buried there.

69. Nodwengu, meaning 'place of revolt and quarrels' to commemorate Mpande's battle for succession, or 'the place of the irresistible'.

70. This aspect of the aftermath of the battle of Ulundi is not mentioned in any of the standard histories. I am grateful to Ian Knight, who unearthed the following childhood reminiscence of H.P. Braatvedt, who accompanied his missionary parents on a picnic and fishing expedition in the Ulundi area in the late 1880s: 'Strolling along the river bank, I was considerably startled by the sight of about two complete skeletons. Probably these men fell in the Ulundi battle, as at one time numerous skeletons lay scattered on the

Ulundi plains. The storekeeper at Ulundi decided to make use of these human remains and offered to barter sugar and salt for old bones. As a rule the Zulus show the greatest respect for the dead, but evidently temptation proved too strong, because very soon long files of women and girls daily wended their way to the trader with baskets full. Eventually a considerable heap of the remains of the gallant Zulu warriors was collected and despatched to what in those days was called a bone manure factory in Durban. But on arrival of the gruesome load there was an immediate outcry against such desecration, so the bones were buried instead.' H.P. Braatvedt, *Roaming Zululand with a Native Commissioner*, Pietermaritzburg, 1949, p. 10.

71. Alligator, an American reptile, used here to mean crocodile.

72. On 3 May 1906, Herbert Munro Stainbank, magistrate of Mahlabatini, was 'foully murdered . . . on the right bank of the White Umfolozi River, and beside the public road'. See James Stuart, *A History of the Zulu Rebellion*, London, 1913, pp. 219–20.

73. uMgungundlovu, Dingane's homestead in the emaKhosini valley, constructed in 1829.

74. George Whitefield Kinsman, appointed assistant magistrate at Babanango, April 1912.

75. This conflicts with Lilias's comment in L.R. Haggard, *The Cloak*, p. 223, on 'how rapidly her generally fastidious parent had reverted to the ways of his youth. He rode the small veld ponies with real enjoyment.'

76. Matiwane was one of several people executed by Dingane as they were perceived to be threats to his authority following the assassination of Shaka. 'Matiwane kaMasumpa of the Ngwane, who returned a suppliant to Zululand in 1829 after the destruction of his following by the forces of the Cape Colony. Dingane did not trust his intentions and he was put to death on a small stony hill across the Mkhumbane stream from Mgungundlovu, a place of execution known ever afterwards as kwaMatiwane.' Laband, *Rope of Sand*, p. 54.

    Hloma amabutho, in Zulu means 'arm the regiments'.

    The emaKhosini Valley or Valley of Kings. Many of the Zulu rulers are buried here, including Zulu Nkosinzulu, supposed progenitor of the Zulu nation. All these locations feature in *Marie*, the first of Haggard's Zulu trilogy set during the reign of Dingane.

77. Nkandla, from Zulu *kandla,* meaning tired or exhausted. 'Throughout Zulu history the Nkandla forest has been a place of mystery, the home of supernatural beings, and a formidable stronghold and place of retreat.' Guy, *The Destruction*, p. 206.

78. *Isigodlo*, king's or chief's private enclosure; women of king's establishment.

79. Piet Retief (1780–1838), Great Trek leader who took a group of trekkers across the Drakensberg into what became Natal. He and his men were killed while negotiating a land settlement and treaty with King Dingane.

80. *Euphorbia ingens,* also known as candelabra tree. A massively branched succulent, it produces a toxic latex (hence the popular name milk tree) which causes blistering on the skin and blindness if brought into contact with the eyes.

    Zulu Nkosinzulu, Senzangakhona's ancestor and supposed progenitor of the Zulus.

81. Haggard visisted the Holy Land in 1900. See *A Winter Pilgrimage*, London, 1901.
82. Francis Owen (1802–54), missionary in Zululand 1837–38. *The Diary of Francis Owen: Missionary with Dingaan in 1837–38*, Cape Town, 1926.
83. The stomachs of the dead were opened to allow the spirit of the dead to escape. For details on this custom and the required cleansing ceremonies see Ian Knight, *The Anatomy of the Zulu Army: From Shaka to Cetshwayo 1818–1879*, London, 1995, p. 226 *et seq.*
84. After the breakdown of Wolseley's settlement plan, Zululand was partitioned in 1883. With the return of King Cetshwayo in the same year, there was renewed conflict between the uSuthu party and Zibhebhu's Mandlakazi. Following the defeat of the uSuthu forces at the battles of Msebe (29 March 1883) and oNdini (21 July 1883) – the latter marking the final destruction of the old order – Cetshwayo fled to Eshowe.

    After the death of Cetshwayo, his son, Dinuzulu, formed an alliance with the Boers who installed him as king on 21 May 1884. A combined uSuthu–Boer force defeated Zibhebhu's Mandlakazi at the Battle of Tshaneni, 5 June 1884. The agreement by which the Boers obtained land was not 'vague' but well-documented. (See C.T. Binns, *Dinuzulu: The Death of the House of Shaka*, London, 1968, chapters 2–5.) The land thus obtained was eventually incorporated into the New Republic, with its capital at Vryheid ('freedom'). Proviso B was excluded from the New Republic but whites were allowed property rights. The Boer settlement, together with German interest in the area, moved the British to act and in May 1887 they annexed Zululand as a British colony. Known as British Zululand, its borders were contiguous with the New Republic in the north and north-west and Natal to the south. However, this did not bring peace, and following further clashes between the uSuthu and colonial authorities who were supported by the Mandlakazi and other 'loyalists', Dinuzulu was tried and found guilty of rebellion and exiled to St Helena. He returned in 1898, a year after Zululand had been formally incorporated into Natal. Implicated in the rebellion of 1906, he was exiled to the Transvaal where he died in 1913.
85. Sir Charles Saunders, see Note 17.
86. *Acacia mearnsii* (black wattle), an Australian tree introduced by the forestry industry.
87. Yellow *Imatophyllum* and *Imatophyllum Sulphurea*, members of the clivia family. These Latin names have since been changed. The orange bloom is *clivia mineata*, the yellow bloom is a variation. See also H.R. Haggard, *A Gardener's Year*, London, 1905, pp. 25–6. A pencilled note in the original typescript reads: 'They have been growing well at Ditchingham. H.R.H. Feb 1915.'
88. Haggard has confused the concluding action of the Zulu Rebellion in the Izinsimba Valley (8 July 1906) with that fought at Mome Gorge on 10 June 1906, where the combined force of Mehlokazulu kaSihayo Ngobese (*c.*1855–1906) and the rebel leader Bhambatha (*c.*1865–1906) was defeated and both men killed. 'The engagement was hardly a battle; it had all the characteristics of a massacre,' Ian Knight, *Great Zulu Battles 1838–1906*, London, 1998, p. 211. One officer was killed and another officer and a trooper died of wounds. Rebel losses were probably in the region of

600. Haggard's casualty figures for the battle at Izinsimba Valley are accurate. See also Walter Bosman, *The Natal Rebellion*, London, 1907; James Stuart, *Zulu Rebellion*, and Shula Marks, *The Reluctant Rebellion*, Oxford, 1970.

89. Miss Nombé appears as Nombi, a central character in *Finished*. '. . . there appeared a tall and graceful young woman, rather light-coloured, with deep and quiet eyes and a by no means ill-favoured face, remarkable for a fixed and somewhat mysterious smile. She was a witch-doctoress sure enough, for she wore in her hair the regulation bladders and about her neck the circlet of baboon's teeth, also round her middle a girdle from which hung little bags of medicines'. H.R. Haggard, *Finished*, p. 129.

Stuart: 'Everything went well until we reached the Umhlatuze river. Here car stuck in middle of river. Whilst there, with a formidable hill before us, Nombi, a young girl, who was qualifying to be an *isangoma* (witch-doctor) turned up, accompanied by her father Sikonyana and another man. The men assisted us whilst Nombi sat on the opposite bank. We were delayed ∫ hr at this place. Reached Empandhleni Magistracy about 6pm and stayed at Nkandla Hotel.' NRO, MC 32/53: 'Diary – Zululand Trip', p. 5.

90. Following the battle of Mome Gorge, Sigananda, who was chief of the Chube in whose area the battle was fought, surrendered. An old man, probably in his nineties, he died in a Natal gaol on 22 July 1906, less than a month after his court martial.

91. Mali-mati or Malimathe, the Zulu name for Osborn derived from his first name Melmoth.

92. *Nkosi! Nkos' enkulu! Nkos' ephakade!* meaning 'Chief! Great Chief! Chief from olden times'.

93. Haggard's Zulu name, see Chapter Four, p. 115 and Note 41.

94. T.A. Jackson (1870–1934), magistrate of Nkandla. Empandhleni was not the name of a magisterial district.

95. Arthur Jesse Shepstone (1852–1912), Natal civil servant, chief Native Commissioner at the time of his death. He was instrumental in Haggard meeting James Stuart. See Introduction, p. 25.

96. Petrus Lafras (Piet) Uys (1797–1838) died at Itala, the site of the Battle of eThaleni (1838) with his son Dirkie. His youngest son, with the same forenames, was killed in 1879 during the retreat from Hlobane in the Anglo-Zulu War (1879).

97. Isandlwana, the name of the mountain dominating the plain where the Zulus annihilated a British force on 22 January 1879. Stuart's interpretation of the mountain's name is the correct one. For accounts of the battle see Knight, *Zulu*, reprinted (minus illustrations and photographs) as *The Sun Turned Black*, Johannesburg, 1995; Laband and Thompson, *The Illustrated Guide*.

98. Mabele or kaffir corn, *amabele*, Zulu for sorghum, millet.

99. Archbishop Carter, see Chapter Five, Note 3.

100. Chief Ntshingwayo kaMahole (then aged 68) and Chief Mavumengwana kaNdlela Ntuli were joint commanders of the Zulu army. Ntshingwayo was killed at the Battle of oNdini, 21 July 1883. The Malagati hills are now known as the Malakatha hills.

101. Charles Evelyn Parr (1885–1953), born in Nottingham, England.
102. Lieutenant-Colonel Henry Burmester Pulleine (1838–79). Pulleine was left in command of the British camp at Isandlwana after Lord Chelmsford had departed with a reconnaissance force in search of the Zulu army. Colonel Anthony William Durnford (1830–79) commanded a force of the Natal Native Contingent and Natal Native Horse during the battle. He arrived after Chelmsford's departure and was senior in rank to Pulleine. Following the defeat there was debate as to whether he superseded Pulleine as commanding officer and was consequently to blame for the defeat.

  George Shepstone (1849–79), son of Theophilus Shepstone, Durnford's political officer.

  Lieutenants Nevill Coghill (1852–79) and Teignmouth Melvill (1842–79) were killed trying to save the Queen's Colour. They were posthumously awarded the Victoria Cross in 1907.
103. Edward Hitchcock, quartermaster, Newcastle Mounted Rifles. He was the innkeeper of the Newcastle Hotel in civilian life.
104. 'Wow', correctly in Zulu, *hau!* Cetshwayo is recorded as saying: 'A spear has been thrust into the belly of the nation. There are not enough tears to mourn for the dead.' See Knight, *Brave Men's Blood*, p. 82.
105. Following the battle of Isandlwana, a Zulu force under the command of Dabulamanzi crossed the Mzinyathi (Buffalo) River and attacked a small British force at the Swedish mission station of Rorke's Drift, which the British had commandeered and turned into a supply depot and hospital. The post was hastily fortified by the occupants who fought off the Zulu attacking force in a battle lasting from about 4 p.m. on 22 January 1879 to dawn on the 23rd. Eleven Victoria Crosses were awarded, a record for a single action and interpreted by some as an attempt to divert attention from the military and political implications of the defeat at Isandlwana.

  In NRO, MC 32/51: 'Rough Diary', 28 April 1914, Haggard notes: 'Rorke's Drift. Zulus passed a hill w. rocky kop now known as Oscarberg. Rorke's Drift masked by patch of old trees on slope of hill. River (Buffalo) at base. Long slope going down to R. Drift. Some miles beyond R.D. Sibindi Mt. in Mankavadui (spelling unclear) Range. Large plain.' There is no such mountain as Sibindi in the area though a stream of that name exists. The range of mountains is also unknown under either the spelling above or that in the text. Haggard gives a factual account of the battles of Isandlwana and Rorke's Drift in *The True Story Book*, edited by Andrew Lang, London, 1900. See 'The Tale of Isandhlwana and Rorke's Drift', p. 132. The battle of Isandlwana features in H.R. Haggard, *Witch's Head*, and *Finished*.
106. The story of 'the old Hottentot washerwoman' is to be found in H.R. Haggard, *The Days*, Vol. 1, pp. 118–19.
107. Black Billy. See Chapter Five, p. 129 and Note 11.
108. In 1879, Canon Robert Mullins was principal of the Native College in Grahamstown.
109. 'All these details about how a person is called by the ancestors to become a diviner are true, and still relevant today. The period of training, as well as the "vague ill-health" itself, is known as *ukuthwasa*. The fetching of a python (or other snake) from the waters of a deep pool is often a feature of the latter part of their training of a diviner.' Information supplied by Adrian Koopman.

In *Finished* (p. 130), Nombi explains her vocation to Allan Quatermain: 'O Macumazahn, I have heard the call, I have felt the pain in my back, I have drunk of the black medicine and of the white medicine, yes, for a whole year. I have been visited by a multitude of Spirits and seen the shades of those who live and of those who are dead. I have dived into a river and drawn my snake from the mud; see, its skin is about me now.'

'Boa-constrictor', a South American snake; its equivalent in South Africa is the southern African rock python that also coils around its prey using compression to suffocate it. The rock python is the largest snake in South Africa, adults averaging between 3 m and 4 m (10 ft and 13 ft) in length.

110. Charles Johnson (1850–1927), Anglican missionary. While still a lay catechist he established a mission at Isandlwana in 1879. In 1881 moved to St Augustine's, Rorke's Drift. Ordained in 1887, he was appointed Archdeacon of Zululand, 1900. He assisted in the translation of *Book of Common Prayer* into Zulu and compiled a Zulu hymnal.

111. John Bernard Farrer (1870–1951), appointed magistrate, Nqutu, in May 1910.

112. Manzolwandle, born 1884, his claim to the Zulu throne was regarded by some as superior to that of Dinuzulu. He later gave his support to Zibhebhu in the conflict between the uSuthu and the Mandlakazi.

113. Dinuzulu's son and heir Solomon Nkayishana Maphumuzana (1893–1933). During Dinuzulu's exile in St Helena from 1890–97 Dinuzulu fathered six children from his two *abalobokazi* or 'female attendants'. Silomo was Solomon's mother.

114. 'The issue of a medal, in recognition of services rendered during the Rebellion, was approved by His Majesty the King. It was granted to those (including nursing sisters), who served between 11 February and the 3 August, for continuous period of not less than 20 days, also to certain civilians, native chiefs, and others who had rendered valuable service. A clasp, inscribed "1906" was issued with the medal to such as had served for a continuous period of not less than 50 days.' James Stuart, *Zulu Rebellion*, p. 406.

115. Those who had killed one of more of the enemy and those who had stabbed a corpse (according to the belief known as *hlomula* that suggested that part of the glory of overcoming a particularly dangerous foe accrued not only to the slayer but to others who stabbed the corpse) were known as *izinxweleha*. Those who had stabbed in battle were called *ingwazi*, one who stabs, or *iqawe*, hero, and were awarded thin willow sticks. Once their bravery was publicly acknowledged they were entitled to cut the sticks into small blocks to be threaded as necklaces known as *iziqu*.

   Xoxa-impi, xoxa is the verb 'discuss' and *impi* is an army (or regiment/battle/war).

116. R. Gordon Cumming (1820–1866), author of *Five Years of a Hunter's Life in the Far Interior of South Africa* (1850).

117. *Inxota, izingxotha,* bronze armbands awarded in recognition of their bravery to outstanding warriors.

118. *Umnaka,* hollow brass rings worn by women of rank.

119. Dundee, established 1882, named after Scottish birthplace of Thomas Paterson Smith, who laid out the town.

'. . . battered, bruised, with its steering gear bent and its starting machinery out of action, that American-made motor car did limp into Dundee, in Natal, where I bade it farewell. I wonder what it cost to put it in repair again?' H. Rider Haggard, 'A Journey Through Zululand', *Windsor Magazine*, 1916.

After Haggard's departure from South Africa, A. Edwards of Berea Livery and Bait Stable, 294 Essenwood Road, Durban, from whom the Overland had been hired, entered into correspondence with the Native Affairs Department following their query of his final account which included a charge for an extra passenger, Mazooku. 'The extra passenger was a valet who accompanied Sir Rider Haggard and who was of considerable service in helping push when the car stopped on heavy roads, and in carrying luggage up hills and through deep rivers,' claimed M.H. Addison, Chief Native Commissioner, Natal, writing on 11 May 1914. 'Although when the car was hired it was not anticipated that extra charge would be made for any person carried beyond the number comprising the originally stated party, I am prepared to pass the item to the Secretary for Native Affairs for payment provided it is reduced, so as to be more commensurate with the extra petrol used and the wear and tear involved in the conveyance of a fourth passenger.'

Edwards responded on 13 May. 'I am, to say the least of it, surprised that you should quibble over the charge made for the extra passenger, which is quite reasonable and if charged pro ratio would be more. On the basis of your argument, it is only right to assume that I should have allowed for a valet for each of the gentlemen without charging extra, which is absolutely ridiculous. No mention is made in your first letter of luggage, but an ordinary amount was anticipated and allowed for but, NOT to the extent of the amount actually carried viz: about 3 cwt. The carrying of this luggage has damaged the paint to such an extent that it will necessitate the car being repainted. In fact the estimated depreciation of the car is considerably over £50/-/- so I am a big loser in the transaction.

'On a journey of this description it is not anticipated that it will be accomplished without difficulties occurring, and as in the case of the crossing of rivers and negotiating almost impossible roads, it is the duty of everyone concerned to lend a hand for their benefit mutually. Both gentlemen made the assertion it was nearly impossible for a motor car to make the journey, and had it not been that the car was a new one, it is questionable whether the trip would have been made so successfully. In conclusion I must say that taking everything into consideration, that I anticipated receiving your cheque by return, and am much disappointed to have you demur at the charges. Kindly let me have cheque without further delay.' CNC 330/1914, Items 41 and 42. Native Affairs Department correspondence on Haggard's tour of Zululand.

'The trip though hurried, with enforced stoppages here and there, was enjoyable and thoroughly interesting at every stage. Owing to lack of time, visit to Nkandla forest, Ofeni gorge and other places of interest had to be abandoned. In addition to our major misfortunes, were the inevitable minor ones, such as my Gladstone bag being filled with water when car stuck in the Mhlatuze. The taking of Masuku proved fortunate all along the route.' NRO, MC 32/53: 'Zululand Trip', p. 7.

120. Tshetsha Umfan, *shesha mfana*, in Zulu meaning 'make haste, boy'.
121. Battle of Talana, 20 October 1899, the first action of the Second Anglo-Boer War (1899–1902). Major-General Sir William Penn Symons, who died of wounds, is buried in a small cemetery attached to the St James Anglican church in Dundee. The other dead are interred in a cemetery at the foot of Talana Hill.
122. Glencoe, railway junction 10 km (6 miles) from Dundee, the site of a train accident in 1895 when 40 people died, mainly women and children who had left Johannesburg due to disturbances prior to the Jameson Raid.
123. East Coast Fever, see Chapter Four, p. 112 and Note 34.
124. Lobola, *ilobolo*, translated as 'bride wealth'. The payment (traditionally in the form of cattle) the prospective groom agrees to pay the bride's father. Only when agreement on the amount is reached does the engagement become official.
125. *Souvent femme varie*, in French it means 'women often change (their minds)'.
126. *Tronk*, Afrikaans for gaol, prison. Colloquial English.
127. Inkoos! baba! (chief father) *Nkosi! Baba!* Chief! Father!
128. 'Caught early train to Glencoe Junction where we joined the "down" mail shortly after 8am. Reached PMBurg about 3.30pm. Here Masuku & I left – Sir R. and Mr Gibson going on to Durban'. NRO, MC 32/53: 'Zululand Trip', p. 6.

Chapter Eight

A Zulu of high blood

డిడిడిడిడి

Haggard's return to Durban effectively marked the end of his southern African sojourn. In a sense it was a fitting place to close the journey since his 'affair' with Africa had begun in the city as a young man of 19, attached to the staff of the Lieutenant-Governor, Sir Henry Bulwer. On that occasion the party had disembarked from an anchorage outside the harbour bar. His departure aboard the Gaika *would be an altogether sedater affair than his arrival in 1875 – embarking from the passenger terminal in the city's impressive and growing harbour facility.*

Thursday, 30 April

On the day after my arrival at Durban where I said goodbye to my kind friend Mr. Gibson, through the good offices of Mr. Binns, the Chief Magistrate,[1] I was fortunate enough to have a long interview with the Rev. J. Dube of Phoenix, near Durban, the Zulu clergyman and leader, whom I have already mentioned, who came to see me on his way to Johannesburg and England.[2] Here I give the *substance* of his remarks which I posted at once to the Colonial Secretary, Mr. Harcourt.

Dube said: 'I am an educator, that is my business. I have been thrust into a semi-political position by my people. Two years ago I was elected President of the South African Native National Congress. Its aim is to unite the natives for political purposes, to consider proposed legislation affecting their interests and to make representations to those in authority. We want an organisation to speak for us as we have no representation in the Union parliament.

'My points of objection to the Land Act of last year are: (1) I regard the refusal to allow us to buy land from Europeans as depriving natives of their rights, since previous to this Act they could buy anywhere except in the Orange Free State. You must remember that we natives today only hold as native reserves 10 million morgen (20 million acres) out of the 400 million morgen (800 million acres) in the Union. (2) That natives are not now allowed to lease land or to farm on shares with Europeans. In fact they may not become rent-paying tenants or

*A page of Haggard's rough diary. This shows the
last page of the interview with John Dube. The last
three lines read: 'Read over to Mr Dube who says
this is a correct summary of his views. HRH'*

squat on farms except on condition that they labour for the farmer.
The law lays down the duration of such labour but its provisions are
frequently evaded by unscrupulous whites to the disadvantage of my
people. The natives have been much deteriorated by contact with low-
class whites. Those of them who have been in Johannesburg and other
mining centres are responsible for what is known as the "black peril";
such men become *izegekbengus* (rascals).[3]

'White women allow natives into their bedrooms when they are
half naked, which they would never do in the case of white men. "A
native is a man as much as a white." I believe in education, both literary and agricultural, as a remedy and desire to bring the natives under
better influences. Christianity is spreading in the country districts and is
likely to continue to spread. The institution of polygamy, which is the
great obstacle in its path, will probably be solved to a great extent by
economic pressure. The expense of it under advanced social conditions
is too great. Also every extra wife means an extra tax. "Of late the

Killie Campbell Collection

*John Dube, first president of the
African National Congress in 1922.*

white people have been tightening the screw more and more." They used to be more sympathetic. This attitude has evoked a like feeling among the natives whose sentiments towards the whites are now harsher than they used to be. They say: "If the whites declare they cannot live with us let them go away and live in their own country." Your people could do more to bring about a better understanding if they chose. They have the power in their hands, and can take us Natives into their confidence. The whites "are so far away from us". We have no means of communication with the authorities or public opinion except through the magistrates who have little time in which to attend to native grievances. My proposition is that in every magisterial division there should be either a magistrate with more leisure, or some gentleman especially appointed to devote himself to native affairs, with whom we could consult on all matters affecting us and our welfare. I should like to see a council in Zululand such as exists in the Transkei. Councils of this sort should have powers of criticism of all laws affecting natives and of spending a certain proportion of the money raised from them on matters of local importance such as roads, commonages, dipping-tanks, education, control of children, etc. etc.

'I do not think there will be any more wars. The white people should be kinder and more generous to natives. £200 000 per annum is raised from natives in Natal by direct taxation and only £15 000 per annum is spent on their education. We natives want a national system of education as in England, but modified to suit local needs. I would not bind

down the natives to any particular sect of Christianity. I am a Con-
gregationalist but I do not insist upon all the pupils in my school becoming Congregationalists. I would make the natives pay a little in this
way or that towards the cost of their education. Our people must be
educated ... "they sit in darkness". I am starting for Cape Town to
present a petition to parliament praying for the repeal of the Native
Land Act. If we fail in this a deputation will sail at once to beg the King
[George V] to repeal the Bill before 19 June next when the year of
grace allowed under the Constitution will expire.'

Such are the views of Mr. Dube which, when I read them to him
from my rough note, he declared to be correctly set down. I should state
that he speaks English perfectly, having been educated in America. He
is a Zulu of high blood. By a section of the white people in Natal he is
mistrusted and accused of personal ambition, which of course he may
possess. There is a great opening for a national native leader and Mr.
Dube may desire to be that leader. However this may be, I am bound to
say that he impressed me most favourably while the case which he
advanced seems to me one hard to answer. Thus, there is no doubt that
this new Land Act inflicts great hardships on the native community and
if an attempt were made to enforce it everywhere I do not know what
would happen. A commission under the presidency of my old friend Sir
W. Beaumont[4] is sitting to determine the native areas but before that
commission has reported this drastic Act is passed.

There is, however, little hope that Mr. Dube will succeed, either in his
petition to the Union parliament or to the King. The Colonial Office at
home will certainly say that it cannot interfere with the discretion of the
Union government and, in effect, that the natives may 'go hang'. But
what will be the end of it all? Seven million of black folk, I think that is
about the number including the population of the protectorates, cannot
be permanently neglected (or is oppressed the word?) by one million and
a quarter of whites.[5] Compressed steam will escape somehow and somewhere. Probably, as Mr. Dube says, it will not be by way of war, unless a
great national leader should arise or the discordant races should be tied
together by some new faith such as Mahomedanism. The effects of moral
pressure exercised by a sullen and discontented multitude robbed of their
inheritance are perhaps more to be dreaded. I enter here a copy of a
passage from a letter I wrote to Lord Gladstone, on my return from Zululand, which touches on these questions:

Marine Hotel, Durban.
30 April 1914.

I hope to send you my impressions of Rhodesia and Zululand in
due course – or rather a copy of what I write to the CO [Colonial
Office]. Meanwhile, as you asked me to do so, I will summarize

the latter in a few lines. I think that the Zulus are in a most unhappy position. Some two-thirds of their land are in the hands of white people: often they are rent-paying squatters on the territory which their fathers occupied. They have no head whatsoever, they 'wander and wander'. They are a people whom we have broken and not mended.

The justice of many of our dealings with them is open to the gravest question. On every occasion and pretext we take more of their land leaving them the worst and most unhealthy portions. And in return what do we give them? They long to be educated but there is no system of education. The little that is done is the work of the missionaries and sectarian. Some general system of education should, in my opinion, be introduced under government control. Again, I think that they should be given a representative voice in their own affairs, such as exists in the Transkei and Basutoland. Why cannot a native council be established on which the Native Commissioner and the magistrates have seats? They have many troubles, many grievances, but their only opportunity of expressing them at present is in the course of a visit from the commissioner, necessarily of a hurried nature, or through an interview with the local magistrate. None of them knows what the rest think throughout their wide land: they have no chance of collective speech.

The present position seems to me to be full of dangers, which are either not understood or are ignored by the political persons who have the practical control of their affairs. Few in Natal take any real interest in the Zulus, or have a sound knowledge of their history, or an understanding of their needs and aspirations, which require to be studied with that sympathetic imagination which enables us to put ourselves in the position of others. One of the few bright spots I see in the general gloom is the recent appointment of Mr. Gibson to the post of Native Commissioner. He *does* understand the Zulus and he does appreciate their wants and needs, if ever a man did. But his powers are very limited. There is much more that I might say but I will not attempt it now. I am extremely glad to have had the opportunity of visiting the Zulus and of forming my own conclusions concerning them, etc. etc.

(sgd.) *H.R.H.*

Friday, 1 May

Today I was conducted by Mr. Donovan, the Superintendent of Police at Durban,[6] round the Native Eating Houses which were established by the municipality eight years ago to give the natives an opportunity of trading in food on their own account. Since the passing of the Native Beer Act, under the provisions of which beer is brewed by the municipality, this drink is also sold at the eating houses.[7] Formerly it used to be brought into the town in pots by the kaffir women, with the result that these girls were exposed to sundry dangers. I should explain that this beer is the old-fashioned beverage made from kaffir corn, which the municipal experts have now learned to manufacture to a nicety on a large scale, not *itishimiana* or treacle beer that makes those who drink it raving mad. This treacle beer is a comparatively new liquor; it was unknown in my day, and the sale of it has been declared illegal because of the crimes and drunkenness which result from its consumption.[8]

These Native Eating Houses, of which four exist in Durban, are very largely patronised. There are also 40 private eating houses in the town, kept by low-class whites and coloured persons, but no more licences are issued for such establishments and whenever a proprietor dies his house is closed. First I visited the largest municipal eating house. It is a big shed-like place divided into two sections separated by a fence of open wirework. In the part to the left food is sold at 3d. a meal, aerated waters at 1d. a bottle, tea at 1d. a cup and two slices of bread and butter also at 1d. There is a white superintendent but no European is allowed here for the purpose of trade. The kaffir stallholders rent a table at 1s. a day and compete for custom with each other. All sorts of meats are provided, including curry which I was surprised to see Zulus eating with appetite. Each stallholder has his compartment in a common kitchen where the food is cooked by Zulus who supply their own fuel and pots. Many natives were taking their meals in this place though it was a slack time of the day.

On the other side of the wire fence is the beer compartment. Tickets are issued by a white man in a box which enables the customers to obtain beer to the value of either 6d. or 3d. from the bar. This they drink from cans, seated at tin-topped tables, generally in small parties and consuming the liquor turn and turn about, loving-cup fashion. The profits from the sale of this kaffir beer, or *tshwala*,[9] which amount to a very large sum in the course of the year – I forget how many thousands of pounds, are kept in a special account by the authorities and must be expended for the benefit of the natives frequenting the borough, such as the provision of kaffir lodging houses and hospitals.

Trade is also carried on at these places, at a rent charge of 6d. a day for a 'pitch'. Here were sundry 'doctors' with their stock in trade spread out before them. This was of a kind that would astonish the average chemist: bottles containing murky-looking mixtures, a great variety of barks, bills of vultures, portions of hippopotamus hides, skins of baboons, snakes and hyenas, assorted roots with various magical or actual virtues and even parcels of asbestos fibre. I asked the medical use of this last substance and was informed by the doctor (who dispenses his own drugs) that it is a cure for the strange *Mandiki*[10] sickness that I have described and for other kinds of hysteria. (The nature of the diseases he made clear to us by realistically imitating their symptoms. How free then from such ailments should be the firemen who are habitually clothed in asbestos cloth. Indeed, now that I come to think of it, as a class they are remarkable for their steady nerves in trying circumstances.) Then there were tobacco stalls, bookstalls where bibles and other literature printed in Zulu are sold, wirework stalls, general merchandise stalls where *muchas*, sjamboks,[11] dancing shields, fibre for head-rings, skin mats, assegai blades (evidently made in Germany or Birmingham) etc. etc. are offered. Further there was such as one sees in hotels and other conveniences too numerous to describe. Altogether this place struck me as one of a most useful nature and calculated to be of great service to natives working in Durban.

Next we went to the Indian market, which is also under municipal control. It is a large place with many stallholders who pay a rent to the corporation. At these stalls all kinds of comestibles are sold, especially vegetables and fruits, the Indians being the great market gardeners of Natal. Many Europeans do their shopping here.

A walk of a few yards brought us to the native women's hostel, a non-sectarian corporation establishment (formerly a tin cement store), which is managed by Mrs. Neilson of the Norwegian Mission.[12] Here accommodation is afforded to three classes of women – (1) Schoolteachers who are mostly half-breeds to whom a separate building is allotted. Such girls have nowhere to go; they are outside of their own people and are not received by Europeans. On this account Mr. Donovan tells me they are frequently driven to prostitution for company and a livelihood. (2) Mission native women who pay 3d. a day for accommodation and bed. These have a sitting room where an electric iron can be hired for 1d. the hour and an electric kettle for °d. a boiling. (3) Kraal women who come into town to visit their relatives. These pay 1d. a night only and sleep on board beds or sometimes on the floor. This place is always full and its upkeep is paid for by the profits resulting from the sale of the kaffir beer which the corporation brews. Mr. Donovan says that there is nothing of the sort in Johannesburg or in any other town in the Union. No men are admitted here save to a wired enclosure where they can talk to their friends through the meshes. An admirable institution, which prevents many native girls from falling into trouble as often happens when they stay at common lodging houses in Durban.

Leaving we motored to the site of the new native quarters or location for single men (others for married people are to be built). The contract price for the first block to hold 800 men is £15 000. The entire building when completed will accommodate from 1 500 to 2 000 men and is to include a common hall measuring 60 feet by 40 feet. The dormitories are to be of different sizes holding from four to 15 beds with 418 cubic feet of space per bed. The rent per bed is to be nominal and preference will be given to needy applicants. The beer profits provide the necessary capital.

Next I saw one of the togt barracks where native day labourers[13] are housed at a price of 5s. a month, which includes sleeping accommodation, cooking and cooking facilities, water, baths and electric lights. This building (an old store) holds 300 men, but the barracks at the Point can contain 2 000. Here are six separate rooms where the wives and sisters of the labourers can visit them for a few days. The rents are paid into the Togt Fund and go towards the cost and upkeep of similar buildings. Lastly I was taken to the New Eating House, which is on the same principle as the one I have described but much more elaborate. It cost £6 000.

Certainly Durban is to be congratulated on these establishments though some purists might object to their being provided out of the profits derived from the sale of beer. Mr. Donovan, their able overseer, informed me that it was through reading my romances that he left Ireland and came to South Africa. I said I hoped that he bore me no grudge on this account. He replied that on the contrary he was most grateful to me since from that day he had 'never looked back'. Out of the comparatively few with whom I have talked since I have been in this country, he is the third (or is it the fourth?) with the same story, so I begin to think that I must have had some hand in providing South Africa with what it so sadly needs, British population, during the last quarter of a century. Many superior persons turn up their noses at my romantic work and for aught I know are justified in that exalted attitude, yet it appears to have some practical influence in the world.

At the conclusion of my morning's round I went to the town hall which is an extraordinarily fine building that cost I know not how many hundreds of thousands of pounds.[14] Still had I been one of the Durban community I should have urged spending the money on the harbour rather than in bricks – or stones and mortar. Here I called on the town clerk and the mayor, the latter of whom pointed out to me the picture of the gentleman who had filled the office when I came here in 1876 with Sir Henry Bulwer on the occasion of the cutting of the first sod of the railway (at least I think that was the function, at which, I remember, I made a speech.) That mayor has long been dead.[15]

Another place I visited was the old military cemetery to look at the graves of those who fell in our 1842 troubles with the Boers at the Congella fight and the siege.[16] Many if not most of these gravestones are of a material so wretched that the inscriptions on them are no longer legible. It is a pity that they have not been renewed while there was yet time but I suppose that there are not many to trouble about soldiers who died for their country in 1842.

In the afternoon the port captain, Capt. Rainnie, took me round the harbour in a tug, as I did not accompany the royal commission to Durban and had not seen it.[17] Truly it is different now to what it was when first I knew it in 1875. Then no large ship could enter, now there is 36 feet at low water on the bar instead of 10 feet. It costs about £10 000 per annum in dredging to preserve this depth, which is done by digging out sand traps. The width at the mouth is 600 feet and at the root of the Bluff 1 100 feet. Capt. Rainnie thinks that this narrowing at the mouth is a mistake as ships of 1 900 feet in length may come to grief there in future. Also by a lack of prescience the quay walls have not all been built deep enough – 3 000 feet of them only carry 23 feet in depth, 700 feet of them carry 27 feet, 1 050 feet carry 30 feet in depth, 1 000 feet carry 34 feet and 700 feet carry 38 feet 6 inches in depth. At the Bluff, 800 feet carry 30 feet in depth and 2 650 feet carry 34 feet in depth. There is nothing in the nature of the bottom to prevent dredging to any depth, the only question being that of the foundation of the quay walls. At Congella, the bottom is heavy clay, elsewhere sand. A new graving dock of 1 030 feet in length, which will cost £750 000 is under consideration. A hundred and fifty acres of land has been reclaimed by pumping onto it the dredged sand and another 60 acres, which I visited, is in process of reclamation, being raised no less than 9 feet in level. The system is wonderfully ingenious and successful, so is that of the ship-coaling machinery which I also saw. Messrs. Lever Bros. (Sunlight soap) have large works on this reclaimed land.[18] They import palm kernels from the West Coast and crush them here. Also there is a whaling industry. I saw the little steamers with their look-out cradles on the masts. I suppose however that they will soon kill out all the whales.[19]

This harbour has cost Natal a vast sum, £3 million if I recollect right, but if its people are wise they will spare no cost to keep it up and improve it. Now that the Union has robbed Natal of her individual importance she has little to rely on save her coal and her harbour, which is one of the great gateways to the interior. But I believe that all these matters are now in the hands of the Union parliament.

I ended the day by calling on Capt. Knight of the *Gaika,* the ship upon which I am to make my long journey home via the East Coast and inspecting the cabin I am to occupy after Mombasa. It is a horrid little hole, dark and without ventilation and of the size of a dog kennel but I must make the best of it. Then I returned to my solitary dinner at the hotel.

Saturday, 2 May

Today I visited the Trappist monastery at Mariannhill, near Pinetown, about 20 miles from Durban, whither I was driven from the station by Mr. Essery, the local magistrate, a very intelligent officer.[20] On arrival

at the great pile of buildings I was shewn into the reception room and
greeted by the abbot, a German, and by Father W. Wanger, also a German as are most of the monks here, both of them fine men of the
Teuton type.[21] The abbot told me that this community are not Trappists
as I supposed, but an independent order modelled on the Benedictines
and named The Religious Missionaries of Mariannhill. 'We eat, drink,
talk and sleep like other people,' he said.

The order, which was started in 1882, just after my time, has 29
stations in Natal, the Transkei, Rhodesia and Griqualand East. It com-
prises 65 white fathers, 15 scholastics and 230 white lay brothers who
wear the brown habit. At Mariannhill itself are about 12 fathers, 15 students, 270 lay brothers. Their object is to Christianise and civilize the
natives and especially to teach them to work. They have altogether
over 5 000 children in their schools, of whom 3 500 are boarders. All
that the natives pay in return is four hours of work *per diem*. No religious pressure is put upon them. In general they are heathens when
they arrive but the greater part of them become Christian. Their Pinetown estate covers 12 000 acres, of which about three quarters is worked
by Christian tenants who pay £2.10s. per annum the family for four or
five acres of plough land and grazing rights. The monastery itself farms
about 3 000 acres but the local soil is too poor in character to pay as an
agricultural proposition. The total population on the place amounts to
at least 1 500 natives, 450 schoolchildren, 80 white sisters and the inhabitants of the monastery. The institution is growing . . . 'there is some
development ever'. It makes something by the manufactured goods it
sells and receives charitable contributions from Germany and elsewhere;
also the government gives a capitation grant to the schools, which
amounts to about 20s. a head a year. Some of the wives of polygamists
who have turned Christian are taken in, also a number of illegitimate
children of all shades of colour. Of these there are about 70 at Mariannhill. The abbot declared that the natives are more and more seeking
after education.

After this interview I proceeded round the various buildings conducted by Fr Wanger, an ecclesiastic to whom I took a great liking. I do
not know that it would serve any useful purpose to describe them all,
though I have the material. Also it would take long, as really they
are very numerous. Churches, abbot houses, refectories, cloisters, hospitals, nunneries, chapter house, sewing and stained-glass factories,
classrooms, tanneries, joiners, smiths and carpenters' shops, boarding
houses, photographic studios – such are some of them, with a campanile
tower and a beautiful vegetable garden thrown in. To my mind however perhaps the most interesting place is a tin shed of about 15 feet
square with a creeper growing over it, in which a brother sleeps. This
was the first abbey, the germ from which all the rest has grown. The
ingenuity of these good monks is great; they make everything from

terracotta plaques and high-class saddlery down to articles such as boys' and ladies' belts manufactured from the skins of snakes and iguanas whereof I purchased a selection as presents, one of which is the beautiful tobacco pouch I am using at this moment. Also they build their own edifices of their own excellent bricks.

We lunched at the nunnery where a dear old lady served us a most excellent repast and here I had a most enjoyable conversation with Fr Wanger, who is a great student of native law and history. He told me a very strange witch story. A deceased brother, a Pole, who investigated such matters, visited an old witch-doctress in the neighbourhood, one of those who say that they are inspired by a 'whispering spirit'. He put to her some questions in Polish. She listened and went through her invocations, which were accompanied by a whistling noise, proceeding apparently from the roof of the hut. Then to the father's utter amazement she proceeded to answer his *Polish* questions perfectly rationally and in good Zulu, prefacing her replies with the statement 'My Lords, the spirits say' etc. Fr Wanger's conclusion about the whole matter is the same as that of Gen. Joubert, that the Devil is at the bottom of it, and that those who attribute all these native witchcraft manifestations to fraud are very much mistaken.

There is a museum at Mariannhill, a very interesting and well-kept place. Two of the exhibits here are, I should imagine, unique. In one of the cases I noticed a small piece of rock and on it a rude painting of three robed men. 'Why,' I said after studying their garments and peaked hats, 'those are Phoenicians.' 'That is what we think,' answered the father in charge. Then he told me that Fr Schweiger of their community found this slab two years ago when investigating a Bushman's cave at Keilands, not far from George in Cape Province. I was taken to another department and introduced to Fr Schweiger, who shewed me a number of coloured facsimiles of these Bushman paintings which he had discovered.[22] They represented women being captured by men in Eastern robes and dragged away into walled places. Now does not this throw some light upon the Zimbabwe problem? Were these men perchance the inhabitants of Zimbabwe and the workers of the Rhodesian mines whom the Bushmen had seen at their man-stealing work and pictured in their rude fashion? At least they were persons who captured women very long ago, perhaps Arabs, and as I have said the trio on the slab (of which I have been promised a facsimile) are extraordinarily like Phoenicians. I only hope that the matter will be followed up by experts. I am glad to say that Fr Schweiger proposes to publish his facsimiles.

The second remarkable object is a copper coin of Samaria found here at Mariannhill in December 1898 at a depth of 9 feet when digging foundations. This coin is said to date from 300BC and has been published in the *Atlas Geographique et Iconographique*. So at the time of the early Ptolemies there was a person travelling or resident in what is now Natal who had in his pouch a coin of Samaria. At least that is undoubtedly the inference as no modern individual could have dropped it 9 feet under the present surface of the ground. Truly Africa has many secrets.[23]

These monks are doing a great work among the natives. All success to them. They wear upon their faces that air of goodness which comes to those who in an utterly unselfish spirit devote their lives to the moral and physical elevation of the ignorant and the fallen. The sight of them and the contemplation of the fruits of their labours makes poor world-lings like myself feel ashamed. They do so much, we so little.

As we drove back to Pinetown Mr. Essery told me that he thought that some apprenticeship law should be introduced under which native lads could be bound to masters for a term of years and taught a trade, their earnings being paid to their parents. At present, he said, many of them learn nothing useful and what they earn they spend upon themselves. We met a number of smartly dressed natives on the road and although they knew well enough that Mr. Essery was the magistrate I noticed that not one of these saluted him in any way. He said that was one of the first fruits of civilization on natives; they became sullen, discontented and insolent.

After dinner Mr. Maurice Evans, CMG [Companion (of the Order) of St. Michael and St. George], the expert on native questions, and the author of *Black and White in South Africa* (Longmans), was kind enough to call to explain his views to me.[24] These, Mr. Evans, who was formerly a member of the Natal parliament, set out fully in an interview which lasted for about an hour and a half. He spoke very sadly of the almost complete ignorance of the electorate on native questions and the remarkable lack of attention given to these by the Union legislators. He advocates the appointment of a non-party council with advisory powers to which all proposed native legislation should be first submitted. I suggested that the advice of this body might not be heeded. He agreed but said he could think of nothing better. He declared himself in favour of the expropriation of white men, and especially of absentee owners, in order to provide more land for natives if the commission, of which Sir W. Beaumont is chairman, should report in favour of such a measure. I pointed out that such an act would bring some into direct conflict with the established interests of white landholders and would have little chance of being passed. Again he agreed. He seemed to think the Land Act of last year utterly preposterous and unworkable in its present form and that before passing it the government should have awaited the report of the commission which is now sitting.

For instance, in one of the Natal coastal divisions, I think that of the Lower Tugela, there are some 30 000 natives living on farms who have *no* location. What is to become of all these people? Often the lands on which they are rent-payers are owned by absentees. How can people in future give labour as a condition of residence to owners who require no labour? It was a most hasty and ill-thought out measure. The whites in his opinion would never admit the natives to the franchise. They had the power and they meant to keep it, independently of any questions of abstract justice. 'The ultimate argument was the gun!' He thought that the relative numerical proportion between the white and black races would remain much what it is at present, as the natives are not increasing so fast as they did owing to the limitation of the number of wives and the spread of diseases such as consumption and syphilis. (On this question I can scarcely agree with him as I am sure that in the future as in the past the kaffirs will breed faster than the whites.) He holds a high opinion of the intelligence and industrial capacity of the native and foresees industrial struggles of which no man can guess the end. Generally he takes a most gloomy view of the outlook. So do I.

The white man has a very heavy bill to pay to the native and certainly he will be called upon it in this coin or in that. Those who persistently sow the wind must expect to reap the whirlwind. Possibly in the end South Africa will become more or less black; the increasing miscegenation that is going on and the very small increase in the white population suggest that this may be so. I know that many thinking men take this view – for instance that able person Mr. Maydon, who told me he was sure it would be so. After all, so far as I am aware, no white race has succeeded in establishing itself permanently in Africa. Or as the whites have corrupted the blacks, so ultimately the blacks may corrupt the whites and bring about their downfall. Or, in this fashion or the other, the blacks may attain to political power. At present the physical superiority of the white man is due solely to the superiority of his means of destroying life by the help of highly perfected weapons. In the future something may occur to handicap him in this respect. It must be remembered that as is shewn by the multitude of poor and degraded whites, taking him in the mass, he is probably deteriorating in South Africa owing to the effects of climate on a northern race and to his ceasing from the hardening exercise of manual toil, which he looks upon as the duty and office of the black. On the other hand the native, taking *him* in the mass is probably rising. His eyes are not shut; he sees a great deal. His brain is not dull, he learns day by day.

Further, Johannesburg may be a university of vice, as Merriman said, but it is also a university of knowledge to the black. He has wrongs to be righted, which gives him a moral advantage, a great support in any national struggle. Most of his land has been seized by the insatiable hand of a million of whites and he knows that it is stretched out towards the rest. A gentleman told me that awhile ago he was discussing the possibility of a Basuto war with an average white farmer. 'It would be a good thing if they did fight,' said the farmer *'for then we should*

get their land!' To my mind the whole position is terrible and, like Mr.
Evans, out of it I see no way, thinking as I do that the time has gone by
when the question can be settled by slaughter on the Insimba valley
pattern.

I do not mean, however, that all the white inhabitants of South
Africa take wrong or harsh views of natives and their problems. This is
not so, there are many who are developing an increasing conscience in
this respect. But after all these constitute a tiny minority in a land that
like our own is ruled by that hard master, a democracy. The kaffir is not
likely to receive much consideration from the backveld Boer, or from
the artisan of the cities with whom he competes more year by year, and
when it comes to elections these rule the Union roost. The amount of
real interest taken in natives, their problems and their troubles may be
measured, roughly, by the inches of space alloted to them in the local
newspapers (excluding reports of crimes and trials). It will, I think, be
found that this is small.

Sunday, 3 May

I went to church (St. Paul's?).[25] Both services very nicely done and a
good congregation. One of the Natal pioneers, I forget which, is said to
have pitched his first camp on the site of this church. All the rest of the
day I spent writing letters home and others of thanks to people who had
been kind to me with the result that I had no time to try to find Phillips,
who came to call on me. I am sorry as he and I, I think, alone remain
of those who were with Shepstone at Pretoria in 1877. He was not on
the staff but the lieutenant in command of the famous 20 policemen.
He is now an elderly man and has retired.[26] However, I wrote him a
note. Oh! what a labour is this constant writing! Now on this ship I
should like to get a little rest after my long journeyings and read some
books, but I must write, write, write to bring my journal up to date,
which I had no time to do while travelling through Zululand, and when
that is done, then there is my Colonial Office private report or rather
'letter' remaining to be tackled in this heat.[27]

On this night Stuart arrived while I was being interviewed by a
reporter, which made me extra glad to see him. He brought me some
splendid Zulu curiosities – head-rings, an *iziqu* with horns, some old
hoes, i.e. made by native smiths which are now so rare, etc. He dined
with me.

Monday, 4 May

I spent the morning shopping, buying a large pilgrim basket to take the
overflow of my luggage, which seems to have swollen (luggage undoubtedly possesses a reproductive quality of its own) and after that in

packing with Stuart's kind help. The curiosities we accommodated in a whisky case. This hot business done I went to lunch with Stuart at the club where I met Dr. Park Ross, who is a considerable authority on native diseases.[28] He assured me that the Zulus are a highly nervous race, especially the women, who it seems are very subject to hysteria, from which, according to all theories, their perfect health and open-air life should keep them free. Then I drove down to the Point, deposited myself and my luggage upon the *Gaika*, said goodbye to Stuart and presently saw my last of Durban Bluff and the Berea.

So ended my visit to South Africa – the last I think that I shall ever make. On the whole it has been successful if sad in some ways, and, as I said to *The Natal Witness* when they interviewed me by telephone from Maritzburg this morning, I am truly and deeply grateful for the excessive kindness with which I have been everywhere received.[29] Indeed, personally I have experienced quite a little triumph but, affectionate as was my greeting, this probably has more to do with the fact that, surviving as I do from a past generation, I am a kind of curiosity, a Rip-van-Winkle, than with my individuality. Also my subsequent career has interested those among whom I spent the first years of manhood, when I was connected with great men, and great events.

And so to South Africa that farewell, which is the dominant word in life. It is a fair land of which the charm still holds me, and whose problems interest me more than ever, if that be possible. How will they work out I wonder, when I have gone to sleep – or maybe to dream elsewhere? Well, my name will I believe always be connected with the country if it remains a white man's home and even if it does not – perhaps! It is impossible for me to avoid contrasting the feelings with which I leave it now that I have grown old, with those with which I bade goodbye to its shores in 1881 while I was young. Then life was before me and I had hopes and ambitions. Now life is practically behind me with its many failures and its few successes. Now I have, I think, no ambitions left and my only hope is that I may end my days in peace and remain of some slight service to my country and others till the last. Not that I am wanted in the world – few are – yet I like to work on and imagine that I am of use. It is, at least, a harmless fantasy. But enough of this.

Notes

1. Percy Binns (1862–1920), chief magistrate of Durban in 1905.
2. John Dube, see Chapter 7, p. 179, Note 13.
3. *Izegekbengu*, more correctly rendered as *izigebengu*, Zulu for bandits or rascals.
4. Sir William Henry Beaumont (1851–1930), chairman of the Beaumont

Commission (1913–16) or Natives Land Commission which investigated the allocation of further land to the Zulus under the Native Land Act (1913). After studying at the Royal Military Academy Sandhurst, he was gazetted to the 75th Regiment but retired from the army after taking part in the so-called Langalibalele rebellion. Thereafter he became private secretary to the Lieutenant-Governor of Natal, Benjamin Pine, and also served on the staff of Pine's successor, Sir Henry Bulwer, which is how he first met Haggard in 1875. The two became friends and Beaumont borrowed Haggard's frock coat for his wedding to Alice Millar in 1876. Beaumont was appointed Resident Magistrate of Newcastle in February 1878. During the Anglo-Zulu War he was appointed Acting Commandant of Colonial Defensive District No. 1 in Natal. In January 1879 he raised African levies for the defence of the border and a troop of mounted black levies called the Newcastle Scouts, for which he received the Zulu War medal. He was later Acting Chief Justice and Administrator of Natal. 'With the passing of Sir William Beaumont, Natal and the Union is all the poorer as the ex-soldier and judge was associated with a group of early colonists who cleared a wilderness and made history', obituary, the *Natal Witness*, 10 January 1930.

5.   In 1911 the population of South Africa was 5 973 394, of whom 21 per cent were white.

6.   Daniel Donovan (1870–1924), served with the Canadian North West Mounted Police before coming to South Africa in January 1900 as a volunteer in the North West battalion of Canadian Mounted Rifles. He joined the constabulary in Pretoria in the same year.

7.   Native Eating Houses, better known as beer halls, were established by the municipality to combat the illicit liquor trade and as outlets for the legal consumption of *utshwala*, a beer made from sorghum. The Native Beer Act (No. 23) of 1908 facilitated the establishment of a municipal beer monopoly in Durban and criminalised others producing alcoholic beverages. The revenue generated by the monopoly was eventually used to set up a municipal Native Affairs Department in 1916. 'Upon the municipal beer monopoly rested the elaboration of the "Durban system": a system of "native administration" which became a model of ruling-class domination and exploitation of African popular classes in urban centres throughout South Africa.' See Paul La Hausse, 'The Struggle for the City', in P. Maylam and I. Edwards (eds), *The People's City: African Life in Twentieth Century Durban*, Pietermaritzburg and Portsmouth, 1996, p. 33; and La Hausse, 'Drink and Cultural Innovation in Durban: The Origins of the Beerhall in South Africa, 1902–1916', in Jonathan Crush and Charles Ambler (eds), *Liquor and Labour in South Africa*, Athens, Ohio and Pietermaritzburg, 1992, p. 78.

8.   *Itishimiana*, more correctly rendered as *shimiyana* or *isishimeyana*, strong beer/liquor made from fermented base of sugar/treacle, together with millet or bread or any other ingredients to hand. This is a very intoxicating brew – the sale and consumption of which were prohibited in terms of Act No. 27 of 1906.

9.   Kaffir beer, *tshwala* or *utshwala*, a thick, traditional home-brewed beer made from fermented sorghum millet and water. The revenue from sale of *utshwala* in 1917 was £28 089.

10. See Chapter Seven, p. 182, Note 28 and Note 109.
11. *Sjambok,* a stout rhinoceros or hippotamus hide whip, used loosely as a riding crop or other whip; from Malay word *tjambok* or from Persian and Urdu *chabuk,* a horsewhip.
12. The Native Women's hostel was established in 1911.
13. *Togt* or daily labourers were required to obtain licenses in order to work. This requirement has been in force since 1870 and is designed to control the influx of Africans into urban areas. In 1902 the *Togt* Labour Amendment Act further tightened controls on *togt* labourers and required them to live in barracks. This system was introduced by Theophilus Shepstone in 1873 to ensure a supply of daily labour at controlled wages. See La Hausse, 'Struggle for the City', pp. 39–40.
14. Durban city hall, completed in 1910 and considered a notable example of Edwardian neo-Baroque architecture.
15. Benjamin Wesley Greenacre (1832–1911), first elected Durban mayor in August 1875 and presided over the turning of the first sod at the ceremony held on 4 January 1876. He was subsequently mayor from 1889–92 and 1897–98; and was a co-founder of Harvey, Greenacre and Co., a famous Durban department store. William Holmes was the mayor in 1914 and William Plowman Moyese Henderson was the town clerk and the author of *Durban: Fifty Years of Municipal History,* Durban, 1904.
16. On 4 May 1842, a British expeditionary force arrived at Port Natal. Defeated at the battle of Congella on 23 May, the force was subsequently besieged by Boer forces of the Voortrekker Republic of Natalia until relieved on 26 June. This was the beginning of a British presence that led to the annexation of Natal the following year.
17. Captain John Rainnie was Port Captain of Durban (1903–19). A testimonial on his retirement acknowledged his 'long, honorable and efficient service during possibly the most important period in the development of our Port'.

    A sandbar had blocked the narrow entrance to the harbour thus restricting the development of the port. 'It was not until the conquest of the bar in 1904, and the subsequent regular dredging of the entrance channel and the harbour in general, that the way was opened for the dramatic growth of the port.' See Anthony Lumby and Ian McLean, 'The Economy and the Development of the Port of Durban' in Bill Guest and John M. Sellers (eds), *Receded Tides of Empire: Aspects of the Economic and Social History of Natal and Zululand since 1910,* Pietermaritzburg, 1994, p. 25 *et seq.* See also Colin Bender, *Who Saved Natal? The Story of the Victorian Harbour Engineers of Colonial Port Natal,* Durban, 1988.
18. Lever Brothers was set up by William Hesketh Lever and his brother James D'Arcy Lever in 1885. Though based in Lancashire, England, the trademark for Sunlight soap was registered in the *Cape of Good Hope Gazette* on 15 December 1887. Apparently William thought 'Sunlight' the perfect brand name and was fearful that others might anticipate its use, not only in Britain but elsewhere. Sunlight soap was introduced to South Africa in 1891. See Eric Rosenthal, *As Pioneers Still,* Cape Town, 1961.
19. Whaling began off Durban in 1908. During 1913 the six stations produced 48 144 barrels of oil, largely 'whale oil' from humpbacks. During the First

World War there was a decline in the whaling industry which subsequently revived until lean catches in the late 1960s and the introduction of quotas saw the industry become unprofitable. Whaling off Durban ended in 1975. See Cornerlis de Jong, 'A History of Whaling from Durban' in Guest and Sellers, *Receded Tides.*

20.   Mariannhill, the largest Roman Catholic mission in Natal in the Pinetown district, was founded by Fr Franz Pfanner in 1882 as a Trappist monastery and named after Mary, the mother of Jesus, and her cousin St Anne. The monks separated from the Trappist order in 1909 and became known as the Missionaries of Mary, though at the time of Haggard's visit they were still wearing the white Trappist habit with a black scapula.

Pinetown, 19 km (12 miles) west of Durban, was established in 1848 and named after Sir Benjamin Pine (1809–1901), Lieutenant-Governor of Natal 1849–56 and Governor 1873–75.

Guy Vivian Essery (1875–1958), appointed magistrate at Pinetown, July 1913.

21.   The abbot was Gerard Wolpert (1855–1945), who held the office from 1900 to 1904. Though technically provost at the time of Haggard's visit, he was still referred to as abbot.

Willibald Wanger (1872–1943) was resident at Mariannhill from 1892. A noted linguist, he was the author of *Konversations-Grammatik der Zulusprache* (Mariannhill, 1917) and *Scientific Zulu Grammar* (Stuttgart, 1927). He was a colleague of fellow priest and linguist Alfred Thomas Bryant, author of *Olden Times in Zululand,* London, 1929. Wanger returned to Germany in 1920 where he continued his research and writing. He was executed by the Nazis in 1943. Beyers and Basson, *South African Biography* record that Wanger died in 1944 and was among those executed following the attempt to assassinate Hitler in July 1944. This conflicts with information obtained from Mariannhill Monastery to the effect that he was executed by the Nazis in Munich on 14 October 1943.

22.   Fr Albert Schweiger (1879–1939) was also a botanist, an expert on native customs and an authority on bushman paintings.

23.   The items discussed by Haggard with Schweiger are still held by the monastery. The coin was found in 1898 during the digging of a well. It is dated to the reign of Simon Maccabeus 143–136BC.

24.   Sir Maurice Smethurst Evans (1854–1929), judge, politician and author of *Black and White in South-East Africa,* London, 1911, and *Black and Whites in Southern States: A Study of the Race Problem in the United States from a South African Point of View,* London, 1915. Haggard met Evans again in 1916 when he visited Cape Town.

25.   St Paul's church, Edwardian Gothic Revival church built in 1909 to replace earlier church that burnt down.

26.   Inspector Fred L. Phillips was in charge of the escort of mounted police that accompanied Sir Theophilus Shepstone and his party on the journey to Pretoria that resulted in the annexation of the Transvaal in 1877.

27.   See Appendix One.

28.   George Archibald Park Ross (1879–1958) was an expert on malaria. In 1910 he was district surgeon at Nqutu, investigating the disease known as Isigwebedhla-Umkhuhlane then ravaging northern Natal. This he proved

was principally the result of malaria infection. In 1921 he carried out the first malaria survey in the Union, which resulted in the division of the country into five areas of malaria risk. He was appointed assistant medical officer of health of the Union of South Africa. See D. Le Sueur, B.L. Sharp and C.C. Appleton, 'Historical Perspectives of the Malaria Problem of Natal with emphasis on the period 1928–1932', *South African Journal of Science*, Vol. 89, 1993, pp. 232–9. See also pamphlet by A.L. Ferguson, 'Park Ross of Natal' (no publisher, no date).

29. On the front of the *Natal Witness*, 5 May 1914, headlined 'Famous novelist's farewell to readers of the Natal Witness':

'Sir H. Rider Haggard, the author of many celebrated African romances, left South Africa by the East Coast route yesterday. Below he says goodbye to his friends and admirers through the columns of the *Witness*.

'I want to say to the readers of *The Natal Witness* that I wish South Africa well. I am very glad to have had the opportunity of seeing it again after so many years, and I shall always have a warm remembrance of the delightful time which the kindness of all whom I met has enabled me to spend. *HRH*.'

Chapter Nine

Running along the coast

&&&&&

Haggard's journey home took him up the East Coast of Africa to present-day Mozambique and then on to the island of Zanzibar. He continued to gather information about the people and places he discovered en route while 'working-up' the rough notes that he had made in southern Africa into an expanded record of his travels. His zest for visiting new places and meeting new people was apparently undiminished even though he had been on the move almost constantly for about 13 weeks.

Tuesday, 5 May

We are running along the coast of Tongaland towards Kosi Bay. Mr. Matravers of the Zululand Police, whom I met at Nongoma and who is going home on leave (after 13 years), says that it would cost a great deal to make a harbour here at Kosi because of the reef across the mouth and the shallowness of the water. St. Lucia bay is, I believe, also a very indifferent harbour with a bad and dangerous landing. The coastline here consists of swelling hills or dunes covered with wood and beneath this white sand running to the sea's lip. It is very feverish and appears to be quite untenanted. Mr. Matravers, as illustrative of the perils of all this Zulu and Tonga country, has been telling me of the fate of his predecessors and companions in office. One died of fever, one was drowned with a friend in a lake and one was killed by lightning. (Bother this monsoon rain!) Personally he seems to be fever-proof as is the case with some fortunate men and, notwithstanding his adventurous life, to have escaped serious accident or wounds.

At 5.30 in the afternoon we were running past the Inyack [Inhaca] peninsula, long, low land with a hill in the centre on which stands a lighthouse. This light shines red when seen from certain points of vision. The town of Lourenço Marques is, I think, situated nearly 25 miles from the mouth of the outer bay and the entrance, which is marked by lighted buoys, is of a somewhat tricky character.[1] There are two channels named the Hope and the Cockburn, with a respective depth of 24 feet and 30 feet at low water. The rise at spring tides is about 14 feet

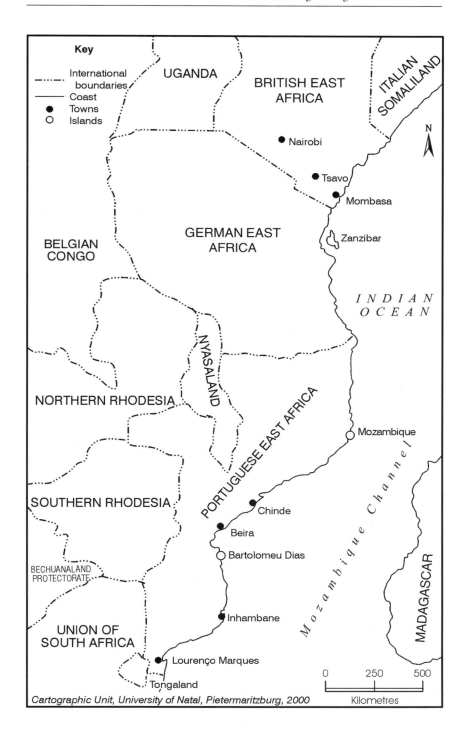

Key

- ----·---- International boundaries
- ——— Coast
- ● Towns
- ○ Islands

UGANDA

BRITISH EAST AFRICA

ITALIAN SOMALILAND

N

● Nairobi

● Tsavo

● Mombasa

BELGIAN CONGO

GERMAN EAST AFRICA

Zanzibar

INDIAN OCEAN

NYASALAND

NORTHERN RHODESIA

PORTUGUESE EAST AFRICA

○ Mozambique

SOUTHERN RHODESIA

Mozambique Channel

● Chinde

● Beira

○ Bartolomeu Dias

BECHUANALAND PROTECTORATE

MADAGASCAR

● Inhambane

UNION OF SOUTH AFRICA

●● Lourenço Marques

Tongaland

Cartographic Unit, University of Natal, Pietermaritzburg, 2000

0   250   500

Kilometres

The Gaika. *Haggard returned to Europe via the East Coast route on this ship belonging to the Union-Castle Line. During the voyage he wrote* Diary of an African Journey *using the rough diary kept during his visit to southern Africa.*

and of the neaps, I was told, 11 feet or 12 feet. On our way in we passed a dredger lying bottom up. Being without lights she was sunk not long ago by a German steamer with some loss of life. The entrance to the inner harbour is between Point Mahone and Point Reuben. It is three miles wide and the harbour is seven miles in length with a maximum depth at low springs of 13 fathoms (about 78 feet). We went under the charge of a pilot with two men sounding in the chains all the way and tied up at the excellent quay, which has accommodation for seven steamers. Another quay is being built with a depth of 35 feet. Take it altogether the harbour is very fine and its trade considerable as a large proportion of the traffic from what is known as the competitive area, which includes Johannesburg, comes this way, the guaranteed quota (I think 60 per cent) being secured by a manipulation of the railway rates. Goods from the Transvaal go through in bond without duty.

Wednesday, 6 May

Mr. Napier Macdonnell, our consul-general,[2] kindly came on board and took me in charge for the day. First he drove me round the town in a motor. It is a nice clean city but the 'boom' in land here has died down. Like everything else it seems to have been engineered from Johannesburg, when the 'Magnates' there got it into their heads that England was about to become possessed of Delagoa Bay. Thus the very finest residential sites in the town of about ° acre, which during the boom would have fetched £4 000 or £5 000, can now be bought for not more than £1 000 and others not quite so eligible for £250.

Having finished our sightseeing we returned to the mosquito-proofed consulate and chatted till luncheon time. Mr. Macdonnell has had a varied experience in the consular service, on the west coast amongst other places. He told me a curious story of an incident he witnessed there. At some village that he visited an old witch-doctor seemed to set a great heap of straw on fire before his eyes. It burnt out (apparently) but when the fire died away, instead of ashes there was the heap of straw *untouched*. The luncheon party was very agreeable and amusing. Amongst others the American consul, Mr. G.A. Chamberlain, was present and Mr. Bayley, the editor of the Lourenço Marques *Guardian*.

After luncheon I had an interview with His Excellency Sir Joachim Machado, KCMG, the Portuguese governor-general.[3] He is a fine old man with large moustachios and speaks English well. He seemed very glad to see me and talked of the difference between the Lourenço Marques of his youth, when it was set in a fever-stricken swamp with a few houses and streets deep in sand, and its state today. All this comparative prosperity has resulted from the Transvaal trade. If ever it should come into English hands under any future international arrangement it will become a great place but in that event I hope that the Imperial government will keep the administration of it in its own hands.

After this interesting visit I was taken up the bay in a steam launch belonging to the Union-Castle Line, and saw the mouths of the three great rivers that discharge their waters into the harbour, or rather that of the Rio d'Espirits Santo with which they seem to join. They are named the Matola, the Umbelozi [Mbuluzi] and the Tembe. It is a splendid sheet of water bordered by mangrove swamps with ample depth for large ships in places. The fine new wharves we passed are being built of ferro-concrete. On one of the banks lies a deserted ship which was blown in a while ago with only a cat and a cock aboard, which died of overeating when they were fed. What became of its crew no man knows. Doubtless they took to the boats and were drowned. The scene here was beautiful beneath the heavy storm clouds. Ahead of us was Refugee island with the Lebombo mountains to the far north-west steeped in blue light. To our left appeared the Tembe river, to our right the Matola, while between them was the Umbelozi, while beyond the flat veld is clothed in heavy bush. On the water not far from the launch floated a flock of the flamingoes which haunt this bay. Returning we reached the *Gaika* just before her sailing time and there I bid goodbye to our kind friends.

At Lourenço Marques we were joined by the Archbishop of Cape Town and Mrs. Carter who are proceeding to Madagascar on some church business.[4] The Archbishop has proved a most interesting companion on the voyage to Zanzibar where he changes for Madagascar. We have had sundry long talks upon various subjects, ranging from the Zulus, among whom he was bishop for a number of years, to religion. I find that on all these matters his views coincide with my own. Thus, as regards the latter he too thinks that there does exist an active 'evil principle', call it the Devil or what you will, that has dominion on this earth, from which we must escape by our own efforts and the aid of faith. That this faith is a very difficult ladder to climb and can in most cases only be surmounted by the surrender of our own wills and the use of the means appointed to us. That in our darkness, speculation and the seeking to understand and explain are useless. All that we can do is to obey and hope for forgiveness of our errors, which come to us by nature and by blood. The gospels or at any rate the spirit of them, if not the *ipsissima verba*,[5] must be taken as they stand, or left, but that those who cannot accept are worthy of all sympathy, etc. etc. So at least I have understood him. I have much enjoyed the society of this good and gentle man. It is helpful and makes one feel better. As I may have said somewhere I used to know his brother at Pretoria in the 1870s. He, poor fellow, was killed by lightning.

Among the other passengers are Mr. Whittet, a young Englishman, who has a coffee plantation near Nairobi in East Africa. He gives a very good account of that country or at any rate of the prospects of coffee there. Certainly he and his partner seem to have done well. They bought 2 000 acres of land at £1 an acre and have sold off 500 acres of it, of which 60 were planted, for £3 000. They have 500 acres under coffee, which are cultivated by 300 natives. At present their only plague has been a cut-worm that rings the bark of young plants and kills them, but these they deal with by planting beans for the creatures to eat, which they prefer to the coffee bushes. Their danger is lest some other pest should develop, as it has done in Ceylon and elsewhere, especially as they have no alternative crop. Mr. Whittet reckons that £15 per acre net is a conservative estimate of his profit on coffee. He says that Nairobi coffee fetches about twice the price of many other coffees on the market and is used for grading up berries of poorer quality. I *think* the figures he mentioned were £80 the ton as against £40 from Brazilian.

A Mrs. and Miss Foley who live at Bulawayo do not give a very cheerful account of that town. Miss Foley, an intelligent girl, tells me that the struggle for a living is hard there and that the place is expensive and has many disadvantages. She says that no one ever laughs at Bulawayo. She lived in London before her father went to Rhodesia and perhaps finds the contrast too great. I believe her mother is going home for an operation, which does not tend to induce cheerfulness in a family.

Thursday, 7 May

We passed Inhambane about 12.30 without calling. A long spit of land on which stands a lighthouse, protects the harbour, which is nine miles long by five miles across. It has a depth of 23 feet over the bar at spring tides, but is said to lack sufficient shelter in gales. There is a considerable township here that trades in ground nuts and tropical produce. Past Bartolomeu Dias we ran, also named after the navigator who first rounded the Cape in 1486. Here is the Sabi river, up which the old Sabaeans or Phoenicians or both, travelled to the gold mines at what is now called Rhodesia (in a direct line Great Zimbabwe is scarce 300 miles away). Past Sofala the Ancient on the south of the delta of the Buzi river also, of which Massonde the Arabian described the glories 1 000 years ago. Its great fortress of San Gaetano, built by Albuquerque in 1505, has been allowed to fall into the sea within the last few years and its harbour to silt up, and where now are its tens of churches? What a history have these places on the east coast of Africa, and concerning it how little there is known.

Saturday, 9 May

We reached Beira at the mouth of the Pungwe and Buzi rivers, a scattered red-roofed town lying on a low, sandy beach and protected by a sea wall from erosion by the sea. The Archbishop, Mrs. Carter and I went ashore with the vice-consul, Mr. Gordon Rule, who gave us tea at the hotel and took us for a ride, or rather a run on the queer little *carros* (the hardest-seated conveyances I know), which travel upon tramlines along the sandy streets.[6] We saw the hospital, which is deserted because a number of the patients have died in it of tetanus; we saw the chancel of the new cathedral, on which all building stopped when the monarchy fell in Portugal, in fact we saw all there is to see, which is not much so far as the town is concerned.[7]

Beira is situated on a huge bay many miles in width. At low springs there is 27 feet at high water on the bar, at high springs 35 feet, at neaps 24 feet at high water and 11 feet at low water. At present there is no dredging done but it is believed that the harbour could be dredged to any depth. So far as the bar is concerned this depends upon the bottom of which the nature is unascertained. If it consists of *matope*, i.e. of hard mud, the task would be simple as the scour would keep it clear; if of sand it would be more difficult as the excavations would silt it up. There is no wharfage for ships, which are loaded and unloaded by lighters and lie at a distance from the shore. Two piers have been built, or partially built, by the railway company but have proved of little use, it is said owing to defects in construction. The Chartered Company, through the Beira and Mashonaland Railway, has a concession for the erection of wharfage and, it is alleged, is prepared to spend a vast sum when Messrs. Coode & Matthews have settled on the scheme to be adopted.

Beira, owing to its geographical position, is the natural port of Rhodesia and also (at present) of the Belgian Congo. An authority I consulted said that in his opinion it can be converted into a first-class port capable of taking the largest vessels at all states of the tide. I was told that it is not liable to heavy gales because of the protection given to it by Madagascar, which lies at a distance of 600 miles. Its hinterland is rich and extensive and when the new railway to Bulawayo is built will comprise all Rhodesia. Another railway which the Chartered Company is reported to have authorised is that from Kafne to Salisbury, which will save much distance and benefit the trade of Beira. It is hoped also that the line from Beira to Sena on the Zambezi, a distance of 173 miles, will soon be constructed and link up with the Nyasaland railway. The concession for this is held by a Belgian company, under an arrangement with the Portuguese Mozambique Company. Messrs. Paulings are the contractors and it will tap the country up to Tanganyika. At present however it seems to be a little in the air and I believe the concession has only about a year to run.

It will be seen therefore that Beira is full of hopes. As a place of residence it strikes me as horrible and its mosquitoes are said to be the worst and most deadly on the east coast, though probably they could be lessened or got rid of by improved drainage and sanitary arrangements. Although we were lying quite 400 of yards from the shore they invaded the ship, which gives the lie to the theory that the mosquito can only fly 200 yards. I killed at least 20 myself and was bitten by them.

I was taken about eight miles up the Pungwe river on a launch, a very interesting trip. The river is enormous with islands in it and bordered by mangrove swamps. In places it is shallow as once we stuck upon a sandbank. I was much disappointed that the state of the tide made it impossible to ascend the Buzi river and see the hippos which frequent it, also perhaps the famous crocodile that is known locally as 'Lloyd George'.[8] Indeed to the benighted natives of these parts that celebrated name applies to this terrible and voracious creature and nothing else. Of the great original they have never heard. Such is fame. Mr. Macdonald, the editor of the local paper, was our guide upon this trip on which we were tormented by hundreds of the big hippopotamus flies whose sting burns like a hot iron. He says that he knew me in 1880 in Newcastle, Natal, but I think it was Arthur Cochrane whom he met. His enthusiasm for Beira even went the length of declaring that there are no mosquitoes there or so few that he had not used a net for 18 years. He did not mention whether his house is 'proofed' against these venomous fever-breeding insects.

Sunday, 10 May

Our next place of call was Chinde, the port, if it may so be called, of Nyasaland and Northern Rhodesia. Chinde, which is situated on one at the mouths of the Zambezi at a distance of 146 miles from Beira, is built on a low sandy coast line that is backed with palms. We did not see much of it however as, owing to the shallowness of the water, we were obliged to anchor five miles from the shore. Our passengers were taken off and others brought on by the German tug *Adjutant*, which draws 10 feet, the charge for landing being no less than £2.10s. They are conveyed from the tug to the steamer and vice versa in a huge basket, a very unpleasant operation in bad weather. Cargo is not landed here but towed up from Beira in lighters but I noted that our passengers brought with them an enormous amount of baggage, probably their year's supply of necessaries. Those who came off to the ship all looked very pale, a hint as to the climatic conditions of Nyasaland. One gentleman took ashore with him six children and nine dogs – the latter I suppose for hunting purposes. They comprised all breeds, including a bulldog which I observed was sent off in great state alone, only the butcher venturing to accompany him in the basket.

Monday, 11 May

This morning I had a conversation with the captain who spoke strongly about the Portuguese, a people for whom he seems to have no liking. Certainly their domestic arrangements seem to be of a peculiar description. He said that at the circus at Beira he had seen the Portuguese officials in uniform with their white wives, while opposite to them and in a bevy sat their black women with the half-caste children. On the other hand I was told on very good authority at Beira that the Portuguese behave very well to their half-caste offspring, often sending them to Europe to be educated. The English and Germans in the interior, it was said, make it a part of the contract for these temporary alliances, which appear to be the custom of the country, that if the lady becomes pregnant she is to be sent back to her tribe. Of the German naval officers, the captain speaks most highly, indeed with enthusiasm. He says that they are 'gentlemen and very able'.

This afternoon I saw the hugest shark I can remember. It was cruising alongside of us looking quite irridescent in that light and must have measured 25 feet or more in length.

Tuesday, 12 May

This morning we reached the island of Mozambique that lies in a gigantic bow of bay, the shores of which are low, flat and sandy with palms growing on them.[9] The harbour is good and spacious, with a depth of from 6 to 19 fathoms in fairway of north channel and of from 5° to 15 fathoms at low water in the outer anchorage and is protected by the two islands of St. George and St. Jago, but unsheltered from southerly winds, though no heavy sea can get up. Ships lie about three quarters of a mile from the shore. There is a 12 feet rise of tide and speaking generally both the outer and inner harbours have great possibilities. Mr. Alfred Martin, the vice-consul, came and breakfasted on the ship after which he took the Carters and myself ashore in his boat. We managed to reach the pier but other visitors from the ship had to be carried for 20 yards or so by natives – a very amusing sight, a stout lady does not look her best wobbling about on the shoulders of a kaffir.

On arrival we proceeded at once to the castle, which was built about 1510, incredible as it may seem when the vastness of the building and the enormous thickness of the walls are considered, of stone imported from Portugal in the tiny vessels of the day.[10] Viewed from the sea this bastioned, medieval castle forms an imposing object with the little white-washed chapel of San Sebastian standing on the beach outside the walls. The chapel is said to be even older than the castle and is built in a somewhat Moorish style of architecture.

At the castle we were received by the newly appointed governor, who has however served here in a subordinate capacity during past years. He is a charming man, so English in his appearance and in the singular directness of his manners and so totally unlike the other Portuguese about him, that it is difficult not to suppose that some of our blood runs in him. I regret to say that I forgot to ask his name. Most kindly he spent the next two hours in showing us over this most interesting and antique building. Its main purpose nowadays is that of a prison to which criminals are brought not only from the east coast but from the Portuguese possessions in India (Goa) and in West Africa and even from Portugal itself. The walls are enormous and on them are mounted a great number of obsolete cannon of about the time of Nelson. There are queer little sentry boxes at their corners with stone crosses on the roofs, which from their lack of height show how diminutive must have been the stature of the old Portuguese. An ordinary child could scarcely stand up in them and there is no place to sit down.

At one angle, that near the chapel, the wall has been recently rebuilt in a slighter style. A few years ago a soldier here entered on an illicit trade with natives on the mainland in powder stolen from the magazine which was in his charge. Hearing that a commission was coming to inspect the stores and knowing that his thefts would be discovered he bribed a kaffir to blow up the magazine with a slow match. The fuse exploded prematurely and the kaffir was killed and with him no less than 200 unfortunate prisoners who were housed near by. The instigator of the plot escaped as there was no legal evidence against him, his confederate having perished, but after he had been dismissed from the army the whole story came out.

It is a terrible one and lacks the quality of poetic justice – or so the annihilated 200 might think. In one of the walls I noticed an ancient inscription about which no one knew anything. With difficulty we made out its purport. It runs: 'In the time of Alphonso VI(?) Antonio Mello de Castro, Privy Councillor was Governor of this Fort. This stone is erected to his memory. Died 20 Dec. 1666'. Another monument which we saw in the town appears to commemorate two of the wives of this old Dom.

We were taken to the chapel, which is very rarely shewn to visitors. It is closed now by order of the republic but in the old days the prisoners were obliged to attend service here. Now they attend no service. Indeed with the exception of two, who are rarely seen, all the priests have been driven from Mozambique and the church in the town which I tried to enter was locked. In short Christianity is, or seems to be, dying. The country, which was once most ardent on its behalf, now by a strange turn of the wheel is its bitterest enemy. This chapel, which is the first built upon this coast of Africa, is dedicated to Our Lady of Baluarte and contains a number of ancient tombstones that no one seems to have tried to read. We discovered that one of these was placed here to the memory of a very early governor. Another engraved with a mitre and cardinal's hat covers the bones of an 'Episcopus Japonensis' (a bishop of Japan) who appears to have died here in 1588. So even in those days there were Christian bishops in Japan.

Another inscription is to Lencastro Conde of Goa, Viceroy of India, doubtless a very great man in his day, which seems to have been comparatively recent if we read the date aright. It appears to be 1765 but the inscription looks much older. Another is to Donna Elena, wife of the governor of the fortress, who died 27 February 1592, while two tablets on the wall by the altar are dated 1516 and 1517, nearly 400 years ago. In a kind of vestry is a box which the sergeant with us opened. It contains the complete skeleton of some grandee, dug up here during repairs.

How much history do these old walls hide! I asked one of the officers in the castle office where the old records were. He replied he thought at Lisbon and the more recent documents at Lourenço Marques. What an opportunity for some new president. Here all things are forgotten, there they might be brought to life again. I wonder what the death-rate must have been in this tropical and unhealthy place during the bygone centuries when mosquito curtains and even the most rudimentary sanitary arrangements were unknown. Something terrific I imagine. Not many can have lasted for more than a few years.

Leaving the chapel, where the door to the confessional is also tiny, we inspected the great cisterns of rainwater, the quality of which they seem to improve by throwing in old iron bedsteads, we went on to the prisoners quarters. There were different coloured badges, those with a green badge being committed to and kept in this place *without any trial*, on the mere complaint of officials. The vice-consul told me that it was only necessary to send up a native with a card and in he went without further inquiry. These convicts were of all races but mostly from India. One had been the mayor of some town there. One a white woman who was kept behind bars, of about 50 years of age, had murdered two husbands, in Portugal and on the west coast respectively, the second in a way too shocking to mention. Yet she seemed to retain some refinement as she had flowers and a canary bird in her window. Mad probably. She most politely asked me to come up to see her but I declined the honour. Another was a Portuguese sergeant who had embezzled the regimental funds. His room was nicely furnished with a mosquito curtain, bookshelves, a photograph of his wife, evidently a lady, and relatives, etc. This poor fellow is in for 15 years, of which he has served two. Probably he will die. Another was an Indian woman who had also murdered her husband. Her child was with her, a pretty little thing of about eight. Another Indian man had the brightest eyes I ever saw, they were almost terrible. Another white man who had stripped himself naked in his cell perhaps because of the heat, was said to be dangerous. Then there were women thieves from the other side of Africa, and I know not who besides. A sad sight. They all seemed to be kindly treated but the most of them work in the town wearing barbarous shackles that chafe their legs.

Lastly we saw the jewels that have been removed from the chapel which were well worth studying. Amongst these was the ancient wand of office of the governors of the castle, which probably had been held by the forgotten dead whose tombs we saw. It is a stick of black wood, ebony I think, mounted with gold and having a gold band twisted round its entire length. Then there was the crown of the Virgin, whose image used to stand in the chapel. It weighs about 3 lbs., is manufactured of the purest gold from Goa and is adorned with really beautiful enamel medallions of sacred subjects and with precious stones. I should say that it dates from the late 15th or early 16th century. Next came a diadem of pure gold from the head of the image of San Sebastian which, as an inscription on its back records, was given to the saint by Donna Missia Devilhena in the year 1651; also the golden arrows which were fixed in the wood of the image. Further there was a gold collar ring and a truly lovely medieval necklace of worked gold and crystal beads. These jewels it seems are never shewn, and there was great difficulty in opening the strong place where they are hidden away, so we were fortunate to have the opportunity of seeing them. I trust sincerely that they will not be taken away by the Portuguese government and melted down or sold.

Altogether our visit to this ancient castle was most interesting. I noticed that the Portuguese soldiers there were very small and yellow, though not so tiny as their predecessors must have been generations ago, if one may judge by the height of the doorways I have mentioned.

Having said goodbye to the governor I went for a ricksha ride in the town. It seems a clean place with squat old houses in the *patios* of which slaves used to be kept till there was an opportunity of shipping them. Lying to the north-east of the castle at a distance of about four miles is an island known as the Isle of Cobras. The sergeant who shewed us the skeleton told me he was there few weeks ago and that the place literally swarms with deadly snakes, in the trees, on the rocks, hidden in the grass and bushes – everywhere. He thinks they live on the lizards and frogs. What a place to land on unawares.

Wednesday, 13 May

This morning we reached Pemba Bay and anchored early off Port Amelia, or rather what had been Port Amelia, for the cyclone of 12 April has wrecked the place. Its aspect is extraordinary. Every house in it is unroofed and some are blown down. The pier is a ruin, three or four dhows lie high upon the beach where also some huge baobab trees are stretched prone. The other baobabs, of which there are hundreds within view, are stripped of their leaves, as are all the trees.

This is what occurred as it was told to me by Mr. Read, the acting head of the Nyasaland Consolidated Company and the agent of the Union-Castle Company. Cyclonic rain began to fall at 3 a.m. on 12 April. At 9 a.m. it commenced to blow badly from the south. At 10 a.m. the cyclone, which was of a terrific character unequalled within the memory of the oldest native, set in furiously and lasted till midday. Then there was a lull till 2 p.m. after which the wind returned from the north and was more awful than before till midnight when it ceased, after which followed incessant rain for three days. In Port Amelia 30 natives were killed, together with 200 more in the neighbourhood, but the white people, of whom there were but a very few, about 20 in all, I believe, escaped by hiding in various places. Mr. Read took refuge in a stone building of which the roof fell in. It was a terrible time and Port Amelia is no more, but so local was the tempest that at Mozambique, 120 miles away, nothing was felt. A German steamer was due in the port but acting on the warning given by the glass her captain stood out to sea and so escaped.

I suppose that this practically unknown place is one of the finest harbours in the world and one that would hold whole navies. Its mouth is about two miles in width and except for a few patches of foul ground, consisting of mushroom-shaped coral reef which could easily be blown up, there is deep water everywhere. Lying quite close to the shore we have, the captain tells me, 40 fathoms under our stern and of this water, with a splendid mud bottom for anchorage, there is an area of about eight miles by five. Moreover a new anchorage is being laid out behind the promontory to give protection from certain winds. Port Amelia, further, is very healthy; there are said to be no anopheles mosquitoes and consequently no fever here, and its appearance is extremely pretty. The country behind according to report is fine, rising in three terraces to Lake Nyasa 500 miles away.

The territory, which is administered by the Portuguese Compania de Nyassa, is bounded by the River Lurao on the south and by the River Ronvuma on the north. It grows cotton and other crops but is practically undeveloped. Indeed there is little trade at Port Amelia; a few bags of corn was the only cargo awaiting us. A railway has, I am told, been surveyed to Mtengula on the Portuguese portion of Nyasa and its best harbours, but there the matter seems to have stopped. Land in the hinterland is apparently obtainable at the moderate price of 2d. a hectare in the Ambaramba and Medo districts, which are excellent for the growth of cotton and tobacco. Labour is cheap and plentiful and chiefly furnished by the peaceable Makua tribe, who are great agriculturists, its price being from 4s. to 8s. the month. The rains begin in October and the best months climatically are from May to September. There are hippos in the bay and big game is plentiful. On the western bank of the bay stand strange-shaped isolated hills, one of which has a huge knob of rock upon its top.

When we reached the place some hundreds of natives were standing on the shore. These had just landed from a steamer, having returned from the Johannesburg mines whither no more of them may go on account of the awful death rate among them there.[11] The natives of these parts seem to be very willing to earn money in distant places. Thus, a ship we saw at Mozambique was taking 1 500 of them to the cocoa plantations of Messrs. Cadbury on the other side of Africa. They are, I am told, apprenticed for three years and Messrs. Cadbury undertakes to ship them, or the survivors of them, home again at the expiration of that time.

As we left this wonderful and lovely harbour I noticed the lighthouse on the north point had been completely destroyed by the cyclone. This night we had pouring monsoon rain so heavy that the darkness kept the foghorn going.

Thursday, 14 May

This morning we reached Zanzibar where Mr. Stirling, the secretary to the Resident, came out to see me on behalf of his chief, Major Pearce.[12] I went ashore with him after breakfast to the government offices, a large ugly building like an hotel, that used to be the Sultan's palace and was there introduced to Major Pearce, who for many years was secretary to the government in Nyasaland and has recently been appointed Resident. He is a keen-eyed man, strong in body and I should say capable. Zanzibar is a collection of oriental-looking buildings of all colours, shapes and sizes crowded together on an island with sundry different flags flying over them, above which rise the double spires of the Roman Catholic cathedral. Beyond these appears the wooded mainland. The harbour has an average depth of 10 fathoms and is protected by reefs and by five islands named Chumbi, Bawe, Prison, Bat and Grave on which last, enclosed by a white wall, are buried sailors who lost their lives in connection with the suppression of the slave trade.

Practically any number of ships can find anchorage in this harbour. It is protected from all ordinary gales and has only cyclones to fear. Zanzibar Island, which is about 50 miles long, lies however just outside the cyclone area, although it was visited by one in 1870 of a terrible nature which destroyed most of the clove trees, especially on the neighbouring island of Pemba. The climate is very tropical and not too healthy but there is a good supply of water from the stream or spring called Chem-Chem where, as I saw afterwards, it is collected in great covered cisterns.

Mr. Stirling took the Archbishop, Mrs. Carter and myself to visit the famous cathedral which was built by Bishop Steere, who lies behind the altar which stands on the site of the whipping post of the old slave market.[13] The building of coral rock is smaller than either the Archbishop or I thought and perhaps a trifle dark even for that climate, but on the whole singularly successful and imposing. I was particularly impressed with the apse, which is very good and appropriate to its general style. Canon and Mrs. Dawe could not remember the name of the architect. Afterwards we drove in rickshas through the narrow streets of the eastern-looking town and Indian bazaars where we inspected curiosities.

Then I was taken to call upon the Sultan, who had signified his desire to see me. He is a member of the Muscat family that ruled in Zanzibar before and since our occupation. His predecessor we deposed a few years ago because of his dissolute habits and general uselessness. He is now said to be drinking himself to death in Paris. The present Sultan who is named (Seyyid Khalifa-bin-Hourub)[14] is a pleasant-faced oriental gentleman of about 35 years of age. He is a British subject having taken the oath of allegiance, but has certain powers reserved to him and is treated with a considerable degree of state, being always addressed as 'Your Highness'. The visitor is expected to bow on entering his presence and to turn and bow at the door on leaving. His reception of me was very courteous. He came to the door to meet me and shook hands, then sat himself down in the centre of a long low room of the palace and having presented me with cigarettes, which he insisted upon lighting matches for himself, sent for sherbet (to me it tasted very like the lime juice of commerce) and entered into conversation in English, which he speaks fairly well. This was after he had asked if I knew Arabic or Somali.

We spoke on a variety of subjects, especially Egypt, which he seemed anxious to visit and he expressed a polite hope that I would return to Zanzibar and stay there some time. Also he shewed interest in my recent travels. When I departed he again rose and accompanied me to the door. Altogether I was favourably impressed with his personality. I am told that unlike his predecessor he gives no trouble at all, also that he has only one wife and no harem. This struck me as odd in an Eastern and from what I heard afterwards I think there must be some mistake in that matter. A fellow passenger of mine, of an investigating disposition, managed to get himself shewn through the women's part of the palace by the distribution of some cash. A eunuch led him and his guide and, under pretext of exhibiting the beauty of the rooms, took him past one in which he saw 15 gaudily dressed young women of various shades of colour who, he was informed, were the Sultan's ladies. He was more impressed with their clothes than by their beauty. I should imagine that His Highness will find that the £8 000 a year he receives from the British government will scarcely provide for the expenses of a Sultana, a palace, eunuchs and the ordinary Eastern female accessories, if these last were his, a point upon which my friend seems to have satisfied himself. I should imagine that the existence of a potentate of this sort on the whole must be somewhat dull.

At the conclusion of my interesting visit I went to the Residence, a really beautiful house which belongs to the British government, with cool, lofty rooms and wide verandahs. Here we had a pleasant luncheon, after which the Archbishop, Mrs. Carter and I were taken out in a motor and shewn the sights by Mr. Stirling. We drove to a place called Bububu where there is a fish market and a clove plantation, passing three ruined palaces. One of these we stopped to see. It is a picturesque and extensive ruin where the blue lotus still blooms in the old cement fountains, but like the others in a very unhealthy situation. There is another deserted palace which I did not see, which is said to be haunted by women (dead). Of the doings at one of those that we did see strange stories are still told.

The clove trees on the shamba (or farm) which we visited are roughly planted and to me did not look at all healthy. Many of the ends of the boughs were dead on all of them. A clove plantation here seems to sell for about 10s. a tree, which includes the price of the land, and a coconut plantation for about 7s. 6d. a tree also with land, but the price varies in accordance with the nearness of the shamba to the coast and the cost of transport. Much of the clove and indeed of all other trade in Zanzibar seems to have fallen into the hands of Indians, with whom few can compete successfully.

The beautiful old carved doorways in Zanzibar struck me very much. I am sorry I had not more time there but at four o'clock I had to say goodbye to Major Pearce and return to the ship. During the clove-picking season here (cloves are the great asset of this part of the coast) labour costs about ls. 4d. per diem and for the rest of the year about half that sum. Indian and Japanese curios and wares are largely imported here and sold to passengers on the ships at very full prices, more indeed than they would cost in Regent Street.

Notes

1. Lourenço Marques, capital of Portuguese East Africa (renamed Maputo after Mozambique became independent in 1975) was a watering station for ships travelling between Europe and the Far East. There were various attempts at permanent settlement but the real growth of the city came in the 1870s with the mineral discoveries in the Transvaal for which the development of the city as a port provided an outlet. With the completion of the railway to the Transvaal in 1895 the city secured a large proportion of the traffic to and from the goldfields. Lourenço Marques was declared the capital of Mozambique in 1902.
2. Edgar Errol Napier MacDonnell (1874–1928), appointed Consul-General of Portuguese East Africa in 1912.
3. Sir Joachim Machado, KCMG, the Portuguese Governor-General. A treaty with the Transvaal in 1869 turned Lourenço Marques into a growth point thanks to its location on Delagoa Bay and its potential as a port. In the 1870s a publics works department created by Joachim Machado set about developing the city. A noted railway engineer, he surveyed the route of the line from Lourenço Marques to the Transvaal.
4. For information on Archbishop Carter, see Chapter Five, Note 3.
5. *Ipsissima verba*, in Latin 'the precise words'.
6. *Carros du bois*, open carriages on runners drawn by oxen.
7. Following a revolution in 1910, which overthrew the monarchy, Portugal became a republic. Portugal's republican constitution officially separated church and state and removed subsidies from Catholic missions.
8. David Lloyd George (1863–1945), British Liberal Party leader; Chancellor of the Exchequer from 1908–15; Prime Minister from 1916–22.
9. Island of Mozambique was the capital until Lourenço Marques was designated the capital in 1902. Mozambique was the first Arab-African town Vasco da Gama touched on his way to India. In 1507 the Portuguese chose it as their final revictualling station for the last leg to India. They built a small fort, a hospital, a Dominican convent and three churches to serve the merchant population. All these buildings were destroyed by the Dutch in raids on the island in 1607 and 1608. The only structure remaining from this period is the chapel dedicated to Nossa Senhora do Baluarte, Our Lady of the Bulwark.
10. The fortress of Sao Sebastio, one of the largest fortifications contructed by

the Portuguese in the East. Construction started in 1558 and the fortress covers an area of 20 234 m² (5 acres).

11.   In 1913, South Africa banned all labour recruitment north of the 22-degree parallel, partly in a bid to cut the high death rate among 'tropical' Africans and also to fend off criticism of South Africa by Mozambican and Portuguese business interests.

12.   Major F.B. Pearce was British Resident in Zanzibar from 1914–22. He was the author of *Zanzibar: The island metrolopolis of Eastern Africa*, London, 1920.

13.   The foundation stone of the Cathedral of Christ the King (Anglican) was laid in 1873 after Sultan Barghash (1870–88) signed a treaty with Great Britain to prohibit the export of slaves from East Africa and to close the slave market. The building of the cathedral was supervised by Bishop E. Steere of the Universities Mission to Central Africa (initiated by an appeal from David Livingstone) and was completed in 1879.

14.   Seyyid Khalifa-bin-Hourub. In both manuscripts the name is not given. A blank space was left for its later inclusion.

Chapter Ten

It is done

చ్చ చ్చ చ్చ చ్చ చ్చ

Haggard's punishing African trek took him next to the British East Africa Protectorate (now Kenya) where he travelled by train through the Travo National Park. By now he was admitting to a degree of weariness. He was still far from home and within a matter of weeks would be joining other members of the Commission for the next stage of their inquiries, this time in Canada. Yet he managed to maintain a keen interest in his surroundings, enthusing about game sightings and probing away endlessly at the thorny problems of land and agriculture in Africa.

Saturday, 17 May

Early this morning we reached Mombasa, the port of British East Africa.[1] The harbour is approached by a deep-water channel between coral reefs and is called Kilindini; also on the north-east of the island on which the town stands is the harbour of Mombasa, shallower water that is chiefly used by dhows. Kilindini harbour is completely sheltered and one of the finest on the coast, with deep water and ample anchorage room. A quay is to be built of 1 200 feet in length at a cost of about £600 000, the money being provided out of the recent loan of £3 million, which is to be advanced imperially to East Africa and Uganda. This will be used for the berthing of ocean-going ships, accommodation that is very necessary as there is no adequate system of lighterage, but there are some who think that it would be better to provide such a system at a smaller cost. Also there is a wharf which, I understand, has been provided by the Magadi Soda Company to ship their product.

The place is pretty in a tropical way when looked at from the harbour but there is not much to be seen in the town, which I had no time to visit. It is however a place of much history. Here the Portuguese were besieged for several years in the fort of Jesus, now a prison, at the end of the 17th century, the poor survivors – 11 men and two women – being massacred two days before a fleet arrived with reliefs, much as Gordon was at Khartoum.[1] I was very anxious to use the two days we had at Mombasa in visiting Nairobi, the capital of British East Africa, about 320 miles from Mombasa but the difficulties with regard to trains proved to be so great that in the end I was obliged very reluctantly to abandon the idea. At the last moment, however, a telegram came from the Governor, Sir Henry Belfield,[3] directing that accommodation should be provided for me to come to Nairobi whereon all difficulties magically melted away as seems to be common in this protectorate where the official element is so supreme.

Accordingly Mr. and Mrs. Carden, Miss Glossop, I and five second-class passengers started at 1.30 in a special train. There was a good deal of confusion in getting off, the promised launch did not arrive, the Indian gentleman in charge of the Customs House notwithstanding all the circumstances shewed a disposition (with the special train waiting) to be inquisitive about our modest baggage, etc. At last we were away, each of the four of us established in a separate compartment like a wild beast in a cage. Like wild beasts also we projected our heads through the bars or rather the window places and conversed with each other. We had been told that we must provide our own bedding and borrowed some blankets and pillows from the ship, but we did *not* know that a paternal government allows no soap or towels or *any* other civilised furnishments on the trains, except a basin and some water, which put us in a quandary. Indeed had I not contrived to borrow a towel and a piece of soap from a friendly guard and to buy a tumbler at a wayside station, I do not know how I should have managed. Since then I have ascertained that the reason for their absence is the constant theft of everything put upon the trains.

A mile or two away from Mombasa the line begins to climb through beautiful scenery with peeps of the harbour below. Then comes bushveld with great antheaps and ashen-hued euphorbias, then large plantations of rubber that look most neglected, perhaps because of the fall in the price of that commodity, then at a distance of 35 miles from Mombasa vast plains covered with rather sparse bush. Meals on the Uganda railway are taken wherever they can be got, which is in few places and are not too plentiful though clean. Indeed they seem to consist chiefly of dry and ancient ham and, if you are lucky, of occasional eggs.

The only game we saw before darkness fell was a flock of beautiful guinea-fowl with greenish necks. We went to bed early, if so the process could be called, but could not sleep much because of the shaking of that rackety train. Also the consciousness that one must be up and watching by daybreak, and that there was no one to call us, did not tend to restfulness. As a matter of fact I rose at 3 a.m., two hours before it was needful. However, I was rewarded for the sea of bushveld looked very mysterious in the light of the waning moon and once I caught sight of some sinuous feline creature bounding up the railway bank and once of some great grey animal standing beneath a tree. Although we were now high above sea level I noticed that the air had none of the crispness of the highveld in South Africa.

At last the light came but to our disappointment it was too cloudy to enable us to see the snows of Kilimanjaro, or later on of Kenya. Now a few buck began to appear among the trees at some distance from the line. Then there was a cry of 'Look! Look!' I looked and there not more than 100 yards away were two herds of towering giraffes, one of six and one of four, their graceful heads rising above the low trees. Yes, these were wild giraffes, perhaps the most wonderful creatures left in the world today. We stared and stared at them till the train left them behind, and blessed our stars that we were there to stare. For many make this journey time and time again and see no giraffe. But we were in luck's path that day for an hour or so later we saw 10 more giraffe, this time to the right of the line which is off the ground of the game reserve. More, for there to the left and within not more than 20 feet was a giant bull, the hugest and most splendid beast I ever saw. What his height may have been I cannot say but I think he had been unable to cross the line because of the telegraph wires, which by the way these beasts often break. As we came up he lumbered off with a curious jerky motion, for 8 or 10 yards not more, then stood and looked back at us with his great soft eyes, his head turned round over his shoulder. Never to my dying day shall I forget the towering grandeur of the form of this gigantic bull or the shining splendour of his striped skin, of which no one who has only seen these creatures in confinement can form much idea. Gladly would I have made the journey to look at him alone there in his natural habitat.

After this we saw no more giraffe (our total visual bag was 21) but we did see many other things. Presently the bush country thinned into endless grassy plains backed by round isolated hills and oh! the place was alive. There were hartebeest in quantity, their curious horns with the ears projecting beneath looking, at a little distance, exactly like the famous Hathor cow in the Cairo Museum wearing the dish of the moon upon her head, fat gleaming hartebeest with white buttocks. There were striped zebra fatter still with their heads held forward and their ears cocked staring at us. There were wild, white-plumed ostriches scouring the plains, there were brindled blue wildebeest, much larger than the white-tailed variety of gnu, looking like small buffalo indeed. The last time I saw these was in 1879 when as an officer of the Pretoria Horse I was out in the bushveld looking for the rumoured Zulu impi.[4] There was a herd of buck like springbucks but not quite the same. There were straight-horned gemsbok and others of a kindred sort but smaller, there were lovely painted creatures of which I do not know the name. Then we came upon impala, two of which rushed in front of the train and departed in huge bounds, each bound taking them apparently from 6 to 10 feet into the air, and other animals I had never seen before. Surely this was the most wonderful journey I ever made in all my life of journeying, in the whole world there can be nothing like to it, nothing at all. For this went on for hours, from shortly after dawn till we reached near to Nairobi about 1.30.

For a space of some 20 miles there was no game, why I cannot say, unless the grass is sour, then they began again thicker than before, hundreds and hundreds of them – although we could see but a little distance on either side of the line. And yet I am told that there are not a third part of what there were some years ago. Were it not for this great reserve by now all would be gone, as doubtless all are destined to go since soon or late the destroying white man will have them upon this pretext or the other. It will be said that they bring tsetse fly, although I observed great herds of cattle which I believe belong to Masai, grazing among them, or that the land is wanted for 'settlement' and the shooters will be let in and glut themselves in the old Boer fashion and these divine creatures will become but a memory. How anyone can want to slaughter such beauteous mammals save now and again for food passes my comprehension. It is nothing but murder, yet I must remember that once when I was young I did it myself.[5]

I have seen the Transvaal veld black with game and 35 years later I have travelled through it without finding so much as a duiker buck and that is what will one day happen in East Africa, or so I fear. I should mention that with the buck is much other life, huge beaked and gorgeous birds, crested mahems [crowned cranes] that I remember in South Africa, but which seem very rare there now, blue crane, wide-winged whitish hawks, guinea-fowl in flocks, partridges, lovely butterflies, and so on. What we were not lucky enough to see were rhinoceros and lion. Both are still common here though no buffalo or sable antelopes live in this veld.

The engine driver of our train told us that only on the previous evening, at a place we passed, there was a rhinoceros on the line holding up a workman on a trolley, who called to him to clear it out of the way. So he steamed on whereupon the bellicose rhino put down his head and charged. He caught the engine on the buffer and got the worst of it (like Stephenson's cow) for his horn was knocked off and he was knocked over and stood for a long while dazed while people from the train took his photograph with Kodaks. Then he turned and made off into the bush defeated, unhorned and probably with a headache. The engine driver gave the horn to one of the passengers. A little while ago this same man who was taking up a gentleman whose name I forget, saw a lion in the bush about 300 yards from the line. He stopped the train and sent for Dr. (—)[6] who had a rifle with him. As the beast was on the non-reserved side of the line the doctor sallied forth and shot the lion, which the driver said was one of the finest he ever saw. They took it on with them in the train. There are plenty of lions here – it was at Tsavo that the famous man-eater lived who came into the train not dead but very much alive.[7] We however only heard one growling in the night and came to the conclusion that if it or another followed the example of its relative of Tsavo, our best place of refuge would be the lavatory – if we had time to get there!

A gentleman informed me that only a week or so since he saw, just as the dawn was breaking, three lions engaged in eating a zebra. They looked up and growled as the train passed, no more. All these animals are perfectly acquainted with the limits of the reserve, and if fired at or disturbed on the northern side of the line cross it and stand quietly in the protected ground. Long may it remain protected. I observed that when we passed back over this ground in the late afternoon no game, practically, was to be seen on the unprotected side, whereas to the south there were hundreds of them as far as the eye could reach. Either this was because the day being Sunday people were out shooting (we saw some with guns in a trolley) or they had moved into their sanctuary for the night.

Amongst other sights we saw some Masai women, stalwart females decked out in their brass ornaments and other finery and a *perfectly* naked man and woman, Kavirondos I think they were, standing in unconscious innocence at a station, like Adam and Eve in the garden.

Shortly after passing Athi River, the town of Nairobi came in sight – a straggling settlement on a plain amidst planted trees backed by a dark range of hills. Half way up the line we were told that instead of our promised three hours we should have no stay at all at Nairobi, even if we got there in time to return and catch our boat at the appointed hour. Telegrams to the governor and a lucky meeting with Mr. Bowring,[8] the government secretary who was coming down the line to be our fellow passenger on the *Gaika*, in the end put this right and arrangements on the Uganda railway being singularly elastic, our return train was held up for an hour and a half.

On arrival at Nairobi I was met by Mr. Brett, the governor's secretary, and after swallowing some food started in a motor to Government House where I had a talk with Lady Belfield, a delightful woman though very deaf, who used to know my brother Will in past years.[9] The governor unfortunately I did not see, as he had not returned from a shooting expedition. She was in grief over the death from heart trouble the previous day of Lady Delamere, the wife of Lord Delamere, a prominent settler in East Africa.[10] This heart disease, or failure, resulting from the altitude of all these uplands, some of which are 7 000 feet above sea level (Nairobi is more than 5 000 feet) is a common evil of the country. Indeed the place seems to be very unhealthy for Europeans – on this point everyone I have spoken to tells the same tale. Typhoid is rife (there is no drainage at Nairobi) and notwithstanding the altitude there is a good deal of malaria which, in part perhaps, is caught in the lower lands and brought out by the cold.

Also everyone, or at any rate most people, seem to suffer from acute 'nerves'. They lose their judgement, they say and do foolish things, they commit excesses or sometimes suicide. This is set down to climatic conditions resulting from the somewhat unnatural combination of a cold climate, hot sun and thin air (the stars shine here with extraordinary brightness) with a situation almost exactly on the Equator. I never heard the health conditions of a place so universally condemned by its inhabitants, unless, perchance, they have land to sell. And yet to a visitor all these conditions seem delightful. In fact, however, this charm and beauty are very treacherous. Major Leggett, the head of the British East Africa Company, who is on board this ship, tells me that in his opinion no white person ought to stay – or at any rate work – in East Africa for more than 15 years. Especially is this the case with women, who go to pieces very rapidly here and, as I remember was the case in Mexico City, suffer much from internal troubles, in addition to the other ailments of the land. Children also should not remain here too long.[11]

The upshot of it all is that this, like much of Rhodesia, is no white man's country, whatever may be said to the contrary by prejudiced persons – at least that is what I gather from those who know it well and I remember that Fred Jackson (who I hear is returning from Uganda sick next week) always said the same thing.[12] An added circumstance of sadness in the case of Lady Delamere is that her husband only reached Mombasa from Europe the day before her death. Whether he arrived at Nairobi before she actually expired no one seems to know. She was to be buried that afternoon, indeed Mr. Brett was going to the funeral after seeing me off.

Saying goodbye to Lady Belfield after my too hurried visit I was motored round the town and shewn all the principal places of interest. Like so many colonial cities it is in the hobbledehoy stage with some fine buildings and many poor ones. Also the Indian bazaar, though curious, is right in the heart of the place and should not be allowed to stay there with its dirt and inconvenience. I stopped for a minute to look at the house where Fred Jackson used to live when he was deputy governor here, a pretty red-roofed building with a nice garden, and then departed to catch our delayed special.

So ended my visit to Nairobi. I wish I could have extended it as far as Uganda but it was not possible. Indeed considering the time at my disposal I have managed to see a deal of Africa since the beginning of March and to travel many thousands of miles. It was a long journey back to Mombasa with little to eat, though we did the 300-odd miles quicker than on our upward trip. The fuel of the engine is wood, which in the end, I should imagine, will cause a great destruction of timber in the country and, after nightfall, it is pretty to observe the glowing sparks passing the carriage windows in a constant stream. Sheer fatigue made me sleep better this night, though having neglected to shut some of the windows I woke to find everything a quarter of an inch deep in red dust, including my hair. It was a grand and gloomy morning and the euphorbias looked particularly ghost-like beneath that heavy sky – pale fingers stretched imploringly to heaven.

At length we arrived hot, shaken, wearied and hungry but glad enough that we had faced our 700-mile journey which, had it not been for official intervention, we never could have done in the time at our disposal. I have a strong impression that the Uganda railway might be better managed than it is and the journey much shortened. The waits at the stations are really intolerable, even on a single line. But it is an official concern, presumably not run with profit as a principal object, and Indians seem to be in charge of all the stations – very stupid Indians.

In fact all East Africa is in a sense official and there is a constant war between this hierarchy and the settlers. No doubt there are faults on both sides. The official clothed in his little brief authority, especially the official of inferior intelligence and calibre, often considers himself the superior of ordinary flesh and blood. This is the tendency everywhere, even in England where the power of the permanent officials, an ever-increasing class, is becoming something of a menace to the public which pays them. It is a common experience that young gentlemen in any office will affect what I believe is called the 'Oxford manner' towards men twice their age and five times their knowledge and experience who are not 'one of ours', and if they need it, receive support of their manners, or of the lack of them, from all their office. It is not wonderful therefore that this traditional attitude should be somewhat accentuated amongst a privileged and dominant band in a place like East Africa. On the other hand settlers are often very unreasonable and very self-seeking and not always quite as straightforward as they might be. In short, as in most human differences, there are faults on both sides.

In Nairobi I obtained a copy of the new land ordnance, which is shortly to become law with or without amendment.[13] It is strangely complicated. Apparently there is in future to be no freehold title but only a 99-year leasehold (which it is now suggested should be extended to 999 years – a very different matter) with an upset price or premium, and periodic revaluations of a rental value, everything ultimately lapsing to the landlord, i.e. the Crown, as London household property lapses to certain dukes. These regulations I understand are inspired by the present government of the United Kingdom to demonstrate the soundness of their recently developed theories. Only then it is odd that in East Africa they should be insisting on the very system which Mr. Lloyd George is denouncing with so much fury at home, namely that of leasehold with an absolute reversion to the lessor, in this case the Crown. However, one may be certain that sooner or later the whole business will break down in a country where the white population is – and must always – remain very sparse. People will desire to own what they acquire unhampered by a multitude of vague servitudes, which must prevent them from raising money on their working property.

It is to my mind a question whether there will ever be much European population in East Africa. I think that the future wealth of that land and of Uganda must lie in the development of the native peoples. Already I believe most of the exports are produced by these, not by the whites, and it is reasonable to suppose that this will be more and more the case in future years. So far East Africa has not been very successful as a white settler proposition. Of the wheat which was to be grown here by the thousand tons not a bag has yet been exported. Cattle and sheep of superior grade are up to the present a failure. Coffee, cocoa and cotton are doing well, the former in East Africa and the latter two in Uganda, but soon the natives will find, and indeed are already finding, that they can grow these crops more profitably for themselves than by working for white masters.

The supply of labour is not abundant. Although there exists a large native population the men will only go out to work in youth and most of them are not laboriously inclined. Why should they be when in this clime they can satisfy all their simple wants off the produce of a little plot of land planted with the banana? Moreover, they do not everywhere multiply very fast, especially on the coastline and in the older and more settled portions of Buganda where, owing to a variety of causes, few children seem to be born. Also in many districts syphilis and other diseases are spreading rapidly and the common unions of white men and native women seem to be unfertile, whether by design or from natural reasons. Thus it comes about that taken altogether the prospects of the labour market are not held to be bright and the crops that pre-eminently succeed (rubber has been proved a failure and scores of acres which I saw planted at great cost near Mombasa have been actually deserted) require a great deal of labour. Meanwhile the native is waking up and especially in Uganda shews a disposition to become a cultivator on his own account. All this taken in conjunction with the climatic conditions, makes the outlook of the white man here more than doubtful. At best it is no country for the settler without capital and, if invested, the earning power of capital, unless most intelligently managed, remains uncertain. Of course if responsible government were granted conditions might be somewhat altered by the usual squeezing of the natives. But I cannot conceive that East Africa will be fit for responsible government within any reasonable time and when it comes, if ever, the native may be in a position to look after his own interests. I think on the whole that this land is an exemplification of the old saying 'Africa for the African', guided and vivified perhaps by constantly refreshed European intelligence, just as India is for the Indian with the same limitations and provisos. Christianity, which has taken a hold, especially in Uganda, may modify the position to some extent, unless Mahomedanism supplants it with its stricter moral laws, or rather enforcement of moral laws (outside of the debated question of polygamy) and its forbiddance of all spirituous drink. But it is difficult to forecast what exact form Christianity may ultimately assume in these latitudes.

Today I heard an interesting and true story which bears upon the point. An intelligent East African native, who had been educated at a mission station, spent two or three years in studying the various forms of Christianity and ultimately returned to his first protestant community where, to the dismay of the white missionaries, he proceeded to develop a sect of his own. The missionaries, fearing this competition, invited him to an interview and, not understanding his language too well, came to the conclusion that his difficulties had something to do with the Trinity. An expert in his tongue was finally called in who explained that the missionaries were ready to resolve his doubts upon this point. For a while he listened with a puzzled air and at last burst out laughing. 'There is a mistake,' he said, 'the trinity I referred to in speaking to these preachers, was not that of the Book, which I accept, but to my *three wives!* I want to start a branch of the Christian religion which will enable me to keep my three wives.' So the controversy ended, like the marriage service, in amazement.[14] If a form of Christianity could be accepted which allowed these people to continue their ancient customs with reference to marriage it would I believe sweep Southern and Eastern Africa. As this appears to be impossible it must be prepared to find in Mahommedanism a most dangerous and often a victorious competitor wherever both faiths are labouring in the same field.

A considerable number of East African officials and their wives came aboard the *Gaika* at Mombasa. All the ladies and children look very washed out and one, Mrs. Leggett, has suffered badly from fever. No one I have spoken to has a good word for the climate. Our ship is now crowded and the cabin or black hole I have been relegated to is as hot as a certain region, being devoid of light or ventilation. However I have been promised a better one after Aden and till then I must sweat and be still – which is more than are the poor children by whom I am surrounded.

Monday, 19 May

Today I made the acquaintance of a very interesting person, a Persian named Henry Ishmael (this sounds Jewish but he does not look like a Jew and are there any Persian Jews?). Mr. Ishmael lives at Tanga, 72 miles south of Mombasa, just over the borders of German East Africa, where he manages a rubber estate called Kamna; also he has a coffee plantation in Uganda and sisal lands in East Africa. He speaks English perfectly and appears to be a man of great intelligence and one who has been a government official and is employed to report on properties. Also he has been a great elephant hunter and held one of the last general licenses to shoot these animals that was issued in the Congo state. On that trip he killed 57 elephants himself, using a small-bore .303 for long shots and a heavy rifle for those that were close. He has found a shot placed just behind the orifice of the ear the most deadly with the .303 and once killed an elephant stone dead with this weapon at a distance of about 500 yards – an amazing thing to do.

He tells me that on one occasion in the Congo he found himself in a vast herd of elephants that could not have numbered less than 600. On these he was too frightened to fire fearing lest he should be crushed to death in the general stampede, so contented himself with watching this stupendous sight. The largest pair of tusks he ever secured weighed 110 pounds and 105 pounds, but of course much heavier ones are known. I think he mentioned one he had seen which scaled 170 pounds. He has not found elephants dangerous, especially where they are unaccustomed to being shot at. On his Congo expedition only two accidents occurred. In one case a boy's leg was broken by a wounded elephant, on the other a native died of fright when pursued by an injured bull – if he was pursued. The bull was running down an elephant path and overtook him and two companions. These threw themselves into the grass: he stood staring at the beast and just as it came up to him dropped dead, as did the elephant. The man's heart had given out.

Elephants are now protected everywhere, except in Portuguese East Africa, where the game laws are not enforced. Mr. Ishmael says that in British East Africa there are quite 100 cows left to every bull, which is twice too many, but it is now unlawful to kill a bull with tusks weighing less than 30 pounds apiece. The sale of buffalo hides is also made unlawful as the natives will give up to £15 for these for shield-making purposes, which caused them to be shot unmercifully. Mr. Ishmael says he very rarely shoots buck now as it is mere butchery which requires no skill. So he has taken to duck and snipe-shooting instead.

What interests me more than his hunting stories however are those he has to tell of the wonders he has seen worked by the Wanyamwezi tribe among whom he is at present living, who have a secret society called *Unyeye* and can cure snakebite apparently with certainty. He describes them as a hard-working, intelligent and industrious people, among whom women have a good position, ruling certain sections of the tribe by hereditary right. Many of them have migrated from German East Africa to British East Africa because of the kind treatment they experience under our rule. They cure snakebite by rubbing in certain *dawa* or medicine, which consists of a black powder whereof he has found it impossible to discover the ingredients. When he asked one of the natives why he would not tell him he answered that he had been assured when he was initiated that if ever he revealed the secret to one who was not of the society he must die, and that die he surely would. This man cured Mr. Ishmael's servant in his presence by rubbing the black powder into an incision made over the wound (he had been bitten three minutes before). In another case he did the same, but as he did not know what sort of snake had bitten the patient made him in addition swallow a decoction of pounded leaves to cause vomiting. The man was instantly all right and walked away. Mr. Ishmael captured and took to him a snake of the cobra variety, which we call ringhals in South Africa.[15] He said: '*Bwana* (master) never you touch one of these again – they are very deadly and if you were bitten and I were not at hand, might die. See,' and he opened the reptile's mouth and let it bite him till his hand bled freely. Mr. Ishmael asked if he were not afraid of consequences. 'Oh, no!' he answered, 'once a year I inoculate myself with *dawa* and fear no snakebite.' As for the magical performances of this *Unyeye* society (which seems to partake of the nature of our free-masonry and to be animated by similar principles) I will let the memorandum which Mr. Ishmael has kindly given me, together with some of the photos referred to (which he took *himself*), speak for themselves.[16]

I should add that he told me of other things which are not described in the paper. Thus the doctor wished to borrow some powder and a bullet from him. He asked what for, and was informed that he might shoot one of the fraternity before his eyes. 'Have no fear master,' he said, 'the bullet will go through him and he will seem to die, but he will take no hurt, in a minute he will be all right again.' Mr. Ishmael declined to be a party to this performance, so the issue remains unknown. He did however see, unfortunately when he had no camera at hand, the doctor drive a sharpened rod of iron quite six inches into the body of one of his assistants, inserting it into the vitals beneath the ribs and pushing it in slowly by a series of efforts. When he drew it out again it was covered with blood and blood appeared on the wound. This was instantly staunched by the application of crushed leaves and presently the man was none the worse!

Also these *Unyeye* are said to be able to walk in fire – like Shadrack and his companions in Nebuchadnezzar's furnace – and take no hurt, though they will stand still and turn about in the flames. This Mr. Ishmael has not seen himself. When he asked the doctor to shew him that particular piece of magic he answered that he had not the medicine necessary to take the sting out of the fire but that there was a greater doctor than he who lived three miles away who would do what he wanted if asked. As yet Mr. Ishmael has not sent for this doctor. Now after studying the above document and the accompanying photos what is to be said? How can a man's head be buried in a hole full of fire for over an hour, with the earth firmly trodden down about the neck and at the end of that time emerge unhurt? If an air passage was left under the neck the fire would have continued to burn and even if the earth immediately extinguished the fire he ought to have been suffocated within a minute and the skin should have shrivelled on his face and his eyes should have scorched up. Yet none of these things happened.

Mr. Ishmael and the vice-consul who I think was with him, might have been hypnotised, but who can hypnotise a camera? And see there he lies in the picture before me. If such things can happen, and happen it seems they do in this wonderful Africa, why should we have so much difficulty in accepting the New Testament miracles? I consider these photos and the accompanying descriptive matter of quite extraordinary interest and think myself most fortunate to have got possession of them. Still there may be some explanation of the business not apparent to me.

Thursday, 22 May

Passed Cape Gardafui – a bald barren headland apparently all sand and no water. Yet the Somalis have villages of huts upon the seashore for we can see them, also their boats. I suppose they live by fishing. They are said to be very fierce and treacherous. It is probable that Italy, to whom this coast belongs, does not make much use of her possession. I had two teeth taken out by the doctor this morning. They have been my companions for half a century but the best of friends must part! They looked very lonely lying there upon the table. The heat in my black hole of a cabin is getting terrible. This afternoon is the hottest we have had. And yet the irrepressible Englishman plays cricket in it and they have asked me to be president of a sports committee. Sports in this temperature! Ye Gods!

Saturday, 24 May

We reached Aden about 5.30 p.m. I went ashore with the Leggetts (I find that Major Leggett, DSO, the managing director of the East African Company is a cousin of mine) and we were driven about by the agent of the Union-Castle Line (Mr. Douglas) in his motor. It is the strangest place. I never landed here before and am glad that I did so now. A couple of miles or so from the landing place is the town of Old Aden, in the crater of an extinct volcano. All around this Eastern-looking settlement rise walls of blasted grey lava. Really it might be a settlement in Hell, to which the temperature (over 90F at night) is quite appropriate. Everywhere run walls built I understand in the first days of our occupation to protect the island, for practically it is an island, from incursions by Arabs across the sands. Also there are long lamp-lit tunnels closed by ancient doors, down which we motored. The place is strongly fortified and I suppose next to Gibraltar is one of the most important of our possessions, being indeed the great gateway to the East.

This has always been recognised, as history shews, by the peoples who went before us, but I am ashamed to say that I am sadly ignorant of the history of Aden. The great tanks it was too dark to visit. They are in good order, but seem to lack a catchment area, or rather no sufficient rain falls nowadays to fill them. Therefore the place depends upon distilled water, though there is now some talk of bringing a supply from miles away. Salt-making is the great industry of the place. It is obtained by evaporating the sea water by means of sun heat and we saw it piled in great white heaps near the shore.

On the ship the scene was very amusing owing to the number of native dealers who came to sell horns, curios, ostrich feathers and the really beautiful baskets dyed in many colours which they make in this neighbourhood. What time it must take a woman to weave a large basket of this sort I have no idea, but I imagine months. I purchased some of these baskets which now I must carry home! But unfortunately I could not get one of the very largest ones which would just about have accommodated my daily supply of wastepaper – or a week's washing. They had been snapped up. Also I bought some ostrich feathers.

Sunday, 25 May

Heat intolerable. Thank Heaven I have been moved into a deck cabin. But I find it hard to work and there is so much to be done. I wonder what it would feel like to have a *real* holiday. Probably I should be bored to death. Work is like dram-drinking – one cannot leave it off, or if one does is apt to leave off everything.

Monday, 26 May

This morning I had a very interesting conversation with Major Leggett and Mr. Spire, a high official in Uganda, who has been showing me his maps of the great district for which he is responsible. Both these considerable authorities allege that where the missionaries have been long established the population is *decreasing*. Also they say that the law of monogamy introduced by them is persistently and almost universally evaded. The only difference is that the open and honest extra wife is turned into a surreptitious concubine and the man into one whose life becomes an acted lie. They both seem to think that in the end an African variety of Christianity will be evolved, which will sanction plurality of wives according to the ancient customs. Meanwhile, the surplus female population which, it seems, is considerable, is drifting into prostitution. The spread of native cultivation of cotton, which Major Leggett has been demonstrating to me, is very remarkable.

Tuesday, 27 May

Yesterday we spent in great heat at Port Sudan. This is a really excellent tideless harbour, of which the following are some particulars: The entrance is 250 yards across at its narrowest part, the depths in the fairway vary from 47 fathoms to 21 fathoms and at the wharf from 4½ to 7 fathoms. The fall here on the edge of the coral reef is very steep. Thus on the inside of the ship against the wharf the water is about 44 fathoms, while on the outside it varies from 7 to 12 fathoms. The new wharf, which is made on a spit of reclaimed land that once was a coral reef, is 680 yards long and will accommodate four ocean-going steamers of ordinary size; indeed that number were tied up there yesterday.

The facilities for dealing with cargo are splendid as trains from the Khartoum railway can run alongside and there are several model electric cranes which lift up to seven tons. There is however no fresh water here and at present the amount of cargo is limited, a matter that will rectify itself as the Sudan develops. Also there is a curious blending of primitive and modern methods. The cranes do not take the stuff direct from the trucks. It is thrown out and lifted by about six men package by package on to the back of *one* man, who sets it down under the crane. The weight that these men, who come from the other side of the Red Sea, can carry in that temperature is something astonishing. I heard it asserted that they can bear as much as half a ton but this I cannot believe. Certainly however they make light, in a literal sense, of huge parcels of hides which must weigh 300 or 400 lbs, which one of them will continue to stagger under for hours without a rest. Five or six of these parcels are then surrounded by a rope and swung into the hold by a crane. It is like setting an elephant to pick up pins as the crane could deal with many times the weight if suitable baskets or trays were provided and much time would be saved. We were kept till about 9 o'clock at night getting on board a very moderate amount of cargo owing to the inefficient management and quality of this black man labour.

Port Sudan is a scattered settlement on burning sand backed by a range of mountains that looked hazy in the heat. We had an exciting episode here. Shortly after arrival Mr. Carden hooked a huge shark, quite a dozen feet long. After it had been played for a matter of an hour and seemed to be growing very exhausted some of the quartermasters took charge saying they knew exactly what to do and began to pass the line forward to get it onto the winch. I told them not once but three times that if they did not keep the rope taut the beast would certainly get off, but they would pay no heed to a landlubber. Result, presently it *did* get off and was no more seen, nor would any other take the bait. The captain was very vexed about it and said the whole stupid business was typical of the modern steamship sailor. Sharks and snakes are the two sections of creation that I take some satisfaction in destroying. They are pre-eminently *hostes humani generis* and devilish-hearted.[17] Well no doubt this one will live on to eat men. Thank goodness there is a strong headwind today so one need not walk about with a towel in place of a pocket handkerchief.

Thursday, 29 May

On our beam are the barren brown mountains of Egypt off which the wind blows fresh and cool. I wonder why they should have such an attraction for me. There is no land I love so well. We ought to be at Suez by 2 p.m. where we are to be medically examined (by a lady doctor) because of the plague which seems to be endemic on the east coast of Africa. The change from the heat of the tropics is a great relief. It is hard to work with the perspiration trickling onto the paper and one's back and arms burning with prickly heat. At breakfast the captain was talking to me of the falling off in the quality of the young Englishmen of all classes who take to the sea nowadays and especially of the officers. Partly he puts this down to the passing of the sailing ship and partly to other and more obscure causes. I do not think this is a mere case of *laudator temporis acti*.[18] Evidently there is much in what he says. Also he laments the loss of touch between shipowners and their servants owing to the inauguration of the huge commercial combines which now rule the sea as well as the land. He says that when he was a young man the officers at the conclusion of a voyage used to go to the owners' house and be entertained by them. Even old Donald Currie,[19] whom I remember so well, was always delighted to see them. Now they see no one except a 'manager' who cares nothing about them and, if it is to the advantage of the business, treats them without consideration and even without mercy.

The personal touch has gone. After all it is the same everywhere. Take the case of publishers and authors. How different it is dealing with a Charles Longman or a John Murray and one of these new firms of tradesmen whom the writer of the book scarcely ever sees and who, individually, look upon the producer of the raw material with the utmost indifference.[20] *Their* only interest in him is the extent to which his work will or will not sell. Well, thus things change and in their sum these changes help to bring about the rise and fall of peoples. Still I hope that the captain is wrong when he declares that in a maritime sense 'we are dead up to the neck!' so far as the Merchant Service is concerned.

Here I may as well end this record of my African travels. During the last few months I have circumnavigated the continent and travelled many thousands of miles in its interior, setting down, often under difficult circumstances, some faithful report of those things that struck me most at the moment. I daresay that I shall never read it through and

whether any one else will who can say? Still it is done and I am glad
that I have found the energy for the work in the midst of so much
employment, hurry and disturbance, for I am sure that I should never
have attempted it afterwards. But in truth I grow weary of journeying
by land and sea!

H. Rider Haggard.
R.M.S. *Gaika*,
off Suez.

29 *May*, 1914

(See letter to C.O.) [21]

Tuesday, 3 *June*

Alas! I must add a postscript. At Naples I received a letter from Miss
Hector [22] which tells me that Ella Hart-Bennett is among the drowned
of the *Empress of Ireland* in the terrible catastrophe of the St. Lawrence
River, in which she was a passenger on her homeward journey from
the Bahamas. [23] Poor Ella! I have known her from childhood, my mother,
whose god-daughter she was, wished me to try to marry her and when
she did marry I made the speech proposing her health and happiness at
the Lodge at Ditchingham. But last autumn she was staying with us as
I hoped she would again this year, and since then we have exchanged
epistolatory jokes for she was a merry and a witty woman. More, although she never knew it, at Madeira I dedicated the new tale I have
written – *The Ivory Child* – to 'The Lady of the New Moon'. Anyone
whoever chanced to read it would understand the allusion. It seems, as
she told us at Ditchingham when I outlined the plot to her, that she,
like its heroine, had on her this mark of a crescent moon. [24]

And now, I suppose, she floats in the icy waters of the St. Lawrence.
She was travelling alone, there would have been none to help her at
the last. It seems that the news of this terrible shipwreck was known by
many on our ship at Port Said. But it seems to have made little impression for I never heard it so much as mentioned. Truly we are an unim-
aginative people. A thousand souls perish in a British steamer off Canada,
but this does not stir those upon *this* steamer, although the same fate
might overtake them tonight. They read of but do not realise the dreadful scene, even, as it is set out, in the special columns of the papers.
They did not know them . . . and 'How terrible! but what about the dance
tonight' . . . and . . . 'Who has won the sweep?' Well, perhaps this lack
of abstract sympathy and vision is fortunate since its abundance does
not make life more cheerful for the possessor. They, or most of them,
cannot see that last terror as I see it and for this they may be glad.
Another old friend gone! One by one they steal or are snatched away,

leaving us ever poorer and more desolate. God grant that we may find them again. Goodbye Ella!

Oddly enough it was also at Naples that I heard of the loss of the *Titanic* two years ago.

H.R.H

Notes

1. The British East Africa Protectorate (later Kenya) was a crown colony from 1896–1920.
2. After a siege of several months, General Charles Gordon was killed at Khartoum on 26 January 1885. A relieving force commanded by Sir Garnet Wolseley arrived two days later to find the town invested by the forces of Mohammed Ahmed ibn Abdullah, the Mahdi.
3. Sir Henry Belfield (1855–1923), Governor of the East Africa Protectorate 1912–17.
4. Following the British defeat at Isandlwana, a mounted corps, the Pretoria Horse, was raised to counter the perceived Zulu threat. Haggard was elected adjutant. See H.R. Haggard, *The Days,* Vol. 1, p. 127. Haggard gives a detailed account of events surrounding the 'rumoured Zulu impi' in 'An Incident of African History', *Windsor Magazine,* December 1900.
5. Though acknowledging 'shooting was my principal occupation', Haggard gave up blood sports in 1904. On the night of 9 July 1904 he dreamt that his retriever Bob was trying to communicate with him. 'In my vision the dog was trying to speak to me in words and, failing, transmitted to my mind in an undefined fashion the knowledge that it was dying.' It subsequently transpired the dog had been killed by a train at the time of Haggard's dream. Greatly moved by the experience, Haggard gave up all blood sports except for fishing. See H.R. Haggard, *The Days,* Vol. 2, pp. 159–67, and H.R. Haggard, 'A Ghostly Connection' in Peter Haining (ed.), *The Best Short Stories of Rider Haggard,* London, 1981. The same volume also contains Haggard's anti-blood sports novella *The Mahatma and the Hare* (first published in 1911), which was also inspired by a dream.
6. A blank space appears in both versions of the manuscript.
7. In 1898 two male lions killed and ate nearly 140 railway workers during the building of a bridge across the Tsavo River thus halting its construction. The chief engineer, Lieutenant-Colonel John Henry Patterson (1865–1947), shot the lions. See his subsequent book *The Man Eaters of Tsavo,* London, 1907.
8. Sir Charles Bowring was appointed Acting Governor, 1917–19.
9. William Henry Doveton Haggard (1846–1923), Haggard's eldest brother. A career diplomat, he retired from the diplomatic service in 1914 and was knighted the same year.
10. Florence, Lady Delamere, wife of Hugh Cholmondely, 3rd Baron Delamere (1879 or 1880–1931), a pioneer of white settlemement, suffered from poor health and in 1911 had a nervous breakdown attributed to

having run the family farm during her husband's absence. Delamere became ill and had returned to England in the middle of 1913 to enter a nursing home, leaving his wife, who was still frail, to run the estate. Her health deteriorated and friends in Nairobi persuaded her to stay with them. Two days after Delamere returned from England, she died at the age of 36. See Errol Trzebinski, *The Kenya Pioneers*, London, 1985.

11.   Haggard visited Mexico City with his wife in 1891 and stayed with John Gladwyn Jebb. It was there that the Haggards received news of the death of their only son, Jock.

12.   Frederick Jackson (1860–1929), brother of Lilly Archer, came to East Africa in 1889 in command of a caravan sent to Uganda by the Imperial British East Africa Company. He held several offices in Uganda including Deputy Commissioner (1896) and Acting Commissioner (1897–98 and 1901–02). In 1903 he was appointed Deputy Commissioner of the East African Protectorate and Lieutenant-Governor in 1907. He was the Governor of Uganda, 1911–17 and the author of *Early Days in East Africa*, London, 1930.

13.   The Crown Lands Ordinance of 1902, which regulated the allocation of land, came under revision in 1910. It was passed in 1915.

14.   A reference to the final paragraph of The Form of Solemnisation of Matrimony in *The Book of Common Prayer* (1662) used by the Church of England of which Haggard was a member. The paragraph gives instruction to wives and ends: 'For after this manner in the old time the holy women also, who trusted in God, adorned themselves, being in subjection unto their own husbands; even as Sarah obeyed Abraham, called him lord; whose daughters ye are as long as ye do well, and are not afraid with any amazement.'

15.   Rinkhals (ringhals), *Hemachatus hemachatus*, stocky snake with broad head, averages 0.9 m to 1.18 m (3 ft to 3 ft 9 in.) in length. Colours vary from banded brown, black and grey to dark brown to black; back sometimes speckled with light brown and grey. In defence it rears, spreads its hood and sprays venom up to 2.3 m (7° ft), usually aiming at the face and particularly the eyes. The venom can cause great pain and even blindness. It is less dangerous than the cobra and fatalities are rare. Common on KwaZulu-Natal grasslands, with relict populations on montane grasslands of the Cape Province and Zimbabwe (Inyanga) and along the southern Cape coast.

16.   The memorandum and accompanying photographs are no longer extant.

17.   *Hostes humani generis*, in Latin 'enemies of the human race'.

18.   *Laudator temporis acti*, in Latin 'eulogiser of times past'.

19.   Donald Currie (1825–1909), Scottish shipowner in the Cape trade and a public figure. In 1875 he met President Thomas Burgers of the Transvaal Republic and hosted him in London. Following the annexation of the Transvaal by the British in 1877, Currie was an active supporter of its retrocession and gave assistance to two Boer delegations protesting against the annexation. During the First Anglo-Boer War (1880–81), he was in frequent contact with Lord Gladstone and Johannes Brand, President of the Orange Free State, the mediator between Britain and the Boer forces.

Today, Currie is probably best-known as the founder of South Africa's premier inter-provincial cricket and rugby competitions.

20. Charles Longman and John Murray both headed family publishing houses. Charles Longman was a friend of Haggard's, as well as the publisher of many of his books.

21. See Appendix One.

22. Ida Hector, daughter of the Irish novelist Annie Hector, who wrote under the pseudonym 'Mrs Alexander', was Haggard's secretary from 1892 until his death. See Introduction p. 15.

23. On 29 May 1914, the *Empress of Ireland* collided in fog with the Norwegian collier *Storstad* in the St Lawrence River while *en route* to Liverpool. Fourteen minutes after the collision the *Empress of Ireland* sank with a loss of 1 012 lives, Canada's worst civil maritime disaster, and the world's third worst civil maritime disaster after the *Titanic* and the *Lusitania*.

24. The heroine of *The Ivory Child*, Lady Ragnall, has a birthmark in the shape of a half-moon – 'a curious white mark upon her breast, which in its shape exactly resembled the crescent moon' (p. 35). *The Ivory Child* was published in 1916 without a dedication.

Ella Hart-Bennett's maiden name was probably Tuck. Ella Tuck accompanied Mary D'Anethan (née Haggard) to Japan in 1893, staying until 1896. Haggard's sister Mary had married the Belgian diplomat Baron Albert D'Anethan in 1886. He was appointed Belgian minister to the Imperial Court of Japan. See Mary D'Anethan, *Fourteen Years of Diplomatic Life in Japan*, London, 1912.

Appendix One

Private and Confidential.

LETTER to the Right Hon. LEWIS HARCOURT from Sir RIDER HAGGARD relating to his visit to Rhodesia and Zululand.

DEAR MR. HARCOURT,

WITH reference to your letter to me of the 29th October 1913, I have now to state, in continuation of my communications to you of 27th March and 27th May 1913,[1] *re* New Zealand and Australia, that at the conclusion of the South African sittings of the Dominions Royal Commission I went to Rhodesia. For some days I stayed with Mr. Inskipp, the representative of the Chartered Company, at Buluwayo [sic]. Thence I journeyed to Salisbury, where I was the guest of Sir W. Milton, the Administrator, after which I travelled to Victoria and to visit the great Zimbabwe ruins and inspect that part of the country. Returning to Durban I made a journey of over 400 miles through Zululand in the company of Mr. Gibson, the Commissioner, and of Mr. James Stuart, the former Under-Secretary for Native Affairs in Natal, finally emerging at Dundee. I now propose to set out the private and personal conclusions at which I arrived in the course of my expeditions, after seeing these places, studying their inhabitants for myself, and conversing with a multitude of persons who are intimately connected with them.

RHODESIA

The first and most dominant impression left upon the mind by a visit to Rhodesia is the vastness of the land. Day and night the traveller passes over immeasurable spaces of bush-veld or of plain, most of which is at present put to little use. Millions, and, I suppose, tens of millions, of tons of rich grass stand there wasted, to become presently food for fire or to rot. In every direction the land rolls on for ever. The second is the semi-tropical nature of most of the country even in its higher areas. I visited it during the first half of April, when the summer is supposed to be done, yet at times the heat was almost unbearable. At Buluwayo, nearly 4,500 feet above sea level, or rather three miles away from it, at Mr. Inskipp's house, the thermometer stood in the neighbourhood of 90 degrees throughout the day and did not seem to fall very much at night. To some extent this may have been owing to the severe drought that was then raging (I can use no other term) for the third or fourth year in succession through all this district, but that it is extremely warm, often almost intolerably so in summer, cannot be denied. Some parts of Rhodesia, however, are better in this respect, but on the other hand others are worse.

Taking the country as a whole, there is, even in many of the healthier parts, still a good deal of malarial fever during a portion of the year. In the towns this can be suppressed in the usual way by sanitary precautions, but I do not quite know how it is to be dealt with over vast areas of veld during, and at the end of, the rainy season, when the anopheles mosquitoes are prevalent. Its presence, with all that this entails, must be reckoned a disadvantage to the country, especially in the lower-lying parts. Thus, at Zimbabwe, I was told that the landlord of the inn there had suffered from blackwater fever; two farmers who went out recently to inspect some land in the neighbourhood, with a view to settling thereon, both returned with blackwater and nearly died, while many people think it desirable to take five grains of quinine a day throughout the summer months – a disagreeable and unwholesome necessity. These remarks, of course, apply with added force to districts that are notoriously unhealthy, though it is possible to visit these and to take no harm. Thus, an official gentleman who had been spending some months in one of them recently returned in very good health. I asked him how he had escaped fever. He replied, by going under his mosquito net at sundown and emerging from it at sunrise, and not before. Such precautions, however, involve the passing of nearly half the twenty-four hours within the circumscribed area of a mosquito net.

On the other hand, many vehemently deny that Rhodesia is in any sense a malarious country. Thus Mr. W., an ex-magistrate, and a large farmer in the Victoria district, whose views I shall have occasion to quote, informed me that he and his family, by taking precautions as to standing water in the neighbourhood of his house, &c, had remained in perfect health in this respect, and that he never got fever unless he were travelling in the veld. Again, on much of the high land there is no fever unless it is brought thither from somewhere else. I have dwelt upon the point because malaria is not, as some seem to think, a disease that can be scorned. It is here, as elsewhere, a very terrible complaint which, even if it rarely kills, wrecks many lives, and, therefore, one the risk of which should be well weighed by an emigrant when considering in what country or locality he will establish his future home.

This brings me to the question of whether or no Rhodesia can be held as what is known as a White Man's country. In my opinion undoubtedly yes, so far as great areas of it are concerned, and, so far as other great areas are concerned, undoubtedly no. In fact the position here is much the same as in Australia, where a large section of the land is tropical and, I think, scarcely suited to the white man. I should add that my remarks, in the instance of Rhodesia, apply to the immediate generation, which is not the case with Australia. Only the passage of time, say, a hundred years, can tell us whether or no Rhodesia will make a good home for the descendants of the present settlers. The question is one much debated, and all that can be said is that as yet it is impossible to speak of Rhodesia as a land suitable to the permanent establishment and reproduction of Europeans, as we do, let us say, of the Cape Peninsula or Natal. Meanwhile, its inhabitants complain of the effect of the altitude and the climate generally on the heart and nerves. The towns also suffer from typhoid, largely owing to the lack of a drainage system, but where there is a sufficiency of water this can be remedied.

Pasturally, owing to the introduction of dipping, which, where practised with persistence, has practically eliminated disease among stock, there seems to be a considerable future for the vast grazing lands of Mashonaland and other portions of the country in cattle raising. In my opinion this will probably succeed best when it is conducted by companies with large capital run by competent and experienced managers. The well-known firm of Liebig has recently embarked upon such an enterprise here, with what success it is too early to say. I do not mean that there is no opening for the individual farmer if he starts on suitable land with sufficient funds, and, what is quite as important, with sufficient knowledge. With reference to the first of these requisites I may say at once (and practically the remark applies to all South Africa) that, in my view, Rhodesia is not a place for the ordinary British emigrant, without means, who belongs to those classes that have a good chance of succeeding in other parts of the Empire, such as Canada and Australasia. A few in the towns might find adequate remuneration and employment, especially if they were trained artisans. On the land they would be placed in competition with the native labourer, working for a nominal wage, and, unless they should be men of unusual enterprise and resource, probably would fail. No land is given to the immigrant in Rhodesia, as is the case in Canada, and no more farms can be acquired as pioneer rights. It must be purchased on the instalment plan or outright, and after purchase, stocked. This means that the newcomer needs considerable financial resources. Such immigrants are few, and for them all the Empire is in competition.

I think it may be advantageous and bring the agricultural position home to you more vividly if here I insert an extract from my private diary detailing interviews that I had with two farmers in the Victoria district. Both of these gentlemen impressed me very favourably, and they were, I am confident, expressing the exact truth as it appeared to them. The first, whom I will call Mr. A., is a young Englishman of about 30 years of age, of high intelligence and education, a singularly attractive personality. The second is a man of about 60, I think colonial born, who for many years was a magistrate in the district in which he now farms, and one who has the advantage of a thorough knowledge of the natives and their language. He is supposed to be a successful man who owns about 3,000 cattle. Now I will let them speak for themselves, each from his own point of view.

> At the inn, which consists of some large Kaffir huts, I had a very interesting conversation with Mr. A., who, with a partner, owns an 8,000-acre ranch in this neighbourhood, and from him at first hand obtained the views of a *bonâ fide* Rhodesian settler of the best type.
>
> His account of the situation was not altogether encouraging, though he said (and I believe him) that he tried to look at the bright side of things. First he went to Canada, which he now appears to regret having left. Then he came to Rhodesia and, to gain experience of the country, enlisted in the Mounted Police, rising to the rank of sergeant. Ultimately he and his partner took up this land from the Chartered Company. On the usual terms, namely, that the purchase price is to be paid after a lapse of five, or, if an extension is obtained, of ten, years, interest only on the capital sum being charged during this period of grace. The cost of the land was, I gathered, 6s. 3d. the acre, which, taking everything into consideration, is, I should say, quite enough for it, although this particular stretch is well watered. Also he has to pay 75l. for the survey fee, which, as the work only occupied two days, is presumably also enough. At any rate he thinks so.
>
> The land is suitable for being used for cattle, which, even if no sickness or accidents occur, take a long while to breed up, and probably I am right in concluding that Mr. A. and his partner, after investing in a nucleus stock, are not overburdened with spare capital, which perhaps accounts for his antiquarian labours at the Temple.
>
> Speaking generally, he said that he was doubtful of the future of Rhodesia, of which the suitability to white folk had yet to be proved. It was enervating and very hot for much of the year and did not, as a rule, agree with white women, many of whom went physically wrong in one way or another. Children also suffered in various respects. Moreover, there was still a good deal of malaria and blackwater fever. The presence of the native popu-

lation, he thought, was not an unmixed blessing, as it lessened self-reliance in the whites, and in the case of young men, exposed them to moral dangers. Further, the great expense of living and building, the high railway rates, and the lack of any but local markets which were not doing too well, even where there had been sufficient rainfall, he pointed out, was obvious from the fact that so many of them tried to add to their income by outside means, such as transport riding, driving motor-cars for hire, &c.

Finally he declared that, after a fair trial of it, he could not conscientiously recommend any young Englishman to settle in Rhodesia, and further, that he thought the price to which the Company was running up land was altogether unjustified by the net return which could be wrung out of the soil. Such were his views, very modestly and quietly expressed, but to them he added the hope that things might turn out better than he saw any present reason to expect.

That evening another farmer, Mr. W., dined with us on the train. His position evidently is very different from that of Mr. A. Once he was a native Commissioner here, a fact, he explained, that gives him command of any amount of labour, since, in the eyes of these raw black people, he is a great chief. Moreover, he likes them and they like him. He holds large areas of land and (I am told) owns 3,000 cattle, in which he deals with the natives and others. Also he is attached to Rhodesia, where he has spent much of his life, and personally, he and his family have remained healthy in the climate. Yet on many points he corroborated Mr. A., saying that to get on, most farmers must do something besides farming, which was why he dealt in cattle. He, too, complained bitterly of the speculative values which were being put upon Rhodesian land, especially by the Chartered Company. He stated that one of the directors whom he saw quite lately told him straight out that they were a commercial company and, as they found that a market in farms had arisen, they intended to make the best of it in the interest of their shareholders, which after all is a natural position. He thought, however, that the land would not pay at the prices now demanded. At the same time nothing would induce him to farm in a country like Canada, where a man's 'hands' considered themselves a good or better than their master, and often enough, that master had to chop his own wood and draw his own water; where, too, his wife must generally cook not only the food of her family, but that of the said 'hands' as well. Rhodesia was more comfortable in all these respects, therefore good enough for him, notwithstanding the narrow markets and high railway rates. He confirmed, however, what Mr. A. told me, that a year or two ago mealies had actually been thrown away be the roadside, because it would neither pay to drag then on or to bring them back to the farm. In this respect things would be better now that the railway had reached Victoria. Of the fever he made light, saying he only got a little when he went on trek in the veld. Generally, it resulted from stupidity and neglect of ordinary sanitary precautions and mosquito nets. I gathered that he saw no sign of any great immediate prosperity for agricultural Rhodesia.

A great disadvantage with which the Rhodesian farmer has to contend is the uncertainty of the rainfall. In the Buluwayo district, I can only call the drought which has endured for three or four years in succession devastating and indeed terrible, adding, as one who has a large farming experience, that nothing would induce me to invest or to advise others to invest capital and labour in a part of the country that is liable to such a scourge. I visited a large farm within about 12 miles of Buluwayo which lies below a massive dam built by the late Mr. Rhodes to supply water for irrigation purposes, at a cost, it is said, of nearly 30,000*l*. To a great extent this dam has failed in its object owing to its catchment area not being sufficient to fill it, especially in a dry year. Still, the farm in question, which is provided with excellent expensive buildings in stone, and, I believe, still belongs to the Rhodes Trustees, being worked by the present occupier under some arrangement, derives a certain benefit from the existence of this dam. Were it not so, ruin would stare the occupant in the face. He informed me that from 320 acres of maize which he had drilled, he did not expect this year to gather a single bag, owing to the lack of rain. The rape he had sown to feed his ostriches in the winter had not come up, and his sunflowers were an utter failure. His cattle, however, still looked well, as there appears to be a good deal of nutriment in the dry grass, but how they will get through the winter I do not know.

The case of this man is that of every farmer over a wide district. I received some valuable, if indirect, evidence of the effect of this state of things from a young doctor, a partner in a Buluwayo medical firm, who is, I believe, a connection of my own. He informed me that his firm had just sent out their accumulated bills, amounting to 'some thousands of pounds', but that they were getting in scarcely any cash, owing to the three years of drought. 'Meanwhile,' he added pathetically 'I have to live.' He said, moreover, that their case was that of every business man and storekeeper in Buluwayo. All were giving credit because they must, and few were being paid their debts. In short, something like ruin threatened the community owing to the persistent lack of rain. It must be remembered, however, that a return to normal conditions of humidity would in time remedy this sad state of affairs, though the loss incurred is already great, and may even cause the financial destruction of some of those by whom it must be endured. Further, matters are better in other parts of Rhodesia, though everywhere there seems of late, and especially during the past season, to have been a shortage and irregularity of precipitation which, as some pessimistic persons think, appear to indicate that the country is drying up. It may well prove, however, that the weather in this part of Africa is subject to cycles of drought that assert themselves from time to time.

Another risk which the Rhodesian farmer has to face is that of the prevalence of a multitude of destroying grubs and insects. When I was at Salisbury I visited the Agricultural Experimental Farm Station, where many kinds of crops were being tested. The lucerne there was covered with butterflies, and is much attacked by their caterpillars. The Indian dhal, which does well here and is cut for green fodder, was being devoured by thousands of terrible red beetles. The castor-oil plants were suffering much from a kind of borer, and the leaves of the mangolds, of which the small return of 15 tons the acre seems to be an average crop, were practically all devoured by grubs. Tobacco flourishes in parts of the country, and last year the Rhodesian Tobacco Warehouse, a venture of the Chartered Company which in future is to be run in conjunction with a co-operative society, treated two and a half million pounds that were grown in the neighbourhood. This year the crop will be smaller, owing to the drought. I am informed it is reckoned that South Africa cannot consume more than 3,000,000 pounds of this Rhodesian product, after which Rhodesia must come into competition with the other tobacco-producing countries in the markets of the world. The question appears to be whether the planters will be able to do this cheaply enough to enable them to compete with the American output.

On the whole, I believe that the principal agricultural output of Rhodesia in the future will be meat and mealies. Cattle it should be able to raise in great numbers upon its illimitable pastures, and maize seems less subject to drought and pests than any other crop. It is evident that the market for beef at remunerative prices is eager and growing throughout the world, a fact that should be the opportunity of Rhodesia, where prime beasts can be grown very cheaply. If, however, these are to be exported, the erection of freezing works on Argentine and New Zealand lines is necessary, since, when the distance of the rearing grounds from the coast is taken into consideration, together with the high cost of transport, it seems impossible that animals could profitably be conveyed thither, and either killed at the port or shipped on the hoof. Such works demand large capital expenditure which could only be faced if an adequate and continuous supply of cattle were forthcoming at a price that would assure a sufficient profit, and this during all seasons of the year, which must involve the cost of winter feeding. Also the grade of beast must be much improved, which will take time.

Meanwhile to my mind Rhodesia, considered as a place of settlement for English farmers, is severely handicapped in comparison with sundry other parts of the Empire by its distance from the seaboard, which makes transport and all the necessities of life very expensive, and by the fact that it possesses no ocean port of its own.

While I was at Buluwayo I had a very interesting conversation with Mr. R.A. Fletcher, who is perhaps the most active and prominent opponent of the Chartered Company régime. Mr Fletcher struck me as a perfectly honest, if a rather narrow man, with the face of one who by constitution generally would be a severe critic in opposition to established authority. He told me that he was in favour of buying out the Chartered Company on fair terms and taking over the railways at *cost*, which seems to me scarcely just after the shareholders have borne all the risk of their government as soon as the country is fit to bear that burden. His views have, however, met with heavy defeat at the recent election, which, in fact, was a vote by the population of Rhodesia against joining the Union and, incidentally, in favour of the continuance of Company rule.

At a dinner-party I sat next to Mr. Forbes, the present head of the Legislative Council, with whom I discussed all these matters. From him and others, also from my own observation, I gathered that about one-third of the inhabitants of Rhodesia is anti-Chartered Company. This opposition, however, is split into three factions:

(1) Those who wish that Rhodesia should join the Union, among whom must be numbered more, if not all, of the Dutch settlers;

(2) Those who wish for immediate Responsible Government;

(3) Those who wish that Rhodesia should be declared a Crown Colony.

Most people admit, however, that it is doubtful whether in the last event the Home Government would do more or even as much for its white population as the Company had done and is prepared to do under the draft Land Settlement Ordinance, which, as you, Sir, are aware, will put a tax upon undeveloped lands held for speculative purposes and enable them to be compulsorily acquired and divided for closer settlement. I wish to add that personally I am much impressed with the work which has been accomplished in Southern Rhodesia during the last twenty years by the construction of means of communication such as railways, roads and bridges, town building, and in every other way. Indeed it is difficult for the visitor to the country to remember that within about a quarter of a century it was absolutely undeveloped, and under the dominion of a savage despotism. I think that the progress which has been made in the face of many obstacles reflects the greatest credit on the Chartered Company and its officers.

The chief and most substantial grievance against the Company seems to be that it is charging too high a price for the land it sells. (Into the matter of its claim to be the absolute owner of lands that have not been alienated I do not enter, as that question is *sub judice* before the Privy Council.) This point of the amount asked by the Company for land is, it will be noted, touched on by Mr. W. in the interview that I have quoted already, together with the explanation of it given to him by one of the Board.

It must be remembered that, however it has been engineered and whether it is or is not justified, there is at present something of a 'boom' in Rhodesian land. Many holders who obtained their farms under pioneer rights or, at any rate, very cheaply, have sold, or say that they have sold, them for large sums, though I am told that not so much cash has changed hands as is reported. This appears to me to be one of those speculative movements which are often the curse of young countries. Still, it is not wonderful if the Company, which has never paid a dividend, has taken advantage of it to turn some of its assets into money, although this yielding to a natural temptation may in the issue prove short-sighted and unwise. I was shown estates not far from Salisbury and elsewhere which, I was informed, were changing hands at not less than 2*l.* the acre, a price that seems to me scarcely justified by what can be made out of them under the present conditions of the country, whatever their ultimate value may prove to be in the course of future years. It appears strange that as much should be asked and paid for farms in Southern Rhodesia as is obtainable for fine properties in the supremely healthy, well-watered, and accessible uplands of Natal, and within one-third as much as they are valued at on fertile soil in the Cape within easy reach of a harbour. The matter, however, is one of an economic nature which, in time, will settle itself.

It is scarcely possible as yet to speak of the future of this great Territory in any certain and definite note. The droughts and pests may disappear, the fever and horsesickness may diminish or die out, an adequate population of the right sort with sufficient capital at command may flow in, the cost of transport, living, and building may decrease; or none of these things may happen. It is a problem that the future alone can decide. Also great and permanent mineral discoveries may entirely change the situation, as happened in the Transvaal, though the general opinion seems to be that, up to the present date, as much, or almost as much, gold has gone into Rhodesian mines in the shape of capital supplied by British investors as has been taken out of them in net profits. In the meanwhile, when its difficulties and the competition of the rest of South Africa and of the entire emigrant-seeking portions of the British Empire are borne in mind, the progress of Rhodesia under the capable and energetic guidance of the Chartered Company has certainly been remarkable.

ZULULAND

From Rhodesia I proceeded to Durban, whence I started on my journey through Zululand. This, thanks to the kindness of the Union Government, I had the advantage of making under the most favourable circumstances possible, in the company of Mr. Gibson, the newly appointed Commissioner and the great authority on Zulu history, and of Mr. James Stuart, ex-Assistant Native Secretary in Natal, who is one of the best Zulu linguists and scholars now alive. Unless he is thoroughly acquainted with the language, has ample time at his disposal and adequate means of transport suited to the horrible roads, it is very difficult and even somewhat useless for the visitor to attempt to travel in a country so undeveloped as Zululand with a view of acquiring information as to the local conditions. I should add that I was accompanied also by a Zulu named Mazooku, now an old man. He became my body-servant in 1876 and remained with me until I left South Africa, where once he saved my life. On hearing that I had returned after a lapse of 33 years he appeared and re-entered my employ, thus affording a conspicuous example of Zulu affection and fidelity. On this journey he was very useful because of his knowledge of the customs of his people, being a native of good blood whose father fought in the great battle of the Tugela in 1856, when Mazooku was little. I mention these facts to show that I had exceptional opportunities of arriving at a sound judgment as to the present state of the country and its people.

One of the first things that struck me was the paucity of cattle in Zululand and indeed throughout Natal. The great herds are no more. Rinderpest and the East Coast fever have destroyed them, though I am glad to say that now that dipping has been instituted they are beginning to breed up again. This has resulted in considerable infant mortality, as for some years there has been and still is but little milk for the native children, whose staple food it used to be. Another result is that by law the *lobola* (*i.e.,* the marriage gift) may now be paid in cash instead of in cattle, a practice that has many bad results. The matter is, however, too complicated to treat of fully in this letter, so I will only touch on the chief of them. Money is liable to be spent, whereas the cattle were, in fact, settled upon the wife and her issue. Here is an example. The man Mazooku, my old servant of whom I have spoken, had accepted some form of *lobola*, or rather propitiatory gift, of 10*l.* from a suitor of his daughter. This 10*l.* he spent, being in difficulties through the death of his cattle from the East Coast fever and owing to very cruel treatment he had received from a white man who, out of revenge for the loss of a lawsuit, destroyed his crops by turning animals into them as they were ripening. Subsequently the young woman appears to have changed her mind and refused to marry her suitor, who thereupon brought an action against the father for the return of the 10*l.*, which action, rightly or wrongly, the suitor won under some provision of native law. The end of it was that, had I not intervened, the father was on the point of being committed to gaol because the daughter declined to take a certain man as a husband. In the old days the cattle would have been there, and in such an event could have been returned, whereas the 10*l*. had gone beyond recovery.

While I was staying with Mr. Gibson at Eshowe, before we started on our journey, I went to his office and studied a large modern map of Zululand. So far as I could discover (and Mr. Gibson informed me that my conclusions were approximately correct), since first I knew the Zulus in 1875 about two-thirds of their territory as it was at that time, including many of the best lands, have on one occasion and another, and one pretext and another, by force, by so-called treaty, and by fraud, passed from them into the hands of white men, Boers and English together. In addition, those of them who wish or are forced to live on farms held by white men, developed or undeveloped, are in future, under the Natives Land Act of 1913, liable to be allowed to do so only on condition that they labour for the owner, the payment of rent and the hiring of land, or its purchase being henceforth forbidden to them. Such is the state of the people of Zululand to-day with reference to the country which their fathers occupied.

Since the year 1879 the history of the Zulus has been one long tale of misfortune. First came the war with the British Power which, whatever may have been the case so far as Cetywayo was concerned, was forced upon the ignorant nation by circumstances. Neither the King nor his people had any real heart in this war, which, many now think, was one of an unnecessary character. It resulted in the deaths of 10,000 or more Zulus and in the break up of the nation and of the military system. Then followed Sir Garnet Wolseley's so-called 'settlement', which set up 13 chiefs in the place of a King, rapidly succeeded by the partial restoration of Cetywayo, and much inter-tribal bloodshed. After the death of Cetywayo by poison, the Boers nominated Dinizulu as his successor, who, aided by some of them, attacked and defeated Usibepu, driving him into the part of the country known as the English reserve. For their mischievous services the Boers claimed and obtained possession of a huge stretch of country, the best in Zululand, namely, the Vryheid District and the territory known as Proviso B. In 1884 [1887] the rest of Zululand was annexed by the Crown, and in 1889 Dinizulu was deported to St. Helena. Four years later he was allowed to return like his father Cetywayo, with the result that other difficulties followed; also Zululand and its people were handed over to Natal instead of being allowed to remain under the direct control of the Imperial Government like Basutoland, which, of course, they would have much preferred, as it is a matter of common knowledge that self-governing colonies look at their responsibilities to native races from a very different standpoint to that which has always been adopted by the Home Government. From this time forward more trouble began to brew, till at length what Sir Charles Saunders, who was once the Commissioner for Zululand, described to me as 'constant pin-pricks', such as land-snatching and the institution of the poll tax, resulted in the rebellion of 1906. This movement was suppressed with the terrible severity that is born of fear, happily without the intervention of Imperial troops. The stories which are freely told by those who know what took place at the last affair in the Insimba valley, when, according to the published reports, some 600 (the unofficial estimate, which may be exaggerated, is about 3,000) Zulus were killed and only one Natal volunteer was wounded in the arm, are too painful to repeat. From that time to the present there has been no armed resistance to the authority of the white man.

But the people are crushed and bewildered. Monarchical by instinct and practice, they have no one visible Chief to whom to give their adherence. When his present Majesty visited Natal as Prince of Wales they went to Maritzburg to declare their earnest loyalty, but in the end, to their wonder and grief, found themselves handed over first to Natal and afterwards to the Union. In the old days there was Sir T. Shepstone (Sompseu) to whom they could turn as an enduring personality who was interested in them, and a Governor who represented the Queen in Natal. Now the first is dead and there is no Imperial Governor in Natal, only an Administrator, and a Minister at the Cape who changes from time to time and whom they do not see. As they say they 'have no head'. Commissions appear and disappear, Ministers come and go, there is no one permanent entity on whom they can fix their eyes as the shadow of their distant King, to whom at heart they are intensely loyal. They were defeated in war, and like a nation of warriors accepted the issue with resignation and without bearing a particle of malice, hoping and believing that they would be taken over and nursed by their victor, the Queen, and her successors and ruled as subjects like the Basutos. Instead of this they were made the bloody sport of a number of rival kinglets, while the Boers and others were allowed to rob them of their hereditary lands. It is not wonderful that, as the say, they 'wander and wander'.

It was very sad at the *indabas* or official talks with the Commissioner, Mr. Gibson, at four of which I was present, to listen to the remarks of some of these chiefs, made in the course of discussing their troubles, of a few of which I made notes. 'We are rejoiced to see you Father,' said one, 'but we can assure you that our grievances are countless.' 'If you can exercise any power as to these lands which have been given away to the white men you would indeed be ruling us for our good,' said another. 'We are left orphaned and owe our existence to the fact that England is,' said a third pathetically. 'It is good that we should find friends among the people to whom we have given our loyalty, for we need them,' declared a fourth, alluding to myself. 'We black people must eat the dust,' exclaimed a fifth. And so on.

It may be said that it is useless to dwell upon the past; that, right or wrong, what is done is done, and, if wrong, since they cannot protect themselves, the Zulus must be content to bear their burden like other shattered and conquered peoples. I think, however, that, in studying the present and speculating as to the future, it is necessary to bear in mind those things which have happened, since, without a knowledge of them, there is much which it is difficult to understand. Thus, those who are unacquainted with the ancient customs of the Zulus, such as their devotion to the profession of arms, their superstitious fear of the witch doctor and the wizard, their courage in the face of death, their splendid loyalty to those whom they hold it to be their bounden duty to serve, their primitive honesty, and so forth, must find it difficult to appreciate the profound change which is coming over the people both here and in Natal. If, as yet, as in a glass and darkly, they have begun to see that the old order is passing away and the new order is at hand, and some among them, especially if they be young, are bracing themselves to meet the altered circumstances. They have studied their masters, the white men, and have come to the conclusion that there exists no unbridgeable gulf between the nature of these and their own. They know that in many essentials they, or, at any rate, the best of them, are quite the equal of the average white, even in intellect. The difference is, they perceive, chiefly one of colour and of the knowledge that comes from education.

That the first of these is no absolute bar between the races the white man is engaged in teaching them by a very practical object lesson. In the old days the Zulu girl who, without special permission from the king or chief, went to live with a white man, would have been severely punished or perhaps have lost her life. Then too, although all the customs resulting from the strict exigencies of their military system were far from admirable, at least there were very few loose women among the Zulus. Now the fear of punishment and public shame has been taken away and many of the girls, actuated by motives that are common to their sex throughout the world, become the temporary wives or mistresses of whites who, in the end, for the most part desert them and their offspring as fancy or circumstances may dictate. 'What are these white things that we see coming to the kraals upon our daughters' backs?' asked an old Zulu pointedly the other day, alluding to the issue of such unions. As yet the habit has not the same hold as in some other parts of South Africa, at the Cape, for instance, where so many of those whom one meets in the streets are half or quarter breeds, because the Zulu break-up is more recent. Still, I have been told on good authority of a case of a white man in Zululand who has no less than 80 half-breed children. That it is a prevalent and growing habit also I have been assured by such observers as the Bishop of Zululand, the Fathers of Mariannhill, near Durban, who take in half-breed children, and many others, and the aspect of it that I wish to emphasise is that it tends, and must tend increasingly, to equality between the races. The legend of the Sons of God and the Daughters of Men may well be applied to the case of the white man and the Bantus. It shows the latter that the gulf between these two sections of humanity is after all not unbridgeable. Moreover, it provokes reprisals. When I was a young man in South Africa I never heard of such a thing as the 'Black Peril'. Then a white woman could have walked alone through the land without fear of hurt, as she might still do in the more unsophisticated parts of Zululand. Now, as the newspaper reports prove, it is far otherwise. What the end of it all will be none can say, but not a few thinking men in South Africa believe that, taken in conjunction with the lack of European population, it will result ultimately in the absorption, or something like it, of the whites by the blacks. For instance, Mr. Merriman informed me he anticipated 'that much of South Africa would in the end become practically native', and Mr. Maydon, the ex-Minister of Railways in Natal, a very able man, was emphatically of the same opinion. Indeed, I heard this view very widely echoed.

I pass to the second problem that is exercising the Zulu mind, that of education. The native has learned that outside of the colour bar, which, as I have pointed out, has been proved passable in the most practical of all ways, he is in many particulars as good a man as the average white. He has as much or more physical courage; he can, if he chooses, work as hard; his health, at any rate under natural conditions, is not inferior; and, lastly, he outnumbers the Europeans by, say, five to one. What he, or his thinkers, know to be lacking are powers of combination, together with practice in the art of government and knowledge of how to make use of the resources of civilisation, among which he would probably set down improved weapons of war as the most apparent. He has become aware by observation in Johannesburg and other cities, that all these and other things are the prerogative of the educated; that, given education, ultimately they may come within his reach, as to some extent they have come within the reach of the Basutos, a branch of his great family.

Consequently the Zulu yearns for education with an almost universal longing, at any rate among the young in the more awakened parts of the country. As Sir Charles Saunders said to me, 'the Zulus have a great thirst for education.' Even the raw 'house-boys' will pay 1s. a month out of their small wages to be 'taught at an evening school', adding 'they cannot be kept back.' It is impossible 'that they should be perpetually suppressed; something *must* be done.' Indeed, I heard the same story in every direction, and from my own observation know that it is true. Their kings have gone and they desire to replace them by a lord called Knowledge; their hereditary customs are going, but this Chief Knowledge will, they think, give them others that are better and more to their advantage, which may enable them to compete with their white masters. Of course this is not the view of the elder men, who served under Cetywayo and perhaps under Panda. Indeed, one of these amused me much by a remark he made at an *indaba* I attended, which I quote as representative of the opinions of his generation. 'Our children try to be white,' he said, alluding to the young Zulus, and to their aping the manners and garments of the English, 'but white they will never be. Black they were born, and black they must remain until they die.' But such conservatives are dying out, and with them will perish their views. The future is to their descendants, who think differently.

It must be remembered also that these hopes and aspirations are not those of a dying people. Since I left Natal in 1881 the Zulu population there has, I believe, doubled. In Zululand proper it is, I am told, now estimated at about 300,000, or more, I suppose, than existed before the war of 1879. Since then thousands, it is true, have been killed, but among these but few were women, and in a polygamous country, where it is customary also for a brother to take over the wives of the deceased in the Biblical fashion, the death of males has little ultimate effect on population. Chaka realised this when he gave instructions to his *impis* not to trouble about hunting down the soldiers of his enemies, but to exterminate every woman. It is true that certain new factors have arisen which may tend to lessen population, such as the spread of lung diseases introduced from the mines and of syphilis as a concomitant of loose living. Also the advocacy of monogamy by the missionaries and its partial adoption owing to economic pressure may have some effect, but for many years to come this will be slight. Indeed all these deterrents to human life taken together can never counterbalance the increase of life resulting from the cessation of the indiscriminate butchery of past generations.

The position is, therefore, that the whites in South Africa are face to face with an increasing native population, among whom the Zulus are perhaps the most powerful section, which refuses to remain in darkness, which insists upon winning through to light. At present that light is denied to them. The Rev. Mr. Dube alleges in the remarks which I have already forwarded to you that, out of the 200,000*l*. per annum which is raised by direct taxation from the natives in Natal, only 15,000*l*. is spent upon their education. It is probable that in Zululand the sum is proportionately even smaller. There the missionaries, who, I believe, are paid a small *per capita* subsidy, are the only teachers, if we except what is being done by the natives themselves in night classes, or in schools like that of Mr. Dube, which, however, is on the Natal side of the Tugela. There is no general system of education and none appears to be contemplated.

It may be urged that, according to my own showing, to educate the native would be to create a new danger, on the principle that know-

ledge is power. But in my view, by this path or by that, he will ultimately attain to that education, if not by the assistance of the whites,
then through the dangerous aid of the Ethiopian Church, or with the
help of black teachers who have contrived to acquire some imperfect
learning, and who will be naturally more or less hostile to European
dominance. Surely it is better that the Bantu should receive his instruction from the ruling European race with whom he is fated to live, than
through these unfriendly elements. Surely, too, this is a duty which
that race owes to him. I am aware that there are many in South Africa,
especially if they be of Dutch descent, who would deny the truth of this
proposition. Even if he does not say so openly, the average farmer, or at
any rate a majority of his class, living perhaps on land originally acquired from natives by means that will not bear examination, thinks
that such people exist to provide him with cheap labour and to pay hut
tax. Indeed, whether by accident or design, the severe provisions of the
Natives Land Act of 1913 must have the former effect if they are ever
generally enforced, since under them henceforth the native who
wishes, or from lack of land is forced, to live on a farm must labour for
the owner, apparently at any wage that owner thinks it well to pay.
Probably, I repeat, the white agricultural classes of the Transvaal, the
Orange River Colony [sic], and even of Natal, would stare amazed if it
were suggested to them that it was their duty to place education within
the reach of every native who desires to learn, even though the native
were willing to pay for it himself. Yet, I suggest that it is not only their
duty; it is also their interest, since, I say again, by hook or by crook, the
black man will get the education, and it is desirable from the white
man's point of view that it should not be of a nature to aggravate national grievances or to breed up national hate.

The general ignorance that prevails in South Africa concerning natives and their affairs struck me as very strange. For instance, even in
Natal there are but few who have any sound knowledge of Zulu history, character, and aspirations. The question is one that excites no
interest, or, at any rate, but little compared to its importance, as is
shown by the small amount of space devoted to it in the local press
unless, indeed, there is some black man's crime to be reported. Again,
in the cartoons and comic papers, whenever there is occasion to represent a native, it is the fashion to picture him as a hideous and idiotic
yahoo, whereas, for the most part, he is nothing of the sort. And yet this
is the most vital problem which confronts the Union at the present
time. Those who are unacquainted with the true conditions of South
Africa imagine that the relations between English and Dutch are all
that matters. In fact, however, as I was assured on every hand, and
rejoice to be able to record herein my belief, these relations are im-
proving day by day. The old racial animosity which culminated in the
Boer war seems to be dying out, although it lingers here and there in

the remoter districts, and there is good reason to hope that if nothing occurs to revive it, in a generation it will be dead. The Englishman has accepted the situation and the Boer has won self-government and everything he can want, plus the support of the fleets of Britain in any national emergency that may arise. Moreover, the socialistic movement on the Rand, and the joint measures taken to combat it by the English and Dutch burghers, have done much to bring them together, as its supposed sympathy with the strikers has done much to weaken the extreme 'National' party. Thus, at Pretoria, I was asked to inspect a body of Boy Scouts, in which I found British and Boer lads serving together in complete amity. It is, I think, felt that the settlement is final and on the whole to the mutual advantage. Indeed, those who attempted to revive the old differences in face of the real South African peril, that has its roots in the existence and attitude of the vast native population, would be as mad as angry children pelting each other with live embers over an open cask of gunpowder.

Upon this point of the overwhelming importance of the Kaffir problem, I found – to take one instance only out of many – that the views of Mr. Maurice Evans, C.M.G., the author of *Black and White in South Africa*, who is an acknowledged authority upon all native questions and especially on those connected with the Zulu race, coincided with my own. He spoke very sadly to me of the almost complete ignorance of the electorate on matters that have to do with the black population, of the remarkable lack of attention given to them by the Union legislators, and of the danger that must result from such a state of affairs. He advocated the appointment of a non-party council of experts with advisory powers to which all proposed legislation affecting natives should be first submitted before it came up for consideration by Parliament. When I suggested that the advice of such a body might not be heeded, he agreed, but said that he could think of nothing better. He declared himself in favour of the expropriation of white men and especially of absentee owners, in order to provide more land for native use wherever it was needed; but when I pointed out that such an Act would come into direct conflict with popular prejudice and the established interests of white landholders and have little chance of being passed, again he agreed. He seemed to think that although its motives might be sound the Land Act of 1913 is preposterous and unworkable in its present form, and that before introducing it the Government should have awaited the Report of the Commission which is now sitting. As an example of its hasty and unpractical character he quoted the case of one of the Natal coastal divisions, I think that of the Lower Tugela, where there are some 30,000 natives who have no location at all but live upon farms largely owned by absentees. What, he asked, was to become of such people, and how could they in future give labour as a condition of residence to landowners who require no labour? He said that in his opinion the white men would never admit the natives to the franchise. They had the power and they meant to keep it quite independently of any considerations of abstract justice, adding that, 'the ultimate argument is the gun'. Further, Mr. Evans holds a high opinion of the intelligence and industrial capacity of the natives, and foresees a fierce future competition in the field of labour between them and the white men of which no one can guess the end.

I have quoted the opinions of this authority because they are similar to those that I have formed during my journeyings in South Africa. Briefly the position may be summed up thus: A million and a quarter whites are occupying a vast territory, holding in subjection enormous hordes of natives. It does not seem probable that the number of the whites will increase greatly for a long while to come, if they ever do so. The English among them do not multiply fast, owing to causes that are in operation all over the civilised world. Even among the fertile land-dwelling Dutch this same leaven is beginning to work. Thus Mrs. Botha, the wife of the Prime Minister, informed me that the Boers, or at any rate the more advanced among them, no longer have the large families that were common in her youth. Emigration cannot be reckoned on in practice to increase the population, for, even if they were welcome there, South Africa is not a country to which working people will migrate from the United Kingdom in order to put themselves in competition with an endless supply of cheap black labour. Therefore the Union can only rely on its present store of white inhabitants, or, at any rate, upon these plus a very slow natural increase. With that population it must work out its destiny. Lastly, the white man in the mass is probably deteriorating somewhat owing to the effects of a warm climate on a northern race, and to his ceasing from the hardening exercise of manual toil which he looks upon as the duty and office of the black. The coloured man, on the other hand, in the mass is probably rising somewhat as the principles of civilisation begin to soak into his primitive nature. At any rate he is learning the arts of his masters. If as yet he is not competent fully to fill that master's place in the more skilled and responsible positions of industry, there are many situations now held by white men which he *is* competent to fill. Of late years he has learned a great deal. Johannesburg may or may not be 'a university of vice', as a great authority has declared; it is also a university of knowledge to the black.

I was much struck with a remark that Mr. Merriman, perhaps one of the shrewdest minds in South Africa, made to me to the effect that after inspecting the Premier Mine he came to the conclusion that the work of the 800 whites employed there could equally well be done by eight, the places of the others being taken by the skilled natives, who receive only a tithe of the white man's wage. Sooner or later the employers of labour will find this out (indeed they are already beginning to do so), and then will come that terrible industrial struggle of which Mr. Evans speaks. The white man will not easily submit to replacement by the instructed Kaffir, but it is probable that in the end the economic argument will win, with the result that the European population will be lessened, especially in the mining centres. Also, there are the half-breeds to be reckoned with. These, with the Malays (a dwindling stock), are, I think, included in the returns as 'other coloured races', and, it appears, increased by about 115,000 between the census years 1904 and 1911, while the proportion of Europeans to the total population of the Union (exclusive, I believe, of the Protectorates, which should, however, be reckoned for practical purposes, such as labour competition) decreased slightly, namely, from 21.58 per cent. to 21.37 per cent. These half-breeds, it may be presumed, inherit some of the characteristics of their fathers, and therefore perhaps will prove more formidable competitors to the European than the pure native. This, indeed, seems to be proved by the force and energy of some of those South African whites whose blood is admitted not to be entirely unmixed, and by the general utility and resourcefulness of the 'Cape boys'.

The white man in South Africa is threatened, then, by a rising flood of coloured people with whom he is intermingling more and more by marriage, permanent or temporary, who, too, in spite of repression or neglect, by degrees are acquiring education and knowledge of his arts. Yet, taken as a whole, he pays as little heed to the danger as it is recorded that the inhabitants of the ancient world did to the rising of another flood, of which those who prophesied its advent to them were looked upon as mad. In the same way such farseeing persons in South Africa who point to the signs and tokens of coming trouble, or who show sympathy and understanding with native wrongs, needs, and aspirations, are often contemptuously defined as 'cranks', and no one makes attempts to build an ark of refuge. As Mr. Dube pointed out in the interview which, Sir, I have already forwarded to you, feeling is hardening between these two great sections of the inhabitants of South Africa; sympathy is dying down, suspicion not unmixed with fear on the one hand, and resentment sharpened by many bitter memories and a sense of injustice on the other, are on the increase.

The issue of it all cannot be even guessed. When he realises his danger the white man, availing himself of his superior weapons, may kill out the black, if the pressure of civilised opinion will allow him to do so, for, as Mr. Evans said, the gun is the ultimate argument between a superior and an inferior race. Or over large stretches of South Africa he may become amalgamated with the black and thus practically disappear as the invaders of the Chinese Empire are said always to disappear; as after the withdrawal of their legions the Roman-bred population disappeared among the Britons, as the builders of the Zimbabwes disappeared; as, higher up the coasts, the Portuguese strain is by constant intermixture disappearing in that of the Bantus and other blacks. It is possible and, as I have said, some students of the problem think it probable; after all there is, I believe, no record of a white race having established itself permanently in Africa, although on sundry occasions it has attempted so to do as in the case of those ancients who occupied Rhodesia. Or the blacks may combine, organise, obtain arms, and conquer the whites by force of numbers and courage. This might well happen if Mahommedanism or some kindred faith should take root among such a nation as the Zulus. Or, through continuous miscegenation, in their turn the blacks may corrupt the whites as in many ways the whites have corrupted the blacks, and make them effeminate and ineffective like the Portuguese. Or in this way or in that the natives may attain to the franchise and political power and thus once more become masters in their own land. It is quite conceivable that some sorely beset political party in the Union might in the future, under conditions that cannot be foreseen, give them the vote to gain an immediate end, of which vote afterwards they could not be deprived again. Or lastly – and this is devoutly to be hoped – the white man, before it is too late, may change his policy and by wisdom and gentleness avert or at the least minimise all these evils. That opportunity is still with him; time has not yet stolen it away. There remains to him the course of educating and guiding the native into the paths of knowledge and of peace. To do this effectively, however, he must first draw the stings of rancour planted by injustice in the black man's soul. He must give him also a fair proportion of the land to be his inheritance.

Nothing is more astonishing to the observer than the insatiable land hunger of the South African white man, especially if it be considered in conjunction with the inconsiderable return that he wrings out of that land. He holds acres by the ten million, and yet to-day South Africa is still a large importer of food stuffs and, save now and again for a few mealies, practically exports none, and still his hand is stretched out for more. A gentleman recently had a conversation with a farmer of the average type as to the possibility of a war with the Basutos. The farmer said that it would be a very good thing, and when asked why, answered, 'Because then we should get their land.' That has been for generations, and still is, the attitude of many in South Africa.[2] Largely, no doubt, it is inherited from the old Dutch ideals (and practice) which laid it down that no man should be able to see the smoke of his neighbour's chimney: or a secret, unexpressed object may be to starve out the black by depriving him of sufficient soil on which to grow his food and feed his cattle, and thus to force him to labour for the white at a miserable wage. Also the mere pride of possession may have to do with it, to say nothing of the hope of successful speculation in farms upon a rising market. At least such is the position, with the result that, putting aside the comparatively small areas left to the natives, there are now hundreds of white men with no land at all. They are called 'poor whites', and of them it may be said that, like the man in the Bible, having lost the habit of labour, which they look on as 'Kaffir's work', they cannot dig, though to beg they are not always ashamed. For the most part, however, they loaf and grumble, doing odd jobs now and again. A Commission, before which I gave evidence, is sitting in the Transvaal to consider what can be done with them, of which the report should be very interesting. If there were more close settlement in South Africa, ten or a hundred times their number might be accommodated and earn their living, especially in irrigated areas. But it is the country of large estates, of which often little or no use is made, so notwithstanding its huge size, both unfortunate whites and natives must go short.

But the black man, if he is to be appeased and brought into line with the white, must receive more than land. He must be given sympathy, and with it, absolutely even-handed justice in every case and particular. He must be given representation of one sort or another. A fair proportion of the money that is raised from him by direct taxation must be spent upon his education and the bettering of his lot. He must be taught to feel that he is no longer looked upon as a dog or a mere 'black creature', but as a man who has within him the capacity to rise and play a worthy part in the world. He must be infused with the ideals of the higher class of whites, and shown that his true welfare lies in working with them for the general welfare and not against them. He must be paid a wage commensurate with the quantity and quality of his labour, not a fixed pittance flung to him under a sort of sumptuary law which says this much, and no more, shalt thou earn, and this work, but no other, shalt thou do. He must be no longer driven to despairing and hopeless rebellion by the process which Sir Charles Saunders described as 'constant pin-pricks'.

All these things and others could be brought about if the best men in South Africa were allowed their way, but the Union is ruled by a democracy which at present takes different views of the Kaffir and his rights – or wrongs. It is, I am sure, the greatest mistake in the world to suppose that the native does not feel or forgets harsh treatment. On the contrary, I believe that at the bottom of that secret mind of his, which so few of alien race have the imagination and the sympathy to understand at all, he feels a great deal. Also, his memory is very long. To know this it is only necessary, as I have, to listen to some old Zulu describing events which took place in the day of Chaka or Dingaan, when his nation was great and ruled the land. He quotes the very words that were said, he acts the very deeds that were done. No syllable, no gesture, is overlooked. It is all there written upon the book of his mind, and so much else is there also, of which he does not speak to the white man – as yet. But a day may dawn when he, or his son, or his grandson, will do so and then it will be found that no single blow, or curse, or humiliation, or act of robbery and injustice, has been overlooked. Deaths in war he will take no count of, for he springs from a race of soldiers, and is prepared to accept what he gives without complaint or malice. Death is, so to speak, the coin of his trade, as victory and defeat are its stakes, but with the rest it is otherwise. For these, in some shape, probably one that is quite unforeseen, an hour of reckoning will surely strike. It is not possible in this, or any other human affair, continually and with intent to sow the wind and always to escape the reaping of the whirlwind that comes after.

I have been obliged to touch upon these points because the Zulu problem is part of a larger general problem and cannot well be considered separately. So far as this race is concerned, however, I think that even now, at the eleventh hour, much might be done to make it, if not contented – for humbled and defeated peoples do not readily reach that state – at least resigned to an altered lot. The reign of chiefs is finished; the pageant, the spoils and the pomp of battle have gone with it to the limbo of the past. These survive only in the stories that for generations will be told round the fire at night, as in the north the Sagas have survived. A new condition has appeared; civilization with its splendours (and its terrors) stares the savage in the face. The white man owns the land that Chaka conquered, white hands have raped the holy graves of kings,[3] and where these issued the word of life or death and decreed peace or war a magistrate fines the small offender ten shillings and the costs. The son of him who slew our soldiers by the fatal mound of Isandhlwana or rushed through a storm of bullets till he fell pierced upon Ulundi's plain. Often the man himself, walks along the Zulu hills and valleys with greasy trousers for his kilted uniform and holding a tattered parasol in the hand that once grasped the shield or stabbing spear.

What can be given to these people to replace all that they have lost, whereof only the glory remains imprinted on the mind, for the horrors; the 'smelling out' of the witch-doctor, the swift and wholesale slaughter by those who executed the command of the King, are quite forgotten. I think that as a beginning they might be granted a Council of their own, such as exists in Basutoland, whereon all the sections of the population are represented. Of this Council, the local Commissioner might be the head, representing the King and the Government, and on it the district magistrates might have seats. To it should be submitted all questions that have to do with the welfare of the Zulus, for discussion if not for final settlement, and it might be given power to devote a certain proportion of the moneys raised from them by direct taxation to objects that would benefit them, such as education, roads, the establishment of dipping tanks, the forwarding of agriculture, and so forth. At present the chiefs and people are not in touch with each other; they have no collective voice and no means of presenting their case to the Authorities except through a casual meeting with the local magistrate, who probably lacks time to attend to their individual grievances, even if his representations meet with consideration from the heads of the Native Department at Maritzburg or in Pretoria. This would be a good beginning and other help or reforms could and probably would follow. I think too that all further alienation of their hereditary tribal territories on any pretext whatsoever should absolutely cease, and where it is necessary the land should be expropriated and reconveyed to them.

In the Hlabisi [sic] district, which I visited, I found that over 600,000 acres are now what are called Crown lands, that is occupied or to be occupied by white men, while about half that area, viz., 334,000 acres, are native reserve. The white inhabitants of the district all told, I am informed, number about 100, while the natives number about 16,000. Surely these figures are disproportionate to the relative needs of the two races. Every authority with whom I have discussed the matter is of opinion that some such Council as I have outlined should be granted to the Zulus, notably Sir Charles Saunders and Mr. Maurice Evans. I gathered also that His Excellency Viscount Gladstone, who has visited Zululand, holds a somewhat similar view.

One of the bright spots in a gloomy outlook is that leading men in the Union, or some of them, are beginning to realise the dangers of the situation and to take more interest in native affairs, among them the Prime Minister, General Botha, if report may be believed and I understood what he said to me aright. But unfortunately the wise and open-minded men are not the electorate of South Africa, of whose callousness and lack of information on such matters I have already written. Another bright spot is the recent appointment to the post of Resident Commissioner in Zululand of Mr. Gibson, the author of a lately published and excellent history of the Zulus, a gentleman who thoroughly understands this people, among whom he had spent most of his life, and who is in deep sympathy with their troubles and aspirations.

It may be argued, of course, that the Imperial power has handed over the Zulus to Natal, and through Natal to the Union of South Africa, and therefore that it is useless to waste time and trouble in discussing their difficulties and destiny. I do not consider that this argument is statesmanlike or sound. They cling to the Crown in a way that is very touching, still looking upon the King as their direct lord and master, which gives them some claim to have their true condition known and weighed at home. Moreover, it is well within the bounds of possibility that a state of affairs might arise among the tribes of Zulu blood which would force the Imperial Government to give earnest attention to their affairs. At the present moment the Reverend J. Dube, himself an educated Zulu with considerable power among his people and the President of the South African Native National Congress, is, I believe, on his way to England with a deputation to lay a hopeless petition before the

King for the disallowal of the Natives Land Act of 1913. This fact alone shows that the Zulus, rightly or wrongly, still look upon the Home Government as a final Court of Appeal. Further, they deserve every consideration, since their misfortunes have been many, and for their wrong-doings they have paid in tears and blood full measure and running over. To their great grief and disadvantage they have been taken from the care of the Imperial Power and given over into the hand of colonial Legislatures. In spite of promises and delimitation Commissions, their land has wasted and wasted beneath the seizures and demands of white people, and there are signs that even now this process is not ended. Upon this point I think it best to quote some paragraphs from the final report of the Zululand Lands Delimitation Commission presented in 1904, as these sum up the matter with authority, and set out very clearly the relative attitudes of the white and black people whose interests are concerned. Moreover, the statements made therein by the Imperial and Colonial Commissioners have as much or even greater force to-day as they had in 1904, since I am told that the awards made by the Commission have not always been respected.

A conspicuous feature in connection with our work of delimitation has been the apparent misunderstanding displayed by almost every European in the country interested in acquiring land, as to the conditions under which Zululand was annexed to Natal, and the object with which this Commission was appointed. The reason for such misunderstanding is somewhat difficult to understand, as the conditions of annexation were published, and anyone wishing to do so had ample opportunity of becoming acquainted with them; nevertheless, very few seem to have done so, and we have been met on all sides by residents and others, who appear to be labouring under the impression that all the Commission was required to do was to indiscriminately throw open the whole of the lands suitable for European occupation, irrespective of the interests of the natives occupying those lands, who, in fact, had hardly been considered as a factor in the settlement.

It is also noticeable that in all the published criticisms on the settlement not a voice appears to have been raised in the natives' interests.

The Commission have experienced no difficulty with the natives, but, on the contrary, have been treated with the utmost respect throughout, and cannot speak too highly of the assistance is has invariably received from the Chiefs and their people. In every instance they have expressed their readiness to abide loyally by the decisions of their ruling power, which they admit to be the British Government, by virtue of its conquest during the

Zulu war. They have, however, over and over again expressed a fervent hope that this will be a final settlement, and urged that ever since the Zulu war they have lived in a perpetual state of not knowing what changes the following day will bring forth. They point to the Zulu war settlement, when they were distinctly promised that Zululand was to be left to its own people: to the acquisition by the Boers of a large extent of the country: to the annexation by the British Government of what remained, when they were again promised that it was being annexed for their use: and, finally, to the annexation of the Province to Natal, under which they are again to be deprived of tribal lands. They freely recognise that the country belongs to the Crown, and that it is for that power to do as it sees fit, but urge that His Majesty has no more loyal subjects than themselves, and that they are therefore unable to understand why these constant changes are made, which have the effect, each time, of curtailing their tribal lands.

Such is the situation in Zululand, which I have set out as briefly and as clearly as I am able to do. I should add that, in my judgment, the Zulus are on the whole likely to benefit by the establishment of the Union, inasmuch as their cause has now been removed to a larger and probably a more impartial tribunal. It will no longer be judged solely by a Province whereof the electors have direct interests that often are opposed to the interests of the indigenous inhabitants, but more as a matter in which general native policy is concerned. This at least is something gained.

Here, too, I would allude to the enlighted and progressive treatment accorded to natives by the Corporation of Durban, which is in striking contrast to that advocated and too often applied to them by the white inhabitants of the rural districts and of some other towns. In that city I was conducted by Mr. Donovan, the able Superintendent of Police, round the native eating-houses, which were established by the municipality eight years ago to give the black people an opportunity of trading in food on their own account. Since the passing of the Native Beer Act, under the provisions of which beer is brewed by the municipality, this drink is also sold at the eating-houses. Formerly it used to be brought into the town in pots by the Kaffir women, with the result that these girls were exposed to sundry dangers, to which often they succumbed. These native eating-houses, that are kept under strict police control, are very largely patronised. The profits resulting from the sale of the municipal *tshwala* or native beer, amounting to many thousands of pounds a year, are kept in a special account by the Authorities, and must be expended for the benefit of natives frequenting the borough; for instance, in the provision of Kaffir lodging-houses and of hospitals.

I inspected one of these lodging-houses, a non-sectarian Corporation establishment known as the Native Women's Hostel. Here accommodation is afforded to three classes of women: – (1) School teachers, who are mostly half-breeds, to whom a separate building is allotted. Such girls have nowhere to go. They are outside of their own people, and are not received by Europeans. As a consequence, Mr. Donovan informed me, they are frequently driven to prostitution for company and a livelihood. (2) Mission native women, who pay 3*d.* a day for accommodation and a bed. (3) Kraal women, who come into town to visit their relatives. These pay 1*d.* a night only, and sleep upon board beds or sometimes on the floor. This place is always full, and the cost of its upkeep is defrayed out of the profits realised on the sale of the Kaffir beer. It is an admirable institution, and one that saves many native girls from ruin, which often overtakes them when they stay at common lodging-houses in Durban. Mr. Donovan stated that there is no Institution of the sort in Johannesburg or in any other town in the Union.

I saw also the site of the new native quarters or location for single Kaffirs, the contract price for the first block of which, to hold 800 men, is 15,000*l.* When completed it will accommodate about 2,000 men, preference being given to needy applicants. It is to be followed by another building for the use of married people, the necessary capital being provided out of the Beer Profits Fund. Further, amongst other places, I visited one of the Togt Barrack establishments, where over 2,000 native day labourers are housed at a price of 5*s.* a month, which sum includes sleeping accommodation, washing and cooking facilities, water, baths, and electric light. I can only express my sincere admiration of all these institutions, on which I think the Corporation of Durban is to be greatly congratulated, though some purists might object to their being provided out of profits derived from the sale of beer.

On another day I visited the great Trappist (it is really Benedictine) Monastery at Mariannhill, near Pinetown, in Natal, where these good monks, who are, for the most part, Germans, do a great work among the Kaffirs. Indeed, speaking generally, I think that the South African natives owe more to the much decried missionaries than to anyone else. Were it not that their interpretation of the laws of the Faith forces them to insist upon monogamy among converts I think that in the end they would gather all the black population of South Africa into the Christian fold, so great is the appreciation of their noble and unselfish efforts, and, I may add, the desire for religious enlightenment, amongst those in whose midst they labour. As it is they have a terrible rival to fear in Mahomedanism, should that creed ever send its emissaries among the Bantus. Of the grave political and social dangers that would then ensue I have already spoken.

Perhaps I may conclude this letter by stating my personal opinion of the Zulus, formed after a somewhat exhaustive examination of that people, of their customs, modes of thought, and mental attitude, conducted under the most favourable circumstances during a long and arduous journey through what is left to them of their land. It can be summed up in few words. So far as the upper classes of them are concerned, they are by nature a nation of gentlemen. No one of discernment can listen to them conducting debate (much more decently and in order than is often the case in civilised public assemblies) and weigh the sentiments they express in their own melodious language and poetic phraseology, without coming to this conclusion. Also their grave courtesy is very striking and their manners are almost perfect. Of this I cannot refrain from giving a single example, which I trust, Sir, it will not weary you to read.

At one of Mr. Gibson's *indabas* I was called upon to make a short speech, necessarily somewhat formal and diplomatic in character, in acknowledgment of the very warm welcome which I received. In the course of my remarks I said that I, who was 'Sompseu's child' (*i.e.* had been intimately connected with Sir T. Shepstone, whose name is still a household word among the Zulus), knew that they had gone through many troubles, of which this was not the hour to speak. I trusted, however, that the storm clouds of the night had broken, that the dawn was at hand, and that in the time unborn the good sun of peace, of happiness and of plenty would shine upon them from day to day and from generation to generation. When the salutes given in the ancient form and words had ceased, a headman in the audience answered that I 'Lundanda u Ndandokalweni' (my native name, given to me nearly 40 years ago, of which the metaphor may be rendered, 'The tall One who travels on the Heights') did well to allude to their sorrows, as they were countless as the leaves and endless as the sky. Then he proceeded to set these out with vehemence and in some detail.

Among those present at this *indaba* was a fine-looking man dressed in military costume, the Chief Manzowandhle (*i.e.* Water of the Sea), Cetywayo's son, and, as many think, the true heir of the Great House of Senzangakona, so called because he was born after his father had crossed the sea to England. Sitting in front of all the other chiefs by virtue of his rank and royal blood, Manzowandhle listened for a while to this man's grumblings. Then suddenly he broke out. 'Who are you,' he asked, addressing the speaker, 'that you vomit all this froth? What kind of breeding have you that you sing so loud a song about the words of the *Inkoosi* Lundanda who has journeyed far to visit us? Surely you must be a low fellow. Do you not know that when the *Inkoosi* speaks it is your part to listen and be grateful, not to weep and whine and make comments upon the acceptable words which he has been pleased to say to us from his heart? Be silent!' he ended sharply, whereon the grumbler collapsed. The incident is very typical of the old Zulu courtesy which will not allow a guest to be cross-examined or his remarks exposed to open question and criticism, and from the expressions of assent uttered by the assembled company evidently they considered the severe reproof administered to the interrupter by the son of Cetywayo to be well deserved.

I trust, Sir, that the views which I have set out above may be of interest to you and to other members of His Majesty's Government who may desire to inform themselves upon these matters. I can assure you that I have not arrived at them without much conscientious thought and investigation; also, although I may have erred or been misinformed upon details, that I believe them in the main to demonstrate the true position of the Zulus at this time. Perhaps, too, I may claim some qualifications to form an opinion on the subject. A whole generation has gone by since first I came in contact with this people. They interested me, and for several years I observed them closely, learning much concerning them also from my late official chiefs, Sir T. Shepstone, Sir Melmoth Osborn, and others, who were the great authorities of the day. Since I left Africa after the conclusion of the Zulu war I have neglected no opportunity of informing myself of all that was passing in Zululand, with the result that I find I have a more intimate knowledge of Zulu history and, I venture to think, a better understanding of the Zulu mind than the majority of those who have passed their lives among them. Needless to say, however, I except such students as Sir Charles Saunders, Mr. Gibson, Mr. James Stuart, Mr. Maurice Evans, and a few others. I was, therefore, very glad to find that the opinions I formed during my recent visit to South Africa are, so far as I can judge, identical with those of these gentlemen, at any rate upon most principal points. At least, I am sure that none of them would differ from me when I say of the Zulus that they are in the main a brave, loyal, and true-hearted people who deserve every possible help and sympathy from Britain, that with difficulty conquered them in war, to enable them to adapt themselves to the changed circumstances which time and the march of events have thrust upon them. Their crimes and errors for the most part have been those of kings and chiefs, and of the witch-doctors preying upon the superstitions of a primitive race, generally in the interest of kings and chiefs. Their virtues are their own and, if encouraged and nurtured with kindness and understanding, these should in the end give them no mean place among the coloured subjects of the Crown. If, however, they are embittered by injustice and ill-treatment; if their proffered loyalty and trust are scorned and rejected; if in the place of help, education and good counsel, they receive from the white man, their master, little save his dislike, his diseases, and his drink; if their lands continue to be taken from them and the morality of their women to be corrupted; ultimately they will add all his vices to their own. Feeling that they are not respected they, in turn, will lose their self-respect and become a degraded folk and a peril to the community in which their lot is cast.

In the case of the Zulus, civilization has one of its great opportunities, for certainly in them there is a spirit which can be led on to higher things. My earnest hope, like to that of all who have given impartial and sympathetic consideration to their case, is that this opportunity may not continue to be neglected in years to come. If so, it seems to me that we shall incur a heavy responsibility towards a bewildered people that we have broken and never tried to mend, and suffer evils to arise of which the effects will not be endured by them alone.

Believe me, &c.,
H. RIDER HAGGARD.

R.M.S. 'Gaika'
The Red Sea,
1st June 1914.

P.S. – In the course of my journey home viâ the East Coast, I also visited East Africa, but, as that country is not mentioned in your letter of 29th October last, I do not speak of it in this communication. I note the wish you expressed to me that I should write you a further letter on my return from Canada. This, all being well, I propose to do.

H.R.H.

Notes by H. Rider Haggard

1. Australian No. 217.
2. It would seem, if the figures I have collected are correct, that in the Union of South Africa, exclusive of the Protectorates, out of a total of over 280 millions of acres, the natives have left to them approximately not much more than 20 millions of acres, less than one-tenth of the land, which tenth must satisfy the needs of over four million people. Out of these four million blacks, nearly one million are stated to have no land at all. When it is remembered that the whites in the Union only number about a million and a quarter, a large proportion of whom dwell in cities, these figures assume a remarkable significance, especially as much of the white man's food is still imported, while the native must, for the most part, grow his own.
3. The skull of King Panda is said to adorn the shelves of an English hospital.

Appendix Two

This article by David Pollock appeared in the Transvaal Leader, *31 March 1914.*

Sir Rider Haggard's Return

In Pretoria Then and Now

'Too Many Fine Buildings, Too Few Men'

(From a Special Correspondent)

PRETORIA, Monday.
Notable amongst the distinguished personnel of the Dominions Commission is Sir Rider Haggard, who is paying a return visit to South Africa after a full generation has elapsed. As a very young man, Sir Rider, then with all his fame as a novelist still unearned, played a commanding part in the moving events which preceded the first Boer War. At the age of 19 he was appointed Secretary to the Governor of Natal, Sir Henry Bulwer. Two years later he accompanied Sir Theophilus Shepstone (the enigmatical 'Somtseu'), who, as Special Commissioner to the Transvaal, rode into Pretoria with his famous handful of Natal policemen. On the Queen's birthday in that year, young Haggard, with Colonel Brookes of the Engineers, formally hoisted the Union Jack over the South African Republic. Still aspiring, the youthful Attache was a few months later appointed the first Master of the High Court of the Transvaal. But not yet was peace to be the portion of our distracted Province. When war became inevitable we find the young 'Master' commissioned as Lieutenant and Adjutant of the Pretoria Horse, and taking a man's part in all the hurly-burly of the famous siege. That story is long since woven into our history; and has not Sir Rider himself distilled the perfume of its romance in 'Jess', the first and most famous of his novels?

A Norfolk Farmer

To resume this brief record of Sir Rider Haggard's career, it may be added that on his return to England he was called to the Bar. His great interest in agriculture and in the condition of the agricultural labourer was first evinced in his book, 'A Farmer's Year', which was published in 1899. It is veritably a modern Georgic. Following this local survey of a Norfolk farmer's life, Sir Rider Haggard journeyed through England in 1901 and 1902, investigating the condition of agriculture and of the rural population; and in the latter year his 'Rural England' was published. It was, and it remains, a classic. Sir Rider, it need hardly be said, is a notable farmer. He is a Norfolk man born and bred; he married a Norfolk woman, and in Norfolk is his home.

Besieged by Venerable Inhabitants

I found Sir Rider yesterday morning at the Grand Hotel, where he is staying during the sittings of the Dominions Commission. He is accompanied by Lady Haggard and their daughter, a typical fair-haired English girl. I wanted to have the opinion of a keen, travelled farmer, as Sir Rider is, on the prospects of farm immigrants to South Africa; and I wanted to know what the author of 'Jess' might be thinking about Pretoria after the lapse of so many fruitful – perhaps, also, fateful – years.

It is not to easy getting a quiet talk with Sir Rider these days, when most of the venerable inhabitants of the capital are wishing to shake the wanderer by the hand, and recall the stirring incidents of the past in which both he and they had shared. But, kindly drawing me into a far corner of the lounge, 'We shall be quieter here,' he said; and we sat down to talk.

Man of Letters and Farmer

Sir Rider talks quickly and well. He is restlessly, almost nervously, energetic. His eyes are ceaselessly observant. The moment a thing strikes him as worthy of retention, is is jotted down in a large flat notebook, which the novelist carries ready for action in his hand. For the rest, Sir Rider is tall, with a slight stoop of the shoulders, thin faced and bearded. He does not look his age, which is 58. He looks what he is, a composite of two high avocations – distinguished man of letters and enthusiastic gentleman-farmer.

Sir Rider heard with interest that great importance was attached by many in South Africa to his having been appointed to the Commission; and it was hoped that he, as a farmer, might appreciate the great prospects awaiting a well-considered scheme of land settlement, and bring South Africa's claims to attract population into notice.

Our Land of Promises

'Ah! but that's about the Commission. I really mustn't say what the Commission will do for South Africa. But I will say there are too many fine buildings and too few people. Of course, every country must arrange its own population. You must breed 'em or import 'em. No other way that I see. But the country is good. There are enormous stretches admirably suited for every class of farming. I say that without hesitation. Not one-fiftieth of the irrigable land is being utilised. The rivers are not used. I wouldn't like to say how many rivers are suitable for irrigation, but the Orange and the Modder notably offer tremendous possibilities. You allow the water to run to the sea. Water is a very valuable commodity here. What with the bush being mostly cut down and the grass burnt off, your rainfall runs away down footpaths and sheep-tracks, and gets to the sea. I see you've got a pretty smart drought here as it is.'

'A Blessed Discovery'

'As for the outlook of South African farming the whole position has been changed with dipping. That was a blessed discovery. It has made what was a most hazardous occupation – South African farming – comparatively safe and remunerative. With ordinary care, now, there is no serious risk in farming cattle. The coast districts which were supposed to be utterly unsuitable, are now becoming available for cattle. This is a tremendous improvement.'

A Jaunt to Jess's Cottage

Conversation turned to the Pretoria of bygone days, when the bearded Commissioner was an eager lad, and great events were toward. 'And it's most interesting,' Sir Rider said, in his quick way. 'They tell me that just where we are now, where we're sitting, my office used to stand when I was Master of the High Court. It was a long, low building. I remember it well.'

'Have you seen Jess's cottage since you came back?' I asked. 'Let's go and see it.'

'No, I haven't – Jess's cottage. Yes, let's go and see it.'

There was time before the Commission would sit. We got into a taxi. As we went up the hill towards the poort, as Sir Rider called the opening in the hills, the novelist's keen, restless glances darted in all directions. But, obviously, it was difficult to reconstruct the past. So much was changed, so little of the old landmarks had stood against the ruthless march of time.

Then and Now

But as we turned off just below the station, and crossing the furrow, drove alongside it, on the east of the railway enclosure. Sir Rider recalled the scene of long ago with vivid touches. 'Ah! this is it,' he said, as the taxi splashed through the sunny water of the furrow. 'Yes, along here. There ought to be some trees, big trees now, in front of it.' Just beyond the senatorial jam factory we pulled up in front of a grassy lawn, along which the furrow flows in a broad stream. We crossed it by a plank bridge. Beyond the bluegums and graceful willows in the tangled copse a long, low white building is set restfully back from the road. A printed card nailed to the trunk of a huge eucalypt announced 'Rooms to Let.'

'These Are My Trees'
Sir Rider stopped at the rickety gate. 'Yes, this is the place,' he said. 'These are my trees. I planted them. There was a row each side of the path. Some on this side are gone,' he added quietly, as we went down the path. 'Let's go in. I shall know the place better from the front.' The good woman who lets the rooms was pleased to see us. 'Yes, this was the sitting-room,' said Sir Rider, as we entered the first room on the right; and, opening an inner door and stepping over a tin trunk which reposed in the doorway – 'Yes, this was my bedroom.' Leading out of that again, a small passage gave on to the diminutive bathroom and the kitchen. 'Yes, that was all there was,' observed Sir Rider thoughtfully – 'two rooms, kitchen and bathroom. It cost £350. I built it. There was a stable and a cowhouse behind,' he added musingly. 'I had two fine horses at the time, I remember.'

'This Is All Different'
By this time the tenant of Jess's cottage had joined the party. He suggested that the stable and cowhouse had been built into the house at the back, thus accounting for the disappearance of those venerable outhouses and for the increased size of the building since the first owner had last gazed upon his home.

On the front stoep the author of 'Jess' stood and looked down into the tangled weed-choked garden. 'This is all different,' he said. 'There used to be a circular flower-bed just in front here, and I planted some vines. I don't see them. Let's go down and look for them.' We picked our way amongst the scrub and tangle. There, amongst some peach trees, we found a few forlorn descendants of the vines for which, it may be, Jess herself had plucked the fruit in her time of love and sadness.

'All Very Sad in a Way'
These straggling vines, it would seem, had power to revive a memory, to evoke some faint perfume of the past. Sir Rider, up to the knees in a riotous tangle of weeds, gazed steadily at them. 'All very sad in a way,' he said between rapid puffs of his pipe. 'It's a long time ago. Well, well!'

With a warm handshake with the good woman who lets the rooms, we passed silently out along the tall avenue of tress. Sir Rider stopped at the gate and looked back. 'Some of them are missing,' he said, pointing to the great trunks of the bluegums. 'One of them is broken in the story, if you remember? Jess, standing in the garden here, sees four men carrying a man, booted and spurred, on a stretcher, killed in a brush with the Boers. She thinks it is John Niel.

'She clasped at one of the bluegum trees that grew along the path to prevent herself from falling . . . "Look," she said, pointing. "Ah, poor man, poor man!" said Mrs Neville, "they are bringing him here to lay him out." Then Jess's beautiful eyes closed, and down she went with the bending tree. Presently the sapling snapped, and she fell senseless with a little cry, and, as she fell, the men with the corpse passed on.'

'Well, well,' said Sir Rider, as he took a last look at the cottage. 'We must be getting on.' And we made our way to the taxi.

Appendix Three

❧❧❧❧❧

This article appeared in the Natal Witness, *28 March 1914.*

Echoes of the past

Famous Novelist's Reminiscences

The Past, Present & Future

(African Club Luncheon)

The African Club entertained Sir H. Rider Haggard as the guest at luncheon yesterday in the Supper Room of the Town Hall.

The interest taken in the visit of the famous author to the scene of his first inspiration added to the undertaking of Sir Rider to recall some of his experiences in the Natal of 33 years ago, caused a record assemblage of members, more than 150 being present. Lady Haggard and Miss Haggard, with Mr G.J. Macfarlane (President), and Mrs Macfarlane were seated at the top table, and three long tables were more than fully occupied by the members and their friends.

The club changed its quarters for the occasion, which was fortunate as the accomodation previously at its disposal would not have dealt with half the number who desired to attend. The feature of the proceedings was the deep attention with which his hearers followed the enthralling recollections called up by the speaker and keeness with which they applauded his earnest appeal on behalf of the historic associations of Government House.

Considering the magnitude of the undertaking the creature comforts of members were admirably and swiftly satisfied by Mr. Christophides, who for the first time undertook the Club's catering.

The club toast 'Our King and Country' having been duly honoured.

A Great Writer

The Chairman in welcoming Sir Rider, Lady and Miss Haggard as guests of the Club, gave a sketch of the author's career. He remarked that Sir Henry Rider Haggard was born on the 2nd of June, 1856, and educated at Ipswich (the birthplace of Cardinal Wolsey), and came out to Natal in 1875 as private secretary to Sir Henry Bulwer, one of the ablest and most popular Governors Natal ever had. He the speaker, got to know a good deal about Mr. Haggard, as he then was, on account of his connection later with the Governor as one of his A.D.C.'s, and it was a great pleasure to find today that the man who was then private secretary to the Governor of a small Colony as it was in those days had now attained an everlasting fame. The following year Sir Rider accompanied Sir T. Shepstone to the Transvaal, and in 1879 returned to England to marry and settled down to a literary life. His first work 'Cetewayo and His White Neighbours', was published in 1882, which vastly pleased the Cape politicians, and then followed work after work until publication of 'King Solomon's Mines' and 'She', which by the novelty of imaginative ingenuity therein displayed won for the author great and immense popularity.

Sir Rider was keenly interested in agricultural conditions and problems and published 'A Farmer's Year' (1899) and 'Rural England' (1903), a somewhat pessimistic survey of the present agricultural position based on elaborate personal enquiries. His study of that subject will, he is sure, be of the greatest value to the Dominions Commission, of which their guest was an honoured member.

On behalf of the African Club, and also, if he might be permitted on behalf of Maritzburg, he offered the heartiest welcome to Sir Henry Rider Haggard on his return to their midst. (Cheers.)

They were honoured by the presence of Sir Henry Rider Haggard as their guest and with that modesty which they always associated with the great, and which was perhaps most strikingly displayed by literary men, Sir Rider has declined to speak of his works and intends to address them solely upon his former experiences in Natal. He would have very many interesting things to say on this subject, but nevertheless, they should have welcomed some reference to the many charming books he had written which has delighted the reading public. For instance, how interesting it would have been to hear something more about the prominent heroes and heroines he has so graphically described, and the sources from which his inspiration sprang.

At least one of those great characters as well known to many of those present referred to the grand old warrior and faithful companion portrayed in that delightful book 'Allan Quatermain', old Umslopogaas, the 'Woodpecker', who was for many years chief Induna and follower to the late Sir Theo. Shepstone – one of the old type of native now fast disappearing, he regretted to say, and who now sleeps the long last sleep buried within a mile from where they were gathered that day.

'Rip Van Winkle'

Sir Henry Rider Haggard, who was enthusiastically cheered, said that during the last month or so he had been compelled to wonder whether his name was really Rider Haggard or Rip Van Winkle. (Laughter.) Consider what had happened to him. The other day he went to Newcastle, where he lived during the First Boer War, accompanying a committee of the Royal Dominions Commission. They were given a civic reception in the Town Hall, and some twenty or thirty gentlemen were deputed to receive them. In his experience Mayors and Town Councillors were not the youngest, and, yet in that room there was not a single man who had been there in 1881. Could they wonder that he looked upon himself as Rip Van Winkle? There were, he was sorry to say, few left whom he knew. It was nearly 40 years since he landed at Durban from a tug – there was no harbour, and he nearly lost his foot by crushing it between the tug and the wharf. He came here by a postcart at a gallop, and they were covered with dust. He supposed that there were few in the room that day who knew of the condition of things then.

Two days previously they came to the City by train, and they trundled comfortably over a spruit or a small river not far from Colenso, and he very well remembered the time time when he and his wife were left on the inhospitable plain after an attempt to cross the river with four natives hanging on to the corners of the cart and the horses swimming. That was one difference between then and today.

Tempora Mulantier

The Chairman has been good enough to review various aspects of his humble career, including his books. He thought that the less a man said about his own work the better, still he would take the opportunity of contradicting one thing which he saw in the paper recently. That was that he had drawn the character of 'She' from a certain chieftainess who lived somewhere near the Soutpansberg. That legend had pursued him for many years. He did not plagiarise the chieftainess – the chieftainness plagiarised 'She'. (Laughter.) He only heard of the chieftainness twenty years after the book was written.

The people of South Africa were now part of the most highly civilised community in the world, the British Empire. The post carts had gone, and the ox-wagons were going. All the way down from Newcastle he never saw an ox-wagon. Even the native dress had changed. He observed that the natives even in their kraals were clad in cast off female fortifications of European origin – (Laughter.) – which bulged out here and there. That might be a mark of the advance of civilisation; it might uplift the moral tone of the native – he did not doubt that it did, but belonging as he did to a past generation he had to admit that he preferred the immemorial fashion of Mother Eve. (Laughter.) They would perhaps be astonished to hear that to his mind Maritzburg was very much the same as when he first knew it. Apart from the fact that it had broken out into an eruption of fine buildings, the essentials of the town were unchanged. When he walked down Loop Street the other evening he could have fancied himself again a lad of nineteen, for the place was intensely silent, and there was no one in sight he could ask to guide him to the hotel except an old Hottentot woman. (Laughter.) They only difference was that they had tramcars which personally, as *laudator temporis acti*, he was not particularly pleased to see. He had always had an idea that the citizens of Maritzburg differed from the rest of mankind in one respect and he had verfied that fact early one morning. Where the rest of the world kept twelve hens and one cock, the people of Maritzburg kept twelve cocks and one hen. (Laughter.) That at any rate was the outcome of his recent experience.

A Plea for the Past
On his first evening here he made an attack on Government House, and that after nightfall. He found that the old house which had been the home of Governors had now become a home of governesses. (Laughter.) From what he saw of them he had no doubt but that the governesses were much more agreeable persons than the Governors used to be. (Laughter.) Governors as a rule were a rather and unbending race of beings, but the young ladies he considered were most genial and pleasant. (Hear, hear.) Still, if he might say one word on the point, he hoped in the end they would not make the old house into a kindergarten or a music-hall. (Cheers.) It had seen much history, but generations changed and history became forgotten; so much so that the caretaker informed him – he trusted it was not the case – that the old visitors' books of his own time had been burned. He could not in the time at his disposal even sketch the interest of the old house and its history.

The last time he crossed the doors of Government House prior to this expedition, was when he and his wife went there to dine with General Colley on the night before he started on his campaign in 1881. There were present thirteen or fourteen persons including young Elwes, and within six weeks or two months ten were dead. All that were now alive were Lady Haggard, Lady Colley and himself. Many years later when dining with James Anthony Froude they met Lady Colley, the three survivors of that historic party before the beginning of that disastrous and most terrible campaign. He could refer to a dozen interesting matters connected with old Government House had he the time, but he would beg of them not to let the old house be lost for it was replete with history. (Cheers.)

The African Talleyrand

Speaking with evident feeling, Sir Rider Haggard proceeded:

This brings me to the memory of some of those I used to know here. I cannot speak now of more than one or two, but I can scarcely refrain from saying a word about some, Sir Theophilus Shepstone, for example. (Cheers.) It is with some emotion that I mention his name because, in truth, I looked on him very much as father, and, in truth, he treated me very much as a son. I do not know what was the bond of sympathy between a young lad as I was then, barely twenty years old and this old, experienced statesman and man of the world, but, as he is long dead and I now am old, I may say that it certainly existed. There was a bond of great affection between us. Somtseu was a silent man and to none would he say much. That was where he got wrong with Sir Bartle Frere, who had a habit of acquiring information, and whenever Somtseu began to feel the vacuum caused by a suction pump he would say nothing. So that it came about that Sir Bartle Frere wrote Home of him as an 'African Talleyrand, whose dark and secret mind it was impossible to fathom', yet that dark and secret mind was ever open to me, and many and many a time he told me things that no wild horses used by Sir Bartle Frere would have got out of him.

Out of that arose an intimacy for which I am grateful and thankful, and honoured to say endured until his death. You know that Shepstone received no good treatment. I will not enlarge on that point but how glad I am to be able to say, as I do, that every year that goes by more and more vindicates his honoured name, and higher and still higher lifts his reputation, until that reputation has become, I tell you, a bright and fixed star in the firmament of history. (Cheers.) If ever a man's purity, if ever a man's high rectitude, and if ever a man's high aims have been justified, then I say the processes of time and the march of political events have justified Somtseu. (Cheers.) Now he has gone, but I confess that one of the hopes of my existence is that there is somewhere a piece of future existence where I can shake his hand again.

There were others, he proceeded, John Bird, the man with the wonderful memory – (Cheers.) – who once bet £10 that he could recite any book of the Iliad without making more than three errors. He heard him once lecture for three hours on English poets, and he thought that lecture was never coming to an end. (Laughter.) John Bird had left behind him a valuable work and a valuable son. There was Osborn, Malimati, with his queer quiet way, and Colenso. The other day he made a remark that the folly of today was the wisdom of tomorrow, a remark which had been widely quoted. Could they have better proof of the authority of that statement than in the case of Colenso! They remembered very well how he was attacked, almost crucified, for his opinions, and yet he believed now, out of all the noble army of Bishops, there was hardly one who would condemn him today. As time had vindicated Shepstone, so (he would not speak of native policy) time had vindicated Colenso. (Cheers.)

A Lifetime's Changes

Let them consider, over this period of forty years, all that had happened here. There in his own memory was the annexation of the Transvaal, in which he, the speaker, took a hand. He believed he was the last survivor of Theophilus Shepstone's staff, the last who knew the secret history of that time, for Henriquez Shepstone did not come until later. Then came the Zulu War and Isandhlwana and the death of the Prince Imperial, then the first Boer War. In that war he and his wife underwent much. They had to sleep with their horses saddled and their rifles by their sides, and finally they were driven into laager. The end of it they knew. He would say no more, but that it was too much for him, and that was why he left Africa. (Hear, hear.) Next came the retrocession, the convention for which, was signed in his own house.

Then there came a long period during which as the Chairman had observed, he wrote 'Cetewayo and His White Neighbours'. In that book he wrote that the end of all that business would be a war which would tax the resources of the Empire. That war came, and once again there was a change in African history. Things were forgotten, and then followed the Union of South Africa, which lifted her to the position of a nation, a position which he knew she would fill proudly and well. All these things had happened in one short lifetime, since he landed with Sir Henry Bulwer.

Advance, Natal!

'That,' Sir Rider said, 'is the past. What of the future? Whatever one may say, anybody who knows Africa will feel that it is most unwise to prophesy that there are no troubles ahead, because without troubles it would not be Africa. (Hear, hear.) There is the question of the increase of the white population; which is not going on as fast as might be hoped. (Hear, hear.) Then you have the increase of the native population, which is a serious and difficult question. (Hear, hear.) What is to be done with a nation just lifting itself up as it were from sleep and looking for the first time upon the dawn! How are you to lead this people? It is not enough just to rig them up in European clothes. I do not think that what I might call a policy of reach-me-downs will entirely satisfy the situation. You cannot build up a civilisation by importing ship-loads of broken-down European corsets. The stay is not strong enough. (Laughter.) It is a question of guidance, of the uplifting of these good people – for many of them are indeed very good people. (Hear, hear.) The races must learn to live together and strive together to an end of the common good.

'What remains? To wish well to South Africa! Well, I do that with all my heart, and perhaps, as an old Natalian, I may be allowed to wish the best of all things to this dear and lovely land of yours – to this fair Natal. She has beauty, great beauty, if ever country had it; she has fertility to a marvellous degree; she has history, such history for so short a career. May she also have peace, prosperity, and progress from generation to generation and from age to age.

'Advance, Natal! God bless Natal, white and black together, and bless her gates of mountain and of sea!'

Sir Rider Haggard resumed his seat amid enthusiastic cheering.

The Chairman, in proposing a cordial vote of thanks to the guest of the Club, announced that Sir Rider had become an honorary member of the Club.

Sir Rider Haggard, in acknowledging the vote, which was carried by acclamation, said that his only regret was that in the circumstances he could not become an active member of the Club.

Select Bibliography

꙰꙰꙰꙰꙰

OFFICIAL RECORDS

1) **Cheyne Collection, Norfolk, England**
   H.R. Haggard to his father, 24 November 1876.
   H.R. Haggard to his mother, 13 December 1876.
   H.R. Haggard to his father, 3 July 1879.
   Lady Haggard's Diary, 'South Africa 1880–81', 27 February 1881.
   H.R. Haggard, 'War Diary of Sir Rider Haggard', Vol. 5, 29 January 1916 to 23 November 1916, pp. 303–8.

2) **Killie Campbell Collection, Durban**
   Stuart Papers, File 19, p. 178. Copy of letter from H.R. Haggard to A.J. Shepstone, 23 January 1911.
   Stuart Papers, File 19, p. 172. Copy of letter from A.J. Shepstone to H.R. Haggard, 30 December 1911.

3) **Norfolk Record Office, Norwich, England**
   MC 32/51: H.R. Haggard, 'Rough Diary', 25 February 1914, 23 March 1914, 30 March 1914. Other items quoted are from undated entries.
   MC 32/53: James Stuart, 'Diary – Zululand Trip', pp. 1, 3, 5, 6, 7.

4) **Pietermaritzburg Archive Repository**
   Shepstone Papers. Vol. 47, pp. 74–80: H.R. Haggard to T. Shepstone, 2 August 1881.
   Chief Native Commissioner (2nd Series), Minute Papers, File No. CNC 330/1914, Item 10: M.H. Addison to J.Y. Gibson, 13 April 1914; Item 41: A. Edwards to M.H. Addison, 11 May 1914; Item 42: M.H. Addison to A. Edwards, 13 May 1914.

5) **Public Record Office, London**
   CO 879/115 and CO 881/14: Letters to the Right Honourable Lewis Harcourt.

NEWSPAPERS

Natal Mercury, 18 April 1914.
Natal Witness, 24 March 1914, 27 March 1914, 28 March 1914, 30 March 1914, 5 May 1914.

Pretoria News, 31 March 1914, 1 April 1914, 4 April 1914.
Transvaal Leader, 31 March 1914.

BOOKS AND ARTICLES

Addy, S.M.   *Rider Haggard and Egypt*, Lancashire: A.L. Publications, 1998.

Bender, C.   *Who Saved Natal? The Story of the Victorian Harbour Engineers of Colonial Port Natal*, Durban: privately published, 1988.

Bennett, D., Brusse, R. and Adams, S.   *A Guide to the History and Architecture of Durban*, Durban: Durban City Council in co-operation with the Natal Architectural Heritage Committee, 1987.

Binns, C.T.   *The Last Zulu King: The Life and Death of Cetshwayo*, London: Longmans Green, 1963.

—— *Dinuzulu: The Death of the House of Shaka*, London: Longmans Green, 1968.

Braatvedt, H.P.   *Roaming in Zululand with a Native Commissioner*, Pietermaritzburg: Shuter & Shooter, 1949.

Branch, B.   *Field Guide to Snakes and other Reptiles of Southern Africa*, Cape Town: Struik, 1988.

Branford, J. with Branford, W.   *A Dictionary of South African English*, Cape Town: Oxford University Press, 1991.

Brookes, E.H. and Webb, C. de B.   *A History of Natal*, Pietermaritzburg: University of Natal Press, 1965.

Bulpin, T.V.   *Discovering Southern Africa*, 3rd edition, Cape Town: Books of Africa, 1983.

Chilvers, H.A.   *The Seven Wonders of South Africa*, Johannesburg: South African Railways and Harbours, 1929.

Coan, S.   'When I was Concerned with Great Men and Great Events: Sir Henry Rider Haggard in Natal', *Natalia* 26, Pietermaritzburg: Journal of the Natal Society, 1997.

Cohen, M.   *Rudyard Kipling to Rider Haggard*, New Jersey: Associated University Presses, 1956.

—— *Rider Haggard: His Life and Works*, London: Hutchinson, 1960.

Collier, J.   *The Purple and the Gold: The Story of Johannesburg and Pretoria*, Cape Town: Longmans South Africa, 1960.

Constantine, S. (ed)   *Dominions Diary: The Letters of E.J. Harding 1913–1916*, edited with an Introduction and Commentary by Stephen Constantine, Halifax: Ryburn Publishing, 1992.

Cope, R.   *Ploughshare of War: The Origins of the Anglo-Zulu War*, Pietermaritzburg: University of Natal Press, 1999.

Couzens, T.   *A Tale of Two Mysteries: The Patterson Embassy to Lobengula*, Brenthurst Archive, Vol. 2, No. 1, Johannesburg, 1995.

Crush, J. and Ambler, C. (eds)   *Liquor and Labour in South Africa*, Pietermaritzburg: University of Natal Press, 1992.

De Kock, W.J. and others (eds)   *Dictionary of South African Biography*, 5 Volumes, Pretoria: Nasionale Boekhandel (for the Human Sciences Research Council), 1968–87.

De La Harpe, R. and P., Derwent, S. and Leitch, B.   *Zulu*, Cape Town: Struik, 1998.

Duminy, A. and Ballard, C. (eds) *The Anglo-Zulu War: New Perspectives,* Pietermaritzburg: University of Natal Press, 1981.

Duminy, A. and Guest, B. (eds) *Natal and Zululand from Earliest Times to 1910: A New History,* Pietermaritzburg: University of Natal Press and Shuter & Shooter, 1989.

Ellis, P.B. *H. Rider Haggard: A Voice from the Infinite,* London: Routledge Kegan and Paul, 1978.

Etherington, N. 'South African Origins of Rider Haggard's Early Romances', *Notes and Queries,* October 1977, pp. 436–8.

—— *Rider Haggard,* Boston: Twayne Publishers, 1984.

Frandsen, R. *Southern Africa's Mammals: A Field Guide,* Sandton: Frandsen, 1992.

Fynn, H. *The Diary of Henry Francis Fynn,* Pietermaritzburg: Shuter & Shooter, 1951.

Gann, L.H. *A History of Southern Rhodesia: Early Days to 1934,* London: Chatto and Windus, 1965.

Garlake, P. *Great Zimbabwe,* London: Thames and Hudson, 1972.

—— *Great Zimbabwe Described and Explained,* Harare: Zimbabwe Publishing House, 1982.

Gordon, Ruth E. *Shepstone: The Role of the Family in the History of South Africa 1820–1900,* Cape Town: A.A. Balkema, 1968.

Guest, B. and Sellers, J.M. (eds.) *Receded Tides of Empire: Aspects of the Economic and Social History of Natal and Zululand since 1910,* Pietermaritzburg: University of Natal Press, 1994.

Guest, W.R. *Langalibalele: The Crisis in Natal, 1873–1875,* Durban: Department of History and Political Science, 1976.

Guide to Rhodesia for the use of Tourists and Settlers, Salisbury: Beira and Mashonaland and Rhodesia Railways, 1914.

Guy, J. *The Destruction of the Zulu Kingdom: The Civil War in Zululand, 1879–1884,* London: Longmans, 1979.

—— *The Heretic: A Study of the Life of William Colenso 1814–1883,* Pietermaritzburg and Johannesburg: University of Natal Press and Ravan Press, 1983.

Haggard, H.R. *Cetywayo and His White Neighbours,* London: Trubner, 1882, 2nd edition with new Introduction, 1888.

—— *Dawn,* London: Hurst & Blackett, 1884.

—— *The Witch's Head,* London: Hurst & Blackett, 1884, reprinted London: Hodder and Stoughton, 1924.

—— *King Solomon's Mines,* London: Cassell, 1885, reprinted Oxford and New York: Oxford University Press, 1992.

—— *Allan Quatermain,* London: Longmans Green, 1887.

—— *Jess,* London: Smith & Elder and Co., 1887 and 1900 edition.

—— *She,* London: Longmans, 1887, reprinted Oxford and New York: Oxford University Press, 1991.

—— *Nada the Lily,* London: Longmans Green, 1892.

—— *A Farmer's Year: Being His Commonplace Book for 1898,* London: Longmans Green, 1899, and 1906 edition.

—— *Swallow,* London: Longmans Green, 1899.

—— *A Winter Pilgrimage,* London: Longmans Green, 1901.

—— *Rural England*, London: Longmans Green, 1902.

—— 'Lost on the Veld', article in *Windsor Magazine*, December 1903.

—— *A Gardener's Year*, London: Longmans Green, 1905.

—— *The Way of the Spirit*, London: Hutchinson, 1906.

—— 'The Real King Solomon's Mines', *Cassell's Magazine*, June 1907.

—— 'The Zulus: The Finest Savage Race in the World', article in *Pall Mall Magazine*, June 1908.

—— *Marie*, London: Cassell, 1912.

—— *Child of Storm*, London: Cassell, 1913, reprinted London: Macdonalds, 1952.

—— *The Ivory Child*, London: Cassell, 1916.

—— 'A Journey Through Zululand', article in *Windsor Magazine*, December 1916.

—— *Finished*, London: Ward Lock, 1917, reprinted London: Macdonalds, 1962.

—— *She and Allan*, London: Hutchinson, 1921, reprinted London: Macdonalds, 1960.

—— *The Days of My Life*, Vols. 1 and 2, London: Longmans , 1926.

Haggard, L.R.   *The Cloak That I Left*, London: Hodder and Stoughton, 1951.

Haining, P. (ed)   *The Best Short Stories of Rider Haggard*, London: Michael Joseph, 1981.

Hamilton, C.   *Terrific Majesty: The Powers of Shaka Zulu and the Limits of Historical Invention*, Cape Town and Johannesburg: David Philip, 1998.

Haw, S.   *Bearing Witness: The Natal Witness 1846–1996*, Pietermaritzburg: Natal Witness, 1996.

Higgins, D.S. (ed)   *The Private Diaries of Sir Henry Rider Haggard*, London: Cassell, 1980.

—— *Rider Haggard: The Great Storyteller*, London: Cassell, 1981.

Hogarth, O.J. and White, R.L.   *The Life of Archbishop Carter: Eton's Gift to South Africa*, England: privately published, 1952.

Jeal, T.   *Livingstone*, London: Heinemann, 1973.

Katz, W.R.   *Rider Haggard and the Fiction of Empire*, Cambridge: Cambridge University Press, 1987.

Knight, I.   *Brave Men's Blood*, London: Greenhill, 1990.

—— *Zulu: The Battles of Isandlwana and Rorke's Drift, 22/23rd January 1879*, London: Windrow & Greene, 1992.

—— *The Anatomy of the Zulu Army: From Shaka to Cetshwayo 1818–1879*, London: Greenhill, 1995.

—— *Great Zulu Battles 1838–1906*, London: Arms and Armour, 1998.

Kotze, J.   *Biographical Memoirs and Reminiscences*, Cape Town: Maskew Miller, n.d.

Laband, J.   *Rope of Sand: The Rise and Fall of the Zulu Kingdom in the Nineteenth Century*, Johannesburg: Jonathan Ball, 1995.

Laband, J. and Thompson, P.   *Kingdom and Colony at War: Sixteen Studies on the Anglo-Zulu War of 1879*, Pietermaritzburg and Cape Town: University of Natal Press and N & S Press, 1990.

Laband, J. and Thompson, P.   *The Illustrated Guide to the Anglo-Zulu War*, Pietermaritzburg: University of Natal Press, 2000.

Lang, A. (ed)   *The True Story Book*, London: Longmans Green, 1900.

Lang, A. *New Collected Rhymes*, London: Longmans Green, 1905.

Lehmann, J. *The First Boer War*, London: Jonathan Cape, 1972.

Le Sueur, D., Sharp, B.L. and Appleton, C.C. 'Historical Perspectives of the Malaria Problem of Natal with Emphasis on the Period 1928–1932', *South African Journal of Science*, Vol. 89, 1993, pp. 232–9.

McLintock, A. *Imperial Leather: Race, Gender and Sexuality in the Colonial Context*, London and New York: Routledge, 1995.

Manthorpe, V. *Children of the Empire: The Victorian Haggards*, London: Gollancz, 1996.

Marais, J. *A Complete Guide to the Snakes of Southern Africa*, Johannesburg: Southern Books, 1992.

Martin, E.B. *Zanzibar, Tradition and Revolution*, London: Hamish Hamilton, 1978.

Maylam, P. and Edwards, I. (eds) *The People's City: African Life in Twentieth Century Durban*, Pietermaritzburg: University of Natal Press, 1996.

Morris, D.R. *The Washing of the Spears: A History of the Rise of the Zulu Nation under Shaka and its fall in the Zulu War of 1879*, London: Jonathan Cape, 1966.

Murray, M. *Union-Castle Chronicle 1853–1953*, London: Longmans Green, 1953.

Newitt, M. *A History of Mozambique*, Johannesburg: Witwatersrand University Press, 1995.

Pakenham, T. *The Boer War*, London: Weidenfeld and Nicolson, 1979.

Palgrave, K.C. *Trees of Southern Africa*, Johannesburg: Struik, 1977.

Pocock, T. *Rider Haggard and the Lost Empire*, London: Weidenfeld and Nicolson, 1993.

Ranger, T. *Voices from the Rocks: Nature, Culture and History in the Matopos Hills of Zimbabwe*, Oxford: Oxford University Press, 1999.

Raper, P.E. *Dictionary of South African Place Names*, Johannesburg: Lowry, 1987.

Rasmussen, R.K. *Historical Dictionary of Rhodesia/Zimbabwe*, New Jersey and London: The Scarecrow Press and Methuen, 1979, and 1991 edition.

Rex, H.M. *Die Strydvraag oor die Bewaring en Restourasie van die Woonhuis van Henry Rider Haggard in Pretoria*, Pretoria: privately published, 1967.

Rosenthal, E. *Encyclopedia of Southern Africa*, 3rd edition, London and New York: Frederick Warne, 1965.

Rosenthal, E. *As Pioneers Still*, Cape Town: Lever Brothers, 1961.

Rotberg, R.I. *The Founder: Cecil Rhodes and the Pursuit of Power*, Oxford: Oxford University Press, 1988.

The Selected Works of Mahatma Gandhi, Volume 3, Satyagraha in South Africa, Bombay: Navajivan Trust, 1968.

Sorrenson, M.P.K. *Origins of European Settlement in Kenya*, Oxford: Oxford University Press, 1968.

Standard Encyclopedia of Southern Africa, Cape Town: Nasou, 1976.

Struben, H.W. *Recollections and Adventures*, Cape Town: Maskew Miller, 1920.

Stuart, J. *A History of the Zulu Rebellion*, London: Macmillan, 1913.

Trzebinski, E. *The Kenya Pioneers*, New York: W.W. Norton, 1985.

Tuchman, B. *The Proud Tower: A Portrait of the World before the War 1890–1914*, London: Hamish Hamilton, 1966.

Tyrell, B. *Her African Quest*, Cape Town: Lindlife, 1996.

Vijn, C. (translated with notes by Bishop J.W. Colenso) *Cetshwayo's Dutchman: Being the Private Journal of a White Trader in Zululand during the British Invasion*, London: Longmans Green, 1880.

Webb, C. de B. and Wright, J.B. (eds) *The James Stuart Archive of Recorded Oral Evidence Relating to the History of the Zulu and Neighbouring Peoples*, 4 Volumes, Pietermaritzburg and Durban: University of Natal Press and Killie Campbell Collection, 1976, 1979, 1982, 1986.

Welsh, F. *A History of South Africa*, London: HarperCollins, 1998.

Whatmore, D.E. (comp) *Rider Haggard's Good Deeds, Pamphlet Four – Letters to the Right Hon. Lewis Harcourt*, Cheltenham: privately published, 1998.

Wills, W.A. and Collingridge, L.T. *The Downfall of Lobengula*, London: Simpkin, Marshall, Hamilton and Kent, 1894, reprinted Bulawayo: Books of Rhodesia, 1971.

Wright, J. and Manson, A. *The Hlubi Chiefdom in Zululand-Natal: A History*, Ladysmith: Ladysmith Historical Society, 1983.

Index

Note: Books, pamphlets and articles by H. Rider Haggard are given under individual titles without author's name. Page numbers in italics have been used to denote photographs.

Wolpert, Gerard, Abbott 244n. 21
Wolseley, Sir Garnet 5, 14, 74, 86n. 36, 211n. 1, 215n. 23, 221n. 84, 279n. 2
  settlement of Zululand 122n. 39, 221n. 84
Wonderboom, Pretoria 132, 139n. 21
Wonderfontein caves 90n. 93
World War One 29
'World's View', Matopos 148, 170n. 19
Wynberg, Cape Town 74, 89n. 79

Young, Arthur 18

Zambia 141
Zanzibar 246, 250, 258–61
Zeerust 175, 212n. 2
Zibhebhu kaMapitha 181, 187, 188, 211n. 1, 215n. 23, 217n. 46, 221n. 84, 224n. 112, 292
Zimbabwe 141
'Zimbabwe' poem by Andrew Lang 172n. 40
Zimbabwe Ruins *see* Great Zimbabwe
Ziwedu 188
Zoutpansberg *see* Soutpansberg
Zulu dancing 177, 181–2, 215n. 27
Zulu diseases 241, 244n. 28

Zulu *indabas* 184–5, *187*, 187–9, 199–200, 206–7, 293, 296, 308
Zulu kingdom, history 211n. 1, 221n. 84
Zulu medicine 232
Zulu Nkosinzulu 193, 219n. 68, 220nn. 76, 80
'Zulu War Dance, A', article in *The Gentleman's Magazine* 6, 119n. 11, 185, 215n. 26
Zulus 1, 7, 25, 28, 29, 62, 74, 97, 105, 108, 175
  Haggard on 181, 291–310
Zululand 2, 3, 13, 17, 25, 27, 28, 64, 74, 75, 80, 105, 112, 113, 119n. 14, 121n. 34, 122n. 37, 124n. 39, 140n. 23, 155, 175, 282, 291–310
  population 296
Zululand Land Delimitation Commission 305–6
Zulu Rebellion *see* Bhambatha Rebellion
Zulu religious beliefs and customs 188, 204–5, 207–8, 210, 217n. 54, 218n. 56, 221n. 83, 223n. 83, 226n. 124
Zulu War *see* Anglo-Zulu War, First
Zweete *see* Zwide
Zwide 189, 218n. 60